Media Sex

What Are the Issues?

LEA's Communication Series
Jennings Bryant/Dolf Zillmann, General Editors

For a complete list of titles in LEA's Communication Series, please contact Lawrence Erlbaum Associates, Publishers, at www.erlbaum.com

Media Sex

What Are the Issues?

Barrie Gunter
University of Sheffield

LEA LAWRENCE ERLBAUM ASSOCIATES, PUBLISHERS
2002   Mahwah, New Jersey   London

Lawrence Erlbaum Associates, Inc., Publishers
10 Industrial Avenue
Mahwah, NJ 07430

Cover design by Kathryn Houghtaling Lacey

Library of Congress Cataloging-in-Publication Data

Gunter, Barrie
   Media sex : what are the issues? / Barrie Gunter.
       p. cm.
   Includes bibliographical references and index.
   ISBN 0-8058-3722-1 (cloth) — ISBN 0-8058-4010-9(pbk.)
   1. Sex in mass media. I. Title.

P96,/S45 G86 2001 ∂ᴏᶜ∂
306.7—dc21

                                          00-068136

Books published by Lawrence Erlbaum Associates are printed on
acid-free paper, and their bindings are chosen for strength and dura-
bility.

Printed in the United States of America

10   9   8   7   6   5   4   3   2   1

Contents

Preface

Public debate about sex in the media has become increasingly vociferous despite the liberal attitudes that prevail within many Western societies at the beginning of the 21st century. Concern about media sex stems, in part, from the perception of increased prevalence and availability of explicit sexual materials produced by a burgeoning pornography industry. For some sectors of society, such material is regarded as distasteful and offensive. The products of this industry are no longer simply identified with salacious magazines, but with a vibrant video and film production business whose output is distributed not only through specialist stores, but also via subscription television channels. It is not only restricted circulation sex material that has been challenged. Conservative lobby groups and associated right-wing press have accused even the mainstream media, television in particular, of turning increasingly to the use of explicit sex in a battle for ratings.

In the United Kingdom, for example, the country's most widely read conservative tabloid, the *Daily Mail*, has waged a major campaign against sex on television. Although virtually no channel has escaped criticism, the campaign has focused principally on the scheduling tactics of the new terrestrial broadcast Channel 5 that has made a point of including significant amounts of risqué content on its late-night (post-10 p.m.) line-up with naked game shows, interviews with porn stars, and exposés on the pornography industry that often include clips from explicit movies that would not normally be deemed appropriate for television. The same channel (though it has not been alone in this) has also televised late-night soft-porn films with full frontal female nudity and simulated sex scenes. Such films would previously have been found only on encrypted, subscription television channels broadcast by satellite or transmitted through cable.

Despite the negative press coverage, public opinion surveys have not supported the view of antimedia sex lobbyists that there is widespread public disquiet over these developments. The new Channel 5 in the UK has quickly established its presence, and the additional publicity it has achieved in the light of its controversial scheduling strategy has undoubtedly helped it to reach a respectable audience share, in an increasingly competitive TV marketplace, by fuelling viewers' curiosity. The public's view about sex on television, however, is fairly open-minded. Subscribers to encrypted television channels have displayed liberal attitudes towards porn channels and displayed an open mind regarding the rights of people to choose for themselves their preferred forms of entertainment. Sex is not widely regarded as unacceptable, though the extent to which it is accepted depends on a range of mediating factors. These include the time of transmission, the channel of transmission, the nature of the program, the appropriateness of its utility in a program, and its treatment when it occurs. Public opinion profiles concerning media sex can also be affected by the form of questioning used in a survey. Survey respondents not uncommonly express greater concern about the possibility of harmful reactions to media sex occurring among other people than among themselves.

Weighing up this evidence, therefore, is there cause for concern about media sex? Whether or not sex on television or in the movies, or the even more explicit depictions of pornography magazines or videos, is acceptable is partly a matter of public opinion. Such opinion serves as a barometer of current social values, and these can shift over time. This is not the end of the story, however. The acceptability of media sex must also be judged according to more stringent criteria that focus on the issue of harm. Regardless of whether people like to consume media sex, or acknowledge that even if it is not something they personally enjoy, others might, there is a separate matter of how viewers might be influenced by the experience. As we will see in this book, a range of possibly harmful, social and psychological consequences of exposure to media sex have been highlighted over the years.

In liberal, democratic societies that enjoy freedom of speech, there is a tolerance for the publication of all kinds of material, regardless of their inherent popularity. The idea of censorship, for example, comes into direct conflict with the fundamental principle of a free press. In the United States, for instance, freedom of speech is one of the founding principles of the society and is a statutorily protected right. The offence that specific publications might cause to the sensibilities of certain sectors of society is not deemed to be a sufficiently powerful reason for restricting the freedom to publish. However, if a solid case can be made that a publication has harmful effects on individuals or society at large, that would present a clear and present danger, then freedom of speech protection could be repealed. The problem here is proving that such harm has occurred or is likely to.

In this book, international evidence is collated about media sex. A number of fundamental questions are asked about sex in the media. Individually, these questions are not new. However, this book represents the first attempt to examine this breadth of questions within a single volume. The book considers questions about the prevalence and prominence of sex in the media, about public opinion concerning that content, about different kinds of effects (usually harmful ones) that allegedly follow exposure to media sex, and about the use of sex as a selling device. The reported or supposed harms of media sex range from short-term effects on postviewing attitudes to sexual aggression and female sexuality or on behavioral aggression to longer term influences on social values, sexual beliefs and sexual practices. Media sex has been accused of undermining social mores, promoting sexual promiscuity, the early onset of sexual behavior and teenage pregnancy rates, and producing distorted male (and female) beliefs about female sexuality. Each of these issues is examined in separate chapters in this book.

As well as these specific questions about provision, tastes, and harms, there are equally important questions to be raised about the quality of the research evidence. Such questions are especially important if research is to be accepted as credible and as being sufficiently robust to inform or guide social policy and media regulation in this area. This book therefore asks questions about how the supposed effects of media sex have been explained in theoretical terms and about the strengths and weaknesses of the research methodologies that have been used to explore the prevalence of and public reactions to media sex.

Finally, the book examines questions more directly concerned with media-related policy and regulation. If there is a serious problem with media sex, what steps can be taken to deal with it? This is a complex area fraught with conflicts of interest and conflicts of value systems that reach to the roots of the founding social principles of some societies. A balance must be struck between the free speech rights of publishers and broadcasters and the need to protect society from undue harm. The freedom and expectation of the public to choose for themselves what types of media content to consume represent further considerations, particularly in a world that is empowering ordinary citizens with greater control over personal media consumption.

Unless there is a clear-cut case of illegal behavior occurring on screen (e.g., depiction of actual sex with under-age children or animals, or real sexual assault), it may be difficult to prove harm in a court of law. In this case, the 'harm' would apply to participants in the sexual depiction rather than to the audience. Instead, alternative measures may be needed that help to protect the interests of the public while not restricting freedom to publish.

Such steps might include clearer labelling and advance warnings or advisories so that members of the public know what to expect and can choose for themselves what to consume and what to avoid.

1

What Concerns Have Been Raised About Media Sex?

Sex has been at the center of many forms of public entertainment for many centuries. Sexual themes have featured prominently in fiction, whether played out on the screen, stage, or page. Ancient Greek comedies were frequently laced with sex. Literary classics such as Chaucer's *Canterbury Tales* and Shakespeare's *The Taming of the Shrew* were filled with sexual double entendres and overtly sexual themes. The blending of sexual titillation with violence, a subject of contemporary concern, was also witnessed in Roman times with the introduction of women to gladiatorial contests. Scantily attired with their breasts naked, such women fought with wild boars and with each other in armed combat or from chariots (Guttmann, 1991; Juvenal, 1958; Robert, 1971).

In recent history, sex has been one of the major themes covered by the contemporary mass media, including books, magazines, newspapers, film, video, and television. Popular dramatic narratives frequently center on relationships between characters that, as often as not, involve sexual interactions—no matter how mild these might be. Sex is also the stuff of news. Sexual scandals involving politicians, media celebrities, and other public figures are featured virtually every week in tabloid newspapers, with such stories regularly spilling over into editorials and other media commentaries or into comedians' jokes. Accounts of the sexual lives of ordinary people and sex advice columns also represent prominent aspects of glossy magazines targeted at various sexually active age groups.

1

Although much of this media preoccupation with sex passes off without comment, the representation of sexual behavior by the media has not received universal acceptance. Complaints have been invoked by certain types of sexual presentation in specific media and under particular circumstances. An alleged preoccupation with sexual issues in magazines aimed at teenage girls, for example, sparked a controversial debate about the role such publications might play in shaping sexual attitudes among young girls. This concern has been focused especially by statistics showing steady increases in the rate of underage pregnancies among teenage girls under 16 years of age and of unwanted pregnancies occurring among girls age 16 and over who are not in a steady relationship with a partner likely to serve as a supportive and responsible father (Harris & Associates, 1986).

Even more widespread concern has been publicly voiced about depictions of sexual behavior in cinema films and television programs that attractive significant audiences. It has been charged that these media have become increasingly preoccupied with sex and that depictions of sexual behavior have become more graphic and gratuitous (Greenberg, 1994). With the growth of cable television and home video, sexually explicit audiovisual materials have become more widely available to the general public, and, more worrisome for some commentators, such materials have become more accessible to young audiences. A number of sexually explicit television channels have launched on cable systems in North America and Europe. Some of these channels, such as *Playboy, Tuxxedo,* and *American Exxxtasy* in the United States and *The Adult Channel* in the United Kingdom, reach large audiences. Such channels depict explicit simulations and, in some case, real sexual intercourse. Latterly, the Internet has emerged as a source of anxiety among parents because of its largely uncontrolled provision of highly controversial, potentially offensive, and even illegal content and the readiness with which children and teenagers are able to gain access to such material.

WHAT CONCERNS HAVE BEEN RAISED?

Concerns about sex in the media have centered on a number of issues relating to offence to public taste, impact on young people, influences on family values and effects on marriage as a social institution, the social and sexual implications for women, and the potential causal agency of such content in relation to the commission of sexual offences. These concerns have been directed towards the representation of sex in mainstream audiovisual media available to everyone and also towards media content for which they is more restricted access. The latter forms of entertainment include encrypted erotic television channels for which subscription charges are levied and explicitly sexual videos available through special outlets or via mail order.

These materials can take on an extremely graphic nature, showing actual sexual behavior involving same-sex and opposite-sex participants, group sex, and sex with violence. Even mainstream entertainment channels such as non-encrypted television services and cinema films have been criticised for a growing emphasis on sexual themes and wider use of nudity and increasingly explicit simulated portrayals of sexual intercourse. Concern about the sheer volume of media sex begs the question of how much sex is actually contained indifferent media. The research evidence on this question is reviewed fully in chapter 2.

Offence to Public Taste

One focal point of concern about media sex is that it can cause offence to large numbers of people. This type of concern has been especially acute with regard to sex on television. Mainstream television channels are freely available to anyone with a television set. Sexual depictions can therefore be seen readily by anyone who tunes in, should such scenes be included in programs. This experience might not just be a source of personal distaste to viewers, but may also cause them considerable embarrassment if they are watching with their children, parents, or other people. The truth is that public attitudes towards media sex vary widely with the nature of the sexual content, the gender, age, social background, and personality of individuals, and the social context of consumption. Furthermore, while some people may object to having media sex thrust before them because they find it personally distasteful, they may nevertheless accept that this does not mean it should be banned. Indeed, many viewers are prepared to tolerate the provision of adult television channels for those with a taste for the material such channels supply, even though they would not wish to watch those channels themselves (Gunter, Sancho-Aldridge, & Winstone, 1994).

Ultimately, if individuals are upset enough by sex in mainstream media, they will let their views be known. In the case of broadcast television, for example, viewers are not slow to complain to the authorities when offended. On some occasions, when a medium goes too far, professional critics join the debate about whether the media are serving the best interests of the public.

By the end of the 20th century, complaints from viewers in Britain about sex on television achieved an all-time high. Of 4,892 complaints from viewers received by the Broadcasting Standards Commission in 1998–1999, 31% were about sex, compared with 18% over the previous 12 months (Harvey, 1999). During the same period, Britain's commercial television regulator, the Independent Television Commission (ITC)received 318 complaints from viewers about sex on the commercial television channels, and the BBC's Program Complaints Unit received 40 complaints about sex on BBC programs (5.1% of all complaints). Not all these complaints were upheld by the regulators (Petley, 1999). Concern focused not simply on the nature of the sexual portrayals, but on the time when they were shown. Much of the public's concern centered on sexual stories creeping into programs aimed at teenagers and sexual innuendo in programs that were popular with children. Another area of concern was the increasing prevalence of sexual themes, often discussed in graphic detail, on daytime talk shows (Harvey, 1999). The ITC (2000) reported a total of 280 complaints from viewers about sex in television drama and entertainment during 1999, the biggest single category of complaint, exceeding violence (121 complaints) and language (133 complaints) combined.

Prominent television commentators joined in the chorus of criticism about broadcasters' apparent growing obsession with sex. Late-night exposés of the sex industry in Europe or reality shows featuring ordinary people talking about their sex lives were billed as investigative journalism with an educational function by their producers, but dubbed as mere 'sexploitation' and titillation by critics (Dunkley, 2000). Even the regulators were dubious about the justification for some of the reality shows with strong sexual themes, even though they were transmitted late at night (Petley, 1999).

One aspect of concern about sex in popular entertainment media is that it can cause offence to members of the public. This concern stems in part from the perception that portrayals of an erotic nature present depictions of (sexual) behavior that would normally remain hidden. For some people, the sexual act is a private behavior. The depiction of graphic sexual portrayals, involving the realistic simulation of sexual intercourse and other intimate sexual practices, is offensive. Herein lies the inherent appeal of sexual depictions in the media. Although media sex is publicly criticised, it is also publicly consumed. By bringing intimate acts out into the open and rendering them available for close scrutiny, they generate extreme curiosity among their consumers who may then seek further exposure to what some scholars call 'forbidden fruit' (Bryant & D. Brown, 1989). Viewers become voyeurs, curious to see other people having sex. The camera brings the details of such activity into close-up. As well as this curiosity, there is the added factor of increased availability of erotica. More people have ready access to such material in the privacy of their own home. They can consume it easily and without embarrassment (Zillmann & Bryant, 1989).

The nature of the appeal of media sex, however, can itself lead to an appetite for more of the same for a while, but then to a demand for more extreme materials. Passive consumption on its own may lose its appeal after a while (Zillmann & Bryant, 1988a). As viewers habituate to one kind of sexual material, they may develop appetites for less familiar types. Sustained interest in explicit sexual material may also be driven by the role it plays as a sexual stimulant or a substitute for the real thing (Glassman, 1977). Erotica can also provide information about sex that its consumers may utilise in their own sex lives (Bryant & D. Brown, 1989; Lawrence & Herold, 1988). The popularity of erotica varies across the population. Sexually explicit materials are not enjoyed equally by men and women (Bryant & D. Brown, 1989; Day, 1988). Males are more active consumers of erotica than are females. Although females will watch sexually explicit material, they usually depend on others to instigate the experience (Lawrence & Herold, 1988). We return to the subject of public opinion about media sex in chapter 3.

Impact on Young People

The concern about the exposure of young people to sex in the media has two main aspects. First, there is a worry that very young children may be upset by seeing explicit sexual scenes that they lack the maturity to interpret. Second, exposure to media content that places emphasis on sexual themes among teenagers is believed to encourage early onset of sexual behavior and contributes, in turn, to the growth in unwanted teenage pregnancies and sexually transmitted diseases (Greenberg, J. D. Brown, & Buerkel-Rothfuss, 1993). Social statistics for the United States have indicated that by the age of 20, 70% of females and 80% of males have had sexual intercourse. One in seven of these individuals has contracted a sexually transmitted disease—in some cases AIDS (Greenberg et al., 1993). The United States has the highest rate of teenage pregnancies in the industrialised world (Bigler, 1989; Jones et al., 1985). By the early 1990s, one in four pregnancies occurred to mothers under 20 years of age (Greenberg et al., 1993). This, in itself, may not be so bad, except that often these young mothers are having children before they have themselves reached psychological maturity or financial independence. Early onset of motherhood may, therefore, prevent them from enjoying their teenage and young adult years free from the responsibilities of child rearing. They may be driven to take steps to recapture their youth in later life, with disastrous consequences for family cohesion. The propensity for engaging in unprotected sex with numerous partners increases the likelihood of infection or further unwanted pregnancies. The impact of media sex on young people is examined at greater length in chapter 4.

Media sex has been identified as a contributory factor in connection with all these behavioral trends. The impact of media sex has been hypothesised to operate through a number of stages. First, the media place sex high on the public agenda. Second, the media prime people to think about sex a lot. Third, the media present role models for emulation. Fourth, the role models do not always behave in a responsible fashion. Thus irresponsible lessons in sexual conduct and morality may be learned. These concerns stem from the observation that the mainstream mass media are permeated by sexual references. These references readily occur in television programs, movies, videos, magazines and song lyrics in popular music (Dorr & Kunkel, 1990; Fabes & Strouse, 1984, 1987; Wartella, Heintz, Aidman, & Mazzarella, 1990). Some media productions present highly explicit sexual depictions. In certain instances, sex is combined with violence or horror. Such materials, as we see later on, can sometimes produce socially undesirable changes in viewers' attitudes towards sex, female sexuality, and the use of coercive or degrading sexual practices.

Effects on Family Values
and the Institution of Marriage

Depictions of sex in the mass media have been accused of taking place outside of a romantic, loving context. Instead, they tend frequently to represent casual sexual couplings or infidelity and convey an implicit message that promiscuity and unfaithfulness are acceptable and normal forms of conduct. Some writers have called attention to the possibility that this pattern of representation could cultivate values among individuals regularly exposed to such content that underpin a wider acceptance of sex outside marriage, childbirth outside marriage, marriage as a temporary rather than permanent estate, and an expectation of many sexual partners in one's adult life (Zillmann & Bryant, 1982, 1984). This, in turn, may contribute to the breakdown of traditional family values and the willingness of people to commit themselves to lasting partnerships and the responsibilities that raising a family entail.

Social and Sexual Implications for Women

For some individuals this trend, and the kinds of portrayals it has brought with it, is an undesirable development because of the kinds of attitudes such material can cultivate among viewers. Feminists claim that depictions of sexual behavior in the mainstream media have tended to show women as sex objects and sexual subordinates to men (Brownmiller, 1975; Diamond, 1985; Longino, 1980). Not only does this convey certain unwanted messages about the role of women in sexual relationships, but it cultivates a broader set of beliefs about the relative power of men and women in society.

Zillmann and Bryant (1984, 1988a) have maintained that continued exposure to explicit depictions of women engaged in sexual activity may activate thoughts about female promiscuity in viewers. Greater availability of these thoughts in memory (Tversky & Kahneman, 1973) may lead to inflated estimates of women's tendency to desire and engage in unusual and abnormal sexual activities, including rape. The probability that these ideas will be accessed and used in evaluations of women increases as a participant is exposed to more of these behaviors in movies.

Research with young college-age males found that when fed a controlled diet of movies for up to a week that contained sexually aggressive rape themes, the men's beliefs about female sexuality and attitudes towards rape appeared to be changed by the experience. Such psychological changes persisted for over a week to a point when they were tested for their perceptions of a simulated rape trial. Those men who had consumed a diet of films with rape themes exhibited more callous attitudes towards female sexuality, stronger beliefs that women enjoy being raped, less sympathy for a rape victim, and more sympathy for the accused, as compared with similar young men who had watched a diet of erotic movies with nonviolent themes (Linz, Donnerstein, & Penrod, 1988).

Whether or not increased rape myth beliefs and more callous attitudes towards women represent normal responses to sexually explicit films aggressive themes has not been consistently demonstrated. A further body of research has found that men are *not* easily affected by sexually explicit materials that portray the sexual objectification or victimisation of women and has detected no relationship between exposure to sexually explicit material and the development of negative attitudes and aggressive behaviors towards women (Becker & Stein, 1991; Fisher & Grenier, 1994; Langevin et al., 1988; Malamuth & Ceniti, 1986; Padgett, Brislin-Slutz, & Neal, 1989). Chapter 6 considers, in great depth, the empirical evidence concerning the role of explicit media sex in shaping male perceptions of women and female sexuality.

Causal Agency in Sexual Offences

The appearance of explicit sexual material in the media has often been linked anecdotally to the prevalence of sexual offences in society and to the onset of sexual offending in individuals. A further and more direct link has been made between the production and distribution of certain kinds of pornographic material and child sex offending. In this context, public concern is not simply focused on the possibility that graphic depictions of sex in audiovisual (and print) media causes the development of sexually deviant propensities among those who consume such material, but that the material itself may contain illegal acts of sexual behavior. The relationship between pornography and sex offending has been examined through four principal methodological approaches: (a) studies of sex offenders' exposure to pornography; (b) laboratory research with offenders and nonoffenders; (c) aggregate statistical analysis of crime figures and pornography distribution figures; and (d) clinical diagnoses of sex offenders in which pornography has been identified as a potential causal influence. This literature is examined in more detail in chapter 7.

Research into the effects of media sex on the occurrence of sex offending has focused on the exposure of known sex offenders to pornography. Some experimental research has also been conducted to find out if sex offenders react differently from nonoffenders to certain types of sexually explicit material. Studies of sex offenders have examined the relationship between men convicted of sex crimes and their exposure to pornography. Surveys of sex offenders have so far produced inconclusive evidence that exposure to pornography was a primary causal agent (Cline, 1974; Cook, Fosen, & Pacht, 1971; Court, 1977; Eysenck & Nias, 1978; Gebhard, Gagnon, Pomeroy, & Christenson, 1965; Goldstein, 1973; Goldstein, Kant, Judd, Rice, & Green, 1971; Kutchinsky, 1971a). One investigation reported that more than eight in ten convicted rapists admitted regular use of pornography, but was unable to prove that pornography triggered sexually violent behavior (Marshall, 1988). Indeed, some survey evidence has indicated that young sex offenders exhibited a history of less exposure to pornography than did nonoffenders as adolescents (Goldstein, Kant, & Harman, 1974).

Laboratory evidence has been regarded by some commentators as more powerful in the context of demonstrating causal links between exposure to pornography and sexual violence. Researchers such as Jennings Bryant, Edward Donnerstein, Dan Linz, Neil Malamuth, and Dolf Zillmann have utilised experimental methodologies to explore the possibilities that exposure to pornographic materials can change men's beliefs about female sexuality, shift men's attitudes to be more accepting of callous dispositions towards women, and even affect men's (nonsexual) aggressive behavior towards women. Studies by these researchers have been conducted largely with nonoffending populations. Experimental methods have been used among dysfunctional and offending populations as well (Abel, Barlow, Blanchard, & Guild, 1977; Baxter, Barbaree, & Marshall, 1986).

Reactions contingent upon exposure to pornographic materials can be explored in a more systematic way in laboratory-based experiments. Investigators exert greater control over variables and can manipulate the nature of the materials to which experimental participants are exposed and the conditions under which exposure occurs. A variety of controlled reactions to pornography have also been investigated including physiological measures of sexual arousal, self-reported arousal or mood, verbal measures of beliefs and attitudes, and simulated aggression responses. This type of research has typically investigated male responses to pornography, although a small number of studies have also measured female responses. The experimental evidence concerning the impact of media sex on ordinary male populations is examined further in chapter 8.

Such experimental studies, based on random assignment of participants to experimental conditions, provide the best methodology for assessing cause and effect relationships in the laboratory. As is shown later in this volume, however, their results have not always been consistent. Furthermore, there are important issues concerned with generalising from their results to the real world, the spontaneity of participants responses, and the choice of responding given to participants that bear close scrutiny in the case of experiments (see Berkowitz & Donnerstein, 1982; Fisher & Barak, 1989).

The third type of study into pornography and sex offenders involves the secondary analysis of aggregate statistics on the distribution and consumption of pornographic materials and the occurrence of sex crimes among a specified population. These studies compare the circulation rates of various magazines or the number of adult theatres with rates of rape and other sex crimes. Mixed results have emerged from this type of research. Evidence has been reported that relaxing restrictions on pornography is associated with a reduction of sex crime rates (Kutchinsky, 1973, 1985), while some investigators have reported no relationship at all (Scott & Schwalm, 1988b) or a positive link in which higher circulation rates of certain kinds of pornography are associated with rape rates (L. Baron & Straus, 1984). In the latter case, however, there were further mitigating factors connected to economic conditions, urbanisation, and gender-related values that may have contributed significantly towards sex crime rates and interest in pornography (L. Baron & Straus, 1984).

The fourth type of investigation involves the collection of data in clinical or therapeutic contexts. Known offenders are interviewed in depth about their background, their urges, their self-perceptions, and their sources of ideas for offending. Such interviews also question offenders about their experiences with pornography. Clinical interviews may reveal evidence of habitual or addictive use of pornography and whether it represents part of a behavioral syndrome that includes other types of unusual sexual proclivities (Colman, 1988; Robertson, 1990). Pornography addiction, for example, may represent an aspect of a wider preoccupation with sex that becomes manifest in a range of sexual practices, not all of which are necessarily violent, including masturbation, prostitution, voyeurism, child sex abuse, and sadomasochism (Carnes, 1991).

Sex and Consumerism

Sexual imagery has been widely used to sell commodities for many years. Sex is used to attract consumers' attention to products and to render specific brands more attractive (Reid, Salmon, & Soley, 1984; Reid & Soley, 1983). Although indecency codes place restrictions on how far advertisers

can go in their use of sex to sell (Lin, 1997), nudity and sexually alluring females are frequently deployed in advertising for a wide range of commodities in most developed nations.

Although the jury is still out on the commercial impact of sex in advertising, with research producing conflicting results about its effectiveness (see
Alexander & Judd, 1978; Baker & Churchill, 1977; Tinkham & Reid,
1988), there has been concern registered about the indirect impact such
imagery might have on perceptions of women. Criticisms have centered on
the objectification of women and the side effects that the focus on certain
types of physical beauty can have on females in the audience. The featuring
of women purely as 'sex objects' in advertising has been supported by evidence showing that much media advertising features female body parts
more than the entire individual and more than their faces (Archer, Iritani,
Kimes, & Barrios, 1983). In contrast, male faces have been found to appear
more often that male body parts (Hall & Crum, 1994; Sullivan &
O'Connor, 1988).

An undesirable social side effect associated with advertising is that the emphasis on slender female body forms may encourage young women to emulate
such icons and become preoccupied with their own weight and body shape.
This may encourage young women with low self-esteem to diet excessively,
with harmful effects on their health (Heinberg & Thompson, 1992; Myers &
Biocca, 1992; Stice & Shaw, 1994). Chapter 9 analyses these issues and the
empirical evidence on sex and advertising in more detail.

WHAT IS SEX IN THE MEDIA?

When examining sex in the media and its effects on media audiences, it is
important to be clear, in the first place, about what type of content is being
studied. Sexual depictions can appear in many forms. They may comprise
verbal references to sex, reports of sex, sexual innuendo, mild sexual behavior, graphic sexual simulations without or without nudity, and depictions of
real sexual behavior, including explicit petting, oral sex, and full sexual intercourse. The sexual depictions may involve members of the opposite sex
or the same sex. They may depict sex between couples, sex in which one
participant has multiple sexual partners, or group sex. Sex may be discussed
in television talk shows, simulated in fictional dramas or sex education materials, or presented in highly graphic form in pornographic films and videos. Some sexual depictions occur in materials labelled as 'sexual' in nature,
whereas other depictions occur in regular entertainment formats in which
sex may not be a dominant theme. Some depictions of sex include unusual
techniques, violence, and even illegal behaviors.

In any review of the evidence about media sex, therefore, it is essential to make distinctions between different forms and contexts of sexual representation. Over successive generations, values change and such social evolution creates a distinct climate of public opinion varying in its tolerance for the overt depiction or discussion of sex. The 1960s witnessed a growth in liberal attitudes towards sex. The introduction of the birth control pill enabled women to take greater control over their sexuality. A perception followed, that may not have been entirely accurate, that an era of sexual permissiveness had opened up in which moral standards were in decline. This trend was believed, by some critics, to have been reflected within the mass media, for example, in the form of greater sexual explicitness on television. In Britain, it is probably true to say that the medium had begun to explore sensitive social issues of which sex was a part. Made-for-television dramas (labelled 'kitchen-sink' dramas) challenged the public to confront issues that normally remained hidden and pushed back boundaries that program-makers had formerly been loathe to cross (Shaw, 1999). For critics, there was too much sex and a potentially damaging erosion of family values. In truth, society was undergoing fundamental changes that television and other media reflected, confirmed and even extended. Equally, although broadcasters dared to feature sex in televised entertainment in ways that would not have been accepted 10 years earlier, 1960s television was relatively tame compared with what was to come in the next 30 years (Shaw, 1999).

Although the attitudes of the public, politicians, regulators, and broadcasters towards the representation of sex in the broadcast media generally underwent a gradual process of modification over time, this evolution of opinion was sometimes given a jolt by specific events. It would also be misleading to assume that public opinion shifted evenly and in a consistent direction in respect of all sexual issues. While increasingly liberal attitudes emerged towards sex in mainstream media, the public maintained a discriminating disposition towards certain sexual issues, particular dramatic treatments of sex, and the depiction or discussion of sex in specific media locations.

Health Risks and Personal Hygiene

There are occasions when critical events cause societies to confront issues that they had previously suppressed. In relation to media sex, the AIDS crisis of the early 1980s brought out into the open subjects that had previously been regarded as taboo. Although sex education in schools, the women's movement, and the shifting balance of power in sexual relations between women and men undoubtedly influenced public attitudes towards media treatments of sex, the onset of the AIDS epidemic was seen by some observers as a particularly key event (Shaw, 1999).

The media were drawn into a major health education initiative that received funding from governments. In Britain, public service and commercial broadcasters collaborated by scheduling a week of special programs in 1984. These programs were mostly designed principally to reach known at-risk groups, especially young people, and were unprecedently frank in the way they tackled certain issues, such as safe sex practices. This kind of treatment was regarded as justified because of the seriousness posed by AIDS. However, it broke through many barriers in the broadcast treatment of sex and contributed to a wider public acceptance of greater openness in dealing with matters linked to human sexuality. Research showed that the multimedia campaign with sometimes explicit sexual imagery and references was accepted by the public as a necessary approach, and increased public awareness of AIDS. Some modification of public attitudes was also registered, but little direct impact occurred on sexual behavior patterns, except among the homosexual community (DHSS/Welsh Office, 1987; Sherr, 1987; Wober, 1987, 1988).

Another ground-breaking event that stemmed from the publicity surrounding AIDS was the relaxation of certain rules regarding advertising for certain personal products. In Britain, given the openness with which the use of safe sex practices had been discussed on air, it became 'old-fashioned' and inconsistent to continue bans on advertising for sanitary protection products (referred to in the NBC code on advertising standards as 'catamenial devices'). The initial introduction of such advertisements caused controversy in Britain because some people regarded them as offensive, an invasion of privacy, and embarrassing. These concerns were reflected in public opinion surveys, whose results urged caution on the part of commercial broadcasters in the advertising treatments that were used for these products and resulted in restrictions on when they could be broadcast. Although such advertising became accepted, even in the late 1990s a large proportion of the British viewing public found excessive bunching of such commercials in the late evening offensive (Svennevig, 1998).

Sex on Mainstream Television

When examining the representation of sex on television, consideration is usually given to two separate matters. The first of these is the overt depiction of sexual activity on screen and the second is the discussion of sex and related topics. Both kinds of representation have given rise to public concern. This concern stems from a belief on the part of some people that certain treatments of sex could subvert traditional moral and family values. There are also worries about the embarrassment caused by bringing out into the open matters that are normally regarded as private. Both of these concerns are particularly acute in contexts involving children. Differences of opinion, however, may be found among different sectors of society. For example, some ethnic and religious groups may also take deep offence at depictions of behaviors that Western cultures would not regard as inappropriate or improper in a public place (see Watson, 1993).

In Britain, scheduling restrictions are placed on broadcasters in regard to the inclusion of certain types of content in programs and advertisements. Nudity is permitted in programs, but only partially in advertisements. Explicit depictions of sexual behavior would not normally be allowed or expected to occur on programs on nonsubscription channels before 9 p.m. prior to this watershed; sex may be spoken about or inferred, and some kissing and caressing may be shown in televised dramas, but nothing beyond that. After 9 p.m. the restrictions on depictions of sex are gradually relaxed and scenes of nudity and simulated sexual activity (including intercourse) are allowed. On subscription channels, even more graphic portrayals of sexual behavior may occur, especially after 10 p.m. However, after 8 p.m. on these channels, films originally made for the cinema may contain sexual depictions that would not be allowed before 9 p.m. on nonsubscription channels.

Types of Sexuality

The acceptance of increasingly explicit sexual representations as the evening wears on does not mean that any kinds of sexual behavior are acceptable. It is important that sex is justified in relation to the story line. Repeated and gratuitous scenes of explicit sex, even though simulated, may enjoy a less positive reception, even among liberal-minded viewers. There may be an uneasy tension here between dramatic licence and voyeurism. There are other areas where the tension between artistic integrity and crossing the barriers of decency is brought into sharp focus. The depictions of homosexuality and sexual violence are two such areas.

Despite increased acceptance of homosexuality in society, there remain sectors of society who regard such behavior as unnatural, morally reprehensible, or socially irresponsible. Public opinion surveys have revealed conflicting attitudes towards the representation of homosexuality on television. In Britain, for example, audiences have been anxious to display liberal, open-minded attitudes, while at the same time exhibiting reservations about such depictions (Millwood-Hargrave, 1992). Once again, the degree of public disquiet over this topic, as with treatments of others kinds of sexuality, is undoubtedly linked to where such material occurs. Late-night broadcasts on channels known for their testing of decency barriers cause less outcry than far less graphic depictions in peak-time broadcasts. Two British soap operas caused a stir by featuring story lines about a sexual relationship between characters of the same sex. In both cases, the controversy over these plot-lines peaked as a result of scenes showing kisses exchanged between the characters (two men in the BBC's *East Enders* and two women in Channel 4's *Brookside*). In both cases, the kisses were brief and discreetly shot. Both scenes, nonetheless, generated a large volume of complaints from viewers.

Public disquiet over the open representation of homosexuality on mainstream broadcast television is not unique to Britain. In the United States, objections were raised about the 'outing' by situation comedy actress Ellen Degeneres of her screen persona (also called Ellen), a short while after the actress herself had declared her homosexuality. The episode in which this occurred received advance publicity and achieved an audience of more than 40 million viewers.

Sex Talk

As we will see later in this volume, talk about sex is more commonplace than actual depictions of sex (Kunkel et al., 1999). Talking about sex is a regular feature of serious drama, especially long-running serialised dramas or soap operas (Greenberg, 1994). In these programs, most of the story lines revolve around personal relationships, and many of these tend to be of a sexually intimate nature. Although nudity and overt depictions of sex are rare in soaps on mainstream television channels (though not so on 'soaps' produced by sex channels such as *The Playboy Channel*), talking about sexual relationships is prominent. Talk about sex in the form of sexual innuendo is also not uncommon in light entertainment programs and is a frequent source of comedy.

PORNOGRAPHY

Among the most controversial forms of media sex is pornography. In the last two decades of the 20th century, the pornography industry expanded significantly. Much of this expansion was facilitated by developments in communications technologies. The growth of the home video market created a wider audience for the consumption of pornographic videos. The later evolution of the Internet provided a further channel, largely uncontrolled, through which a significant market for pornography could be reached. The production and distribution of explicit sexual materials thus became transformed from 'a seedy cottage industry' to a more technically sophisticated, mass production business serving a large international customer base (Hebditch & Anning, 1988).

Debates About Erotica

Media theorists have debated the effects of sexual material in the media, and especially the influences of highly erotic content. One central area of contention about erotica is whether the balance of its effects can be considered socially positive or negative. While much emphasis in public debate has been placed on the offensiveness and potentially harmful effects of media sex, there is an alternative view that erotic material can have important educational or therapeutic functions. These benefits include the provision of valuable lessons in sexual technique that can enhance a consumer's own sex life or be of assistance in the treatment of sexual dysfunction (Gagnon, 1977; Kaplan, 1984; Wilson, 1978). Such material may also be of use in helping individuals overcome guilt and anxiety about sex that may impair their ability to establish or maintain meaningful emotional relationships (Buvat, Buvat-Berbaut, Lemare, Marcolin, & Quittelier, 1990).

The beneficial effects idea has been roundly rejected by other writers. According to critics of media sex, particularly that featuring realistic depictions of sexual behavior, erotic materials can be damaging to women, cultivate detrimental perceptions of female sexuality, and encourage the use of violence against women as an aspect of sexual intercourse. Erotica that divorces sex from loving relationships and portrays it as a physical act performed purely for hedonistic reasons may also socialise irresponsible values that undermine the importance of stable marital and family relations, and encourage permissive sexual behavior both inside and outside marriage (Attorney General's Commission on Pornography, 1986; Committee on Sexual Offences Against Children and Youths, 1984; Lederer, 1980; Scott, 1986).

The sexual callousness model has been voiced repeatedly, especially in major government-backed commissions of enquiry into pornography (Commission on Obscenity and Pornography, 1970; Attorney General's Commission on Pornography, 1986). This perspective on the hypothesised effects of pornography has been strongly espoused by feminists. Their concern has focused on pornographic themes that emphasise the sexual promiscuity of women. Women are depicted as obsessed with sex, and willing to engage in any kind of sex act with any partner. A further characteristic typical of this entertainment format is that women present themselves to men as easy sexual conquests whose principal role is to gratify male sexual needs (Brownmiller, 1975; Diamond, 1985). Such portrayals, it is argued, can send the wrong messages about women and their sexuality. At the very least, this may cultivate perceptions among men that women prefer a subordinate sexual role and, for some men, only further reinforce already callous attitudes about the opposite sex (Russell, 1988).

Early commissions of enquiry into pornography reached the controversial conclusion that exposure to explicit sexual materials is not a cause of social or individual harms (Commission on Obscenity and Pornography, 1970; Williams Committee, 1979). This conclusion was not readily accepted within the scholarly community (Cline, 1974; Eysenck & Nias, 1978). This view changed in later years with increased recognition being given to the potential harms caused by sexually violent material (Attorney General's Commission on Pornography, 1986). Whereas pure sex may be harmless, the combination of sex with violence could prove to be a far more damaging cocktail. By the mid-1980s, it was claimed that sexually violent materials had become so widespread that a rethink was necessary about the effects of pornography. Whether sexual violence was as prevalent as the 1986 Attorney General's enquiry claimed, however, was questioned by other researchers prominent in the field (Linz, Donnerstein & Penrod, 1987; Malamuth, 1989).

Differentiating Forms of Explicit Sex

It would be misleading to treat all forms of explicit media sex as the same. There are clear distinctions that can be made between different types of sexual portrayal that are associated with the degree of explicitness, whether the sex is real or simulated, whether the sex is nonviolent or violent, whether sex scenes are heterosexual or homosexual, and whether sex scenes depict unusual sexual practices or involve children.

In the context of pornography, Harris (1994) noted that the U.S. Attorney General's Commission on Pornography (1986) identified five classes of pornographic material:

> 1. Sexually violent materials portray rape and other instances of physical harm to persons in a sexual context. 2. Non-violent materials depicting degradation, domination, subordination or humiliation constitute the largest class of commercially available materials. These generally portray women as 'masochistic, subservient, and over-responsive to the male interest.' 3. Non-violent and non-degrading materials typically depict a couple having vaginal or oral intercourse with no indication of violence or coercion. 4. Nudity shows the naked human body with no obvious sexual behavior or intent. 5. Child pornography involves minors and, though illegal to produce in the United States, still circulates widely through foreign magazines and personal distributions (p. 248).

Elsewhere, three mainstream themes have been identified in pornography. These are termed *standard, violent,* and *idealised.* In the case of standard pornographic themes, the emphasis is placed on a macho culture in which males are sexually dominant and females are sexually submissive (Day, 1988). Sex is a preoccupation in these productions and the story lines tend to be thinly veiled stratagems that result in sexual couplings with minimal build-up. Emphasis is also placed on the physical side of sex, with little time or plot devoted to the establishment of emotional relationships between characters (Palys, 1984; Prince, 1990; Slade, 1984; Winick, 1985). Women tend eagerly to give themselves to men (or other women) and engage in multiple sexual encounters (Abeel, 1987; Palys, 1986; Rimmer, 1986). Sex is depicted as a purely hedonistic activity.

In violent themes, the usual erotic scenarios occur, but also include an emphasis on violence as an aspect of the sexual act. Often women are shown responding to coercive sex with pleasure. The perpetrators rarely suffer adverse consequences or penalties for their actions. The 'rape myth' is promoted in many of these films whereby a woman is forced to have sex, displays initial expressions of disgust, but eventually becomes sexually aroused and experiences apparent enjoyment. This typical scenario reinforces a cultural myth that women enjoy being raped (Burt, 1980).

Idealised sexual themes present compassionate portrayals of sexuality with emphasis on emotional aspects of heterosexual sex. While graphic displays of physical sex may still be shown, they tend to be contextualised within a story line that provides a strong romantic or affectionate background to the relationship (Steck & Walker, 1976; Abeel, 1987; Hazen, 1983; Senn, 1985).

Sex and Violence

One particular genre that has proved highly controversial is the so-called 'slasher' movie. This horror genre depicts graphically displayed gory violence, often with erotic overtones. Women are frequent targets of extreme aggression, but their vulnerability is magnified by featuring them as naked or scantily clad at the point at which they are attacked. In some scenes, the female victim's sexual allure is emphasised prior to her violent demise (Weaver, 1988).

The 1986 Attorney General's Commission on Pornography voiced concerns about the possible link between sexually violent media and violent behavior. The Commission concluded that, 'in both clinical and experimental settings, exposure to sexually violent materials has indicated an increase in the likelihood of aggression. More specifically, the research ... shows a causal relationship between exposure to material of this type and aggressive behavior towards women' (p. 324). The Commission concluded that the increase in aggressive behavior occurred not only in research settings, but also included unlawful sexually violent behavior by some subgroups of the population. In making this case, the Commission referred primarily to experimental research that showed evidence of short-term increases in laboratory aggression among young college students following their controlled exposure to sexually violent media content—usually film clips (Donnerstein &

Berkowitz, 1981). This part of the Commission's report, however, failed to include the findings of the only study of that period that examined possible long-term effects of repeated exposure to sexually violent media content on laboratory aggression (Malamuth & Ceniti, 1986). That study did not find any such long-term effects. A further element of the 1986 Commission's conclusions related to research into the effects of exposure to violent pornography on attitudes to rape. The conclusion reached here was that the research had demonstrated that such material could shift male attitudes towards female rape victims and the act of rape itself in a more callous direction.

Criticisms of such entertainment-oriented material have stemmed from particular ideological perspectives in which a range of effects on public values have been hypothesised to occur, though have not always been empirically tested by their supporters. Nevertheless, a significant body of empirical research emerged during the 1980s that explored, through largely quantitative research methodologies, specific psychological effects of pornographic materials. These effects included measures of perceptions, attitudes, beliefs, and behavior (Krafka, 1985; Linz, Donnerstein, & Adams, 1989; Malamuth, 1984; Zillmann & Bryant, 1982, 1984; Zillmann & Weaver, 1989).

This volume examines a number of important questions about media sex. These questions relate to the amount of sex that the mainstream media contain, whether such material is acceptable to the public, and what kinds of effect media sex has on different groups of people. Most of the attention devoted to media sex has concentrated on its potentially harmful effects. In considering whether media sex does cause harm, however, a blanket view that all sexual portrayals or all media consumers are the same is unhelpful. In reviewing the evidence therefore distinctions are made between different types of media sex, different types of influence, and different types of individuals who might be exposed to it. Media sex can have distinct influences on women, on men, on young people, and on individuals with particular personality profiles. The influences of media sex can take the form of attitudes, beliefs, self-perceptions, values, and behaviors. behavioral effects may involve sexual proclivities or aggressive dispositions. Media sex may also be involved in consumer behavior, when sex is used to help sell products in advertisements.

Finally, having examined the different types of media sex effects in relation to different types of media consumer, the book turns to other significant issues of theory, method, and practice. Questions are asked about how media sex effects can be explained, whether the research evidence can be trusted, and whether the evidence points to the need for tighter social policies and regulatory controls over the media and media depictions of sex. While a number of different explanations of media sex effects have been put forward, there have also been disagreements among social scientists and clinicians working in the field over the conceptual and methodological rigor of the published research. Chapter 10 examines the theories and explanations of media sex effects, and chapter 11 considers the methodological debates about the empirical evidence.

Uncertainty over the findings of research into the effects of media sex has, in turn, produced mixed opinions about the need for more or less regulation of media. Regardless of what the effects of media sex might be, there continues to be debate about the legitimacy of censorship. In a world in which communications technologies have undergone revolutionary development, and will continue to do so, perhaps the most significant change has been the increased empowerment of media consumers. With control over the distribution of media content becoming decentralised, the debate about controversial content has placed greater emphasis on the provision technologies to facilitate control over reception at the level of the individual and on the need for better quality advance information about content, enabling individuals to make more informed choices for themselves. Whether or not the freedom of choice should reside with the producers of content and with the consumers of content, or with a centralised legislator or regulator, depends ultimately on whether it is possible to prove that harm is being done. To date, governments and legislators have paid some lip service to the harms of media sex, but have not yet acted as though fully convinced by the scientific and clinical evidence.

2

How Much Sex Is Shown?

In considering how much sex is shown in the major media , such as films, videos or television programs, one approach has been to ask the audience. This, as we will see in chapter 3, is usually done in the context of enquiring as to whether people believe there is too much sex in these media. The sub-jective opinions of media consumers, however, may not reflect the reality of what the media actually contain. Thus, we need to examine findings from research that has attempted to quantify how much sex is depicted in the media. Most of this evidence has been produced for broadcast television, al-though research has also been conducted to measure the prevalence and prominence of sexual behavior in magazines, films, and videos as well. In the latter case, the focus of attention has usually been on the availability of pornographic material. Some studies have also investigated the frequency with which sexual content occurs in pop music videos.

QUANTIFYING SEX IN THE MEDIA

Most of the evidence based on objective, quantitative measures of sex in the media has been obtained through the research method of content analysis. This perspective uses a simple counting method. Researchers using this method begin by defining the range of behaviors they intend to subsume un-der the general heading 'sexual' for the purposes of their analysis. Trained observers are then employed to monitor television programs, films, videos, or publications, identify actions or incidents that qualify as sexual behavior, and catalogue them. Distinctions are generally made between different categories of sexual behavior such as kissing, touching, petting, and full intercourse. Talk about sex has also been distinguished from overt depictions of sexual behavior. Sexual portrayals may also be classified in terms of factors such as whether they are heterosexual or homosexual, whether they take place between married or unmarried couples, whether the actors are nude, the age and ethnicity of participants, and the circumstances surrounding the behavior (e.g., a loving relationship between permanent partners, a one-night stand, prostitution, and so on). Researchers usually distinguish the type of program or film in which the behavior occurs (e.g., soap opera, action-adventure, comedy, horror, science fiction, etc.).

Where sexual behavior in videos and films is concerned, much of the focus has been placed on measuring the prevalence of pornographic materials. In this context, interest centers on the extent to which depictions of more unusual sexual practices are shown. There has also been a great deal of attention given to erotic film and video scenes that feature violence. Depictions of rape have been a source of much concern and hence much of the research into video pornography has studied the frequency and nature of such portrayals. Analysis of themes of sexual aggression against women has not been restricted to pornographic material. Such themes, and the often graphic images that characterise them, can be found in mainstream entertainment media, including general release cinema films and television programs.

Historically, trends in media depictions of sex have focused on print media. Longitudinal analyses of sex references in mass circulation magazines, such as *Reader's Digest, McCall's, Life, Time,* and *Newsweek* have indicated increased volumes of references to sex across the decades since the Second World War. Sex references have also become progressively more liberal. This was evidenced by a decline in references to censorship of sex and increased references to extramarital sex (Scott, 1986). Sex therefore became a more prevalent theme in the mass media between the 1950s and 1980s. Whether this coverage was instrumental in producing more liberal attitudes towards sex that were observed over this period (e.g., Godenne, 1974; Scott, 1986; Scott & Franklin, 1973), or whether the media were merely reflecting social trends caused by other factors is less clear. In later years, trends in the depiction of sex in broadcast media have emerged as well (Lowry & Towles, 1988; Kaiser Family Foundation, 1996; Sapolsky & Tabarlet, 1991).

SEX ON TELEVISION

Most of the research into the amount of sex in the media has studied the frequency of sexual portrayals on television. Most of that research has, in turn, derived from the United States. Given that American television programs are broadcast widely in other countries, however, the findings from this work are probably relevant to readers beyond the United States.

Initial research about sex on mainstream television began in the United States in the mid-1970s. Since then, American writers have observed steadily increasing amounts of sex on television—whether in terms of verbal references to sex or depictions of one form of sexual conduct or another. Franzblau, Sprafkin, and Rubinstein (1977) analysed 61 prime-time U.S. network programs from one full week in October 1975. They examined 13 categories of physical intimacy ranging from intimate behaviors (sexual intercourse) to more casual behaviors (embracing). The behaviors that appeared most often were kissing, embracing, aggressive touching and nonaggressive touching. The most controversial acts, such as intercourse, rape and homosexual behavior, had virtually no behavioral appearance. Only verbal references to rape and other sex crimes occurred, usually in the context of discussing crimes to be solved in dramas and crime adventure shows.

Situation comedies contained more kissing, embracing, nonaggressive touching, and innuendoes than any other type of program. Variety shows also displayed frequent nonaggressive touching, but contained only moderate amounts of kissing and embracing; the most distinctive feature of the variety show was the use of innuendoes, particularly in those without canned laughter. Drama programs were more conservative, containing low to moderate amounts of kissing, embracing and nonaggressive touching, but almost no sexual innuendoes. There was no differentiation of sexual behavior on screen by gender of characters.

In a 1981 study, Sprafkin and Silverman (1981) found a sharp increase in the amount of sexual content in 1978–1979 prime-time network programs: 'Specifically, contextually implied intercourse increased from no weekly occurrences in 1975 to 15 in 1977 and 24 in 1978; sexual innuendoes increased in frequency from about one reference per hour in 1975 to seven in 1977 and to almost 11 in 1978. Most dramatically, direct verbal references to intercourse increased from two occurrences per week in 1975 to six references in 1979 and 53 in 1978' (p. 37).

In another study, Fernandez-Collado, Greenberg, Korzenny, and Atkin (1978) focused on drama series from prime-time U.S. network television. They coded intimate sexual behavior and found that sexual intercourse, whether shown or implied, occurred much more often between unmarried partners than between married partners on television. Nearly all sexual behavior or references to such behavior were heterosexual in nature and deviant forms of sexuality were rare. Verbal and visual displays of intimate sex behaviors on television were largely confined to acts of intercourse between mutually consenting heterosexual partners. Sexual deviancy in the form of rape and alternative sexual lifestyles such as homosexuality were rarely portrayed.

Further studies of sex on American network television in the late 1970s were confined largely to touching, embracing and kissing. References to sexual intercourse were implicit and never explicitly depicted (Silverman, Sprafkin, & Rubinstein, 1979). By the end of this decade, however, a significant increase was measured in the rate of occurrence of sexual innuendoes and verbal references to sexual intercourse. This increase in sexual suggestiveness was primarily located in situation comedies (Sprafkin & Silverman, 1981).

A later study of prime-time television drama series in the United States reported an average of just under three sexual behaviors per hour. Television series included in this research were *Dynasty, Hill Street Blues, Riptide,* and *Miami Vice.* Two types of sexual behavior—intercourse and kissing—were most prevalent. Most sexual activity in prime-time drama series (63%) was verbal rather than visibly depicted. Thus, sexual intercourse was usually talked about and not shown on screen. Among those sexual behaviors that were actually shown, the great majority comprised kissing (70%). Just one in five (21%) were intercourse acts (Greenberg, Stanley, Siemicki, Heeter, Soderman, & Linsangan, 1993).

Sex in Soap Operas

Long-running, serialised dramas represent some of the most popular programs on television. Thematically, much of the drama centers on relationships among the central characters, with these relationships, in turn, frequently being sexual in nature. Focusing specifically on afternoon soap operas, Greenberg, Abelman, and Neuendorf (1981) concluded: 'Soap operas have more sexual content than do prime-time programs, but the types of intimacies portrayed differ' (p. 88). Lowry, Love, and Kirby's (1981) study of soap operas from the 1979 season found an average of more than six sexual behaviors (i.e., erotic touching, implied intercourse, prostitution) per hour. Like several earlier studies, they found more than three instances of sexual behavior involving unmarried partners for every instance involving married partners.

Greenberg and his colleagues documented an increase in rates of sexual content of 103% in the 5 years from 1980 to 1985 in television soap operas popular with adolescents. They estimated that the average adolescent American viewer in 1985 was exposed to between 1,900 and 2,400 sexual references on television, depending on his or her viewing patterns (Greenberg, Stanley, Siemicki, Heeter, Soderman, & Linsangan, 1986; Greenberg, Linsangen, Soderman, Heeter, Lin, & Stanley, 1987).

Lowry and Towles (1988) replicated the 1979 study of sexual behaviors on soaps and found a substantial increase in sex between unmarried persons and a norm of promiscuous sex, with few attendant consequences. There was a generally higher rate of sexual behaviors per hour in 1987 compared with 1979, up to 7.4 behaviors per hour from 6.6. In terms of who was engaged in various forms of sexual behavior, there was a major increase in the ratio of sexual behaviors between unmarried and married sexual partners from 1979 to 1987. Although there was an increased amount of sexual behavior on prime-time television, there was no major increase in soaps.

In furthering their work on sex in soaps in the 1990s, Greenberg and his colleagues reported on depictions of sex in the most popular serialised dramas among teenagers in the United States—*All My Children*, *General Hospital*, and *One Life to Live*. Across ten episodes of each serial, these researchers found a total of 110 acts involving some form of sexual behavior. This represented an average of 3.7 acts per hour. Nearly nine in ten of all sex acts (88%) in these programs comprised long kissing and intercourse. Prostitution, rape, and petting (distinguished from long kissing) were virtually nonexistent (Greenberg, J. D. Brown, & Buerkel-Rothfuss, 1993). Much of the sexual behavior was talked about or referred to rather than visibly shown. Talk about sex focused most of all on the subject of sexual intercourse (62% of sex-related talk). Visibly depicted sexual behavior was usually restricted to kissing. In only one in four sexual couplings were the participants married to each other. Otherwise, they were individuals engaging in extramarital or premarital sexual contact (Greenberg et al., 1993).

An update on the 1980s figures emerged from the same research group in the mid-1990s, covering the three television drama serials from the earlier analyses plus two more: *The Young and The Restless* and *Days of Our Lives* (Greenberg & Busselle, 1996). Ten episodes were analysed from each soap opera in 1993 yielding 333 incidents involving some kind of 'sexual' behavior. There was an hourly average of 6.6 sexual incidents in 1994 compared with 3.7 in 1985. With intercourse, just over one in four scenes contained visual depictions (27%). Intercourse was far more likely to be talked about (73%) than shown. A summary of the distribution of sexual incidents in these serials is shown in Table 2.1.

Sapolsky and Tabarlet (1991) found that television had not diminished its portrayal of sex in an age when teenagers and adults were being urged to approach sexual intimacy with caution. Comparisons were made with an analysis by Sapolsky (1982). Network prime-time television offered viewers 15.8 instances an hour of sexual imagery or language in 1989 compared to 12.8 an hour in 1979. Noncriminal sex acts in both years were dominated by less sensuous forms of touching, kissing, or hugging. There were few instances of sexual intercourse in either program sample: four depictions in 1979 and nine in 1989.

TABLE 2.1

Sex in American TV Soaps in the 1980s and 1990s

Nature of Sexual Act	1994 (5 soaps)	1994 (3 soaps)	1985 (3 soaps)
Unmarried intercourse	2.40	1.83	1.56
Rape	1.40	1.07	0.10
Long kisses	1.14	1.00	0.93
Married intercourse	0.72	0.67	0.73
Miscellaneous	0.70	0.13	0.16
Prostitution	0.14	0.23	0.10
Petting	0.14	0.03	0.07
Homosexuality	0.00	0.00	0.00
Total	6.64	4.96	3.67

Note. Source: Greenberg and Busselle, 1996.

Research reported by the Kaiser Family Foundation and Children Now compared sexual messages contained in television programs in the United States between the mid-1970s and mid-1990s during the 8 p.m. to 9 p.m. time slot on the major networks. A great deal of talk about sex was found, with more than three incidents per hour. Actual sexual behavior occurred much less frequently and was largely restricted to kissing and caressing. There were a few, rare incidents of simulated sexual intercourse. Over a 20-year spell from the mid-1970s, sexual depictions became increasingly prevalent on network television programs during the mid-evening time slot, with 43% of programs containing any sexual material in the 1970s and 75% doing so in the 1990s. This overall increase in sex on mainstream television was largely attributable to a greater amount of talk about sex in situation comedies and drama series (Kaiser Family Foundation, 1996).

The latest research attempting to quantify sex on television has emerged from the United States under the direction of Dale Kunkel of the Department of Communications, University of California at Santa Barbara. He compared the depiction of sex on American Family Hour television in 1996 with figures for 1986 and 1976. These comparisons were only possible for the three longest-established television networks, ABC, CBS, and NBC (Kunkel, Cope, & Colvin, 1996). This study analysed 128 network family hour programs in 1996, and compared sex in these with earlier program samples from the 8 p.m. to 9 p.m. period in 1986 ($n = 31$) and 1976 ($n = 23$). The earlier samples were obtained from research conducted by George Gerbner and his colleagues under the 'Cultural Indicators Project.'

In a further analysis, however, Kunkel and his team examined additional television channels in their own analysis for 1996. Kunkel and his colleagues monitored a larger sample of 1,351 television shows over a 6-month period from four major commercial broadcast networks, one public broadcasting station, one local independent television station, and four cable channels (Kunkel et al., 1999). All programs except sports and news were monitored.

Across the studies conducted by Kunkel and his colleagues, attempts were made to improve upon previous research methodologies both in respect of program sampling and content coding. At the same time, certain elements had to be retained from earlier research in order to facilitate comparisons over time. Sex was defined as any depiction of sexual activity, sexually suggestive behavior, or talk about sexuality or sexual activity. Portrayals involving talk about sex were measured separately from those that included sexual actions or behaviors. To be considered sex behavior, actions had to convey a sense of potential or likely sexual intimacy. Thus a kiss of greeting between two friends did not count. But a passionate kiss between two characters with a discernible romantic interest would be counted.

With sexually related talk, any comments about sexual incidents that had already occurred or involving sexual suggestiveness were cataloged. For example, if one character told another that he went to bed with a woman the previous night, this would be counted as a sexual incident. Similarly, seductive conversations between potential sexual partners, even when no overt sexual behavior was depicted, would also qualify. Sexual behavior was categorised in a similar fashion to methods used in earlier studies. This approach was taken to ensure that the data obtained for the 1990s would be directly comparable to those obtained in the two previous decades (Kunkel et al., 1999).

The type of sexual behavior was measured using a range of six categories that began with physical flirting (behavior meant to arouse or promote sexual interest), and also included passionate kissing (kissing that conveys a sense of sexual intimacy), intimate touching (touching of another's body in a way that is meant to be sexually arousing), sexual intercourse strongly implied, and sexual intercourse depicted. A final category of 'other' captured highly infrequent behaviors that meet the definition of sexual behavior indicated above but do not fit in any other category, such as self-gratification.

A further distinction was made between intercourse implied and intercourse depicted. Talk about sex was divided into six categories: comments about own or others' sexual actions/interests; talk about sexual intercourse that has already occurred; talk toward sex; talk about sex-related crimes; expert advice; and other. For any material involving either sexual dialogue or behavior, the degree of *scene focus on sex* was judged, differentiating minor or inconsequential references and depictions from portrayals in which there is a substantial or primary emphasis on sex. All scenes were also coded for *degree of explicitness,* which indicated the physical appearance of the characters involved in the behavior. Finally, all scenes were classified in terms of their depiction of *sexual risks or responsibilities.* This term was used to describe the issues surrounding the serious outcomes that could be associated with human sexual activity such as unwanted pregnancy or sexually transmitted diseases.

The measurement system applied by Kunkel and his co-workers did exhibit some modifications to earlier methodologies. Three levels of analysis were deployed to measure sex on television. Distinctions were made between sexual interactions, scenes depicting sex, and the overall sexiness of an entire program. The fundamental level of measurement was an interaction between two or more characters on screen. An interaction endured so long as it continued within the same scene and maintained the same characters as the primary participants. Thus, two characters kissing would represent an single sexual interaction. As soon as they stopped kissing the interaction would end. If the camera shifted to another scene while they were kissing (even though they had not finished), this would mark the end of the interaction. A single interaction could also represent a single scene. However, a scene could contain more than one interaction presented in a relatively unbroken sequence.

The Family Hour Study

The significance of Family Hour stems from the fact that the greatest concentration of young viewers is normally found at this time. During the mid-1990s, audience ratings showed that the four major television networks in the United States (ABC, CBS, NBC, and Fox) could attract more than 6 million children and teenagers between 8 p.m. and 9 p.m. Family Hour was the subject of broadcast industry self-regulation in the 1970s designed to ensure that programs shown at this time would be suitable for all viewers (Wiley, 1977). There was widespread concern to control the appearance of sex and violence on television in the early parts of the evening. The industry's commitment to Family Hour protection was abandoned in the 1980s following legal challenges by the creative community responsible for producing most television entertainment content (Cowan, 1979). The courts ruled that scheduling restrictions on content violated the First Amendment because the Federal Communications Commission (the industry regulator) had pressured the industry to adopt it.

Decisions about appropriate standards for sexual portrayals were then made at the network level. Some observers have argued that, in response to increased competitive pressure from other television services, particularly cable channels, sexual content on the networks has become both more frequent and more explicit. Inasmuch as the great majority of Americans believe that sexual portrayals on television contribute to young people having sex and to the even more serious problem of teenage pregnancies (Impoco, 1996), it is not surprising that calls were heard for a tighter grip on the use of sex in mainstream television entertainment. It was against this background that Kunkel and his colleagues undertook their research.

Kunkel, Cope, and Colvin (1996) found a marked increase, over time, in the proportion of programs on the three television networks that contained any sexual behavior at all. Figures for 1976 showed that 43% of programs contained at least some sexual content, and this increased to 65% in 1986 and to 75% in 1996. The proportion of shows with *no* sexual content at all diminished from a majority (57%) in 1976 to one in four (25%) in 1996. All movies analysed on these networks contained sex in both 1996 and 1986, whereas only half (50%) did in 1976. Drama showed a more substantial increase in the presence of sex over time. In 1976, none of the dramas analysed contained sexual content, but a little over half (54%) did so in 1986 and an overwhelming majority (81%) did so in the 1996. Situation comedies also contributed to television's sexual content. Once again, the prevalence of sex increased over time, from 33% of sitcoms containing sexual material in 1976, to 41% doing so in 1986, and 60% in 1996 (see Table 2.2).

Two types of sexual representation were differentiated in this analysis—one known as 'talk about sex,' and the other labelled 'sexual behavior.' The latter covered physical actions ranging from kissing or caressing to sexual intercourse. In 1976, talk about sex was found in a larger proportion of Family Hour programs (39%) than was actual sexual behavior (26%). In 1986, both types of portrayal had increased with depictions of sexual behavior (48%) found slightly more often than talk about sex (46%). By 1996, an even larger percentage of Family Hour programs contained sexual behavior (61%), slightly outnumbering those containing talk about sex (59%). Family Hour programming in 1996 contained an average of 8.5 sexually related interactions per hour (3.1 involving talk about sex and 5.4 involving sexual behavior), compared with 3.9 in 1986 (1.8 and 2.1), and 2.3 in 1976 (1.2 and 1.1).

It was not only the amount of sex depicted in mainstream television programs on major networks that changed over the 1970s, 1980s, and 1990s, but also the nature of that behavior. A trend was noticed between the mid-1970s and mid-1990s away from characters simply talking about sex and towards actually doing it. In 1976, a larger proportion of programs contained talk about sex (39%) than actual depictions of sexual behavior (22%). By 1996, although there were more programs containing sex in general, the proportion of programs depicting overt sexual behavior of one form or another (61%) was greater than the proportion containing just talk

TABLE 2.2

Prevalence of Sexual Messages Across Types of Programs
Broadcast During 'Family Hour'

	Sitcoms	Drama	Film	Reality	Total
1996 number of Programs	78	31	3	16	128
	%	%	%	%	%
Talk about sex	69	55	33	19	59
Sexual behavior	60	81	100	19	61
None	21	16	0	62	25
Either	78	84	100	38	75
1986 number of Programs	17	13	1	0	31
	%	%	%	%	%
Talk about sex	47	38	100	0	46
Sexual behavior	41	54	100	0	48
None	35	38	0	0	35
Either	65	62	100	0	65
1976 number of Programs	15	6	2	0	23
	%	%	%	%	%
Talk about sex	53	0	50	0	39
Sexual behavior	33	0	50	0	26
None	40	100	50	0	57
Either	60	0	50	0	43

Note. Source: Kunkel et al., 1996. Reproduced with permission of Kaiser Family Foundation.

about sex (59%). Having said that, it should be borne in mind that when sexual conduct was shown on screen, it usually involved little more than kissing or flirting.

Of course, even talk about sex can get erotic at times. However, Kunkel and his colleagues observed that intimate or seductive conversations (8% of all sex talk) were quite rare. Instead, most conversations that touched on the subject of sexual matters represented observations about other people's sex lives on the part of television characters (32% of all sex talk), or comments about the character's own sex life (28%) or past sexual history (21%).

Turning to actual sexual behavior, more than eight in ten incidents of sexual behavior comprised physical flirting (46%) or kissing (39%). More intimate touching was the next most frequently occurring sexual behavior (12%), whereas sexual intercourse was rarely shown on screen (3% of sexual incidents).

Across all examples of sexual behavior observed in 1996, two out of three included characters who shared an established relationship with each other. An established relationship was defined as characters having shared close interpersonal activities and experiences together, which could range from a dating relationship to a long-term committed situation. While it was common for those involved in the full range of sexual interactions to have an established relationship with one another (67%), it was uncommon for the characters to be married. Individuals engaged in sexual behaviors were much more likely to be unmarried (71%) than married (23%).

Relationship fidelity was sometimes violated in television programs. Roughly one case out of six involving sexual behaviors (17%) included a character who had an established sexual or romantic relationship with someone other than the partner in that situation. In more than one in five cases (22%) where sexual intercourse was depicted or implied, at least one of the characters had an established relationship with another person.

The "Sex on TV" Study

This later and much bigger study by Kunkel and his colleagues analysed sexual content 'presented across the overall television landscape' (Kunkel et al., 1999, p. 4). This study covered both network and cable channels. The analysis revealed that there are two primary types of portrayals involving sex—talk about sex and sexual behavior. Both types of portrayals have the potential to influence viewers' beliefs and attitudes about sexual issues. Across the composite week sample of 942 programs, more than half (56%) contained some sexual content. Of all programs studied, 39% contained one or more scenes with a substantial emphasis on sex. Sex was often not just an isolated incident in a program. Of the 528 programs that contained any sex at all, there was an average of 3.2 scenes per hour involving sex. More than half (54%) of all programs studied contained talk about sex, with an average of 3.0 scenes per hour containing sex talk; 23% of all programs studied contained sexual behavior, averaging 1.4 scenes per hour with sexual behavior shown.

Among programs containing any sexual content, the sexual material was rated in terms of its degree of explicitness along a four-point scale, encompassing provocative dress, some disrobing, discreet nudity, and nudity. Across all programs including any sexual behavior, the average level of explicitness was low at 0.9. In programs with precursory behaviors only, the explicitness score was 0.4; in those depicting sexual intercourse, it was 1.9. Although this difference is significant, even in cases of depictions of sexual intercourse, the level of explicitness was fairly mild.

Turning to talk about sex, two thirds of such scenes (66%) involved an individual making comments about his or her own or another's sexual interests. In 15% of cases, the talk was about sexual intercourse that had occurred. In just under one in ten cases (9%), the talk was about sex-related crimes. In smaller proportions of cases, the talk concerned 'talk towards sex' (talk leading up to sex; 4%) and expert advice or technical information about sex (2%). On sexual behaviors, three out of four cases involved physical flirting (26%) or kissing (50%). Much smaller proportions of cases involved more explicit sexual behavior such as intimate touching (7%), implied sexual intercourse (12%) or depicted sexual intercourse (3%).

SEX ON TELEVISION
OUTSIDE THE UNITED STATES

A small number of studies have been carried out beyond the United States in which sex on television has been quantified. In Britain, the Broadcasting Standards Commission (formerly the Broadcasting Standards Council) conducted regular monitoring of sex on television during the 1990s.

An initial content analysis was reported by Millwood-Hargrave (1992) of seven days' evening output (6 p.m.–midnight) on the four main UK television channels (BBC1, BBC2, ITV, Channel Four) to assess the depiction of sexual activity and nudity on British television. Out of a total of 277 programs and 524 advertisements, 57 scenes of sexual activity were catalogued. All portrayed heterosexual sex. The most frequently occurring sexual behavior was kissing, which was represented in over half the scenes (53%). Just under one in four scenes (23%) depicted the coital act. Other scenes were noted to be precoital (11%) or postcoital (9%). There were also two scenes (4%) where sex was implied through sound though not actually seen on screen.

A further classification of sexual activity in terms of context and characterisation revealed some evidence of gender differences in the depiction of sexual behavior on British television. Although more than one third of the relationships in which sexual activity occurred were established relationships, few involved married couples (see Table 2.3). This pattern is consistent with findings in North America. Men were much more likely than women to be depicted having an extramarital affair. Women and men, however, were equally likely to be shown engaged in sexual activity on a first date.

Millwood-Hargrave (1992) compared these objective content analysis results to the subjective opinions held by the British public towards premarital and extramarital affairs. The former was largely accepted (54% of re-

TABLE 2.3

Context of Sexual Activity on UK Television

Type of relationship	Number	%
Established married	5	9
Established nonmarried	15	26
Extramarital affair: men	13	23
Extramarital affair:women	1	2
Extramarital affair: both	1	2
First time pick-up by male	3	5
First time pick-up by female	3	5
First time pick-up mutual	6	11
Rape or sexual abuse	1	2
Prostitution	2	4
Other	7	12

Note: Source: Millwood-Hargrave, 1992.

spondents saying it was rarely or not at all wrong and 23% saying it was mostly or always wrong), but the latter were roundly rejected (85% saying it was always or mostly wrong and 3% saying it was rarely or never wrong).

Other work on television sex has emerged from New Zealand. An analysis of sex on television based on all programs recorded on the three New Zealand broadcast television channels during one week in February 1991 found 287 sexual images, events, or sequences. On Channels 1 and 2, sexual images occurred around once every 90 minutes, and on Channel 3 they occurred once every 45 minutes. In this study, coders were asked to code each image, sequence, and event by the level of public offence they believed it would cause. They assessed this by reference to past objections filed with the Broadcasting Standards Committee. They were invited to decide the likelihood that an objection would be raised, not whether it would be sustained. Ratings were made along a five-point scale: 1 being 'sure not to cause complaint' and 5 being 'certain to cause complaint.' Fifteen scenes were rated at the 3 and 4 levels, but none at 5 (Watson, Bassett, Lambourne, & Shuker, 1991).

Most of the sexual material was found to occur in films that were largely broadcast in the afternoon or in the late evening or late-night slots. There were 24 films scheduled in the week of the analysis. Thirteen of these films supplied 90 out of the total 287 instances of sexual imagery. Most of the sexual imagery seen during this week was not of a violent nature. More than one in two sexual scenes (56%) were classified as depicting loving relationships; more than one in three (35%) were classified as casual relationships. Nine per cent of scenes contained any angry or coercive behavior.

The great majority of sexual scenes comprised kissing (84%) and a further one in ten (9%) contained some petting (hugging, cuddling, stroking, etc). Nudity was infrequent and any that did occur was carefully staged to avoid giving offence. The only full-frontal images to include pubic hair were within the movie *Body Double*, which was screened after midnight. In scenes that depicted lovemaking, the camera tended to show no more than the top half of a naked body and from behind. There was only one instance when the camera showed almost full-length nudity in a scene depicting intercourse. Women's breasts, however, were shown on 11 occasions.

The authors concluded that the amount and nature of sexual activity shown on television was not of a quantity or type that would cause concern to most people. Furthermore, programs that contained more explicit sexual imagery were scheduled late at night, thus keeping within the requirements of the guidelines provided by the broadcast regulator.

GENDER DIFFERENCES IN DEPICTIONS OF SEXUAL BEHAVIOR

Few of the early studies of sexual behavior on mainstream television differentiated between genders in terms of the nature of their sexual behavior. One exception was a study by Silverman and her colleagues. Following up an earlier study, Silverman et al. (1979) analysed prime-time network programs from the 1977–1978 season in the United States. They found no overt portrayals of intercourse, but there were occurrences of implied intercourse, where intimate sexual behavior was about to take place or had just happened. Touching, embracing, and kissing were again the most common acts. On this occasion, comparisons were reported between male and female characters. Females represented 32% of the character population studied. Females also accounted for a greater proportion of the categories of physical kiss, physical hug, physical affectionate touching, and implied intercourse than would have been expected on the basis of their overall representation.

The most likely explanation of this is that these types of interactions are typically done heterosexually, and as the likelihood of male–female reciprocal actions increases, the male–female ratio of performers will reach one to one. Therefore, for the category of implied intercourse where, by definition, a coded instance involves a heterosexual couple, the ratio reaches an even split. In addition, females accounted for a disproportionate amount of the physical suggestiveness and references to affectionate touching.

Research by Sapolsky and Tabarlet (1991) shows that, in interactions between men and women, the male predominated as the initiator. In 1989, male characters were found to initiate two thirds of sexual behavior and conversation. Male characters initiated three fourths of the noncriminal sex acts in 1989. In contrast, in the 1979 season, equality of the sexes was in order. Males initiated 110 sexual acts; females precipitated an additional 111 (see Table 2.4).

Later research reported a near even split between males and females involved in talk about sex (49.2% vs. 49.7%) and overt depictions of sexual behavior (50.5% vs. 48.9%) in Family Hour network television the United States (Kunkel et al., 1996).

TABLE 2.4

Frequency of Sexual Incidents on U.S. Television—1989

| | Gender of Initiator–Receiver | |
	Male–Female	Female–Male
Noncriminal sex acts	204	76
Touching	87	35
Hugging	36	9
Kissing	72	29
Implied intercourse	6	2
Explicit intercourse	3	1
Criminal sex acts	3	0
Sexual language	79	53
Touch-hug-kiss	15	11
Intercourse	11	16
Prostitution-rape	32	22
Sexual innuendo	21	4
Atypical sex practices	116	99
Sexual responsibility	9	5
Categories combined	416	240
Rate per hour 1989	7.23	4.17

Note: Source: Sapolsky and Tabarlet, 1991.

MARITAL RELATIONS AND SEX
ON TELEVISION

From the earliest studies of sex on television, a preponderance of sexual action and talk was found to take place among unmarried characters. One
analysis of American network television found that three out of four noncriminal sex acts featured unmarried characters in 1979, and that 10 years
later, this figure had increased to eight in ten characters engaged in sexual
interaction. Furthermore, all instances of implied or explicit sexual intercourse involved unmarried partners. In 1989, only one verbal reference to
intercourse (out of a total of 91) occurred between a married couple
(Sapolsky & Tabarlet, 1991).

Many of the analyses of sex on television in which the marital status of
characters has been a focal point have examined soap operas. This prominent and popular genre has proved to be a rich source of sexually oriented
story lines. By the 1990s, soap operas on American television were shown
frequently to depict sex outside of marriage. Around one in five sexual incidents (21%) in these soaps involved fictional characters who were, within
the context of the story, known to be married to each other, whereas in all
other such incidents the participants were either single, married but not to
each other, or had an unknown marital status (Greenberg & Busselle, 1996;
Greenberg & D'Alessio, 1985; Greenberg & Woods, 1999).

During the 1990s, evidence emerged that trends were changing. Sex was
depicted as something engaged in more often by characters who were in established sexual or romantic relationships. Heintz-Knowles (1996) found
that sexual activity was increasingly depicted as a part of an established romantic involvement between partners, and that one-night stands were rare.

Another American study of a wider sample of programs, by Kunkel and
his colleagues (1999) found that more than half the characters involved in
the depiction of sexual intercourse-related behaviors (53%) were in an established relationship (even if not actually married), more than one in four
(28%) had met before their initial sexual encounter but had not yet established an intimate relationship, and one in ten (10%) had only just met.
This study analysed a composite week of television programs video-re-
corded from ten channels, including the major networks.

The same research group conducted an analysis on a small sample of 15
television shows designed specifically for the teenage audience. The shows
analysed were known to be the most-watched among that age group. In this
case, most physical behaviors occurred between participants who were not
married (79%). However, most of those involved in some kind of sexual interaction (71%) were in an established relationship. Furthermore, in most of
these relationships (74%), the characters remained faithful to their romantic

partners. A minority of characters (10%) were depicted as being unfaithful to their established romantic partner in the show (Cope & Kunkel, 1999). This same study found just six instances of sexual intercourse taking place among characters. In every case, these interactions occurred between characters who had an established sexual or romantic relationship with one another.

Some researchers have gone beyond simple descriptive counts of the extent on involvement in sexual interactions of characters within or outside of established relationships, to explore the reactions of participants to their sexual relations. Greenberg and Woods (1999) reported that married couples in televised fiction were depicted as overwhelmingly satisfied with their sexual relationship. For the most part, husbands were older than their wives. More than half the husband characters (54%) were in their 40s, whereas less than a quarter of the wives were in this age group (23%). The initiation of sex was evenly divided among married men and women.

In those instances where sexual relations occurred among characters who were not married to each other, there was a tendency for the men to be older than the women. The attitudes of participants towards their sexual relationship were also less clear-cut than was the case with married couples. Fewer than half the men (46%) and women (40%) who engaged in sexual relations with someone to whom they were not married were positive about the experience, whereas a minority in each case (men, 14%; women, 18%) were not completely satisfied with their relationship. In contrast to earlier studies, however, having sex with someone who was married to someone else was a minority activity for women (12%) and for men (15%).

The significance of these patterns of sexual portrayals stems from evidence that they may shape viewers' beliefs about the status of sexual relations, faithfulness, and the institution of marriage. Regular exposure to soap operas in which volatile relationships, marital infidelity, divorce, abortions and pregnancy outside marriage are depicted as frequently occurring if not the norm, can encourage viewers to believe that the world really is much the same as this (Buerkel-Rothfuss & Mayes, 1981). Although the extent to which such social conditioning effects occur may be dependent on the reasons that bring viewers to these programs to begin with (Carveth & Alexander, 1985; Perse, 1986), there is some suggestion that certain categories of viewer, who rely on television for much of their entertainment, information about the world, and companionship, could be especially susceptible to such influences.

SEX-RELATED RISKS AND RESPONSIBILITIES

Public opinion about the depiction of sex on television has challenged broadcasters to take a more responsible line by building safe sex messages into sexual portrayals. This treatment is believed to be particularly important given the role that television might play in the sex education of children and teenagers (Millwood-Hargrave, 1992). Concerns have been about the morality of television's depictions of sex as well as its health implications. The mass media have been criticised for showing sex as glamorous or exciting and risk free (Furstenberg, Moore, & Peterson, 1985) and cited as one of the causes of increased risky sexual activity among the young (Hayes, 1987).

Over many years, however, content analysis studies have indicated a tendency for television to represent sex as a largely hedonistic pursuit rather than as part of a loving, established, and long-term romantic relationship, and one publicly sealed through marriage. Instead, sex is frequently depicted as an activity indulged in more often by unmarried than married couples. Contraceptives are rarely referred to or used, yet women seldom get pregnant, and men and women rarely contract sexually transmitted diseases unless they are prostitutes or homosexuals (J. D. Brown & Steele, 1995; Fernandez-Collado et al., 1978; Greenberg, Abelman, & Neuendorf, 1981; Greenberg, Graef, Fernandez-Collado, Korzenny, & Atkin, 1980; Lowry et al., 1981).

Between the mid-1980s and mid-1990s, soap operas on American network television depicted increased incidence of sexual relations (particularly intercourse) between unmarried partners and introduced of date-rape story lines. Discussions of safe-sex practices or use of contraception were identified on five occasions across 50 episodes from five drama serials (Greenberg & Busselle, 1996). Although much TV sex focused on sex between partners who were not married, a great deal of this content was spoken rather than visually depicted. Interestingly, spoken dialogue revealed signs of an increasingly responsible attitude towards sex among soap characters. Positive attitudes towards sexual activities declined from 69% in 1985 to 50% in 1994. Positive attitudes towards married sexual intercourse, in contrast, rose sharply. Sex outside marriage was increasingly frowned upon. Themes of pregnancy—wanted and unwanted—became more prominent and were reminders of sexual responsibility and irresponsibility.

Across 50 soap opera episodes, Greenberg and his colleagues looked for special references to safe sex and the use of contraception. Five references were detected. One case involved a lengthy, multiscene discussion between a mother and her teenage daughter about the merits and demerits of having sex with her boyfriend, and one specific mention of AIDS occurred. Twenty out of the 50 episodes included scenes that referred to pregnancy. There were 15 different pregnancies in all. Pregnancies were twice as likely to be unwanted as wanted, and in most cases, the identity of the father was known. In half these cases, the parents were married to each other and in one in four cases they were not. In other cases, the marital status was unclear. The researchers noted that given the centrality of pregnancy to most soap operas, it was curious that half of the pregnancies they cataloged were portrayed as being a surprise (Greenberg & Woods, 1999).

The risks and responsibilities factor was regarded by Kunkel et al. (1999) as an important contextual feature in relation to the portrayal of sex. They measured three possible types of themes concerning risks and responsibilities of sexual behavior: (a) *sexual patience*: waiting until a relationship matures and both people are equally ready to engage in sex; (b) *sexual precaution*: pursuing efforts to prevent AIDS, STDs, and/or unwanted pregnancy when sexually active; and (c) *depiction of risks and/or negative consequences* of irresponsible sexual behavior.

There were 45 scenes containing depiction of risks or negative consequences (2% of sexual scenes). There were 35 scenes of sexual precaution (2% of all sexual scenes). There were 13 scenes depicting sexual patience (1% of all sexual scenes). Those scenes ($n = 78$) that included risk or responsibility concerns were categorised as placing either minor or substantial emphasis on such topics. A further 37 scenes were classified as minor emphasis and 41 scenes were classified as a substantial portrayal. Talk shows (23% that had any sexual content) were most likely to contain discussion of risks and responsibilities of sex. Comedy (3%) and drama (5%) were least likely to include any such caveats associated with sex.

Kunkel et al. examined the ages of the characters involved in sex, their apparent relationship to one another, and any association between sex and drugs or alcohol. Nearly three quarters of all characters involved in sexual scenes (73%) were classified as adults aged 25 or older. Nearly one in four (23%) were classified as young adults, age 18 to 24 years. Just 3% were classified as teens age 13 to 17. There was just one scene in which a child character (under 12) was involved.

In more than half the scenes depicting sexual activity, the characters were in an established relationship (53%). In more than one in four cases (28%) the characters had met before but were not yet in an established relationship. In one in ten cases (10%), they had just met. There were just two scenes in which drugs were involved and 13 scenes in which alcohol was involved.

Kunkel et al. found that the majority of shows on television that involve intercourse present no information at all within episodes regarding the consequences for the characters. This held true both for programs than presented talk about intercourse (63% showed no clear consequences) and for those that depicted or strongly implied the behavior (59% showed no clear consequences). When intercourse was the topic of talk, there was relative balance between the programs that included primarily positive and primarily negative consequences of intercourse (14% positive vs. 16% negative in programs featuring talk about intercourse that has occurred). When intercourse behavior was shown rather than discussed second-hand, there was a much stronger tendency towards positive than negative outcomes (27% vs. 7%).

VIOLENT SEXUAL PORTRAYALS
ON TELEVISION

Content analysis studies have indicated considerable variability in the prevalence of violent sexual portrayals in different types of sexually explicit media, as research discussed later in this chapter shows. Around a third of 'adult' books were found to contain references to such behavior (Smith, 1976), as compared to a little more than one in ten 'adult' movies (Palys, 1986; Slade, 1984; Yang & Linz, 1990), and about one in 20 soft-core magazines (Malamuth & Spinner, 1980; Winick, 1985). On broadcast television, however, such depictions are seldom shown in an explicit way.

Following the discussion of 'risk factors' associated with the depiction of sex on television, however, in addition to risks concerned with avoidance of pregnancy and sexually transmitted diseases, there has been concern voiced about violent sexual depictions on mainstream television programs. A study of daytime soap operas indicated that although violent sexual behavior was the second most frequently occurring type of sexual conduct, it was nearly always implied rather than shown on screen (Lowry et al., 1981). A later analysis revealed that even implied sexual violence or references to rape were not common, occurring about once in every 11 hours of broadcasting. In contrast, the sexual activity most frequently referred to—verbal mentions of sexual intercourse—occurred 1.5 times every hour in soap operas (Greenberg & D'Alessio, 1985).

During the 1990s, date rape emerged as a prominent theme in television soap operas. A nonevent in the 1980s, within 10 years it emerged as a key issue. Greenberg and Woods (1999) reported two date rape stories in soap operas from the mid-1990s. Both dealt with date rape of teenagers. In one case, the date rape involved multiple assailants and viewers witnessed remorse and guilt from two of the male characters, but not from a third. The pain of the victim was relived frequently in subsequent episodes. Another story line portrayed a teenage boy holding his potential victim hostage and tormenting her, having raped her sister some time earlier. The episodes in this story ended with the accused rapist stating that he would testify he never had sex with the victim and verbally menacing both sisters.

SEX IN MOVIES AND VIDEO

Content analyses of the most popular movies in the United States of 1959, 1969, and 1979 demonstrated a trend towards increasing explicitness in depictions of sexual themes, but the themes themselves remained stable. Sex in the movies was more about physical gratification than about expressing affection (Abramson & Mechanic, 1983). Movies made for the theatre are frequently shown on television. Analyses of televised films have shown them to be among the most 'sexual' genres on broadcast or cable television, and the most explicitly sexual of any genre in terms of depictions of overt sexual behaviour (Kunkel et al., 1999).

Much R-rated (and even some X-rated) material to which they would be denied admission in a theatre can be watched by children and teenagers on cable channels (Yang & Linz, 1990). Furthermore, with R-rated and X-rated films shown in the theatre, most individuals experience a single viewing, whereas on cable television, movies enjoy repeat showings, giving opportunities for repeat exposures.

Video entertainment has become increasingly popular since the early 1980s. Mainstream cinema films, originally produced for theatre showing, are eventually distributed through video releases. However, concern about sexual portrayals in video has focused more emphatically on pornographic movie releases that are exclusive to this medium and on music videos. The pornographic video releases contain a greater quantity of sexual content that is generally far more explicit than anything found in cinema films. Music videos have caused concern because sex is one of the dominant themes in popular music and the addition of sexual images may increase the excitement they can arouse in viewers (Zillmann & Mundorf, 1987). They are also especially popular with teenagers. The potential risk of socially undesirable effects on young viewers may increase when already powerful music and lyrics are mixed with visual images (Hendren & Strasburger, 1993). Together, the newer media of cable television and video present increased opportunities for exposure to material of an extreme sexual nature. Against this background, it is important to have data on just how much explicit sex these media present.

Sex in Music Videos

The growing popularity of music videos during the 1980s, stimulated by the increased availability of economically viable products in music stores and promoted through specialised television services such as MTV, led a number of researchers to turn their attention towards this category of video entertainment. Research into music videos was further encouraged by anecdotal observations that sex and violence appeared to be prominent themes. As the market for these products became established, investment in their production grew, with the result that their professional quality also improved.

As they became more firmly established on the entertainment scene, music videos were the focus of more concerted criticism. Groups such as Women Against Pornography and the National Coalition on Television Violence argued that the videos were even more sexist, pornographic, and violent than conventional television (Jaeger, 1984). Others argued that MTV (Music Television) was racist because it did not play adequate numbers of videos of Black performers (Wolmuth, 1983). There was particular concern about the potential impact of these videos given that most of their audience comprised adolescents.

Music videos can be divided into performance videos and concept videos. In a performance video, a musical performer or group sings a song in a concert or studio setting. A concept video consists of a story that goes along with the song, which may or may not add a plot to the lyrics (Strasburger, 1985). Both types of video have been found to display sexual content. In performance videos, popular music artists wear revealing attire designed to enhance their sexual allure make sexually suggestive movements, and in some cases even simulate sexual behavior on stage. Concept videos may display more explicit sexual imagery, involving nudity, and display behavior such as kissing, erotic touching, and simulated intercourse. When such images are combined with explicitly sexual lyrics, the overall effect is a highly sexualised medium.

Only a limited number of studies have been published in which the prevalence of sexual content in music videos was measured. An analysis of concept music videos in 1985 found sexual intimacy in more than three quarters of the music videos examined. Visible sexual activity consisted mostly of touching, kissing, hugging and flirting. However, sex was more often implied than overtly shown (Sherman & Dominick, 1986). The same study also found that around half of all the women featured were dressed provocatively and tended to be displayed as sex objects. Another study conducted around the same time reported that nearly 60% of concept videos sampled contained sexual themes (Baxter, De Riemer, Landini, Leslie, & Singletary, 1985).

This study was limited, however, in that it restricted its analysis to detecting the presence of sexual content in music videos and did not provide measures of how much sexual material individual video productions contained. Even so, it did provide a breakdown of the types of sexual behavior that were identified. Sexual content was signalled by provocative clothing (31% of videos with sexual content), embraces (31%), sexually suggestive dancing (27%), other sexually suggestive movements (21%), scenes of dating or courting (15%), kissing (11%), scenes depicting males chasing females and vice versa (11%), and finally, someone using a musical instrument in a sexually suggestive manner (8%).

Music videos were found to be not only sexual but also sexist (Gow, 1993; Vincent, Davis, & Bronszkowski, 1987). The earliest studies that emerged in the mid-1980s corroborated less formal, nonscientific evidence about the violent and sexual themes that ran through many of these videos (Baxter et al., 1985). At this time, however, the fusion of sex and violence was relatively rare. Analysis of a random sample of videos from one week of output on MTV in 1984, for example, found sadomasochism themes in 5% of videos and sexual bondage themes in just 2% (Baxter et al., 1985).

J. D. Brown and Campbell (1986) conducted a content analysis study to establish what kinds of portrayals music videos contained. They sampled videos from MTV and Black Entertainment Television (BET) and compared how men and women were portrayed. They distinguished two broad categories of music video. Performance videos contained images of the musical performer or group in concert, with or without a live audience. Concept videos were based on a story line or subject of the story and featured the song's artist(s) as the main performer(s).

Love emerged as the dominant theme of performance and concept videos on both television channels. In one in three cases on MTV, sexual relations were featured prominently, and this was also true of four in ten videos from the BET channel. Altogether, just under half (47%) of the songs featured in the videos in this sample were about love, in the context of courting, desiring a sexual relationship, or severing a relationship.

Further research by Vincent and his colleagues expanded on these early findings, and produced more detailed results on the nature of sexual themes and depicted sexual behavior in music videos. In one study, they analysed 300 rock videos selected from MTV and classified the different forms of male–female contact. This varied from simple touching (53.8% of videos) through kissing (26.9%), hugging (25.2%), heavy petting (4.2%,) to implied lovemaking (1.7%). Nearly one in ten videos contained suggested nudity (9.2%), nearly 4 in 10 (38.7%) used highly seductive clothing, and one in ten (10.1%) used women in undergarments (Vincent et al., 1987).

Vincent (1988) published another analysis of MTV rock videos 2 years later to find out if the themes noted in the earlier study had changed at all. He found that the prevalence of implicit or explicit nudity (15.6% of videos), of women in lingerie (16.4%), and of women in bathing suits (13 cases) had all exhibited marginal, nonsignificant increases over time. The frequency of nonintimate, sexual touching actually decreased, while kissing and heavy petting remained largely unchanged. Implied lovemaking still occurred only in a small minority (4%) of videos, but had become twice as prevalent compared with 2 years earlier.

Films Aimed at Teenage Audiences

Analysis of mainstream television in the United States has indicated that one in ten scenes containing sexual material involved teenagers. In the great majority of such scenes (83%), teenager characters simply talked about sex, although in some of these instances (13%), talk centered on sex that had occurred. About one in six sexual scenes (17%) involving teenagers depicted sexual behavior. For the most part, these scenes comprised kissing (63%) or flirting (27%), and none were found to depict sexual intercourse between teenagers, although in a few cases (8%) sexual intercourse was implied (Kunkel et al., 1999).

Analysis of R-rated films known to be popular among adolescents has indicated the presence of more explicit sexual content. Greenberg and his colleagues looked at the sex content of movies such as *Friday the 13th, Best Little Whorehouse in Texas, Risky Business, Porky's II,* and *Bachelor Party.* All the movies ($n = 16$) selected for analysis had previously been identified by a teenage sample as being among the most liked movies among their age group. An average of 12.5 acts involving sexual behavior were found per film (or 10.8 scenes per hour). Nude scenes were quite prevalent (9.8 per film), with female nudity exceeding male nudity by four to one. The main category of sexuality was sexual intercourse between unmarried partners (8 acts per film). In sum, these R-rated movies typically contained far more sex than television programs (Greenberg, Siemicki, Dorfman, et al., 1993).

Sex in Explicit Videos

Sexual content has traditionally been associated with restricted adult forms of entertainment. Prior to the popularity of entertainment videos, explicit sexual content could be obtained through printed media, including books and magazines. Much explicit sexual material could be found, for instance, in adults-only paperbacks. During the 1960s and 1970s, the amount of sexual material being made available in this form increased by a substantial margin (Smith, 1976).

With the rapid expansion of the home video market in the 1980s, pornographic videos superseded print media as the preferred form of explicit sexual entertainment. Several published studies have reported analyses of sexual depictions in these videos. While adult videos contain large quantities of explicit sex, almost by definition, researchers have been interested in the particular types of sexual behavior portrayed.

The bulk of pornographic material, published in the form of still photographs or video and film productions, is nonviolent. Predominantly, it depicts revealing shots of female nudity and acts of heterosexual intercourse.

Themes tend to be highly masculine, preoccupied with the sex act and with little surrounding story line or development of romantic relationships. Typical portrayals show heterosexual intercourse, oral–genital contact, lesbianism, group sex, and anal intercourse (Hebditch & Anning, 1988). There tends to be minimal communication between partners and little expression of emotion apart from lust and desire (Brosius, Weaver, & Staab, 1993; Prince, 1990; Rimmer, 1986).

Palys (1986) examined adult and XXX-rated videos commercially available in Vancouver, Canada. More than 4,200 separate scenes were identified with 150 videos, of which about half could be coded for sex, aggression, and/or sexual aggression. The triple-X videos frequently depicted explicit sexual acts among the actors, including genital–genital intercourse, oral–genital contact, and the fondling of breasts and genitals.

Palys found that XXX-rated videos portrayed more egalitarian and mutually consenting sexual depictions than adult videos. For example, although in adult videos men usually played the dominant role in sexual scenes, in the XXX-rated videos men and women were depicted in the dominant role about equally often. Second, the adult videos had higher percentages of aggressive scenes and more severe and graphic forms of aggression than the XXX-rated videos and more often depicted scenes in which at least one participant did not engage in sex freely or scenes involving overt aggression. Finally, although Palys found no indication of an increase between 1979 and 1983 in nonsexual aggressive images in either type of video, the percentage of *sexual* violence appeared to have declined in X-rated materials but remained constant in adult videos. Palys found that females were more likely to be the targets of sexual violence in adult-rated videos than in X-rated videos.

In another study, Cowan, Lee, Levy, and Snyder (1988) analysed more than 400 explicit sex scenes taken from 45 X-rated videos. They found that more than half the scenes they examined depicted themes of domination or exploitation. Four major themes were identified: domination, in which the sex act was controlled by one person (28% of all sex scenes); reciprocity, in which sex took place between equal and mutually consenting participants (37%); exploitation, in which one person used status or coercion to get their own way (26%); and finally autoeroticism, which depicted scenes of self-stimulation and masturbation (9%). Most of the sex scenes were heterosexual (78%). Bisexual or homosexual acts featured female actors only. There was a clear presence in many scenes of aggression—either verbal (20%) or physical (23%). Six per cent of scenes depicted rape. The analysis showed that men were usually the dominant actors, whereas females were submissive recipients of what was sometimes seen as abusive treatment.

A later study by Yang and Linz (1990) analysed a sample of 90 R-, X-, and XXX-rated videos selected at random from a pool of more than 1,600 titles. behavior portrayed in these videos was classified for the presence of sex, violence, sexual violence and pro-social activity. Nearly 2,800 behavioral sequences were coded of which 52% were coded as either sexual, violent, sexually violent, or prosocial. Sexual behavior was most frequently portrayed in X-rated and XXX-rated videos. Violence was most prevalent in R-rated videos. Sexually violent behavior was infrequent in all categories. The predominant form of sexual violence overall was individual or group rape (33% of such scenes) followed by exploitative and coercive sexual relations (26%, and sadomasochism (19%). Female and male homosexual rape was the predominant theme in around 5% and 6%, respectively, of sexually violent behaviors.

A breakdown by video type showed that in X-rated videos the predominant sexual theme was rape (either individual rape or group rape of a single female by a group of males). Exploitative and coercive sexual relations not coded as rape comprised 21% of the remaining sexually violent depictions, and sadomasochism an additional 1% in the X-rated videos. The scenes on XX-rated videos were exploitative and coercive sexual relations (39%), followed by group rape and sadomasochism. In R-rated videos, group rape and exploitative coercive sexual relations, portrayed with nearly equal frequency, were the most frequently portrayed sexual themes. Male homosexual rape and sadomasochism, the next most frequent categories, were also portrayed with about equal frequency in R-rated videos.

Among the four types of behaviors examined here—violent, sexual, sexually violent, and prosocial—the predominant behavior in both X-rated and XXX-rated videos was sexual, while in the R-rated videos it was violence followed by prosocial behavior. Sexually violent behavior was infrequent but equally likely to be portrayed in R-rated, X-rated, and XXX-rated videos. When R-rated videos were compared to X- and XXX-rated types, combined in a slightly more powerful statistical analysis, no difference was found.

Pornographic films and videos are highly sexual in nature. They depict frequent acts of sexual behavior, and most of these acts are very explicit. Sex in such material tends to be heterosexual rather than homosexual, but homosexuality is not uncommon and tends predominantly to involve lesbianism. The availability of pornography with coercive or violent themes is limited (D. Brown & Bryant, 1989). Nevertheless, such materials are not unknown and tend to depict women getting enjoyment out of being raped (Cowan et al., 1988). In a rape myth scenario, women's initial reactions of distress during rape are transformed into sexual arousal and pleasure. Few sexually explicit materials depict idealised sexual themes in which sex occurs as part of a romantic relationship and where male and female partners are equals in the relationship.

CONCLUSION

This chapter has reviewed research into the way sex is shown in the media. It has focused on the representation of sex on television, films, and videos. The overriding impression to be gained from studies conducted during the past three decades is that the amount of sex in these media has increased. Television programs contain more overt sexual activity, but more especially more talking about sexual matters. In addition, the degree of explicitness of sexual depictions in mainstream media, such as television and popular films, has also increased. Although much of the sex shown on nonsubscription television channels is mild in nature, rarely going beyond kissing and cuddling, there has nevertheless been a growing propensity to push back the barriers by developing story lines that tackle controversial subject sexual matter, such as homosexuality, rape, prostitution, and even incest.

Explicit depictions of sexual intercourse have remained rare in mainstream entertainment media, though not so in materials made for adult audiences. Sex in pornographic videos tends to be graphically portrayed. Indeed, in many of these 'adult only' productions, little is left to the imagination. The real concern with such sexual depictions lies not with the tastefulness of the nudity and sexual simulations, but with the hidden messages that may be conveyed about women and female sexuality. As we will see in later chapters, this concern has been reinforced by audience research on public opinion about such portrayals (especially that of women viewers) and on the effects that exposure to this type of sexual depiction might have on the beliefs and attitudes of young men about women and female sexuality.

Other characteristics of media sex portrayals are related to the occurrence of sex outside of established emotional relationships and the tendency for sexual couplings to take place with little consideration being given to the risks of casual sex. This pattern has been found to characterise sexual portrayals in media aimed at younger audiences. As such, concern has centered on the lessons that these sexual representations may teach young people at a time of life when they are becoming sexually active and media role models are significant sources of influence.

The analysis of media content can identify and describe regularly occurring patterns of sexual behavior in television programs, films, and videos. It does not represent a measure of the impact of media sex, however. To understand the significance of media sex as a social phenomenon, it is necessary to turn to research conducted among media consumers. This research should tell us something about the way viewers perceive media content for themselves and react to what they see. In the next chapter, we continue the analysis of media sex by examining public opinion about sexual content in the media.

3

What Is Acceptable to the Public?

Studies of media output have clearly demonstrated that sex represents a prevalent feature of motion pictures and other productions that are shown in theaters, on video or on broadcast television. Studies of the representation of sex on screen have distinguished between different kinds of sexual behavior. Most of what appears on mainstream audiovisual media productions tend to take the form of fairly mild depictions of sexual behavior. More graphic depictions also occur, but tend to be restricted to films and videos with adult classifications or programs broadcast late at night and on more specialised subscription channels. Having shown that depictions of sexual behavior occur with some regularity and that sex has increased in its presence on screen over the past two decades, the next important question is whether sex per se or different types of sexual portrayal are acceptable to viewers. Do viewers display concerns that sex is too much of a preoccupation in films and programs? Do they perceive that it has increased in prevalence and in graphic detail over time? Are such developments generally welcome or should they be discouraged and reversed?

Establishing whether the depiction of sex in films, television programs, and videos is acceptable to the public has been attempted mostly through public opinion surveys. In addition, qualitative methodologies have been deployed to explore in greater depth the opinions that ordinary people hold about sex on screen. Attempts have also been made through laboratory-based studies to measure viewers' perceptions of different types of sexual portrayal and to relate these perceptions to the nature of the portrayal and to the personality of the viewer.

PUBLIC OPINION ABOUT SEX ON SCREEN

Numerous surveys have explored public opinion about sex on broadcast television. This research has examined the public's views about whether there is too much sex in the audiovisual entertainment media and attitudes towards different kinds of sexual portrayal. Surveys asking about the amount of sex in the media tended to be used most frequently with television. This is understandable given the ubiquity of the medium, but more especially given the way it enters people's homes. With cinema films, movie-goers have to attend screenings in a theatre and often will have read advance notices about the films they go to watch. The movie-goer therefore exerts a considerable degree of personal control over what to see, when, and in whose company. With videos, consumers must take a deliberate decision to purchase or rent a film on video. The choice of when to watch and with whom to watch is also very much under the viewer's control. With television, in contrast, programs are scheduled by broadcasters, others with whom one shares one's home may enter and leave the viewing situation at will, and controversial or salacious content can occur without warning.

Public opinion, of course, merely reflects the personal views of media consumers. Opinions can vary widely across television audiences and may shift over time. Nevertheless, opinion surveys about public perceptions of sex on television have provided useful snapshots of the climate of opinion that exists at different times. Television, for example, has been identified by members of the public in the United States as a major source of learning about sex for children and teenagers. While not unduly critical of this role, there was some concern voiced about the accuracy of the sex-related information presented by television (Roberts, Kline, & Gagnon, 1978).

In the United States, for example, such surveys have revealed a marked degree of public concern about the amount of sex shown on television (Greenberg, Graef, Fernandez-Collado, Korzenny, & Atkin, 1980; Sprafkin & Silverman, 1980). This concern does not just take the form of being personally offended by sex on television, but also stems from the perception that television can encourage young viewers to become sexually active earlier than they would otherwise, often without taking adequate precautions (Planned Parenthood Federation of New York City, 1986). Contrasting opinions have been expressed by some writers who have claimed that television has become more responsible in its depictions of sex and has turned to traditional themes of commitment and love, while giving less emphasis to bed-hopping (Hill, 1987).

In Britain, surveys have addressed the question of the perceived amount of sex on television head-on. In the early 1990s, more than half a nationally representative sample of British television viewers (54%) claimed that the amount of sex shown on television was about right. Of those who dissented from this opinion, the great majority (41% of all viewers) said there was too much sex on television; only a few (2%) felt there was too little (Millwood-Hargrave, 1992). By the end of the 1990s, opinions about the amount of sex on television became more relaxed. There was a gradual decrease in the percentage of British viewers who felt there was too much sex on television and an increase in those who felt the amount was about right (see Table 3.1).

Opinions about the amount of sex on television are not uniform in their distribution across different population subgroups. Millwood-Hargrave (1999) reported that people age 65 or more years (73%) were much more likely to think there was 'too much sex' on television than viewers in general (36%). By the late 1990s in Britain, concern about the prevalence of sex on television centered on levels of explicitness, too much talk about sex, and the complaint that it had become almost impossible to avoid it.

Viewers perceived the problem of 'too much sex' on television to be more acute in relation to particular categories of broadcast than others. Millwood-Hargrave (1999) reported that British viewers were especially likely to single out confessional talk shows (47%), television advertising (37%), films on television (33%), television drama (29%), soap operas (29%), and comedies (21%) as containing excessive amounts of sex. Women were more likely to say there was 'too much sex' shown in films (43%), drama (32%), and comedy (27%). Men were more likely to disagree (28% of men said these was *not* 'too much sex' in any of these genres compared with 15% of all women).

By the early 1990s, British viewers expressed the general belief that standards in broadcasting were becoming more liberal and depictions of sex

TABLE 3.1

British Viewers' Opinions About the Amount of Sex on TV

	1991	1992	1993	1994	1995	1996	1997	1998
	%	%	%	%	%	%	%	%
Too Much	41	41	40	38	35	41	32	36
About Right	54	54	55	58	58	53	62	57
Too Little	5	4	4	4	7	6	6	7

Note. Data are from Millwood-Hargrave, 1999.

more explicit. Most respondents (71%) expressed the view that the amount of sex on television had clearly increased compared with the past. More than one in three (36%) also felt that television had a strong influence in encouraging sexual and moral permissiveness and a similar percentage (35%) felt that it had some influence in this respect. This opinion was particularly likely to be supported by viewers aged 55 and over, of whom 60% believed that television had a strong or very strong influence in cultivating a climate of permissiveness (Millwood-Hargrave, 1992).

By the end of the 1990s, slightly more than one in two British viewers (54%) said they did not enjoy watching sex on television, compared to approximately one in three (36%) who did. In contrast, nearly three out of four viewers (72%) did not usually find sex on television offensive, compared to one in four (24%) who did (Millwood-Hargrave, 1999). Older viewers went against this trend, with four in ten of those age 65 and over (40%) agreeing strongly that sex on television was offensive, compared with 14% of the general sample. Although most British viewers were not offended by sex on television, more than four in ten (41%) questioned whether it was necessary to show it. For most viewers (58%), while sex was acknowledged to be a part of everyday life, they did not want to be confronted by it on television.

What emerged from the early 1990s' research, however, was that many people thought about their opinions carefully and were not inclined to give blanket endorsement or rejection of sex on television. Most viewers (61%) denied that they found it offensive to see sex on television, though a marked minority (39%) did find it offensive. Even so, there were mixed views about the possible impact that televised sex could have, especially on young people. More than half of British viewers (56%) in the early 1990s agreed that showing sex on television only encourages the young to experiment with sex themselves too young, but more than four in ten (43%) rejected this opinion. Opinions were even more equally divided on the issue of whether sex on television encourages immoral behavior, with around half saying that it did (48%) and half saying it did not (51%).

Opinions about sex on television were further mediated by the nature and intention of its inclusion in programs. In the early 1990s, many British viewers thought that sex on television could have an educational role. However, the perceived educational benefits of televised sex depended on the context in which they were used. On balance, British viewers were slightly more likely to agree (53%) than disagree (47%) that sex scenes give parents a good chance to talk about these things with their children. In contrast, the belief that showing sex on television is a good way of helping to educate children about the facts of life was rejected (52%) more than it was accepted (45%). Where most viewers were clearly in agreement (81%) was in their endorsement of the opinion that sex scenes on television should imply, as much as possible, that condoms were used and thus give encouragement to safe sex practices.

Regardless of the beneficial functions televised portrayals of sex might fulfill, viewers' opinions were also affected by the nature of the production treatment. For most British viewers (75%), sex on television was tolerable provided sex scenes did not go on for too long. Equally, it was important for the great majority of viewers (78%) that sex scenes were necessary to the story (Millwood-Hargrave, 1999). There was less general agreement with statements that suggested that the depiction of sex was acceptable because it was acting (48%) than with the importance of sex being depicted as part of a loving relationship (63%).

In Britain, attitudes to sex on television have been tracked over many years, alongside opinions about violence and bad language on television, by the commercial television regulator (see Gunter, Sancho-Aldridge, & Winstone, 1994; Independent Television Commission [ITC], 1999). Public sensitivities to sex on television have been investigated in this survey in relation to a question that asks viewers about what has offended them on television. Although this survey does not pin down in precise terms what kind of sexual material is being referred to, it does serve as a measure of the relative importance of sex, as a television-related issue, in the public's consciousness. By the mid-1990s, around one in ten British viewers expressed concern about sex or nudity on the commercial terrestrial television channels, with around 1 in 20 expressing the same concerns about this on the BBC's two national terrestrial channels. Around one in 20 viewers also made specific reference to sexual violence as a source of offence across these channels. One in five viewers (20%) indicated they had seen programs on television over the past year that had contained an unacceptable amount of sex or nudity. One in four (24%) said they had switched off the television or changed to another channel because of the amount of sex or nudity in the program they had been watching (ITC, 1998).

In a recent review of this survey's findings Svennevig (1998) noted that sex—by which was meant sexual acts and sexual innuendo—was as much a cause of concern as bad language during the 1970s, whereas in the 1980s the proportions of viewers complaining about sex on the main television channels fell. During the 1990s, sex was of less concern to viewers than bad language or violence on television. Yet, by the end of the 1990s, sex was the cause of more complaints from viewers about drama and entertainment on commercial television in Britain than any other single category of content, including violence and bad language (ITC, 2000). Such complainants are a self-solicited group of individuals, of course, who do not comprise a representative sample of the viewing population in any normative sense.

Svennevig (1998) also examined opinions about steps broadcasters take to safeguard children. Respondents were asked to say whether, when young people under the age of 11 might be watching, programs had been shown on television which the children should not see. In 1970, when asked to give reasons for saying programs were unsuitable, 22% said because they contained too much sex, 16% said because of too much violence, and 16% said because of too much swearing. By 1988, these percentages had shifted to 13% for sex, 24% for violence, and 8% for bad language. This indicated a more relaxed attitude about sex and language and more concern about violence. By 1997, the relaxed attitude towards sex on broadcast television in Britain was further illustrated by the finding that 65% of viewers who could receive terrestrial television channels and 80% of those who lived in homes with cable and/or satellite broadcast reception felt that people should be allowed to pay extra to watch sexually explicit programs not available on other channels if they wanted to (Svennevig, 1998).

This more relaxed attitude towards sex on television has been supported by other surveys carried out in Britain. A study by the Broadcasting Standards Council indicated that an overwhelming majority of viewers agreed that if people want to watch sex on television, they should be allowed to do so (78%) and that people who do not like watching sex can always switch the set off (88%). There was a more mixed reaction to the view that it is alright to show sex on television because it is what people do in everyday life (51% agreed and 49% disagreed). A majority of respondents in this survey (61%) rejected the notion that sex on television is offensive, though nearly four in ten (39%) did find it offensive. Furthermore, four in ten viewers aged 55 and over (40%) found seeing sex on television very offensive. Another concern about sex on television lay in perceptions of its possible harmful influences. Nearly half the viewers interviewed in this British survey (48%) felt that showing sex on television could encourage immoral behavior, and a majority (56%) worried that sex on television could encourage the young to experiment with sex too soon (Millwood-Hargrave, 1992).

Even though a more relaxed attitude towards sex on television emerged during the 1990s, certain sections of the public nevertheless voiced some concerns about particular kinds of sexual content on television. Many public opinion surveys have examined viewers' attitudes about sex on television in a fairly generalised fashion, divorced from the actual viewing experience. Furthermore, distinctions among viewers have centered on demographic measures. Yet, attitudes towards sex on television may reflect attitudes towards sex in general, in many respects. If this is true, then one should expect variations in opinions about televised representations of sex to be explained in terms of psychological differences among members of the audience. Later in this chapter, research findings are reviewed that derive from studies in which respondents have given opinions about sexual media content that was presented under more controlled conditions, and where differences in reactions were linked to specific psychological characteristics of individuals.

How Reliable Are Opinion Surveys?

One of the problems faced by public opinion surveys is that the opinion profiles they yield not only change from one point in time to the next, but more
significantly, can vary with the type of question asked. Question framing
can make a marked difference in the apparent level of concern people have
about sex on television.

In analysis of American and British public opinion survey data, Gunter
and Stipp (1992) demonstrated how views about sex on television can vary
widely within the same survey in response to differently framed questions. In
a British survey of causes of offence on television, more than half (57%) a national sample indicated that they had been offended by something they had
seen on screen in the past year. Fewer than half of these respondents (46%)
mentioned that the source of their offence had been a depiction of sex.

Next, a different question was used which provided a different frame of
reference. Respondents were asked to name any material they *would not like
to see* on television. On this occasion, less than one in five (18%) mentioned
sex scenes. Finally, a third open question asked respondents to name any
subject matter that, in their opinion, *should never be shown* on television.
Nearly half the sample (48%) were able to mention something in response
to this question, with 14% mentioning sex scenes in this context. Thus, responses mentioning sexual material were clearly less likely to occur in the
context of sources of offence, than in connection with things respondents
said they would not like to see or that should never be shown. Table 3.2
shows that variations occurred in the extent to which a number of potentially controversial types of scene were mentioned in relation to these three
frames of reference.

These questions required respondents to supply their own answers. In
the same survey, further questions were asked about these issues in which
ready-made response options were provided. In the case of each question, a
list of items was presented to respondents and they were asked to choose
any that, first, represented items they personally would not want to see on
television and, second, represented items that they believed should never
be shown on television.

Rape, explicit sex, certain forms of violence, and bad language were the
most often selected items. Three points were of special interest here. First,
more items were chosen from the items that had been self-generated by respondents. Second, items that had earlier been self-generated by survey
respondents were selected by many more respondents from the prompt
list. Third, the rank order of items of concern from prompt list selections
was different from that derived from self-generated choices. Thus, sexual
material was more often chosen as the type of content respondents said

TABLE 3.2

Public Opinion About Sex and Other Matters on Television

	Should Never Be Shown	Would Not Like to See	Found Offensive
Base:	1,195	1,195	1,195
	%	%	%
Violence/brutality/cruelty	16	27	25
Explicit sex scenes	14	18	11
Factual scenes of violence	5	7	3
Child abuse	5	–	–
Bad language	4	9	22
Nudity	1	2	–
None/nothing	52	34	11

Note. Source: Gunter and Stipp, 1992. Reproduced by permission of publisher.

they would not wish to see than were violent items when a list of options was provided, whereas violence was more often mentioned than sex when respondents had to supply their own answers (Table 3.3a).

A similar comparison was made between items mentioned and item choices in response to a question asking respondents to select items that should never be shown on television (Table 3.3b). Again, more respondents made a response of some sort, items were mentioned more often when chosen from a prompt list than when self-generated, and the rank order of items common to prompted and self-generated questions varied. Rape was once more the most often mentioned item from the prompt list, followed by explicit sex scenes.

The differences in public opinion that occurred as a result of variations in the frame of reference offered by questions are important. One feature all the types of question have in common is that they required respondents to consider the acceptability of different categories of behavior in an abstract context. The reality of television viewing, however, is that viewers watch programs and programs can provide varying contexts for the depiction of sexual behavior. Research into public perceptions of violence on television has repeatedly shown that context is a key factor that viewers take into account when judging the seriousness and acceptability of on-screen violent behavior (see Gunter, 1985; Morrison, 1999; Van der Voort, 1986). The same principle can reasonably be expected to apply with respect to public perceptions of sexual behavior on television.

TABLE 3.3a

Content Viewers Would Not Want To See on Television

	Prompted	Unprompted
Base	1,195	1,195
	%	%
Woman raped by man	55	–
Explicit scenes of love making	31	18
Killing of innocent victim	29	27
Animals fighting /killing each other	28	3
Bad language	26	9
Frontal male nudity	16	–
Killing of criminal	14	27
Frontal female nudity	13	–
Close-up of childbirth	9	–

TABLE 3.3b

Items Viewers Think Should Never Be Shown on TV

	Prompted	Unprompted
Base:	1,195	1,195
	%	%
Woman raped by man	60	*
Explicit scenes of lovemaking	36	14
Killing of innocent victim	32	16
Animals fighting/killing each other	27	–
Bad language	25	4
Frontal male nudity	23	1
Frontal female nudity	21	1
Killing of criminal	20	16
Close-up of childbirth	12	*

Note. Source: Gunter and Stipp, 1992. Reproduced by permission of publisher.

* Less than 0.5%

Despite some public concern about showing explicit sexual material on television, the degree to which audiences object to such material can depend on the treatment afforded the subject matter by particular programs. Wober (1990) reported a study of public opinion about a television series called *Sex Talk* that appeared over 15 weeks on Channel 4 in Britain. This series dealt with a range of sex issues and included explicit discussions of safe sex practices, orgasms, prostitution, sadomasochism, and a number of other sex-related topics. Although broadcast late at night (11 p.m.), the series was ground-breaking and contained material that some observers felt exceeded the boundaries of good taste. Research among a large national television viewing panel of more than 4,000 viewers found that opinions about the series varied dramatically.

More than one in four panel members (28%) had watched at least one edition of the series and 6% of panellists had seen three or more editions. More frequent viewers were also more likely to have discussed it with family and friends. General attitudes towards the series were measured and found to divide the audience into two groups that Wober labelled *reticence* and *openness*. The first group exhibited some reservations about the series and the way it have dealt with its subject matter. Many panellists (60%) felt that the series had focused on the sexual experience and failed to pay sufficient attention to the moral aspect of sexual relationships. Others (54%) were concerned that some participants in the series were discussing intimate details about their sexual relationships without having obtained their partners' consent. The second group, characterised by openness, felt that young people were lucky that they had healthier, more open attitudes towards sex today (56%), that no aspects of sex should be excluded from examination on responsible television (45%), and disagreed that such programs lowered moral standards (44%).

The variation in public response to programs that deal, in explicit terms, with sex on television has been observed elsewhere. Research in New Zealand, for instance, underlined this point, using more qualitative lines of enquiry. Watson (1993) prepared a report for the Broadcasting Standards Authority in which he analysed the comments of participants in ten focus groups who watched the final edition of the first series of the Australian sex education program called *Sophie's Sex*, presented by Sophie Lee. The members of each focus group watched one episode without interruption and then they were taken through the program, section by section, with small 'trigger' extracts to remind them of the main stories. They were asked for their general reactions to each segment and then their specific responses to certain issues raised by each story (e.g., the language used, the level of nudity, or the sexual activity depicted). They also discussed their feelings as to the appropriateness—for themselves and for other groups—of each of the segments shown. In addition, the groups with no members under the age of

18 were asked for their reactions to three explicit sequences from *The Lovers' Guide* (a popular English sex education video) to see whether they would object to the transmission of material even more explicit than that screened in *Sophie's Sex*.

The final edition of *Sophie's Sex,* broadcast on Tuesday, 13 October 1992 at 9:30 p.m., aroused much interest and little wrath among the focus groups of polytechnic students, night clubbers, and the parents of teenagers who watched it. Most perceived it as essentially educational and believed it was authoritative and factually correct. They also admitted to being entertained and informed by it. The material cut by the broadcaster (scenes of genitalia) also would have been accepted as educational by most focus group participants, but only a few were willing to see images of real sexual intercourse being broadcast. Two of the three groups chosen on the basis of ethnicity, Pacific islanders and Asians (Indians), were embarrassed by the subject matter, both for its frankness about recreational sex and its depictions of nudity. Both groups added that the objections that they had to this material stemmed from aspects of their cultures' approach to sexual matters. Both observed that their own children would have to adapt to the local mores, and they acknowledged that they could not protect them from such depictions. The Maoris in these groups also said that there were aspects of the program with which they were not comfortable, but they, too, suggested that there were educational aspects of the program that might have been of benefit to their young people.

ATTITUDES TOWARDS EXPLICIT EROTICA IN FILMS AND VIDEOS

Up to this point in the chapter, we have explored public opinion about sex on broadcast television. As we have seen, much of this work has comprised standard surveys of one-shot samples of viewers or established viewing panels. Many of these surveys considered sex on television in a fairly broad sense, though a few studies investigated public response to specific programs. Compared with most television channels, much more graphic and explicit depictions of sexuality can be found in films originally made for cinema or video distribution. Some of these productions may eventually be shown on television as well, though they are usually shown at restricted viewing times (late at night) and on subscription channels, and even then will often have the most explicit scenes cut.

Public opinion evidence has indicated that explicit sexual material is regarded as an important source of entertainment and sexual information (Press et al., 1985; Stengel, 1986). Such materials can serve as marital aids and a useful outlet for sexual frustration. Many people, however, also believe that such materials could contribute to sexual promiscuity, loss of respect for women, and increases in acts of sexual violence. Thus, public opinion is divided over such materials.

There is little doubt that there exists a healthy market for erotica. Pornographic magazines enjoyed considerable popularity from the 1950s to 1980s. Latterly, videos seem to have replaced magazines as sources of such entertainment. The pornography business was one of the first to adopt videotape technology as a distribution outlet for its products (Hebditch & Anning, 1988). By 1988, around 1,250 sexually explicit videos were released within the United States (Weaver, 1991).

How do public attitudes towards these more sexually explicit materials compare with attitudes towards the kind of sexual material that usually occurs on mainstream broadcast television? So far, much more sophisticated research has been carried out into public attitudes towards sexually explicit cinema films and videos than towards sex on television. This research has also displayed greater methodological variety. Survey research has been complemented by experimental, laboratory-based studies and qualitative research using in-depth individual or group interviews. Furthermore, more concerted attempts have been made to explain the nature of public attitudes through psychological theory. One important content distinction has also been drawn in the context of explicit films and videos—between depictions of a purely sexual nature and depictions of sexual violence.

There have been numerous surveys of attitudes towards the acceptability of sexually explicit materials over the past three decades. Most surveys have relied on verbal descriptions of erotic materials (Abelson, Cohen, Heaton, & Suder, 1971; Athanasiou & Shaver, 1971; Diamond & Dannemiller, 1989; Eysenck, 1976; Gallup, 1985; Herrman & Bordner, 1983). Some studies have supplemented survey methods by showing respondents specific examples of erotic materials and eliciting their reactions to these illustrations (Linz et al., 1991; Wallace & Wehmer, 1973). A number of early surveys that did not distinguish between sexually violent and purely erotic sexual films found that older people, individuals with stronger religious beliefs, and women had more negative attitudes towards sexually explicit materials than anyone else (Athanasiou & Shaver, 1971; Diamond & Dannemiller, 1989; Herrman & Bordner, 1983).

Employing a field study methodology, Zurcher, Kirkpatrick, Cushing, and Bowman (1973) compared the attitudinal and demographic characteristics of ad hoc antipornography and anticensorship groups. Cowan, Chase, and Stahly (1989) examined the similarities and differences in attitudes towards pornography control of self-defined feminists and fundamentalists using a structured interview format.

A limitation of most of these studies is that researchers did not systematically explore differences in attitudes towards sexually explicit media and sexually violent media. The distinction between them has emerged as central in the literature on the effects of exposure to sexually explicit media (Donnerstein, Linz & Penrod, 1987; Malamuth & Donnerstein, 1982).

Linz (1989) concluded that the evidence of harmful effects from exposure to (nonviolent) sexually explicit media is weak and inconsistent, whereas the evidence consistently shows that exposure to depictions of violence towards women, whether sexually explicit or not, produces acceptance of rape myths and desensitization to the suffering of rape victims. Researchers who have examined public opinion toward sexually explicit materials and made the distinction between violent and nonviolent examples have found that public opinion is considerably harsher toward depictions of sexual violence (Gallup, 1985; Linz et al., 1991).

In the Gallup poll, respondents were told that the interviewer was going to read to them several descriptions of adult entertainment, and the respondents were asked to indicate whether they thought 'laws should totally ban any of the following forms of activity, allow them so long as there is no public display—or impose no restrictions at all for adult audiences' (1985, p. 60). The percentages of respondents willing to ban 'magazines that show sexual violence' (73%), 'theatres showing movies that depict sexual violence' (68%), and 'sale or rental of video cassettes featuring sexual violence' (63%) were much higher than the percentages of respondents willing to ban 'magazines that show adults having sexual relations' (47%), 'theatres showing X-rated movies' (42%), 'sale or rental of X-rated video cassettes for home viewing' (32%), and even more so 'magazines that show nudity' (21%).

Linz et al. (1991) conducted a public opinion survey to assess viewers' and readers' opinions about pornographic films and a porn magazine that had been the subjects of a criminal case. A cross-section of residents of a regional community were randomly allocated to view one of the films or to look at the magazine or to view a control film.

Before and after viewing, the participants judged the materials' appeal to a prurient interest (a shameful, morbid, unhealthy interest in sex) and patent offensiveness (community tolerance for such material). The legal standard at that time required that offensiveness be judged against 'community standards.' This meant that rather than giving personal opinion, jurors were required to consider whether pornographic material would be a probable cause of offence to people in their wider community.

In some obscenity cases, social scientific evidence was called upon as expert testimony. Thus public opinion poll data on the perceived offensiveness of certain types of material were used to reinforce judgments about what fell short of community standards.

Linz et al. (1991) presented findings from one such case. From a random telephone sample of over 600 adult contacts, 129 individuals eventually participated in viewing sessions in which they gave opinions about pornographic film and the magazine content. The results on this occasion found that respondents felt that the films and magazine did not appeal to a shameful, morbid, or unhealthy interest in sex, nor did they perceive these materials as going beyond the level of tolerance regarding depictions of sexual conduct for the average adult in their community.

After viewing these materials, a lower percentage thought that the community would tolerate the materials they had just seen than when they were asked if they personally would tolerate such materials. Before viewing specific pornographic films charged in this particular case, 59.1% of respondents felt that the average adult in the community did tolerate adult movies, videos and magazines showing nudity and sex; 52.7% endorsed this opinion after viewing pornographic material themselves. Before viewing porn films, 74.5% of respondents felt that a person should definitely be able to see any such showing of actual sex in adult movies, videos, or magazines if they wanted to, and 75.2% believed this afterwards.

Fewer people felt the films appealed to shameful, morbid, or unhealthy interest in sex after they had an opportunity to see them than before viewing. Beforehand, 43.6% felt that pornographic films, videos, and magazines that depicted sex acts and close-ups of sexual organs would appeal to an unhealthy, shameful, or morbid interest in sex, whereas 16.4% endorsed this view afterwards. The researchers argued that there were certain advantages to providing jurors in obscenity cases with information about community standards based on summations of personal tolerance for materials actually charged in court cases, rather than on hypothetical judgments about the community and obscenity.

TYPES OF MEDIA SEX PORTRAYAL

Measurement of the enjoyment of sexual content can be indicated through verbal reports usually filed after the film or program has finished and via actual sexual arousal while watching. Sometimes these two indicators have been used together. Not all sexual portrayals in film, television programs, or videos are the same, or even of the same type, however. Instead, a variety of different types of behavior are possible, with portrayals occurring in a variety of different contexts and settings. An important aspect of assessing audiences' evaluative reactions to media sex, therefore, is to consider thematic elements within films and programs that can influence viewers' enjoyment.

Public opinion surveys have indicated that television audiences are largely accepting of nudity, somewhat less accepting of explicit scenes of lovemaking, and display fairly widespread concern about scenes showing rape (Gunter & Stipp, 1992). Further survey research conducted amongst British viewers provided a number of descriptions of television scenarios involving different types of sexual behavior. In each case they were invited to indicate whether they thought the scene was acceptable or not acceptable for showing on television (Millwood-Hargrave, 1992). Respondents expressed greater caution as the sex became more explicit. Only 4% felt it was *not* acceptable to show a scene in which a couple were clearly preparing for sex, but the sex itself was not shown, as compared with 10% who objected to a scene in which a couple were having sex but were completely covered by bedclothes, and 34% who could not accept a scene in which a couple were shown completely naked obviously having sex.

As Table 3.4 shows, the acceptability or otherwise of televised sex scenes for viewers is also determined by more specific contextual factors concerning not only the degree of sexual explicitness, but also the social context, nature of the characters, and the relationship shown. Five of the six descriptions used in this study were found to be acceptable for transmission by minorities of respondents only. The least acceptable scene was one that depicted coercive, homosexual behavior, which was regarded as acceptable by fewer than one in five respondents. The only scene accepted by a clear majority of viewers was one that dealt with the subject of child abuse within a factual context. The other significant point about this scene was that it was described as a radio broadcast rather than a television broadcast.

The reaction to the scene that depicted homosexual behavior was one illustration of a wider negative reaction that was found among British viewers when questioned about the portrayal of homosexuality on television. More than seven in ten British viewers (71%) indicated that they would find it

TABLE 3.4

The Acceptability of Different Types of Sex Scene on Television

---

Scenario One

A scene from the dramatized version of a novel by a well-known and respected author, shown late in the evening. One of the female characters is having an affair with a friend she has known for a long time. They peel each other's clothes off in front of the living room fire, then he lies on the sofa and she climbs on top of him to have sex. The camera remains fixed on them as they achieve a mutual climax.
Very acceptable — 7%; Quite acceptable — 35%
Not very acceptable — 27%; Not at all acceptable — 30%

Scenario Two

An episode of an historical drama shown late in the evening. Set in Ancient Rome, it is based on a true story. During the program there is a scene in a brothel, where lots of wine, women and song result in a full-scale orgy. Characters are seen swapping partners, in unconventional sexual positions, and having sex with more than one person at a time. Although there are a range of characters involved, most are overweight, wealthy Romans, whereas the prostitutes are all young and beautiful.
Very acceptable — 6%; Quite acceptable — 35%
Not very acceptable — 27%; Not at all acceptable — 38%

Scenario Three

A scene in a dramatized documentary about a boys' school, shown in the late evening. A young boy is in the showers alone, having been kept behind for a detention for misbehaving in class. An older boy comes in to the shower, sees the younger boy, and decides to take advantage of the situation. He slowly corners the frightened boy, talking reassuringly to him as he starts to kiss and caress him. His embrace becomes stronger as the scene fades. The next scene shows the smaller boy crying on his bed.
Very acceptable — 2%; Quite acceptable — 15%
Not very acceptable — 26%; Not at all acceptable — 57%

Scenario Four

A scene from an early evening soap opera. One of the main female characters is committing adultery with the next-door neighbour. She is a very glamorous 40-year- old, but he has only just left school. They go into the bedroom in a passionate embrace, and the door closes on them. They are next seen lying in bed after having sex.
Very acceptable — 7%; Quite acceptable — 31%
Not very acceptable — 32%; Not at all acceptable — 39%

Scenario Five

A scene from an early evening drama series. A newly married couple are about to make love for the first time since the wedding. They can be partly seen in the low, romantic lighting as they slowly undress and have sex. Soft music is playing in the background and sounds of pleasure can be heard.
Very acceptable — 7%; Quite acceptable — 31%
Not very acceptable — 32%; Not at all acceptable — 39%

Scenario Six

A radio documentary in the early evening about child abuse. The physical and emotional effects on the child are discussed in detail, and a lively discussion follows among social workers, doctors, and program makers.
Very acceptable — 24%; Quite acceptable — 48%
Not very acceptable — 17%; Not at all acceptable — 11%

Note. Data are from Millwood-Hargrave, 1992.

embarrassing to watch homosexual sex scenes with some of the people with whom they would normally watch television. More than six in ten (62%) claimed they would find the screening of any physical contact between gay men offensive. Despite these opinions, respondents in the same survey were not completely intolerant of homosexual sex scenes on television. Six in ten (60%) believe that it is important to show homosexuality if it is necessary to the story. More than six in ten respondents rejected the view that either gay characters (62%) or lesbian characters (61%) should not be shown on television at all. More respondents disagreed (61%) than agreed (29%) that programs and films about gays and lesbians should be banned (Millwood-Hargrave, 1992).

Such surveys were dependent on people's responses to verbal descriptions of film or program content, however. Reactions to actual footage may be quite different and depend crucially on contextual factors that might be regarded as justifying the use of a certain type of portrayal or degree of explicitness.

Using verbal reports elicited immediately after viewing sexual film material, Sapolsky and Zillmann (1981) found that male viewers were disturbed by scenes of petting but not by scenes depicting sexual intercourse. Female viewers displayed the opposite reaction. Other studies in which respondents have reported their feelings verbally immediately after watching sexual media content have found that images of nudes or semi-nudes and scenes depicting sexual behavior up to and including heterosexual intercourse cause viewers few problems (R. A. Baron, 1974a, 1974b; Zillmann, Bryant, Comisky, & Medoff, 1981). Portrayals of masturbation and homosexuality, on the other hand, are more likely to be rated as distasteful (Mosher & O'Grady, 1979a). Scenes that depict oral sex, sadomasochism, and bondage also elicit negative verbal reactions (Malamuth, Haber & Feshbach, 1980; White, 1979; Zillmann et al., 1981).

Even within the category of otherwise acceptable heterosexual sex, there are depictions that are regarded as unacceptable by some viewers. One might expect to find that scenes depicting mutually consenting sex will be found more pleasurable than scenes of rape. Even with rape depictions, however, whether the ultimate audience reaction is one of pleasure depends on how the victim in the scene responds. Social psychological experiments conducted in the early 1980s, for example, found that film portrayals of female rape produced little immediate sexual arousal in male college student viewers when the victim was depicted as being distressed. In contrast, when the rape victim became involuntarily aroused, so too did male viewers. Indeed, this kind of scene was more sexually arousing than one showing male and female actors engaging in mutually consenting sex (Malamuth & Check, 1980a, 1983). Thus, even with a theme such as rape, which survey evidence has indicated to be a source of concern to many people, immediate reactions to actual media portrayals depend on subtleties within the portrayal itself to which survey questioning is usually insensitive.

By the early 1990s, research with college students in the United States revealed that portrayals of male dominance and the treatment of females as sex objects in unequal male–female relationships were found offensive by male and female viewers alike. Degrading pornographic portrayals of females in which initially unwilling female characters are coerced into having sex and violent sexual attacks on subordinate female targets produced negative reactions and mood states (Cowan & Dunn, 1994; Stock, 1991).

Varying Preferences for Viewing Pornography

Evidence has emerged from research conducted by Zillmann, Bryant, and their colleagues that viewers can become bored with one form of pornography if regularly exposed to it. In consequence, their tastes may shift towards more explicit forms of sexual entertainment. Experiments by Zillmann and Bryant (1982, 1984) show that a heavy diet of standard, nonviolent pornography produced habituation and lowered satisfaction with the entertainment value of such material. Consumers remained interested in less common forms of erotica that featured more extreme and unusual types of sexual behavior, such as sadomasochism and bestiality.

Zillmann and Bryant (1986) reported further data on this issue with student and nonstudent populations. Participants in their studies were shown one movie per week for 6 weeks and gave evaluations of what they had seen at the end of each viewing session. Some participants viewed a diet of exclusively pornographic films, while others viewed only nonpornographic films. After this 6-week film exposure spell, participants were tested for their selective exposure to different types of video entertainment. They were left in a room by the researcher who asked them to wait until called to assist with another part of the study. While waiting, they had access to a selection of videotapes that could be played over a TV monitor in the room. There were entertainment choices ranging from nonpornographic material through soft porn to more hard-core material featuring bondage, sadomasochism, and bestiality. The equipment was able to register which tapes were played and for how long.

Results showed that participants exposed to 6 weeks of standard pornography exhibited less preference for more of the same, and were more likely to choose something else to watch, whether sexual or nonsexual in nature. In fact, they showed some preference for hard-core pornographic materials. For participants not fed the diet of pornography, their selections exhibited a preference for soft-core pornography or nonsexual materials, and they were much less inclined to select hard-core material depicting unusual sexual practices. It was not entirely clear why these shifts in entertainment preferences occurred. Repeated exposure to soft-core pornographic films may lead to habituation whereby they fail to excite viewers, or it may be that after a while they no longer ignite curiosity.

INDIVIDUAL DIFFERENCES
IN RESPONSES TO SEX SCENES

Not everyone responds to sex scenes in a similar fashion. Consistent differences in the way people react to such material have been associated with gender, attitudes towards women, sexual socialisation style, and sexual personality type. Much of the work on individual differences has centered on the way viewers react to explicit erotica, and especially to those scenes in which the sex takes on an aggressive tone.

Gender Differences

Men and women exhibit largely different orientations towards pornography in terms of tastes, sources of offence and postviewing effects. In general, females have been found to display a weaker appetite and liking for sexual media content than males, whether there is violence present or not (Malamuth, Heim, & Feshbach, 1980; Sapolsky & Zillmann, 1981). Erotic content enjoyed by males will be disliked by females, and sexual material that even males find distasteful will be disliked to a stronger degree by females (Sapolsky & Zillmann, 1981). Thus, males may like or dislike sexual media content, but females tend usually to dislike it (Byrne, Fisher, Lamberth, & Mitchell, 1974).

When married couples were invited to evaluate a series of pictures or verbal descriptions of heterosexual, homosexual, and autosexual acts and to indicate their feelings afterwards, differences emerged between the opinions of men and women. These differences centered on both the nature of their emotional arousal and their opinions concerning these sexually explicit items. Opinions were measured about how pornographic each sexual theme was judged to be and about participants' support for legislation restricting the dissemination of pornography.

Following exposure to the erotic stimulus materials, women who experienced strong negative feelings (anger, disgust, depression, nausea) judged them to be more pornographic and exhibited stronger support for restrictive legislation. Among men, however, negative opinions about pornography occurred only for those individuals who experienced strong negative and weak positive emotional reactions to the stimulus materials. Women high on negative emotional reactions rated pornography negatively even when they also experienced some positive affective reactions (excited, entertained, sexually aroused; Byrne et al., 1974).

Female inexperience and discomfort with sexual material may be explained partly as symptomatic of their conditioning not to display sexual excitement overtly to avoid sexual exploitation by males. Females avoid appearing to be sexually aroused by erotica because such a reaction may encourage unwanted sexual approaches from males (Byrne, 1977). In addition, cultural, gender-related values discourage females from acquiring erotica or using it to stimulate their sexual fantasies (Fisher & Byrne, 1978b).

Despite these observations, it is not true to conclude that females never show an interest in erotica or that they never enjoy the experience of being exposed to it. It is safe to observe, nevertheless, that females and males do display different tastes in sexual media content. Women prefer softer erotica over hard-core material, whereas men often show the opposite taste. Women dislike sex scenes with violence or in which the woman is shown in a submissive role (Cowan & Stahly, 1992). Men show greater liking for sex scenes with female subordination themes in which male sexual gratification is the primary concern, whereas women prefer sex scenes in which the man and woman are equals and the sexual behavior grows out of a loving relationship (Cowan & Dunn, 1994).

Gender differences also emerge in the way pornography is used. One study found that pornographic videos served four different purposes: sexual enhancement (to create the right mood for sex or to provide ideas about sexual technique); diversion (as an escape or relief from boredom); sexual release (to stimulate sexual fantasies); and substitution (replacement for a sexual partner). College men were more likely than college women to report using sex videos for sexual release and substitution. Men who used sex videos for sexual stimulation and foreplay with their partners were more likely to hold sexist views about women and sex. Use of sex videos as a substitute for a sexual partner was related to rape myth acceptance on the part of men, whereas using them for sexual release was associated with rejection of the belief that all women secretly want to be raped (Perse, 1994).

Sexual Socialisation

Gender has already been identified as an important factor in relation to the way viewers respond to pornographic films and videos. One reason for this difference in opinion about and reaction to such material is that men and women receive different social conditioning in relation to their sexuality. They are socialised according to different 'scripts' (Gagnon & Simon, 1973; Mosher & MacIan, 1994). Such sexual scripts determine the kinds of behaviors that are deemed to be appropriate for each gender. Put simply, men are socialised to be sexual initiators and women to be more sexually reserved (Mosher & Tomkins, 1988). Such sexual scripts can also vary within genders, with some men displaying more feminine scripts and some women displaying scripts more usually associated with men.

According to one school of thought, a person's dominant sexual script may influence the way they react to sex scenes. The degree of liking for a sex scene is dependent on the 'goodness of fit' between the sexual script played out by the men and women in the scene and the individual's own dominant sexual script (Mosher, 1980; 1988a, 1994a). When there is a disparity between the viewer's own sexual script (i.e., the manner he or she has been socially conditioned to display) and the one being acted out on screen, the more likely will the viewer find the scene unpleasant (Mosher & MacIan, 1994). A failure of fit explains why most individuals do not become sexually involved in paraphilic fantasies when these are portrayed in pornography. Similarly, low goodness of fit reduced the involvement in heterosexual men who watched gay male pornography (Mosher & O'Grady, 1979a).

This theory has been invoked to explain why so many women dislike typical sex scenes in pornographic films. The women in such scenes are much freer with their sexual favours than most women in the audience would be, and the sex scenes tend to be devoid of emotional depth or involvement. Reinforcing this explanation are findings that women respond more favorably to erotic films made by women directors for women, which, though sexually erotic, adhere more closely to dominant feminine sexual scripts (Mosher & MacIan, 1994).

The origins of this sexual involvement theory are located in script theory. Tomkins (1979, 1987, 1991) defined a script as a set of rules for ordering information in a family of related scenes that produce, interpret, direct, enact, and evaluate actions and outcomes in those scenes. All psychological processes in any scene are amplified by affect. When these affect-invested scenes are connected in a family of scenes, they are psychologically magnified by fresh affect that reamplifies the family of scenes and their rules for ordering information in the connected and growing set of scenes that define the script.

Script theory posits gender (Mosher, 1994b) in the differential socialisation of emotions in boys and girls (Mosher & Tomkins, 1988). Traditional gender socialisation entails a punitive socialisation of discrete emotions that are split and stratified into sets of so-called 'superior masculine' emotions (excitement, surprise, anger, disgust) and 'inferior feminine' emotions (joy, fear, distress, and shame). The socialisation of emotions by parents who endorse a normative ideology of gender requires that they manage and inhibit so-called cross-gendered emotions within any socialising scene. Parents thus reward their children for displaying gender-appropriate emotional responses. Any emotional responding deemed to be not normal for the child's gender will be discouraged. Thus, it is less acceptable for a boy to cry than for a girl to do so.

When emotional socialisation is guided by a normative ideology of gender, it produces a differential magnification of the two discrete positive emotions: Men magnify excitement over enjoyment, whereas women magnify enjoyment over excitement. In addition, the negative emotions form contrasting pairs in men and women. The contrasting pairs are anger versus distress, surprise/excitement versus fear, and disgust versus shame. Moreover, the first emotion is differentially magnified over the second in men, whereas the second is magnified over the first in women. A gender script is a modular component of the sexual scripts of men and women. Given a traditional normative ideology in parents and a consequent differential punitive socialisation of gender-stratified emotions, traditional gender scripts in men and women reflect this differential magnification of invidiously stratified sets of emotion that indirectly preserve an unjust hierarchy of gender.

For men, the differential magnification of excitement invests excitement for many men in physical attractiveness of the partner and affect-amplified sexual drive—scripts of sexual excitement that promote sexual interactions with many partners. For women, the differential magnification of enjoyment is invested for many women in familiar and sensual kinesthetic experience, familiar and loved sexual partners, and parenting.

A sexual script is the set of rules for ordering information in a connected and psychologically magnified family of sexual scenes to predict and produce, to interpret and understand, to direct and defend, and to justify and evaluate the happenings in any ongoing, imagined, or past sexual scene. Goodness of fit between the person's sexual script and the events, actions, and affects occurring within the sexual scene deepens involvement, which, along with optimal physical stimulation, produces sexual arousal and potentiates orgasmic response. Similarly, goodness of fit between scene and sexual script is required to produce deep involvement in erotic fantasy or pornography.

To measure the potential for involvement in sexual scenes, Mosher (1988b) introduced the Sexual Path Preferences Inventory to measure three different paths for deepening involvement: (a) role enactment, (b) sexual trance, and (c) partner engagement. These paths are sexual scripts that map the contours of generally preferred elements in sexual scenes. Prior researchers found that men, compared to women, preferred the path of role enactment for exciting, novel sexual performance, whereas women preferred the path of partner engagement for a familiar, loving union (Earnest, 1988; Lenderking, 1991; Sirkin, 1985).

Mosher and MacIan (1994) assessed the psychosexual responses to X-rated videos intended for male or female audiences. Two hundred male and 195 female undergraduates were randomly assigned to view one of six videos: three X-rated videos intended for men and three X-rated videos designed by and for women. Reactions were assessed on measures of sexual arousal, emotional responses, absorption, and sexual behavior.

As predicted, men reported more positive psychosexual responses to all X-rated videos than did women. Women were less likely than men to express enjoyment and more likely to display disgust. Men were significantly less likely than women to experience shame, anger, guilt, fear, or surprise in response to pornographic movies. In comparison to videos intended for men, which activated negative affect, women reported more sexual arousal, more positive and less negative affect, more absorption, and more frequent intercourse after viewing videos designed for women. Men were aroused by both types of movie, whereas women responded more favorably to those movies made for women by women (i.e., *Femme* movies).

A preference for the sexual script of role enactment, which is more common in men than women, was related to psychosexual responsiveness to X-rated videos of both men and women. But the script of partner engagement, which is more common in women than men, did not predict responsiveness to the videos. Those who adhered to a script of role enactment were more likely to enjoy X-rated pornography movies, whereas those for whom this script was not characteristic enjoyed these movies far less.

In summary, men were more psychosexually responsive to videos intended for either men or women than were women. The women were less sexually aroused, experienced stronger negative emotions, and were less absorbed by pornography aimed at men. In the 48 hours after watching the videos, the men masturbated more and experienced more orgasms, apparently mostly from masturbation after viewing the videos intended for men. In contrast to the women, these men reported more frequent weekly masturbation, sexual fantasy, and use of pornography during masturbation as typical behavior.

On the other hand, women were far less responsive to conventional X-rated videos intended for men but were relatively more responsive to the Femme videos. Compared to their responses to videos intended for men, women were mildly sexually aroused; became more absorbed in the videos; experienced more enjoyment and interest; experienced less disgust, shame, anger, guilt, fear, surprise, distress, and contempt; and had intercourse more frequently after viewing the Femme videos.

These women's psychosexual responses to the Femme videos stand out from most prior reports of sex differences in which men, who reported nonconflicted excitement, were more psychosexually responsive to sexually explicit films than were women, who reported conflicting interest and disgust (Mosher, 1973, 1994c; Mosher & O'Grady, 1979b; Schmidt, 1975; Schmidt & Sigusch, 1970; Sigusch, Schmidt, Reinfeld & Weidemann-Sutor, 1970).

Only Mosher and Abramson (1977) found that women were more emotionally and sexually aroused than men to two films, one of a man masturbating and one of a woman masturbating, apparently because they were less turned off than the men by the film of same-sex masturbation. In a subsequent experiment, men experienced both homosexual threat and masturbation guilt to this same film of a man masturbating (Mosher & O'Grady, 1979a). Mosher and MacIan (1994) believed that psychosexual responsiveness to pornography is a function of the goodness of fit between sexual scene and sexual script, which means that pornography—or at least erotica—can be constructed that either appeals to or disgusts any individual by matching or mismatching that person's sexual script.

These two processes may explain these women's psychosexual responsiveness: (a) the women's sexual scripts were more compatible with the sexual scenes in the Femme videos, generating greater depth of involvement, emotional enjoyment and excitement, and subjective sexual arousal; and (b) the Femme videos were more psychosexually arousing simply because they generated less negative affect—particularly, less disgust— that would attenuate and conflict with positive affect and form a barrier to deepening involvement (Green & Mosher, 1985). Although women reported far less exposure to pornography in their everyday lives, their experience with mass media, sexual fantasies, and sexual activities was sufficient to develop their capacity for responding to the Femme videos. Conventional X-rated films intended for a male audience include elements and themes that women may consider offensive to women as a social category or to be personal turn-offs, making such male-oriented videos harder to assimilate to their sexual scripts.

These women may have desired intercourse after the Femme videos because they were aroused without being as turned off as is the case with the typical X-rated video. It should be noted that the Femme videos still triggered mild disgust and other negative emotions in women. In contrast to the men, most of these women did not appear to have a pattern of masturbating to pornography. Their sexual arousal to the femme videos may have been translated into sociosexual behaviors because they were in an established relationship that permitted intercourse whenever they chose. (They were not questioned on this point, however.)

From script theory Mosher and MacIan argue that the results of their research could be explained by referring to differences in the gender socialisation of discrete emotional responses and in the gendered socialisation of sexual scenes. The punitive socialisation of enjoyment, fear, distress, and shame in boys leads many men to embrace an ideology of machismo and a macho personality script that ordains a daring, exciting, aggressive, tough, and calloused sexuality (Mosher, 1991b; Mosher & Tomkins, 1988).

The punitive socialisation of excitement, surprise, anger, disgust, and contempt in women produces a more relaxed and enjoyable but also more fearful, distressed, and shameful sexuality that favors seeking union with powerful men. Gagnon (1990; Gagnon & Simon, 1973) proposed important and relevant differences in sexual scripts stemming from women's socialisation into heterosociality before heterosexuality, in contrast to men's socialisation into masturbation and heterosexuality before heterosociality. Men and women differed in their use of masturbation and pornography because of scripted personality differences that lead men, on the one hand, to view sex as an exciting entitlement and as necessary to their manhood and that lead women, on the other hand, to view sex as part of love and an intimate act that provides familiar and enjoyable sexual union.

Gender is an important subcultural influence on sexual norms. According to claims for gender-specific sexual socialisation 'scripts,' men are socialised to be hyperresponsive sexual initiators and women are socialised to be more reserved inhibitors (Gagnon & Simon, 1973; Laws & Schwarz, 1981). Early data on gender differences in sexual behavior supported this idea (e.g., Kinsey, Pomeroy, & Martin, 1948; Kinsey, Pomeroy, Martin, & Gebhard, 1953). Subsequent work suggested a narrowing of the gap on various indices of sexuality (Hopkins, 1977; Tavris & Sadd, 1978).

Both gender scripts and sexual scripts are always particularised within persons within sexes. For example, although Mosher and MacIan (1994) found a typical pattern of gender differences between men and women in psychosexual responsiveness to pornography, they also found similarities within the men and women who preferred the path of role enactment as compared to those who did not. The pattern for role enactment was qualitatively the same pattern, although quantitatively somewhat less intense, as was the pattern for gender differences. That is, women high on role enactment had a pattern of psychosexual arousal to pornography similar to men's in general, just as men who were low on role enactment responded less to the pornography, like many of the women. From the perspective of script theory, it is the affect socialisation of individual men and women by parents that accounts for each person's preferences for sexual scripts and for how traditionally gendered they become.

The characteristics of the path of role enactment (Mosher, 1980) include the following: (a) sexual fantasies are scripted for novelty, drama, and exhibition; (b) sexual techniques display variety and skill in oral sex and intercourse; (c) the sexual style favours active expression in movement, sounds, and facial expression; (d) good sex is ecstatic and nonvolitional expression, with dramatic orgasms; and (e) the meaning of sex is to be a real man or a real woman, fulfilling an archetypal role. Therefore, both the use of pornography as a sexual aide and the novelty in partners and sexual activities in pornography achieve better goodness of fit with the path of role enactment.

A sexual script (Mosher, 1980, 1994a) may specify the attractive features in a cast; the appropriate time and place for sex; the preferred sexual activities and their sequencing and style; the role expectations for the sexual partner; the sexual talk, fantasies, and other psychological functions; the conception of sexuality; the criterion of good sex; the interpretation of the meaning and the evaluation of the outcome of a specific sexual scene; and more. For commercial pornography to succeed in generating sexual arousal, it may need to match these scenic elements or, at least, to not trigger negative affect that will attenuate the positive elements in the scene.

Sexual Personality

This heading is used to distinguish another form of audience differentiation from the sexual script. A distinction has been made between *erotophilia* and *erotophobia*. This distinction refers to a personality measure—a permanent psychological characteristic that predisposes individuals to act in a certain manner across a range of situations. Erotophiliacs are people who generally display a more open, liberated, and positive disposition towards sex and towards erotica. In contrast, erotophobes are characterised by being sexually more uptight, conservative, and reserved. The latter are also less comfortable viewing erotic material. These dispositions are again believed to arise largely out of early socialisation experiences with parents (Fisher, Byrne, White, & Kelley, 1988).

Sexual arousal plays a role in enjoyment of erotica. It is, therefore, understandable that sex differences might be found in levels of appreciation of sexually explicit material in films and television programs. A common theme across psychosexual models of sexuality is the notion that, from birth, individuals undergo a person-specific sexual socialisation process that shapes their pursuit of, attitude toward, and response to sexual experiences. Through exposure to direct and indirect communications from family, friends, authorities, and media and through learning experiences with their sexual responses, individuals develop a dispositional or trait-like constellation of sexually related attitudes, expectancies, and behaviors. In one model of sexual behavior development, the erotophobia–erotophilia dimension serves as a central construct (Byrne, 1977, 1983; Fisher, 1986; Fisher & Byrne, 1981).

Erotophobia–erotophilia is defined as 'the disposition to respond to sexual cues along a negative-positive dimension of affect and evaluation' (Fisher et al., 1988, p. 124). It is measured by the 21-item Sexual Opinion Survey. Erotophilia relates negatively to sex guilt and authoritarianism (Greendlinger & Byrne, 1985). Both men and women with negative attitudes towards sex have been found to display less taste for pornographic films than those with more positive sexual orientations. Individuals characterised by erotophobia, with relatively restrictive sexual socialisation experiences behind them, did not enjoy sex scenes depicting oral sex and full intercourse to orgasm to the same extent as erotophiliacs who had more liberal and active sex lives (Fisher & Byrne, 1978a).

In relation to audience enjoyment of erotica, some evidence has emerged that measures of 'sexual personality' in the form of erotophilia and erotophobia can discriminate between viewers. Not all the research evidence on this topic to date has been consistent, however. Sapolsky (1984) reported a study in which erotophobe-erotophile measures failed significantly to predict enjoyment of either violent or nonviolent sexual materials on film. In contrast, frequent church attendance, the expression of opposition to the showing of sexual films on film or television, and low personal experience of exposure to X-rated films all signalled greater dislike for the erotic film sequences that were shown.

Other laboratory studies, however, have shown that, compared to erotophobic individuals, erotophilic individuals exhibit more willingness to consume erotica (Becker & Byrne, 1985) and exhibit more positive emotional reactions when talking about sex (Fisher, Miller, Byrne, & White, 1980).

In a further test of the significance of this personality dimension to the way people respond to erotic material, researchers invited male and female undergraduates to view and evaluate a number of photographic slides, some of which depicted explicit sexual activity between a man and a woman with genitalia clearly visible. Some slides also depicted the man and woman engaged in more devious sexual practices, including sadomasochistic behavior. Differences in the length of time spent viewing these slides were found between men and women and between respondents whose replies to personality tests had identified them to be either erotophiliacs or erotophobes. Men tended to spend more time viewing the erotic slides than did women. The more deviant the erotica, the more polarised did men's and women's responses become. In addition, and cutting across gender differences, men or women who exhibited erotophiliac profiles were clearly more comfortable than were those with erotophobic profiles with viewing graphic and deviant sex scenes (Lopez & George, 1995).

NATURE OF MALE RESPONSE

It is worth reiterating at this point that the male response to violent sex scenes can vary with the nature of the scene itself. For some researchers, it is the violence in violent erotica, and not the sex, that is crucial to the way men respond (Donnerstein et al., 1987). Women, in addition, are also sensitive to the way their sex is depicted even in nonviolent sex scenes. However, evidence has emerged that degrading pornographic portrayals, even with no violence, can adversely affect male attitudes towards women (Check & Guloien, 1989). One reason for the inconsistency in these findings may be that some researchers failed to use nonviolent scenes that were sufficiently degrading to women.

A number of specific thematic elements in sex portrayals have been identified to produce distinctive emotional reactions and aggression-modifying effects. Men prefer to watch graphic penetrative sex scenes, whereas women prefer to watch scenes depicting loving foreplay (Sapolsky &

Zillmann, 1981). However, there are certain scenes that men and women often both display negative emotional reactions to. These include portrayals of masturbation and homosexuality (Mosher & O'Grady, 1979a), oral sex (White, 1979), sadomasochism (Malamuth, Haber & Feshbach, 1980), and bondage and bestiality (Zillmann, Bryant, Comisky, & Medoff, 1981).

With sexual depictions of an extremely graphic nature in which sadistic motives are apparent, the immediate emotional reactions of male observers can depend on the response of the female recipient. According to a sexual sadism model, for example, men with sadistic or sexually aggressive tendencies enjoy scenes that depict females in distress more than men not characterised by such tendencies (Heilbrun & Loftus, 1986). Research evidence has emerged from male judgments of photographic slides of women displaying a range of facial emotions from happiness, through anger and fear, to disgust. Nonsadistic males found women with happy faces the most sexually attractive, but men with sexually aggressive tendencies were more attracted to women showing distressed reactions (Heilbrun & Loftus, 1986).

Further evidence emerged from a study that obtained young college males' reactions to photographic scenes of female bondage taken from pornographic magazines. In these scenes, young, White females were shown scantily clad and bound hand-and-foot, helpless to avoid the impending sexual advances from a male. These scenes were preclassified by independent judges for the level of distress displayed by these female models. A sadistic component surfaced even within the sexuality of apparently normal males. Pictures of distressed women were found to be more erotic and sexually alluring than those of less distressed women. Males who also exhibited antisocial dispositions on a personality test enjoyed the pictures of distressed, bound women more than average (Heilbrun & Seif, 1988).

Attitudes Towards Women
as an Individual Differences Factor

Pre-existing attitudes towards women can influence the way men respond to violent sex scenes. Men who reveal a likelihood of raping, as measured through a clinically developed test (Burt, 1980), tend to exhibit similar patterns of sexual arousal to and attitudinal acceptance of rape scenes to those of known sex offenders. Men who score high on the rape likelihood scale hold more callous attitudes towards rape and believe that women secretly desire to be raped to a greater degree than men who score low on this scale (Malamuth & Check, 1980a; Malamuth, Haber, & Feshbach, 1980). Higher scorers on the rape likelihood scale are also more likely to believe that men would rape if they knew they could avoid getting caught, they identify with rapists in depictions of rape, and they attribute more of the responsibility for rape to victims who they believe derive pleasure from such assaults.

Not surprisingly, given this background, men who score high on the rape likelihood scale show greater enjoyment of sex scenes in which a woman becomes involuntarily aroused, as compared with men who score low on this scale. Indeed, such men may enjoy rape depictions more than portrayals of mutually consenting sex (Check & Malamuth, 1983; Malamuth & Check, 1980a, 1981a, 1983; Malamuth, Heim, & Feshbach, 1980). This finding is especially true of self-reported sexual arousal, although similar results have been obtained with physiological measures of penile erection (Malamuth & Check, 1980a, 1981a). Men who score low on rape likelihood tend to react to rape scenes with displeasure, even when the woman is shown as becoming sexually aroused (Malamuth & Check, 1981a).

In a study by Malamuth and Check (1983), male college students were administered questionnaires concerning their sexual attitudes and behaviors. One of the items enquired about the likelihood that the participant himself would rape if he could be assured of not being caught and punished. Several days later, the same men listened to one of eight audio tapes containing an interaction that involved sexual acts between a man and a woman. The contents of these depictions were systematically manipulated along the dimensions of consent (woman's consent vs. nonconsent to sex), pain (woman's pain vs. no pain), and outcome (woman's sexual arousal vs. disgust).

The findings highlighted the importance of the interaction between characteristics of male listeners and variations in the depiction of the sex act. When the woman was portrayed as experiencing disgust, male listeners tended to be much less sexually aroused themselves as compared with the scene in which the woman consents to sex. This was true regardless of pre-existing male attitudes about women or rape. In the example in which the woman was forced to have sex, initially against her will, but then eventually became sexually aroused, the men became sexually aroused themselves. This arousal was greatest, however, among men who had initially exhibited high scores on the rape likelihood scale.

Laboratory results were confirmed by a field study in which college students were bought tickets to attend either two movies with violent sex scenes or two alternative movies with no such scenes. All movies were viewed in a normal cinema environment. Afterwards, all respondents were administered a questionnaire to measure attitudes towards women and rape. Greater acceptance of rape myth beliefs materialised among those men who watched the two movies with violent sex scenes (Malamuth & Check, 1981b).

MEDIATING EFFECTS OF OTHERS

Reactions to sex portrayals can vary with the social context in which they are seen. Whether or not an individual displays enjoyment of sex scenes depends on whom he or she is viewing them with. Furthermore, if an individual receives information that other people have been sexually aroused by a particular scene, this too can make a difference to their reaction to it.

In a test of this social influence on reactions to sexual material, Norris (1989) found that men and women reported feeling more aroused by reading a nonviolent sexually explicit story when they had received a message telling them that other men and women had become aroused by it, but were less aroused by the story if told that others had not become aroused by it. Men generally reported higher arousal to this story under the condition when told about the strong reactions of a reference group. This enhanced sexual reaction was stronger for both men and women when told that men had become aroused by it than when told that women had become aroused by it. One explanation of this effect of reference group gender could be that consumption of pornography is normally associated more closely with men than with women. Thus, men may be perceived as a more credible information source about such material than are women (Fisher, 1983; Norris, 1989).

In a follow-up experiment, Norris (1991) compared the reactions of men and women to explicit written material that contained violence as well as sex. In different versions of a story in which a woman was forced to have sex, she displayed either pleasure or disgust as an outcome to the attack. Both versions contained explicit heterosexual acts, including intercourse, genital fondling, and oral sex, with violent elements, such as the male actor tearing off the female actor's clothes and forcing her to engage in various sex acts. Although initially reluctant to yield to the male character's advances in both versions, the female character in one gave in and expressed pleasure, whereas in the other she remained reluctant and conveyed shock, disbelief, and general distress.

Prior to reading the story, all participants were given a bogus research report indicating that same-sex young adults had become either highly aroused or not very aroused while reading the story. They also answered a brief questionnaire to ensure that they had understood the key elements of the report. This information influenced male and female participants' reactions to both versions of the story. In the pleasure-ending version, participants perceived less force, greater acceptability, and greater enjoyment by the woman in the scene than did those who read the version in which the woman displayed extreme distress. The reaction to the pleasure ending version was further enhanced by reading that other similar people had responded in a positive way towards the scene.

CONCLUSION

This chapter examined public opinion about media sex. Although most people do not seem to find sex on television offensive, many more people are likely to believe that there is too much rather than too little sex in programs (Millwood-Hargrave, 1999). Sex is seen as being a part of everyday life, but many viewers question the necessity of featuring it so prominently and so often on television. Sex may render programs unsuitable to watch, in the opinion of a minority of people, but most tend to agree that sex on television should not be censored out of existence. Most viewers agree that although sex may not be to their taste, others who wish to watch it should be given the opportunity to do so (Millwood-Hargrave, 1992; Svennevig, 1998).

Films and videos can provide far more explicit sexual materials than would normally be found on mainstream television channels. Public opinion has indicated, however, that most people would not ban X-rated movies featuring purely sexual content. Most people do object to videos or films for theatre viewing that depict violent sexual material (Gallup, 1985). As with television, personal tolerance for sex may not be as widespread as tolerance on behalf of others. With explicit pornography, individuals may often eschew opportunities to watch it themselves, but still feel that others should be able to do so if they wish (Linz et al., 1991).

Public opinion about sexually explicit media content varies with the nature of the sex portrayals, the social context in which it is experienced, and with the psychological make-up of the individual. Scenes of mutually consenting, heterosexual sex are generally regarded as acceptable, even though explicit. Scenes depicting rape, sadomasochism and bondage, masturbation, and homosexual sex, in contrast, are much more likely to be rated as distasteful (Malamuth, Heim, & Feshbach, 1980; Mosher & O'Grady, 1979a; Zillmann, Bryant, & Carveth, 1981). The enjoyment obtained from sex scenes can be enhanced when individuals are told that others found it arousing (Norris, 1989).

Men tend to be more tolerant of media sex than women, and prefer hard-core pornography, whereas women prefer soft-core depictions. Men and women tend to be socialised to different sexual scripts. The result of this socialisation is important to preferences for viewing erotic content. Women prefer sexual themes that represent a feminine sexual script in which sex is depicted as part of a romantic relationship (Mosher & MacIan, 1994). Men, in contrast, gain more enjoyment from watching explicit sex scenes in which the sex act is central and men are shown as being readily able to obtain sex with beautiful and receptive women. The individual's sexual personality is another important factor underpinning enjoyment of media sex. Individuals who display a more open and liberated disposition towards sex (erotophiliacs) enjoy watching sexually explicit films and videos more than do individuals who display a more conservative and awkward sexual disposition (erotophobics; Fisher & Byrne, 1978a; Fisher et al., 1988). Among men, in particular, those with pre-existing cynical attitudes towards women obtain more pleasure from scenes that depict coercive sex, especially when the female victim is seen to suffer (Malamuth & Check, 1980a, 1981a, 1983).

In determining the acceptability of media sex, therefore, it is important to bear in mind that overall public opinion about broad sexual labels or descriptions may disguise many important differences between individuals in what they enjoy for themselves or regard as acceptable for others. Although certain kinds of sex scenes may be regarded by most people as acceptable, the numbers of people expressing such an opinion may become progressively smaller as the nature of the scenes becomes more explicit or unusual. At the same time certain categories of individual exhibit exaggerated sensitivities to sex scenes of all kinds, and other categories of individual display strong preferences for particular types of sexual scene. Much more research is needed that cross-references the defining psychological characteristics of media consumers with types of sexual portrayal to establish those depictions that should be taken most seriously by media regulators.

4

Does Media Sex Influence
Young People?

One of the concerns about depiction of sex in the media is the effect that long-term exposure to it might have on viewers. The concern about long-term effects has been focused most especially on young people for whom the mass media represent potentially important sources of learning about social as well as purely sexual relationships.

Although sex is a prevalent feature of many mass media, exposure to sex tends to occur mostly via restricted rather than mainstream media output. Thus, the amount of sex to which teenagers in the United States, for example, were found to be exposed on broadcast television was fairly minimal. However, 15- and 16-year-olds were nevertheless found to have seen R-rated movies that carried frequent depictions of sex and where portrayals were usually far more explicit than on television (Greenberg et al., 1993). At the same time, it was found that family structure was important with teenagers from households with nonworking mothers tending to watch less sex content on television. Indeed, family circumstances had an impact on teenage exposure to sex both on broadcast television and in R-rated movies. Families in which there was a divorced parent (usually the mother) exhibited less parental supervision of children's television viewing. This relaxation of vigilance did not extend to teenagers' consumption of movies outside the home, however. Even single parents were likely to ask their offspring about the movies they were going to see (Stanley & Greenberg, 1993). Despite parental monitoring of teenagers' out-of-home media con-

80

sumption, most late adolescents and young adults have acknowledged consuming explicitly sexual media content in the form of books, magazines, and videos (Buerkel-Rothfuss & Strouse, 1993). Indeed, the most popular R-rated videos among this age group tend to be the ones with the most problematic sexual content, in which stories revolve around themes of violence and male dominance (Palys, 1986; Yang & Linz, 1990).

The attraction of sexual content in the media to young people stems from a natural curiosity in learning about sex. Traditional childhood and adolescent experiences may often provide only limited opportunities for learning about sex (Bandura & Walters, 1963; Kinsey, Pomeroy, Martin, & Gebhart, 1953). In addition, the socialisation process often attaches a degree of negativity to sexual behavior. This may, in turn, transfer across to opinions about media portrayals of sexual activity. In this traditional frame of reference, sex has been classified as something that is private. For many people, it is a source of discomfort or embarrassment to talk openly about sex or to be in the presence of others doing so. Sex may thus become associated with guilt, shame, and even disgust (Dienstbier, 1977). A psychological climate is then created that further fuels the young persons curiosity. This may then lead young people actively to seek out opportunities to find out about this mysterious forbidden fruit. In the absence of adequate information being derived from family, friends, or school, the media provide an available and necessary information source. Carried to an extreme, this drive to find out about sex through the media can lead to a preoccupation with not just mild sexual depictions, but more graphic erotica later in life (Dienstbier, 1977). In contrast, for some individuals, it can lead to the rejection of activities divergent from approved sexual practices (Mann, Sidman, & Starr, 1973) or a strongly negative disposition to sexual depictions (Fisher & Byrne, 1978a). A number of theories have been invoked to identify and explain different kinds of media effects in this respect.

Television has been identified, for example, as shaping cultural norms through its depiction of sexuality in stereotyped ways (Gerbner, 1985; Greenberg, 1982). Television can influence viewers' conceptions of social reality by displaying certain patterns of behavior on screen, especially when these portrayals are credible and relevant to the lives of viewers (Hawkins & Pingree, 1982; Wober & Gunter, 1988). Television and other media can convey messages to their consumers concerning how to behave in different settings. Thus, individuals can learn through observation and may subsequently copy what they have seen if appropriate circumstances should arise in their own lives (Bandura, 1977; Roberts, 1982). Television also has a role as a socialising agent. Rather than teaching specific behaviors, it imparts entire scenarios or sequences of behavior to individuals. Some writers have called these sequences of displayed activity 'scripts.' In the context of sexual socialisation, therefore, the emphasis is not placed simply on specific behavioral actions that viewers might imitate for themselves, such as kissing. Instead, the learning that occurs covers a whole range of activities and activity sequences in a sexual context, such as meeting a prospective sexual partner, engaging in a courtship ritual that involves spending time with that person in different situations where each can get to know the other, creating the conditions in which progressively more intimate physical contact takes place, and then establishing a relationship beyond sexual intimacy (Silverman-Watkins, 1983). Each of these theoretical models is now examined in more detail.

CULTIVATION THEORY

According to *cultivation theory*, a steady diet of television can influence viewers' conceptions of social reality such that heavy viewers' beliefs about the real world are shaped by the images of television (Gerbner, Gross, Jackson-Beeck, Jeffries-Fox, & Signorielli, 1978). The cultivation perspective suggests that television offers a consistent, stable set of messages that serves as a common socialiser (Gerbner, Gross, Morgan, & Signorielli, 1980). Furthermore, heavy consumption of the highly repetitive messages of television can create a distorted picture of social reality (Carveth & Alexander, 1985). According to Sapolsky and Tabarlet (1991):

> Looked at from the cultivation perspective, prime time television offers a consistent and repetitive set of messages regarding sexual behavior. Sixteen times an hour, entertainment programming adds to its particular vision of the sexual world. This world is noted for its overemphasis on sexual activity between unmarried characters and a disregard for the issue of safe sex. Adolescents and teenagers who regularly watch prime time television are offered a steady mix of marital infidelity, casual sex, the objectification of women, and exploitative relationships. As traditional avenues for sexual socialisation have diminished in influence, television has become the electronic educator (p. 514).

Operating within a cultivation effects model, there are numerous published investigations that provide empirical evidence for media influences on gender-role conceptions. Television has been identified as a particularly potent force in this context (Durkin, 1985d; Gunter, 1995). Among pre-teenage children, stronger gender-stereotyped beliefs have been repeatedly correlated with heavier television viewing (Beuf, 1974; Frueh & McGhee, 1975; McGhee & Frueh, 1980). These early studies did not distinguish between exposure to different kinds of programs, however. Furthermore, their results were challenged on the grounds that their measures of gender stereotyping were weak (Durkin, 1985b). More sophisticated studies revealed that television's cultivation effects among children could be moderated by the child's intelligence or educational attainment levels. Even here, though, closer inspection of the results indicated a far from consistent pattern of relationships between the child's own gender, IQ, television viewing, and gender-role stereotyping (Durkin, 1985b).

Research among adolescents within a cultivation model found that the correlation between the reported amount of television viewing and gender-role stereotyping was mediated by social class and strength of peer group affiliation. Adolescents of either sex, from lower social classes and with few friends, exhibited stronger gender-role stereotyping when they also watched a lot of television (Morgan & Rothschild, 1983). Although heavy viewing of sexist television might influence teenagers attitudes concerning gender-appropriate behavior (such as cleaning the house, washing the dishes, and mowing the lawn), there was no link between television viewing and how much teenagers tended to perform these chores (Morgan, 1987).

Admitting to stereotypically inappropriate behavior among pre-teenage children has been linked to their holding less stereotyped ideas about each sex. A contributory role for television was also identified in that the strongest correlations between gender-role attitudes and behavior occurred among children who were the heaviest television viewers (Signorielli & Lears, 1992).

Gender-role stereotyping embraces a wide range of beliefs and attitudes about masculinity and femininity. Much of the research on gender-role stereotyping touched only peripherally on the issue of sexuality as an aspect of gender-role conceptions. Within a cultivation effects model, exposure to the symbolic environment of television should contribute to viewers beliefs about the nature and frequency of sexual behaviors in the real world. Adolescents are believed to be especially susceptible to the sexual messages contained in adult television programming. In that regard, the types of messages conveyed by television, film or video are of paramount importance when aimed at or, in any case, are likely to be consumed by young audiences. One issue surrounds the responsibility with which sexual behavior and sexual relationships are depicted. Considered within the cultivation model, for instance, a television world that depicts casual sexual couplings, women as easy sexual conquests, or sex as a means to ends other than a loving relationship between committed partners, might be hypothesised to cultivate sexual beliefs and attitudes that encourage young viewers to behave in a similar fashion.

What evidence exists for a cultivation-style influence of television and other media on public conceptions of sexuality and sexual behavior? Not surprisingly, given their hypothesised susceptibility to media messages, much of the research on this subject has been conducted with adolescents. In many cases, researchers have confronted perceptions of sexuality directly; in other cases, measures of sex-related attributes and behaviours have formed part of a more extensive investigation of gender-related beliefs.

One early indication that perceptions of sex-related attributes could be influenced by television derived from an experimental study by Tan (1979). This investigation found that adolescent girls aged 16 to 18 years, who were fed a heavy dose of beauty product commercials emphasising feminine beauty, were more likely than a control group of girls who saw commercials containing no beauty messages to believe that being beautiful is an important female attribute. Those girls who watched commercials that focused on sexual qualities of women were primed to rank sex appeal attributes as being especially important in the context of being liked by men.

Evidence has emerged from other studies that media images of beautiful women provide points of comparison for men as well as for women. In the case of men, comparisons are made between the women in their own lives and those seen in the media. Male college students who viewed a single episode of *Charlie's Angels* were harsher in their evaluations of the beauty of potential dates than were males who had not seen the episode (Kenrick & Gutierres, 1980). Male college students were also reported to find their own girlfriends less sexually attractive after being shown centerfolds from *Playboy* and *Penthouse* (Weaver, Masland, & Zillmann, 1984).

Another aspect of cultivation theory and research has been the demonstration that regular exposure to television, with its stereotyped and often exaggerated portrayals of behaviors, can affect viewers' conception of the prevalence of similar behaviors in the real world. This relationship has been indicated in relation to public perceptions of violence (Gerbner & Gross, 1976; Gerbner et al., 1980). Given the findings that have been reported about television's depiction of sexual behavior, similar cultivation effects might be expected to occur with regard to viewers perceptions of sex-related behaviors. The world of television has been found to exaggerate the prevalence of premarital sex, extramarital sex, rape, and prostitution (Greenberg, 1994). The cultivation hypothesis would therefore predict that regular exposure to such patterns of sexual behavior on television might affect teenagers perceptions of the prevalence of these behaviors in reality and alter their self-perceptions in that they might become less satisfied with their own sex lives and have higher expectations of their prospective partners (Greenberg, 1994).

One suggestion from the United States is that American teenagers are exposed to far more media messages about sex than their peers in most other countries. This may lead them to believe that more of their own age group are sexually active than is really the case. This adds to the pressure on them to become sexually active (Jones et al., 1985). Teenagers tend to overestimate how many of their peers are sexually active anyway (Zabin, Hirsch, Smith, & Hardy, 1984). Regular viewing of television programs that emphasise teenage preoccupation with sex may further accentuate these perceptions. This phenomenon may contribute to the gradually but steadily decreasing age at which both males and females first have sexual intercourse that has been observed among American teenagers since the 1970s (Braverman & Strasburger, 1993).

Research has been published in which this type of effect was documented. In this case, heavy viewing of programs depicting stereotyped pattern of sexual behavior, was associated with an increased perception of the frequency of sexual activity in the real world (Buerkel-Rothfuss & Strouse, 1993). College students who were heavy viewers of soap operas estimated higher percentages of people in the real world who are divorced or have illegitimate children than did light viewers (Buerkel-Rothfuss & Mayes, 1981; Carveth & Alexander, 1985). In another study, pregnant teenagers were twice as likely to think that television relationships were like real-life relationships than were nonpregnant teenagers, and that television characters would not use contraceptives if involved in a sexual relationship (Corder-Bolz, 1980).

SOCIAL LEARNING THEORY

Another perspective on how television or film might influence young people's sexual attitudes and behavior is *social learning theory*. Whereas cultivation theory posits an influence of media representations of sex on general public perceptions about the prevalence of different sexual practices, social learning theory focuses instead on the specific behavioral influences of individual media portrayals. This theory holds that actions depicted as rewarding, in the sense that they obtain status, success, or personal gratification, have greater potential as exemplars that others might copy. Successful behaviors performed by attractive characters can serve as role models for others to follow. Thus, adolescents who see young adults, a little older than themselves, gaining prestige and peer popularity as a result of their sexual exploits may be encouraged to engage in similar behavior themselves (Bandura, 1977, 1994). To what extent, though, does mainstream television and the films and programs it broadcasts provide the kinds of role models in relation to sexual conduct to which teenagers are likely to be attracted?

One of the significant concepts in social learning theory is identification. The greater the perceived similarity between the viewer and the actor or model on screen, the greater the likelihood that the former may imitate the latter. To what extent do teenagers and sex mix on television? One way of finding out is to monitor television output and catalog how often and in what way such scenes appear.

Studies of sex-role portrayals on television have indicated that male characters tend to outnumber female characters by a significant margin (Gunter,

1995; Liebert, Sprafkin, & Davidson, 1982). Male characters have been found to portray more authoritative and superior roles than female characters. Furthermore, the status of women on television has more often been defined in terms of their relationships with men (Greenberg, Richards, & Henderson, 1980). It has, therefore, been suggested that the consequences of sexual behavior presented in the media, especially on television, are usually positive. This is particularly true for male characters. Among the few instances of negative consequences resulting from sexual behavior on television is unwanted pregnancy for women (Liebert et al., 1982).

In a content analysis of American network and cable television stations, Kunkel et al. (1999) studied the extent to which teenagers were depicted in scenes involving sexual behavior. They reported that out of a composite weeks television output, one in every ten scenes with sex involved a teenager. More specifically, one in ten scenes of talking about sex (10%) and a slightly smaller proportion of scenes depicting some form of overt sexual behavior (8%) involved a teenager. Most of the scenes containing sexual content and involving teenagers comprised just talk about sex (87%) with only a minority of these scenes (17%) depicting sexual behavior. Of the scenes involving sexual behavior ($n = 40$), just three contained implied sexual intercourse and none at all contained actual sexual intercourse. Among these scenes, most ($n = 25$) comprised kissing, a few (11) depicted physical flirting, and one comprised intimate touching.

If teenagers turn to television and films for role models in the context of their sexual development, it is important that these models set responsible examples. Some writers have argued that television's sexual role models often lack sufficient responsibility in their conduct (Elkind, 1993). In television serials popular with young audiences in which story lines revolve around intimate relationships, attractive role models are depicted as sexually active, but lacking in social and moral responsibility. Sexual behavior is depicted with infrequent references to the use of contraception, for example, and sex often occurs spontaneously with little planning at all (Wattleton, 1987). There is an absence of social learning messages that emphasise safe sex. Later in this chapter we return to this subject to examine evidence for risks and responsibilities in sexual portrayals on television in more detail.

The need for responsibility is underlined by findings that indicate that adolescents do make comparisons between television role models and themselves. Adolescents who identify closely with television personalities and believe that their television role models are more proficient at sex than they are, and who think that television's sexual portrayals are accurate and realistic, report being less satisfied with their status as virgins or with their own intercourse experiences. No relationship was found between the way television portrayals of sex were perceived and satisfaction in virginity (Baran, 1976a, 1976b; Courtright & Baran, 1980).

Given the significantly greater frequency, status, and favorable sexual consequences for male actors in the media, researchers have predicted that men are more likely to select media models than are women. When college students were asked to identify models of responsible and irresponsible sexual behavior, they selected primarily media figures (Fabes & Strouse, 1984). This study was conducted with college students. They tended to select both responsible and irresponsible sexual models from the media based more on the context in which sexual behavior took place than the fact they were or were not sexually active. This finding raised important questions regarding not only the type of sexual behaviors displayed by models but also how these behaviors are perceived and interpreted by those who observe them.

In a subsequent study, Fabes and Strouse (1987) asked students to provide information regarding their perceptions of models of sexual behavior. They were asked to name two individuals who they personally felt represented models of responsible or irresponsible sexual behavior. These selected models could be real or fictitious people, famous or ordinary members of the public, male or female. Participants were then asked to explain their reasons for their selections. In addition, participants were asked questions about their own sexual behavior.

Parents were rarely identified as models of irresponsible sexual behavior (7%), but were more frequently identified as responsible sexual models (30%). Men identified media celebrities as sources of irresponsible sexual behavior most of all, followed by peers. Women identified peers as sources of irresponsible sexual behavior most of all, followed by media models. For men, responsible sexual models were most likely to be found among peers, followed by parents and then the media. For women, responsible sexual models were primarily found among peers and then parents, with media models a long way behind the other two. Men's preference for media models may arise out of the fact that they have more models of their own sex to choose from on television, as compared with women.

Both men and women identified reasons for selection of irresponsible and responsible models based mainly on the intentions and motives underlying a model's sexual behavior (67%), rather than on the nature of the person's sexual experiences or the resulting consequences (33%). Men's reasons varied more as a function of model type. Men tended to identify reasons based on intentions significantly more often for their selection of irresponsible sexual models than they did for their selection of responsible sexual models. In addition, men tended to identify responsible sexual models proportionately more often according to the model's sexual acts and proportionately less often according to the model's underlying intentions for the behavior than did women.

Respondents who identified media models or peers as primary examples of responsible sexuality also reported relatively more permissive sexual attitudes, higher rates of sexual intercourse, greater numbers of sexual partners, and lower rates of contraceptive usage. Among young people of both sexes, media models and peer groups represented the majority of both responsible and irresponsible sexual models. However, television may represent a more important source of motivation and behavior styles for men than it does for women.

The findings regarding young adults reasons for choice of sexual models have important implications for the ways in which men and women tend to judge irresponsible sexual behavior primarily on the basis of an individuals' motives and intentions. Research has shown that men and women exhibit different motives for sexual intercourse. Men's motives more often include pleasure, fun, and physical gratification, whereas women's motives more often include notions of love, commitment, and emotion (Carrol, Volk, & Shibley-Hyde, 1985). Parallels also exist with sex differences in judgments about sexual behaviors and morality. Women appear to give greater consideration to the human relationships involved in moral dilemmas and are less likely to apply absolute moral rules than are men (Gilligan, 1982).

SEXUAL SOCIALISATION

A third approach to explaining the potential influences of television and film depictions of sex on young people is offered by the *sexual socialisation model.* Some observers have suggested that significant changes have occurred in the past 30 to 40 years in the sexual socialisation process. They point to the sexual liberalisation of the 1960s with its emphasis on greater permissiveness and shifting sexual norms (L. K. Brown, DiClemente, & Peck, 1992; H. T. Christenson, 1962; Johnson & Goodchilds, 1973). As a result, there may be a convergence in the responses of males and females and a lessening of guilt and disgust associated with sex and sexual images (Schmidt & Sigusch, 1970). Such speculation must be treated cautiously, however.

There is mounting evidence that adolescent and young adult populations are able to experience increased exposure to sexually explicit material. Bryant (1985) and Bryant and D. Brown (1989) reported a telephone survey with 600 respondents age 13 to 15 years, 16 to18 years, and 19 to 39 years. The aim of the questioning was to obtain normative data on amounts of exposure to various types of R- and X-rated media content. Findings indicated that by age 15 years, 92% of males and 84% of females had looked at or read *Playboy* or *Playgirl* and that by age 18 years, the proportions rose to

100% of the males and 97% of the females. The average age of first exposure for males was 11 and for females was 13.

High levels of exposure to sexually explicit films were also reported. Nearly 70% of 13- to 15-year-olds, even though underage, reported exposure to an average of 6.3 sexually oriented R-rated films before the age of 13. In regard to X-rated media, among all respondents the average age of first exposure to a magazine that depicted couples or groups in explicitly sexual acts was 13.5 years. In regard to X-rated films, 92% of 13- to 15-year-olds said they had already seen such a film, with an average reported age at first exposure of 14 years 8 months.

Evidence has emerged, long after the swinging sixties sexual revolution, that college-age populations still find more unusual sexual themes disturbing (Zillmann, Bryant, Comisky, & Medoff, 1981), and females remain more displeased than males even with depictions of normal sexual practices (Mosher & MacIan, 1994). Some studies have examined the impact of filmed sexual content on attitude formation. For example, college students shown sexually explicit films reported a greater acceptance of sexual infidelity and promiscuity than did controls (Zillmann, 1994). Adolescents viewing music videos with sexual content were more likely to agree with the notion that premarital sex is acceptable (Greeson & Williams, 1986).

In two further studies, college students' disapproval of rape could be lessened by exposure to just 9 minutes of scenes taken from television programs and R-rated movies or viewing 5 hours of sexually explicit films over a 6-week period (J. D. Brown, Childers, & Waszak, 1990; Zillmann & Bryant, 1982). Finally, both male and female college students exposed to hour-long nonviolent X-rated videos over a 6-week period reported less satisfaction with their intimate partners (Zillmann & Bryant, 1988b). The researchers concluded that 'great sexual joy and ecstasy are accessible to parties who just met, who are in no way committed to one another, and who will part shortly, never to meet again' (Zillmann & Bryant, 1988a, p. 450.).

Whereas social learning theory focuses on the possibility that young people may copy specific behavioral examples seen on screen, the sexual socialisation perspective examines the longer term influence potential of the media in conditioning generalised norms and values surrounding sex. This model recognises that young people can learn about sexual practices not only through witnessing sexual behavior played out on screen, but also by tuning in to talk about sex. Conversations about sex have been identified as representing a significant aspect of all sexual portrayals on television (Kunkel et al., 1999). Such talk can contribute to norms and expectations concerning how to be sexual, why and when sex is appropriate, and with whom. Television can thus provide an agenda for sex and represent sexual 'scripts' that youngsters can learn and then utilise themselves at an appropriate later date (Roberts, 1982).

Before reviewing the evidence for how television and films can influence the sexual mores of young people, how responsible are these media in their depictions of sex? In particular, is any emphasis at all given to the potential health risks known to be associated with casual or promiscuous sexual behavior?

RISKS AND RESPONSIBILITIES
IN SEXUAL RELATIONS

One of the biggest concerns about television's depictions of sex—and the same point applies to much sexual content in films and videos as well— is that high-risk sexual behavior is often portrayed. Risky sexual behavior can include sexual practices that increase the likelihood of unwanted pregnancy, especially where this occurs among underage families, or contracting a sexually transmitted disease. Observers in the United States, for example, have noted that risky sexual practices appear to be quite prevalent among American teenagers. Use of contraception among sexually active teenagers is inconsistent (L. K. Brown, DiClemente, & Peck, 1992) and sexual intercourse with multiple partners is not uncommon. These risky sexual behaviors have resulted in a relatively high teen pregnancy rate in the United States compared to other industrialised nations (Trussel, 1988) and a steady increase in sexually transmitted disease rates (Alan Guttmacher Institute, 1991). Full-blown AIDS during adolescence is rare because of the long incubation period. However, more and more health experts believe that many individuals contract the virus during their teen years (Family Planning Perspectives, 1990).

At a time when sexually transmitted diseases are widespread, television's typical depiction of sexual relationships projects a message that appears to run counter to the warnings put about by health education campaigns. Television itself can serve as an incidental sex educator. Although teenagers generally indicate getting information about sex from parents, school, or peers, the media have often been cited as the next most important information source (Louis Harris & Associates, 1986). Indeed, these different sex information sources do not provide consistent advice. There is some concern, for example, that the lessons being taught through formal sex education programs may be undermined by counter examples supplied through peer groups and the media (Strouse & Fabes, 1985). Avoidance of sexually transmitted diseases and the prevention of their spread can be facilitated by adopting safe-sex practices and by a nonpromiscuous lifestyle. Another social problem that stems from unprotected sex is the increased occurrence of unwanted pregnancies, particularly among teenagers. To find out more about how responsible a medium such as television has been in its depiction of sex, researchers once again turned to content analysis methodologies.

At a time when increased sexual responsibility is called for in society, studies of television programming have revealed that appropriate sexual role models have been generally inadequate. Not only has sexual behavior in general increased in prevalence on mainstream television, more importantly, depictions of explicit intercourse have grown in number and frequently take place between partners outside of a permanent or long-term emotional relationship and without any apparent use of protection (Sapolsky & Tabarlet, 1991). Issues of safe sex, sexually transmitted disease, and contraception were rarely addressed on American television between 1979 and 1989. The subject of homosexuality was rarely dealt with. The preponderance of sexual action featured unmarried characters.

Lowry and Towles (1988) analysed a sample of programs from prime-time network television in the United States in 1987. They were particularly interested in the extent to which sexual portrayals contained references for sexually transmitted disease prevention, unwanted pregnancies, and AIDS. They found 14 references to pregnancy prevention and 18 references to sexually transmitted disease prevention, of which 13 dealt with AIDS, out of a total of 722 sexual incidents coded.

The Planned Parenthood Federation of America conducted another study of network television at about the same time in 1987. This investigation found that references to sex education, sexually transmitted diseases, or abortion were extremely rare, comprising less than a tenth of 1% of sexual incidents.

Research conducted during the mid-1990s by Kunkel and his colleagues at the University of California, Santa Barbara explored the prevalence, distribution, and character of sexual portrayals on American network and cable television, and paid particular attention to depictions of risks and responsibilities associated with sex (Cope & Kunkel, 1999; Kunkel, Cope, & Colvin, 1996; Kunkel et al., 1999).

In a 1-week composite sample of television output comprising 1,170 programs broadcast on 10 television channels, Kunkel et al. (1999) found sexual content in 56% of monitored programs, with an average of 3.2 scenes containing sex occurring per hour. More than half the sample of program (54%) contained talk about sex, and just under a quarter (23%) contained sexual behavior. In total, 420 scenes were found with sexual behavior, of which just 45 scenes contained depiction of or reference to risks or negative consequences (2% of all sexual scenes). There were 35 scenes in which reference was made to the use of safe-sex precautions and 13 scenes that depicted waiting for sex until a relationship had developed more fully in other ways. Out of 78 scenes in total that included any reference at all to risks or responsibilities linked to sex, this subject was given substantial emphasis in 41 of these scenes. In the remainder it received little emphasis.

The idea that mainstream television depicts a world of rampant promiscuity characterised by frequent casual couplings between partners who hardly know one another was not upheld by Kunkel et al.'s (1999) analysis of mid-1990s American programming. In more than half (53%) of the scenes depicting sexual activity, the characters were in an established relationship. In more than one in four cases (28%), though the characters had not yet established a long-term relationship, they had met before. In only one in ten cases (10%) had they just met.

Despite this character-relationship profile of television's sexual couplings, Kunkel et al. (1999) also observed that most television programs that contained scenes of sexual behavior presented no information about the consequences of such behavior for characters. This finding was true both for programs that presented talk about sexual intercourse (63% showed no clear consequences) as well as for those that depicted or strongly implied such behavior (59% showed no clear consequences). When intercourse was the topic of conversation, there was relative balance between the programs that included primarily positive and primarily negative consequences of intercourse (14% positive vs. 16% negative). When intercourse behavior was shown rather than discussed second-hand, there was a much stronger tendency toward positive than negative outcomes (27% vs. 7%).

Out of a total of 456 scenes involving sexual behavior, just 9% were found by Kunkel and his colleagues to contain any mention at all of risk or responsibility, although some of these cases involved jokes or minor references that clearly would not convey a serious message about the topic to viewers. Although this represents only a modest degree of attention to such concerns, it does contrast with their treatment in previous decades. In 1976, only a single scene of 27 involving sexuality (3.7%) addressed any risk or responsibility topic, and that involved a humorous remark about abortion. In 1986, again only a single scene out of 48 (2.1%) was observed, and this comprised a discussion about a possible abortion. In contrast, in 1996, 12 scenes were cataloged in which the use of a condom was mentioned. In five of these cases, it was referred to as protection against AIDS or other sexually transmitted diseases.

Cope and Kunkel (1999) used the same general methodology to analyse the depiction of sexual content in 15 television shows that were top-rated among young people age 12 to 17 years in 1996. Three out of four of these shows were situation comedies; the remainder were dramas. Three episodes of each series were analysed, giving a total sample of 45 programs. In 37 of the programs, scenes were found that contained either talk about sex or depiction of sexual behavior. Within these 37 programs, 262 separate interactions were cataloged involving talk about sex or physical sexual behavior across 179 scenes, giving an average of 5.8 sexual interactions per program, or 9.2 interactions per hour. Most physical behaviors that were portrayed were restricted to kissing and flirting. Even so, the authors concluded that more intimate behaviors such as heavy petting or intercourse occurred often enough to provide adolescents with an opportunity to learn from them. In fact, there were only six portrayals of implied or simulated intercourse in just three of the programs. None of these scenes could be classified as explicit and in every instance, the participants were portrayed as being in established relationships (in three cases they were married to each other).

Of 80 scenes containing talk about sex, only 11 (14%) contained an emphasis on a sexual responsibility theme. The most prominent theme, occupying around two thirds of cases, was waiting to have sex or abstinence. Three scenes made reference to using a condom and two scenes made reference to protection from AIDS. There was just one mention made of other sexually transmitted diseases and one mention of abortion. Of the 99 scenes containing overt sexual behavior, only 3 contained a responsibility theme. This study indicated that programs popular with adolescents contain regular references to sex and sexual relations, but relatively modest attention is devoted to messages concerning risks and responsibilities associated with being sexually active.

IMPACT ON YOUNGSTERS

As the content analysis evidence has indicated, television does comprise repetitive sequences of activity related to sexual behavior. Entertainment programming emphasises extramarital sex and displays an apparent disregard for safe sexual practices. Thus, adolescents and teenagers who regularly watch prime-time television are offered a steady mix of marital infidelity, casual sex, the objectification of women, and exploitative relationships.

In a survey of 15- and 16-year-olds in three Michigan cities, more than half had seen the majority of the most popular R-rated movies released between 1982 and 1984 either in cinemas or on videocassette (Greenberg et al., 1986). Compared with prime-time television, these movies had seven times more sexual acts or references, which were depicted more explicitly (Greenberg et al., 1993). The ratio of unmarried to married people engaging in sexual intercourse was 32 to 1. As Greenberg (1994) observed, 'What television suggests, movies and videos do' (p. 180).

A growing number of researchers have investigated the relationship between exposure to sexual media content and adolescents' perceptions, beliefs, values, and sexual behaviors (Baran, 1976a; Buerkel-Rothfuss, &

Strouse, 1993; Newcomer & J. D. Brown, 1984; Peterson, Moore, & Furstenberg, 1984; Walsh-Childers, 1991). In general, these studies have shown that there is more evidence for the impact of sexual content on perceptions than on values and behaviors.

Television has, according to some writers, become an important sex educator because of both its frequent, consistent, and realistic portrayals of sexuality and the lack of alternative sources for learning about sexual behavior (Roberts, 1982). Young viewers are provided with frequent lessons in how to look and act sexy. As a consequence, television has become an important sexual socialisation agent (Baran, 1976a, 1976b; Courtright & Baran, 1980). Media depictions of sex can create expectations in the minds of young viewers about the pleasures of sexual activity that contribute towards dissatisfaction with their first sexual experiences. Baran (1976a) surveyed adolescents about this subject and found that the more highly they evaluated the sexual prowess of television characters, the less satisfied they were with their own initial sexual experiences. This negative correlation between the perceived sexual pleasures obtained by fictional characters on screen and satisfaction with ones own sex life was repeated in a subsequent survey among college students (Baran, 1976b). The degree to which media depictions of sex are perceived as realistic is also important in this context. This, in turn, may be linked to the individuals own sexual experience. Adolescents who were sexually experienced perceived media depictions of sex as less realistic than did virgins, and saw television characters as having less sexual prowess (Courtright & Baran, 1980).

In the absence of alternative sources of information, the sexual lessons young viewers derive from television foster an inaccurate image of sex that can lead to unrealistic expectations, frustration, and dissatisfaction (Baran, 1976a, 1976b; Fernandez-Collado, Greenberg, Korzenny, & Atkin, 1978). Documenting the specific nature of sexual portrayals on television thus becomes an important step in establishing the reality that influences the perceptions of young viewers.

PROBLEMS WITH TEENAGE SEXUALITY

A number of Western countries have witnessed increased prevalence of births outside marriage and premarital sexual activity, especially among teenagers (Baldwin, 1982). In the United States, researchers have observed that teenagers are engaging in sex earlier and take more partners in the early part of the sex life, often without contraception (Courtright & Baran, 1980; Planned Parenthood Federation of New York City, 1986). Between 1971 and 1979, for example, the proportion of never-married women, aged 15 to 19 years in American metropolitan areas, who had ever had sexual intercourse rose from 28% to 46%. Comparable trend data were not available for men during this period, but it was known that the proportion of 15- to 19-year-old males who were sexually active in 1979 was 69% (Zelnick & Kantner, 1980).

A number of factors have been found to be associated with the timing of initiation of sexual activity. For instance, those starting early are more likely to be males and to be Black (Zelnick & Kantner, 1980), to have reached physical maturity earlier (Billy & Udry, 1983), to place greater value on independence and less on achievement, to be more tolerant of deviance, to be less religious, and to be more involved in problem behaviors (Jessor & Jessor, 1975; Jessor, Costa, Jessor & Donovan, 1983), to have lower self-esteem, to come from a single-parent family and to live in a poor neighborhood (Hogan & Kitagawa, 1983), and to have lower educational aspirations (Devaney, 1981; Furstenberg, 1976).

For some writers, television has had a part to play in this social phenomenon. Television viewing is thought to be a factor contributing to the high incidence of sexuality among teens. Television has been accused of allowing producers to push back the boundaries of what is acceptable (Beschloss, 1990; Polskin, 1991). Increasingly, risque network programming was attributed to reduced censor staffs, and audience erosion was attributed to more permissive cable and videos (Beschloss, 1990; Polskin, 1991). Prime-time dramas and movies were observed to venture ever more graphically into intimate and detailed conversations about sensitive sexual subjects such as impotence and orgasms, while even situation comedies were becoming increasingly filled with sexual innuendo and suggestiveness (Beschloss, 1990; Franzblau, Sprafkin, & Rubinstein, 1977).

As we have seen already, sexuality on television is a broad topic that includes not only suggestive and erotic behavior, but is also wrapped up with the representation of gender roles, intimacy and affection, and marriage and family life as well (Roberts, 1982). As such, the picture of sexuality presented by television is often a distorted one (Greenberg, 1982; Roberts, 1982). For example, most references to sexual intercourse on television have tended to involve extramarital relationships and references to prostitution. Sex and violence are linked from time to time, although more especially in video sex depictions than on television. Erotic relationships are frequently depicted as occurring outside of warm, loving, and committed relationships (Fernandez-Collado et al., 1978).

Studies of the impact of televisions depiction of sex on adolescents sexual attitudes and behavior have usually taken the form of surveys in which samples of teenagers report on their viewing habits and sexual activity. Peterson, Moore and Furstenberg (1991) used data from the National Survey of Children in the United States to examine the amount of time children spend viewing television and the extent to which the content viewed that is sexual in nature is related to the initiation of sexual activity. These researchers considered a number of theoretical explanations for the effects that television might have on young viewers inclinations to begin sexual relations at an early age.

Television was hypothesised to provide sets of role models and a source of social learning. It was felt that children could learn about sexual behavior by observing it performed on television. Television was regarded as an agent of social conditioning, that could provide children and teenagers with attractive examples of how to behave. Another view was that televisions effects might operate by reducing socialised inhibitions against engaging in sexual behavior before a certain age, or against committing oneself too readily to sex before a relationship had become sufficiently well developed. It was also felt that television could arouse latent tendencies. As teenagers reach puberty and experience physical and hormonal changes, sexual drives naturally emerge. Viewing sexual scenes on television could serve as a stimulus, adding directly to natural urges and increasing the likelihood that those urges will be acted upon. Finally, it was also hypothesised that television could serve as an instrument of tension release. Viewing sexual scenes in programs could provide a channel through which sexual urges could be vicariously expunged, thus attributing a cathartic effect to television.

The study carried out by Peterson and his colleagues utilised National Survey of Children data at two points in time, nearly 5 years apart. The same children were surveyed on both these occasions, enabling the researchers to investigate relationships between television viewing and the onset of sexual behavior longitudinally as well as at one point in time. Initial soundings were taken when the children were between 7 and 11 years old. At that time, the children were interviewed with a parent (usually the mother) present. The second interview was carried out when the children were 12 to 16 years old. In this interview, all respondents age 15 to 16 years were asked about the sexual experience of their friends and about their own sexual experience. A question was also asked about teenage pregnancies among their friends.

During the second survey, 16% of 15-year-old and 20% of 16-year-old girls reported having had sex. The initiation of sexual behavior among these girls, however, was not found to be linked in any significant way to their history of television viewing. Among 15- to 16-year-old boys in the survey, a curvilinear relationship emerged between reported television viewing and sexual experience. The heaviest viewers had the highest prevalence of sexual experience (35%), whereas moderate viewers had the lowest rate of sexual experience (12%). These relationships were found both in regard to television viewing in mid-teens and during the respondents pre-teenage years.

Finding a relationship between being sexually active in mid-teens and amount of overall television viewing does not provide enough evidence by itself to demonstrate that television was an influential agent in this context. We also need to know something about the kinds of material to which teenagers have been exposed on television that might be relevant to the shaping of their sexual behavior. The same study probed further for teenager girls and boys program preferences to find out whether or not they especially enjoyed watching programs known to contain sexual portrayals. Evidence of this kind of relationship did emerge in this study, but only for girls. Fifteen- and 16-year-old teenage girls who admitted to being sexually active were more likely to name programs with sexual content among their favourites.

Among both boys and girls, the strength of association between overall television viewing and sexual activity varied as a function of other factors in their lives. Among the girls, sexual experience and television viewing were especially strongly linked for those girls who had low self-esteem, who watched television apart from their parents a lot of the time, and whose parents had a more permissive attitude to sex. Among teenage boys, the association between television viewing and sexual experience was stronger for those who tended to watch television apart from their parents and who also had low educational aspirations.

The conclusions reached from this study were that television viewing appears not to act in any direct way to influence teenagers sexual behavior. Any effects it might have are likely to be indirect, taking the form of teaching sexual values and sexual scripts. This role of television in the socialisation of sexual behavior among teenagers is probably most powerful when other potential influences, such as from parents, are largely missing. Values and scripts that encourage engaging in casual sexual behavior, taking many partners, and in which there is little emphasis on using protection, may encourage some teenagers, for whom counterexamples are not present in their own lives, to be less concerned about the risks associated with unprotected sex with partners they barely know.

Another survey of American teenagers reported that those who chose heavier diets of television programs that contained sexual behavior were more likely than those who viewed relatively little of this material to have had sexual intercourse (J. D. Brown & Newcomer, 1991). The data on which this analysis was based were obtained through questionnaires from nearly 400 teenagers age 13 to 18 years. Once again, repeat surveys were carried out on three separate occasions spread over 3 years. Measures of peer and media encouragement to have sex were used. Respondents looked at a series of sentences that described sexual activity and decided if TV and movies, your best male friend, and/or your best female friend do that activity, and whether each of these three sources of potential influence encouraged them to learn about sex, set rules about sex, or encourage them to be more sexually active or to be less sexually active. Further questions were then asked about television viewing habits. Finally, each adolescent respondent was asked about their own degree of sexual experience, progressing from kissing to necking to petting to sexual intercourse.

Television viewing patterns were found to differ by the sexual status of the respondent. Nonvirgins in all but the Black male group, were significantly more likely than virgins to seek sexy programming. Having had sexual intercourse was related to seeking out such programs, but not to actual frequency of exposure to them.

When a regression analysis was carried out in which various predictor variables were linked to sexual intercourse, the model achieved significance only when the ratio of viewing sex on television was added in. This suggested that the relationship between viewing a high proportion of television shows containing sex and engaging in sexual intercourse held even after controlling for the perceived influence of male and female friends and previous noncoital experience. Although this is not a conclusive test of the causal sequence between television viewing and adolescent sexual behavior, it does suggest that teenagers who selectively view television programs with sexual content are more likely to have had sexual intercourse, regardless of their friends encouragement or discouragement to have sex and regardless of their previous sexual experience.

In an attempt to shed more light on the direction of any potential causal relationship between viewing television programs that contained sex and adolescents personal experience of sexual intercourse, the researchers examined the viewing of sex-containing programs as a dependent variable. When reported experience of sexual intercourse was added to the predictor variable list, it did not significantly improve the amount of variance explained in sexual activity. This finding, therefore, strengthened the conclusion that the direction of causality flowed from a high degree of viewing sex-containing programs to onset of sexual intercourse rather than vice versa.

CULTIVATION OF BELIEFS ABOUT SEXUAL BEHAVIOR

Mass media are among the sources of information about sex mentioned by teenagers (Thornburg, 1981). Teenagers do not all turn to the media for sex information in the same way. For some teenage girls, for example, media depictions of sex are regarded as very useful sources of guidance by which they are intrigued. For others, media sex portrayals are perceived to have little relevance to real life. Indeed, for those girls who are sexually experienced, media depictions of sex may be regarded as overromanticised and as not reflecting their own experience (J. D. Brown, White, & Nikopoulou, 1993).

Although dispositions towards the media may vary, there is evidence that media sex portrayals may influence young viewers perceptions of sexual activity in reality. Quite apart from any impact that media sex depictions might have on individuals perceptions of their own sex lives, there may be wider effects on social reality perceptions. Regular exposure to televised portrayals of sexual behavior, for instance, has been linked among American teenagers with their perceptions of the frequencies with which those behaviors occur in the real world. Buerkel-Rothfuss and Strouse (1993) measured relationships between television viewing patterns and teenagers perceptions of a range of male- and female-linked sexual behaviors.

College students in the high teens were asked to report on their viewing of television in general, and viewing of daytime serials, action-adventure series, evening serial dramas, situation comedies, and high-brow dramas. They were also asked to indicate their views on aspects of male-related behavior (e.g., having an affair, bragging about their sexual experiences, picking up women in bars, fathering illegitimate children, committing rape) and female-related behaviors (e.g., having abortions, talking about sex, feeling guilty after sexual encounters, using sexual favors to achieve goals, and sleeping with multiple partners).

Reported watching of daytime serials or evening serial dramas emerged as good predictors of a wide range of nonerotic sexual perceptions about both males and females. Serial drama viewing predicted perceptions about problems with sex, sex without love, frequent sex, and perceptions about virginity for both males and females. Viewing of MTV was related to perceptions that males and females brag about sex, and consumption of X-rated movies, sex manuals, and MTV were the best predictors of perceptions of the prevalence of erotic sexual behavior. In sum, this study indicated a strong link between the nature of the media selected and the social construction of reality by individuals in their late teens. The real world perceptions that appeared to be influenced were those that involved behaviors portrayed in the media. There was no evidence that perceptions of sexual behavior not depicted in the media were in any way affected by patterns of media exposure.

In a related analysis, Buerkel-Rothfuss, Strouse, Pettey, and Shatzer (1993) reported a number of relationships between television viewing habits and attitudes to sex. General media consumption was unrelated to such attitudes, but the extent to which young adult males and females watched MTV and television soap operas was linked to holding sexually permissive attitudes. This finding applied to both males and females. Although neither

MTV nor television soaps depict explicit sexual content, sexual themes are prevalent in both cases. Even so, the data reported in this analysis were inconclusive as to the direction of causality, and whether the media were causal agents or whether sexually explicit media content was selected by already permissive individuals.

TELEVISION SEX AND ADOLESCENT MORALITY PERCEPTIONS

Television depictions of sex can provide fictional examples of sexuality, sexual relations, and sexual behavior that teenagers may learn from and even try to emulate. Apart from the social learning through the observation of overt behavioral depictions on screen, televisions fictional representations of sexual relationships may convey implicit messages about morality. In other words, are certain types of sexual liaison deemed to be socially or morally acceptable forms of conduct? Content analysis studies of sexual portrayals on television have indicated that sexual relationships often occur outside marriage and even outside of any established emotional relationship (Greenberg, 1994). What kinds of lessons might this teach young people who are just becoming sexually active themselves?

Bryant and Rockwell (1994) reported three experimental studies designed to investigate adolescents moral judgments about sexual liaisons between characters in popular fictional series broadcast on prime-time U.S. network television. They began by manipulating the television viewing diet of teenage boys and girls, and then had each participant view and evaluate a series of brief video vignettes extracted from television series, some of which depicted sexual behavior. They also examined the mediating influences of family communication style, family value systems and the participants own viewing styles on their reactions to television's sexual scenes.

Following a forced diet of television programming 3 hours a night for 5 nights, which covered themes of pre-, extra-, or nonmarital sexual relations, young viewers rated the sexual indiscretions or improprieties depicted in video vignettes as less bad compared with same-age peers who had viewed nonsexual material. These effects were much weaker, however, among teenagers who were active and selective viewers, whose families had an open, democratic communication style and well established value systems.

In another examination of the acceptability and value of different televised depictions of sexual conduct, Greenberg, Linsangan, and Soderman (1993) found that teenage viewers felt that they learned something worthwhile from sexual vignettes about sexuality or about sexual terms. There were variations among different types of sexual scene in terms of how much they were enjoyed or regarded as acceptable for showing on television. Four categories of sexual scene were used in this study, with three scenes adopted in each case: married intercourse, unmarried intercourse, prostitution, and homosexuality. Each scene was rated for enjoyment, realism, humour, sexiness, and suitability for viewing. Synopses of each vignette are presented in Table 4.1.

The prostitution vignettes were the most enjoyed, and the segments involving intercourse between married couples were the least enjoyed. In the latter case, scenes of intercourse involving married couples, along with such scenes involving unmarried couples, were regarded as the least humorous. Scenes of homosexual activity were rated as the least acceptable, whereas the other three types of sexual conduct were all rated about equally acceptable. The scenes involving unmarried couples engaged in sex were rated as the most sexy scenes overall.

YOUNG PEOPLE AND PORNOGRAPHY

Despite legal restrictions placed on the rental of pornographic videos to adolescents, survey evidence has shown that underage viewing of explicit sexual materials, designated as suitable for adult audiences only, does take place. One survey of American high school students in the mid-1980s found that 46% of junior high school students and 84% of high school students interviewed had reportedly seen an X-rated film (see Bryant & D. Brown, 1989).

A Canadian survey reported that among adolescents in their mid-teens, nine out of ten boys and six out of ten girls claimed they had viewed explicit pornographic videos. The boys indicated that they were frequent consumers of pornography and that they had learned about sex from such material. These regular adolescent users of pornography were also found to be more accepting of rape myths and violence against women, as well as being more likely to believe that forcing girls to have intercourse is acceptable (Check & Maxwell, 1992).

Further evidence emerged from a sample of Californian teenagers (age 14 to 15 years). This study indicated that exposure to pornography was linked to beliefs that rape is often brought on by the actions or appearance of women themselves and that it can be excused in part because men have stronger sexual needs, that are more difficult to keep under control, than women do. This pattern of linkages between rape-related beliefs and reported exposure to pornography was found among both female and male adolescents. Indeed, correlations between claimed pornography exposure and rape beliefs were stronger for girls than for boys, especially for those girls who claimed also to have used pornography to learn about sex (Cowan & Campbell, 1995).

TABLE 4.1

Television Sexual Vignettes Rated by Adolescent Viewers as Used by Greenberg, Linsangan, and Soderman, 1993

Prostitution

Scene One

Scene from *Hill Street Blues* in which a young woman is arrested by an undercover policeman for solicitation. During the hearing, the public defender explains to the judge that the young woman's family situation is not too good and that she is pursuing job opportunities in California. She convinces the judge that the young woman should be tried as an adult. The young woman pleads guilty to disorderly conduct and is given a $200 fine. The young woman is then seen with her boyfriend, who slaps her and calls her a whore. The public defender consoles the young woman and talks to her boyfriend, explaining that the young woman was only trying to help him so they could start a new life.

Scene Two

Again from *Hill Street Blues,* the scene shows a more stereotypical looking prostitute—wearing a red low-cut and skin-tight dress—who also tries to solicit an undercover policeman. She is arrested and jailed. A police officer drops by her cell. The prostitute asks him why he is staring at her breasts and tells him that he is a horny cop looking for a freebie. She undresses and offers herself to him in exchange for her release. At her hearing, she pleads guilty to solicitation, is fined $200 and warned that if she is arrested again, she will be given 90 days incarceration. She is later arrested.

Scene Three

From *Night Court.* Comic context. Group of prostitutes are brought to court. The prosecutor informs the court that a complaint from a disgruntled former employee led to the arrest of the women in a house of prostitution. The defense attorney moves for postponement pending the location of the owner of the building. Scene ends when Madame of the house arrives.

Married Intercourse

Scene One

Taken from *Cheers.* Revolves around Norm, one of the regular characters, who is trying to start a family. Banter and one-liners directed at Norm and his wife's attempts at having a baby.

Scene Two

From *All My Children.* Talk concerns one of the main character's attempts to have a baby. Her dialogue with various relatives centers on this topic. Her husband wants a baby but she is not so sure about it.

Scene Three

Taken from a soap opera; features a couple talking about how much they enjoyed the previous night together after the children had gone to bed and how close they felt to each other.

Unmarried Intercourse

Scene One

From *Facts of Life*. Radio show hostess has a young caller who asks her for advice about going on a camping trip with her boyfriend who has asked her to sleep with him. The hostess tries to avoid the question, but the caller asks if she should have sex with her boyfriend. The hostess says it is a very difficult question for her. She advises the caller to think of the consequences and consider her feelings.

Scene Two

From *One Life to Live*. A man and a woman are talking about their relationship. The discussion centres on the man's understanding of what the woman needs and the woman's confusion about her feelings. Scene ends with man asking woman to stay and go to bed with him.

Scene Three

From *General Hospital*, this scene opens with a man and woman dancing to slow music. They talk about the situation being cozy and becoming even cozier. They kiss. The man is then seen in bed waiting for the woman. She then gets in the bed and under the covers. They embrace, talk, kiss again, and whisper to each other. The woman then gets undressed under the covers and the man discards her nightgown. There follows more caresses and kissing.

Homosexuality

Scene One

From *Night Court*. A gay tells Dan he finds him attractive. Dan tells his co-workers about this incident and one of his co-workers tells everyone else about it. Dan gets stuck in the elevator with the gay and tells him that he is wasting his time. Dan gets cold and the gay gives him his overcoat.

Scene Two

From the sitcom *Gimme a Break*. A short scene with the police chief telling his housemaid about his problems at work, one of which concerns a cop who wants to 'come out of the closet.'

Scene Three

From *Dynasty*. Opens with Luke telling Steven that he has figured out why Steven has been distant with him. To the question whether he was 'coming on' to Steven, Luke replies that he is capable of a platonic friendship. Adam accuses Steven of having an affair with 'the little fag' he is working with and that is why Steven's marriage is crumbling. The two fight. The scene ends with Steven going to Luke's apartment, with the fairly explicit indication that he wants to be with him again.

Note. Data are from Greenberg, Linsangan, and Soderman (1993).

MUSIC VIDEOS

Rock music videos are complex stimuli that combine music with visual content. They can be expected to produce a blend of emotional reactions. Stronger sexual feelings, for instance, might be provoked by very sexy videos than by videos with little or no sexual content. Because music videos are aimed at and consumed primarily by the youth market, and teenagers are regarded as more susceptible to a range of potential social and psychological influences of mass media, there is understandable interest in and even concern about the impact of these videos. The possibility of a link between exposure to music videos and teenage sexual activity was indicated by an American survey that showed that teenagers who exhibited a strong liking for Music Television (MTV) were also more sexually experienced (Peterson & Kahn, 1984).

In addition to the sex component of rock videos, many have an additional factor—namely their capacity to create physiological arousal through the nature of the music and the volume at which it is played. This factor deserves attention because of the theoretical status of such physical arousal when paired with certain types of content. The theory of excitation transfer, for example, captures the way in which arousal produced by rock music might contribute to wider emotional effects of visual sex or violence within video productions (Zillmann, 1978, 1984). Within excitation-transfer theory, physiological arousal is related to both the intensity of emotional responses to an event (Zillmann, 1978) and the strength of its appeal (Cantor, Zillmann, & Einsiedel, 1978). Thus, both the intensity of the viewers' emotional responses to sexual or violent videos and how appealing viewers find them should be related to the level of arousal or excitation provoked by the sexual or violent images.

Sexual images can become compounded with the music in a music video to enhance its audience appeal. Zillmann and Mundorf (1987) conducted an experiment in which they edited R-rated sex and violence into a rock music video, either independently or together. Sex was found to increase the appeal of the music, but not so violence. Sex and violence together decreased the music's appeal.

Hansen and Hansen (1990) conducted two experiments to examine the effects of sex and violence in rock music videos on viewers' judgments of the appeal of the music and other aspects of the production. In the first study, audience reactions were compared across videos with high, moderate, or low levels of visual sexual content. Visual sex had substantial effects on degree of liking for the music and visual production. Overall, the visual content of videos judged as high in sexual content was rated as more enjoyable than the visual content of videos judged to have less sexual content. The presence of more sexual content also enhanced overall liking for the music. Viewers also reported feeling more sexy after watching the videos with higher sexual content.

Combining sexual and violent imagery in music videos had the opposite effect of sex on its own. The appeal of music videos declined in the presence of high levels of violence, even though sex was also present. This result confirmed the earlier findings of Zillmann and Mundorf (1987). The latter also observed, however, that the effect of sex was felt mostly in the emotional responses of video viewers to the music being played, rather than to the visual elements of the production. In fact, the presence of sex appeared to diminish the appeal of the visual production among women viewers. Hansen and Hansen (1990), in distinction, found that sex had a strong positive effect on the appeal of both music and visual production. The main difference between these two studies was that Zillmann used R-rated sexual inserts, whereas Hansen and Hansen used milder forms of sex content that had occurred naturally in the original video productions. This difference in methodology, taken together with their respective findings, suggests that the mere presence of sex per se is probably less important to audience reactions to music videos than is the nature of that sexual content.

COMPREHENSION OF MEDIA
MESSAGES ABOUT SEX

Survey investigations of links between verbally reported media consumption habits, perceptions of sex, and self-reports of personal sexual practices among young people can reveal where possible associations exist between such measures, but really only scratch the surface in terms of improving our understanding of the ways in which media messages about sex can influence them.

One important aspect of media influence in this context is the way messages about sex are apprehended and processed by members of the audience. Content analyses of the representation of sex in film and television have identified regular patterns in these portrayals that may present not simply behavioral models to be emulated, but also social scripts that are committed to long-term memory to be invoked to guide behavior in a more general fashion when the right occasions arise. Sexual depictions in the media are not always overt and explicit. Often they are implicit and have to be presumed on the basis of depicted action. It may be more important to understand the extent to which different sexual scripts are being learned from the media than to demonstrate copying of specific incidents shown on screen in relation to establishing how far-reaching media effects on sexual practices can be.

Another relevant factor is that distinct gender-related sexual scripts can be identified. Males tend traditionally tend to be sexual initiators and females are sexual delimiters (LaPlante, McCormick, & Brannigan, 1980). Males are significantly more likely to report that their main motives for sexual intercourse are to have fun and achieve gratification, whereas females report that their main motives are love commitment (Carrol, Volk, & Shibley-Hyde, 1985). The learning that takes place from media depictions of sex, therefore, may take the form of schemas or broad frames of reference to guide thinking about male and female sexuality and to inform sexual conduct in different situations. Factual information about biological matters linked to sex, such as menstruation and the reproductive process, can be conveyed to young viewers by documentary programs (Greenberg, Perry, & Covert, 1983). Teenage attitudes toward issues such as premarital sex and birth control have been modified through a specially produced film about birth control (Herold & Thomas, 1980). However, there may be wider scripts about sex than can be effectively communicated not just through factual media productions but also through fictional portrayals.

In some instances, the nature of the media's impact on young people's sexual awareness and understanding depends on the specific type of cognitive information processing in which they engage. One relevant distinction that has been made in this context is between content-centered processing and content-stimulated processing (Hawkins & Pingree, 1986; Thompson, Pingree, Hawkins, & Draves, 1991). Content-centered processing involves cognitive activities related to thinking about the content of the message. This might include selectively attending to or focusing on certain information or drawing particular inferences about information missing from the content. Content-stimulated processing occurs when individuals make connections between media content and their own past experiences or when they imagine being in a character's place.

One interesting study on comprehension of media sex investigated young women's interpretations of implicit sexual portrayals in movies. A small sample of female college undergraduates ($n = 39$), all in their late teens and early 20s, were interviewed about implicit sexual portrayals in clips taken from three movies. Participants were shown either a clip from *About Last Night, Dark Man,* or *An Officer and a Gentleman* (Meischke, 1995). The clips contained scenes in which sexual intercourse had apparently taken place but was not actually shown on screen. The scenes depicted events leading up to and then following sex between a man and woman.

After viewing one of these clips, each female respondent was interviewed in a fairly nondirective fashion in which a series of open-ended questions were posed about the scenes depicted. Meischke was interested in the schemata viewers used to explain the events seen on screen and to reach a conclusion that sex had or had not taken place. According to schema theory, people can reach judgments about what happened in television programs even though a film or program itself may have provided them with only partial information about the events depicted. Schemata are cognitive structures gained from past experience with events, issues, and topics that represent a form of organised and often quite generalised knowledge about those domains of experience. They are used to help make sense of new encounters and underpin the drawing of inferences about events where all the information about them is not present.

Some schemata focus on persons featured in films. Person schemata focus on knowledge about the traits and goals that shape other people's behavior (Fiske & Taylor, 1984). For example, a trait for the schema 'promiscuous' might include what promiscuous people do. Person schemata also include schema for people's goals, or for the motivations and intentions associated with their actions. A goal schema is useful for predicting a particular person's behavior in a particular setting based on the notion of *what* behavior goes with *what* goal.

Mieschke was interested in finding out to what extent young female viewers drew conclusions about not just whether sex had occurred, when the physical act itself was not shown on camera, but also whether perceptions emerged that safe sex had occurred. In the case of the latter perception, what kinds of clues on screen and internal schemata were used to reach this conclusion? During open-ended interviews, it became apparent that these young female viewers were able to infer that sex had taken place, even though they had not seen it. This conclusion was not reached in a consistent fashion, however. Among some viewers, the sex judgment was based on broad generalisations about sexual behavior. For example, in one movie, the woman was believed to be sexually promiscuous and therefore was also believed to have had sex with the man with whom she was depicted, even though they had not known each other long, because that is what promiscuous women do. Other viewers picked up on production cues and cues from the events that took place on screen. For example, the characters were witnessed dancing, then kissing, and then finally taking each other's clothes off. Afterwards they were shown getting dressed. Thus, one logical conclusion from these signs was that they had had sexual intercourse. Such a sequence of events represented a sexual script—a sequence of behaviors associated with having sex.

On the question of whether the sexual behavior that transpired was 'risky,' judgments were more difficult to make. There were no overt clues presented on screen that the actors talked about using or were seen applying contraceptives or other behaviors typical of safe sex. Instead, viewers relied on their schemata of the kinds of sexual behaviors that go with certain relationships or sexual goals. Even then, different schools of thought emerged. For example, some respondents argued that promiscuous women take precautions because of their high-risk lifestyle. Other respondents countered this by arguing that such women tend not to take precautions because they are risk takers, fateful, or do not care much for themselves.

The significance of television portrayals of sexuality for young people can vary with age. As they progress through their teenage years and move into young adulthood, young men and women are attracted to media messages about sexual relationships in different ways. One qualitative study of this topic, grounded in reception theory, has found that teenage girls and young adult women exhibit different reactions to the same television serial in which the lead characters were supposedly in their mid- to late teens (Granello, 1997).

In a series of focus group interviews with viewers of *Beverly Hills 90210*, the degree to which respondents were attracted to the lead male characters, or identified with the lead female characters and their relationship problems, varied between 12-, 17-, and 21-year-olds. The 12-year-olds focused mainly on female friendships in the show, although they showed early signs of being attracted to some of the male characters. The 17-year-olds were interested primarily in the male characters whom they regarded as sex objects. This emphasis grew out of a heightened focus at this age on male–female relationships. The 21-year-olds were not interested in the male characters whom they regarded as too immature. They were seen as boys rather than real men.

The young age group displayed early signs of understanding the importance of relationships, particularly between members of the opposite sex, but were still embarrassed to talk openly about such matters in front of their own peers. They were aware of the status of sexual relationships among the characters on the show, however. The mid-teens group emphasised male–female relationships in their comments more than any other group. Even the 21-year-olds focused on sexual relationships between the characters in defining the way different characters related towards one another, even when there were nonsexual relationships and nonrelational story lines featured in the series. The 12-year-olds displayed their sexual immaturity in their reluctance to discuss sexuality openly, and were critical of too much overt sexuality in the program. Interestingly, the 21-year-olds also felt there was too much emphasis on sex in the series, but they reached this opinion from a different perspective to the pre-teenage girls. For these young adult women, the sexuality depicted was inappropriate because of the potential influence it could have on young girls who might treat some of the lead female characters as role models. The 17-year-olds were the only group who did not seem to think that *Beverly Hills 90210* paid too much attention to sexual issues. However, this age group was probably the one most interested in sexual technique and information about sex (Moffitt, 1987). Consequently, they could be expected to welcome story lines that provided this sort of material.

The importance of this exploratory study lies in the differences that emerged, albeit with a limited sample of respondents, among female viewers of a popular, relationship-oriented television show in their modes of response to its sexual content. All three age groups were aware of the sexual content in this show, but the significance of sexual relationships for these groups varied as a function of their own stage of psychological maturity and sexual socialisation. Among pre-teenage and teenage girls and young adult women, relationships were an important and defining aspect of their lives (Gilligan, 1982). There were, however, developmental differences in the kinds of relationships to which most weight is attached. For pre-teenage girls, female–female relationships were most important, whereas for 17-year-old girls, male–female relationships were critical. Among 21-year-old women, relationships with the opposite sex retained a position of paramount importance, but their greater maturity and experience meant that they questioned the realism of some television portrayals of sexual relationships in a way 17-year-olds did not. According to Granello (1997), this factor may be especially important in the way teenage girls and young adult females react to relationship portrayals in a series such as *Beverly Hills 90210* in which female subordination and inferiority typify many story lines.

CONCLUSION

Sexual portrayals in the media may serve as sources of information and learning for young people as they embark on sex lives of their own. Media sex may therefore act as an instrument of social learning and sexual socialisation. This form of influence may act not merely through overt depictions of sexual activity, but also through talk about sex. Sex in media aimed at young people often occurs in the form of conversations about sexual relationships and experiences. This talk about sex can provide an agenda for sex and presents sexual scripts from which young people can learn. Thus, the influences of media sex stem not simply from showing graphic depictions of sexual technique, but from scripts that play out the role of sex in the context of wider interpersonal relations.

The concerns about media sex and teenagers center as much on the kinds of scripts that are played out on television, film, and video as on their early exposure to nudity and scenes of simulated sexual intercourse. In the context of rising teenage pregnancies and the spread of sexually transmitted diseases, the media have been identified as often presenting the wrong kinds of examples to young media consumers. Depictions of sex rarely emphasise the risks and responsibilities that accompany sexual relations. Sex is depicted as fun and largely as risk free. Safe sex practices are rarely allowed to surface, nor are the potential risks associated with casual sexual relations among partners who have not known each other very long. The accompaniment of sex with violence in films and videos has been widely criticised for cultivating a set of beliefs surrounding coercive sexual relations, that support the myth, for example, that women enjoy being raped. Yet, films that present sexuality in a way that runs counter to these more prevalent themes can be effective at drawing the attention of teenagers and young adults to the importance of sex as part of a lasting and committed emotional relationship with someone and that even when sexual partners know one another well, there may still be good reasons to observe safe sex practices.

5

Is Media Sex
Degrading to Women?

One of the concerns raised about the depiction of sexual behavior in the media has centered on the way women are represented. For many years, there has been widely voiced criticism of sex-role stereotyping on television and other media in which women are frequently depicted in subordinate positions to men. The media treat women as objects, primarily as sex objects, who are to be admired, manipulated, and used by men.

Women have long been underrepresented in mainstream television in most major genres of programming. This pattern has been traced back to the 1950s (D. M. Davis, 1990; Head, 1954; Tedesco, 1974). However, it is not so much the extent to which women appear on screen as the way in which they are presented that has caused the greatest controversy. Women have tended to be shown in a much narrower range of roles than men. The traditional pattern has been one in which the domestic role of women is played up and any professional role is played down (McNeil, 1975; Butler & Paisley, 1980; Tuchman, Daniels, & Benet, 1978). Even when women are shown in employment, the occupational roles in which they appear have tended to be traditionally female occupations and positions in which they are subordinate to men (Ceulemans & Fauconnier, 1979).

Another aspect of sex-role stereotyping has been manifest in the personality and emotional characteristics of women and men. Women have been depicted as more emotional and less rational than men. As such women have generally been shown as more preoccupied with personal relationships, family, and emotional conflicts (McNeil, 1975). Women were observed to require more emotional support than men (Greenberg, Richards, & Henderson, 1980). Women are more likely than men to be oriented towards marriage. Although some women would be shown in occupations, work was usually secondary to home life (Kuchenhoff, 1977).

Men were observed to exude greater authority and competence than women across a variety of situations. Men were more likely to give and women more likely to receive advice (Turow, 1974). If women were successful professionally, the price they paid was failure in their private lives. Females who were successful at work were unhappily married. The same pattern was not so pronounced for men who were portrayed more often than women as being able to achieve a successful balance in both their private and professional lives (Manes & Melnyk, 1974). Women were less likely than men, across a range of fictional genres on television, to be shown as having control over events in their lives. Women were more likely to lack control or to be portrayed as believing that they lacked control over their lives (Hodges, Brandt & Line, 1981).

These stereotyped portrayals on television persisted throughout the 1950s, 1960s, and 1970s to the late 1980s (Pribram, 1988). At around this time, however, published research began to emerge that signalled shifting patterns of sex-role portrayal. Women were observed to be as prominent as men in genres such as situation comedy and serialised drama. They remained in a subordinate position to men in action–drama series, however (Steenland, 1990). Where women were beginning to achieve parity with men, though, this was manifest not only in terms of the prevalence on screen, but also in terms of the kinds of roles they played. In particular, there were signs that the occupational variety of women's roles was broadening (Huston et al., 1992). Indeed, single, professional women had started to appear in lead roles, demonstrating equal competence with male leads even in action-oriented series (Atkin, 1991; Reep & Dambrot, 1987).

The depiction of sexuality is one important element of the representation of the sexes. Much attention has focused on the subordinate position women tend to occupy vis-à-vis men in sexual situations in the media. This type of depiction becomes acutely focused in scenes in which men force women to engage in sexual activity and sex becomes mixed with violence. Depictions of sexual violence feature most prominently in pornographic materials. However, influential feminist writers have argued that in pornography, women tend to be featured as subordinates of men even when there is no overt violence present. Women are depicted as existing primarily for the sexual satisfaction of others (usually men) and as willing to accommodate any and every male advance (Dworkin, 1981; MacKinnon, 1989). Continued exposure to this kind of representation of women may result in the acceptance of women in a subordinate sexual role and ultimately lead to be-haviors that reflect this perception.

SEXUALITY AND THE SEXES

The stereotyping of sex roles and sex traits by television might be expected to characterise representations of sexual behavior. Few such comparisons have been made between male and female characters. One study reported that females accounted for a greater proportion of kissing, hugging, and af-fectionate touching, and of implied sexual intercourse than would have been expected on the basis of their overall representation (Silverman, Sprafkin, & Rubinstein, 1979). In a later examination of female and male involvement in sexual behavior, men were found to initiate a far greater proportion of sexual acts than did females. This finding for American net-work television in 1989 showed an increase in the propensity of males to ini-tiate sex relative to females, as compared with 10 years earlier, when both sexes had been shown to be equally likely to initiate sexual acts (Sapolsky & Tabarlet, 1991). Research in Britain found that while males and females were equally likely to make a first-time approach to a member of the oppo-site sex, males were much more likely than females to engage in an extra-marital affair (Millwood-Hargrave, 1992).

PORTRAYALS IN MORE EXPLICIT MATERIALS

The expanded popularity and availability of pornography have been key factors rekindling and fuelling public scrutiny of and debate about video pornographic materials (Attorney General's Commission on Pornogra-phy, 1986; Committee on Sexual Offences Against Children and Youths, 1984; Joint Select Committee on Video Material, 1988; Lederer, 1980; Special Committee on Pornography and Prostitution, 1985; Zillmann & Weaver, 1989). One predominant and recurrent point of contention in-volves classification and interpretation of the content characteristics of sexually explicit materials.

One view of pornographic materials is that they are simply entertaining, innocuous communications that pertain to sexual behavior. Advocates of this position contend that modern sexually explicit materials offer only pos-itive images of sexual pleasure and abandon (Gagnon, 1977; Kaplan, 1984; Stoller, 1976; Wilson, 1978). Proponents of this perspective maintain that the social and sexual 'reality' portrayed in pornography is so accurate and detailed that these productions provide important educational and thera-peutic aids that help eradicate 'puritanical attitudes about sex that have long dominated our society' (Goldstein, 1984, p. 32).

Alternatively, it has long been 'asserted that a distinguishing characteristic of sexually explicit materials is the degrading and demeaning portrayal of the role and status of the human female' (Commission on Obscenity and Pornography, 1970, p. 239). Many feminist analysts, in particular, argue that the social and sexual 'reality' conveyed by contemporary pornography portrays women as sexually and socially subservient to and dominated by men.

From their vantage point, these analysts maintain that such materials disparage and demean women by portraying them as 'malleable, obsessed with sex, and willing to engage in any sexual act with any available partner' (Diamond, 1985, p. 42); that sexually explicit materials require 'that women be subordinate to men and mere instruments for the fulfillment of male fantasies ... that our pleasure consists of pleasing men, and not ourselves' (Longino, 1980, pp. 45–46); and that they consistently depict women as 'anonymous, panting playthings, adult toys, dehumanised objects to be used, abused, broken and discarded' (Brownmiller, 1975, p. 394).

Defining the Problem

Special concern has been reserved for the way women are portrayed in sexually explicit or pornographic films and videos. Such concern stems not only from the 'objectification' of women, but also from a trend within this category of material to depict scenes of violent sexual attacks on women. Within the psychology literature there have been theoretical disagreements and empirical inconsistencies regarding the effects of nonviolent but degrading sexually explicit material. There is no objective criterion regarding what is 'degrading,' although there may be a consensus about the types of images that are regarded as degrading.

Although limited, the available empirical data show that contemporary pornographic productions typically involve a narrow range of highly stylized content conventions that strongly emphasize a 'chauvinistically male or macho orientation' towards sexual behavior (Crabbe, 1988; Day, 1988). Most notable among these conventions is a seemingly complete 'preoccupation with sexual activity to the exclusion of all other facets of human social behavior' (Hebditch & Anning, 1988, p. 15). Many analysts have noted, for instance, that pornographic materials typically feature all variants of heterosexual intercourse in innumerable circumstances (D. Brown & Bryant, 1989; Palys, 1984, 1986; Prince, 1990; Slade, 1984; Winick, 1985).

At the same time, however, depictions of other basic aspects of human sexuality—such as communication between sexual partners, expressions of affection or emotion (except fear and lust), depictions of foreplay, afterplay, or friendly cuddling, and concern about sanitation or the consequences of sexual activities—are minimised (Cowan, Lee, Levy & Snyder, 1988; Prince, 1990; Rimmer, 1986). Furthermore, within this context, women are normally shown as eagerly soliciting participation in, and responding with hysterical euphoria to, any of a variety of sexual encounters (Abel, 1987; Palys, 1984; Rimmer, 1986).

Zillmann and Bryant (1982) proposed that degrading but nonviolent pornography has pervasive attitudinal, if not behavioral, effects. Zillmann (1989) and Zillmann and Bryant (1982) reported varied negative effects of degrading pornography in both men and women, including sexual and victim desensitization and changes in broader attitudes and values towards sex and towards women. Later research indicated that exposure to degrading sexually explicit material was as likely as violent sexual material to increase male proclivity to coercive sex, and both types of material were more likely to do so than nondegrading erotic portrayals (Check & Guloien, 1989). Another study using college women indicated increased mood disturbances in response to nonviolent as well as to violent pornography (Senn & Radtke, 1990) and more negative feelings towards rape victims as a function of exposure to sexually explicit nonviolent films than either eroticised (nonexplicit sex) violence or covert violence (Borchert, 1991).

Perceptual consequences have been found to occur following consumption of both sexually explicit (X-rated) and suggestive (R-rated) materials portraying the standard nonviolent pornographic theme. Sexual coercion and violence, and idealised sexuality have also revealed strong negative shifts in perceptions of female sexuality and victims of sexual assaults (Weaver, 1991; Zillmann, 1989). Research by Weaver (1987) and Zillmann and Weaver (1989) found that exposure to depictions of both sexual and coercive and/or violent media depictions can induce adverse shifts in perceptions of women and dispositions about punishment of a convicted rapist. Men also rated rape victims as sexually more promiscuous after exposure to media portrayals of sex or sexual violence. Women responded differently. They did not perceive a rape victim as more permissive after viewing sexual themes. However, they did tend to perceive greater permissiveness after viewing scenes of coercive and/or violent sex.

A major problem in research on degrading, nonviolent, X-rated pornography has been how to define 'degrading (to women)' material. Different researchers have used quite varied material in investigating the effect of degrading depictions of women. Researchers have also disagreed on the terminology to be used for this class of pornography, which is distinguished from erotica and violent pornography. Some prefer the use of the word *dehumanising* (Check & Guloien, 1989), others *common pornography* (Zillmann, 1989), and still others *degrading* pornography (Attorney General's Commission on Pornography, 1986).

Antipornography feminist writers, such as Steinem (1980) and Dworkin and MacKinnon (1988), have contended that the inequality, domination, and objectification of women in pornography are degrading. For example, Steinem (1980) used mutuality and equal power versus inequality as the major distinction between what she labeled erotica versus pornography. To Steinem, erotica occurs between equals, whereas pornography is unequal sex. Hill (1987), a philosopher, suggested that a public display of low status is degrading—that is, a loss of personhood by being treated as a means, not an end.

In contrast, Dworkin and MacKinnon's (1988) views are based on a political rather than a moral argument. In their view, pornography sexualises the subordination of women and is a form of sex discrimination. Their proposed civil ordinance spelled out in a more detailed way their definition of pornography. Some of their criteria included the 'graphic, sexually explicit subordination of women in pictures or in words that also includes women dehumanised as sexual objects, things or commodities, in postures or positions of sexual submission, servility or display, or women's body parts ... exhibited such that women are reduced to those parts, or women presented as whores by nature or inferior or hurt in a context that makes these conditions sexual' (p. xxxiii).

A point of view about what constitutes degrading pornography that does not fully capture the feminist view is that of Zillmann (1989). To him, degrading (common) pornography 'depicts women as sexually insatiable and socially nondiscriminating in the sense that they seem eager to accommodate the sexual desires of any man in the vicinity and as hyper-euphoric about any kind of sexual stimulation' (p. 135). Donnerstein et al. (1987) also defined degrading sexually explicit material as that which depicts women as 'willing recipients of any male sexual urge (excluding rape) or as over-sexed, highly promiscuous individuals with insatiable sexual urges' (p. 4). Then, according to Cowan and Dunn (1994), 'These definitions focus on unbridled sexuality as itself constituting the degradation of women. The extent to which men's availability and insatiability are degrading to them is rarely discussed. When the degradation of women is associated primarily with their display of sexuality, rather than by the ways in which sexuality portrays their subordination, not only is a double standard of sexuality being used, but also subordination is discounted' (p. 12).

Cataloging Degrading Portrayals

Among the earliest published evidence on this topic were studies of the representation of female sexuality in printed media. Smith (1976) found a repeated pattern of male dominance in sexual acts and a perpetuation of the 'rape myth,' wherein the woman initially resists forcible intercourse, but eventually enjoys it. Of 4,588 sexual episodes identified in 428 paperbacks, one in five (20%) involved rape, and one third of the sex depicted in these novels involved the use of force to obtain sex, usually with no punishment of the aggressor. Fewer than 3% of the attackers were repri-manded for their crimes. Smith found that descriptions of forcible sex in-creased from the late 1960s to the mid-1970s, with rape scenes doubling in prevalence during this time.

Later, a study of 1,760 adult magazine covers from 1970 to 1981 found an increase in domination and bondage themes in which the object of sexual domination was usually a woman (Dietz & Evans, 1982). In another study of magazines, Malamuth and Spinner (1980) observed that levels of sexu-ally violent themes in certain sex magazines decreased after reaching a peak in the late 1970s. They found that depictions of rape, sadomasochism, or exploitative coercive sexual relations in Playboy and Penthouse pictures and cartoons increased from 1% in 1973 to about 5% in 1977. No further in-crease was observed after that. Following the study by Malamuth and Spin-ner, a study of violence in cartoons and pictures in Playboy from 1954 to 1983 found that the violence level with women as targets rose until the mid to late 1970s, and then descended again (Scott & Cuvelier, 1987). Sexual violence occurred in about 1 page out of every 3,000 and in fewer than 4 out of every 1,000 pictures. The increase in sexual violence in erotic magazines observed by Malamuth and Spinner (1980) may, therefore, have covered those years in which such content peaked, before dropping off again.

There is relatively little evidence on the gender role portrayals in sexu-ally explicit film and video materials. Some studies have shown relatively high levels of violence; others have found less violence and more sex be-tween mutually consenting partners.

Depiction of Women in Restricted Videos

A number of content analysis studies of pornographic videos carried out during the 1980s provided interesting descriptive data, but used nonrepresentative samples of sexually explicit videos (Cowan et al., 1988; Palys, 1984; Prince, 1990; Yang & Linz, 1990) or nonsystematic analytical procedures (Rimmer, 1986). Palys (1984) for example, used a procedure purposefully biased to permit oversampling of potentially violent porno-graphic materials from the rental stock available on the shelves at several outlets in a Canadian metropolitan area. Cowan and colleagues used a simi-lar sampling procedure. Prince (1990) and Yang and Linz (1990) sampled only the 'classic' or more notable 'feature-length' productions. Although widely viewed, such productions included only a small proportion ($n = 800$) of the approximately 5,000 sexually explicit videos available in the contemporary marketplace ('Charting the Adult Video Market,' 1989).

In an examination of the 'stag' film genre (the 8mm films now shown more often in peep shows), Slade (1984) noted that, between 1915 and 1972, rape depictions constituted 5% of this material, on average. During this time period, violence never went beyond an upper boundary of 10%, and there was no indication of any increase in violent images over time. Slade did note that the violence since 1970 had become more graphic and brutal.

Stag films were popular before the mid-1970s. Since then they have been replaced by videos. There have been several investigations, using content analysis, of the representation of male and female sexuality in sexually explicit videos. A number of these studies were reviewed in chapter 2 as part of a discussion about the amount of media sex on distribution. However, it is relevant to examine these studies again at this point, with special reference to what they revealed about portrayals that were degrading to women. This review also introduces some studies for the first time in this volume because of their specific relevance to the theme of the present discussion.

In a Canadian study, Palys (1986) analysed more than 4,000 scenes from 150 adult-rated and commercially available triple-X-rated videos. Although the commercially available videos contained scenes of explicit sex and sexual violence, there was greater equality between the sexes in these videos, as compared with adult-rated materials, in sexual scenes. In contrast, in adult-rated videos, men were dominant in most sex scenes. Over the 4-year period covered by this study, from 1979 to 1983, Palys found a decrease in violent sexual imagery in commercially available videos, but no such change in more restricted adult-rated videos. A further study in the United States of videos rated R, X, and XXX found sexually violent behavior, in which female victimisation was the norm, to be present in all three categories of production (Yang & Linz, 1990). Sexually violent scenes mostly comprised depictions of rape, coercive sexual relations, and sadomasochism.

For all three types of videos, the predominant theme in the portrayal of sexual violence was either individual rape or group rape of a single female. Further examination of sexual violence against females (female homosexual, individual, or group rape) showed no differences across R-rated and X-rated (combined) categories. A comparison of the frequency of sexual violence across year of production revealed no statistically significant increase in this type of portrayal for either R-rated or X-rated (combined) videos. Sexually violent behavior sequences were much shorter in R-rated videos than in others, however. There were no statistically significant changes in duration for either R-rated or X-rated (combined) videos across the years.

Computation of 'recipient–initiator' ratios indicated that females were more often the recipients than the perpetrators of violence and sexual violence in both R-rated and X-rated (combined) videos. But this ratio was different for different ratings categories. Females were more often recipients of sexual violence in R-rated than in X-rated videos (4.33 vs. 2.72). Finally, there was generally a greater number of violent (combined) behaviors than prosocial behaviors in both types of videos. An exception was in R-rated materials, which had more than three times as many prosocial as sexually violent behaviors.

In another analysis of X-rated videos in the United States, Cowan et al. (1988) focused on the prevalence of debasing portrayals of women. More than half the sexually explicit scenes identified were coded as predominantly concerned with domination or exploitation. Specific indicators of domination and sexual inequality, including physical violence, occurred frequently.

Dominance and exploitation as major themes comprised 545 of the sexually explicit scenes. Men did most of the domination and exploitation. Of 124 scenes characterised as dominance, 78% were commanded by men, and 22% were female dominated. Of the latter, 37% were depictions of women dominating other women. In 68% of the exploitation scenes, a man exploited one or more women. Women appeared as exploitative in 23% of such scenes, with 38% representing women exploiting other women. Of the total of 40 autoerotic scenes, 38 depicted women and 2 depicted men. Some sexual scenes depicted incestuous relationships. These never took the form of father–daughter—but did include mother–son, sister–sister, brother–sister, aunt–nephew, and uncle–niece. Of the 14 bondage scenes, 10 showed female bondage. When a man was bound it was done playfully, whereas when a woman was in bondage, it was more often done in a violent, abusive manner.

A rape occurred in 51% of the films. All rape scenes were rapes of women. Of these scenes, 90% presented a man raping a woman. The remaining scenes depicted a woman being raped by another woman. Nearly one in four of the sex scenes (23%) contained some violence—all directed towards women. Reinforcement of the rape myth that women enjoy being forced to engage in sex occurred in 14% of the scenes, which showed women submitting to dominant, often coercive, acts and ultimately responding with acceptance and even pleasure.

Two other aspects of these investigations also tend to limit their usefulness. First, in published reports (Cowan et al., 1988; Palys, 1984; Rimmer, 1986; Yang & Linz, 1990), attention has focused primarily on quantification of the manifest behavior presented in sexually explicit productions. Consequently, although considerable detail about the occurrence of various sexual and/or violent behaviors is available, only limited information on the more basic social and relational milieux of these behaviors is provided. This omission emerges as a particularly weak aspect of previous research because it is the social 'reality' projected by pornography through the depiction of social roles and contexts—not sexual behavior per se—that is the focus of controversy.

A later analysis of the prominent themes in pornographic films attempted to deal with this issue by utilising more than one level of analysis (Brosius, Weaver, & Staab, 1993). In this study, a random sample of 50 pornographic videotapes was selected from an archive of such materials targeted for heterosexual consumers, during the 1979–1988 period. The research used a three-tier coding system.

In the first tier, information was collected about each movie, such as length and year of release. In the second tier, information was coded about the sexual scenes within each movie. A 'scene' was defined as an uninterrupted sequence of activity (a) by a fixed number of participants and (b) in a given location. If either of these characteristics changed, a new scene was recorded. The beginning of a sexual scene was defined either by actors removing their clothes or by their initiating of sexual behavior. Each sexual scene was coded for length, number and gender combinations of participating individuals, the nature of the relationships, the nature of the persuasive efforts used to initiate sexual activities, dominance and subordination in institutional relationships, the reasons for engaging in sexual activities, and the type of sexual activities depicted. In the third tier of the coding system, various characteristics of each participant in the sexual scenes were recorded. These included gender, age, somatic features, ethnic background, and clothing.

In all, 72 movies were included on the 50 videotapes sampled. Of these, 30 films were made during the 1979–1986 period, and 42 were released post-1986. More female (288) than male (227) actors participated in the sexual scenes. The movies contained a total of 436 sexual scenes (6.1 per film). Overall, 67.6% of the typical movie was devoted to sexual scenes. The average length of sexual scenes was 5.28 minutes.

Individual women were more sexually active and appeared in more scenes than their male counterparts. Female actors were almost exclusively young (under 35). Approximately two thirds of the men and women were naked. Women were more expressive than men and made two thirds of the utterances in these movies. More than half (52%) of utterances referred to the sexual activities, 30% consisted of utterances of pleasure, and 16% instructed partners' actions through requests or demands.

More than half the sexual scenes (52%) depicted heterosexual couples; about 13% featured a male with two female partners; a female alone was shown in about 12% of the scenes, and 11% involved two or more females. Almost 38% of all sexual scenes depicted intercourse between casual acquaintances or colleagues, and about 30% involved strangers.

Persuasion was not generally needed. However, between the two production periods, scenes depicting females persuading males into sexual activities increased significantly. Males persuading females remained unchanged. The most frequent institutional relationships portrayed females as subordinate to males (16%). Females subordinate to females seldom appeared (2%).

In more than three quarters (77%) of scenes, sex was engaged in purely for pleasure. Coitus was depicted at least once in 61% of all sexual scenes. Across all scenes Fellatio (54%), cunnilingus (40%), fondling of female genitalia (digital stimulation of the vulva, vagina, and or clitoris; 37%), and fondling of male genitalia (digital stimulation of the penis and/or scrotum, 22%) were also commonly portrayed behaviors. One or more of these behaviors were involved in 96% of scenes.

The findings also revealed that some thematic aspects of modern pornographic movies have shifted over time. Significant increases were evident in the frequency of portrayals of sex between casual acquaintances, males engaging in sex with female subordinates, female characters persuading males into sexual activities, and the performance of fellatio as the initial sexual behavior among heterosexual partners. Over time, a significant decrease in the number of depictions involving sex between colleagues in a workplace or a prostitute–client relationship was also apparent. Taken together, however, the data showed that contemporary pornographic movies continue to spotlight the sexual desires and prowess of men while consistently and persistently portraying women as sexually willing and available.

In the pornographic reality, women were shown as more sexually active with a greater variety of partners than were men. A strong age bias (young) was noted for women but not for men. Women were far more expressive than men during sex scenes. The pornographic reality frequently depicted sexual behavior as occurring outside the bounds of the cultural norms of most Western societies. More than half the sexual scenes portrayed intercourse between total strangers or casual acquaintances. Sex between married partners was infrequently presented.

There was a significant decline in portrayals of sex between colleagues at work. Women initiated sex more often across the two time periods. Depictions of women as superordinate to men in institutional contexts, however, increased. This view of pornographic reality was different from the one promulgated by feminist commentators.

Slasher Movies. The subordination of women in videos that contain sexually explicit material and receive adult or restricted-adult ratings often focuses on overt depictions of coercive or violent sexual behavior in which female actors are portrayed as victims. Although women can be subordinated in more subtle ways, to what extent are women victimised by violent male attackers? Are women proportionately more likely to be victims of violence than men in these films? In slasher movies, in which a prevalent theme is the violent victimisation of women by a male attacker who apparently enjoys inflicting pain and suffering on his victims, the violence often involves close-up aggressive acts, frequently including the use of knives and other cutting or sawing instruments. Contrary to popular belief, however, recurrent evidence has emerged from systematic empirical studies of these films that female characters are no more likely to be victimised than male characters.

Cowan and O'Brien (1990) analysed 56 slasher films to reveal no difference in the overall number of male and female victims. This result called into question the belief that slasher films contained scenes of explicit violence primarily directed toward women (Linz et al., 1988). However, their finding that one third of nonsurviving females were presented in a sexual context before or at the time of their attack supports the claim that slasher films often juxtapose sex and violence.

Weaver (1991) examined the 10 slasher films with the highest box-office earnings in 1987. In terms of the death of the protagonist in slasher films, females were no more often portrayed as the victim than were males. However, the duration of death scenes was significantly longer for female characters. There were only six scenes (out of 406) that depicted a female victimised after sexual activity. Weaver provided further evidence counter to the assumptions that had been posed regarding slasher films. First, in line with findings of Cowan and O'Brien, women were not inequitably portrayed as the victims of violence in slasher films. However, female victims were shown suffering longer than their male counterparts. Second, females rarely fell victim to the slasher subsequent to sexual actions. On the latter point—the degree to which violence was mixed with sex—the two studies were in conflict.

Molitor and Sapolsky (1993) analysed 30 slasher films released in 1980, 1985, and 1989. This study revealed that females were not featured most often as the targets of slashers; a significantly higher number of deaths and injuries were suffered by males. Females, however, were shown in terror for longer periods. Sex and violence were not commonly linked in these films. A death or severe attack of a female during or after depictions of sex occurred infrequently. There were 92 instances recorded of sexual display or behavior preceding or at the time of violence, regardless of the gender of the victim or the outcome of the violent act. Less than one in four of these instances featured full nudity or implied intercourse.

When female victims were considered, there were 38 instances of death and two instances of major injury juxtaposed with the portrayal of sex. Around one in seven (13.6%) of all sexual incidents in these films were linked to the death of a female and fewer than one in 100 (0.7%) were linked to a female's serious physical harm. Just over one in five (21.6%) of all innocent female actors were kicked by a slasher during or following a sexual display or act. In answering the central question of the study about the link between sex and violence, one in three of the sexual images found in slasher films were connected to at least one act of violence. When focusing on female victims, however, the sex–violence linkage was substantially smaller.

THE PERCEIVED IMPACT
OF DEGRADING PORTRAYALS

Although the following chapters examine evidence for postexposure psychological effects of sexually explicit or pornographic media content on consumers of such material, it is worth saying something at this point about immediate emotional responses of viewers of degrading portrayals of women at the time of watching them. A small amount of research has been carried out to investigate whether male and female viewers judge particular sexually explicit portrayals as degrading to women.

In one such study, Stock (1991) found that for both females and male college students, the viewing of unequal sex (themes of dominance, objectification, and penis worship) led to more negative mood states (depression, hostility, confusion) than did exposure to either female availability without inequality, violent pornography or sexually explicit erotica depicting mutuality. Among the women specifically, compared to erotica, exposure to both nonviolent but degrading (unequal) pornography and violent pornography increased negative moods. Stock's research supports the conclusion that female subordination, more than female sexual availability, is seen as degrading to women.

A series of studies conducted by Cowan et al. (1989) among different groups of women indicated that the explicit sexual portrayals found in pornography are generally regarded with some disdain by female viewers. In an initial investigation, in-depth interviews were carried out with 44 women—who comprised 29 self-designated feminists and 15 fundamentalist women (including Baptists, Jehovah's Witnesses, Mormons, and Pentecostals)—explored their opinions about pornography. Feminists were also divided into those who favored tighter regulation and censorship and those who did not. All three groups felt extremely negatively about pornography. Themes that involved battery, rape, and incest were the most strongly criticised, but even nonviolent sexual themes were perceived by many of these interviewees as degrading, demeaning, and dehumanising women.

There were differences between fundamentalists and feminist thinking. Fundamentalists' answers were influenced by their strong religious beliefs and conservative ideology. They believed that pornography contributed to violence against women and that it presented a distorted image of female sexuality. Explicit media sex was perceived to be immoral and wrong. Pro-censorship feminists also believed that pornography harmed women. They wanted to see much tighter regulation of pornography in consequence, and they regarded such control as outweighing the principles of freedom of speech. Feminists who believed that tighter regulation or more censorship would lead to greater repression of women, also regarded pornography as degrading women and therefore as a source of potential harm. Although they were concerned about the welfare of women, they perceived that there were more significant issues of freedom of speech at stake should censorship be tightened here, that would not benefit women (or men) in the longer term.

A second study surveyed a sample of recipients of the National Organisation of Women newsletter about their opinions concerning pornography. This survey was primarily concerned with attitudes about regulation and censorship of pornography that are dealt with in chapter 12. However, one question relevant to the subject matter of the current chapter asked respondents to indicate whether they would regard any of six classes of content as 'pornographic.' These six categories, together with the percentages of respondents who found them pornographic, were: (a) partial female nudity (8% rated this as pornographic); (b) full female nudity (13%); (c) male nudity (13%); (d) nonviolent, noncoercive, nondegrading, explicit sexual activity (33%); (e) highly degrading or dehumanising, explicit sexual activity (e.g., sexual activity in which one partner is depicted as unequal and/or exploited or presented as an object to be used; 96%); and (f) violent, sexually explicit activity such as rape, use of force, or threat of force (95%). Thus, for most of these women, nudity or mutually consenting sexual depictions (even though explicit) were not seen as 'pornographic.' Degrading and violent sex acts, in contrast, were labelled as pornographic by an overwhelming majority of the women surveyed here (Cowan, 1992).

In a third study, Cowan and Dunn (1994) assessed ratings of nine themes in commercial pornography to test feminist theory about what is degrading to women in pornography. On this occasion, the respondents were 94 female and 89 male college students, who rated nine brief excerpts of sexually explicit material. Seven of the nine themes depicted two types of inequalities—active subordination and status inequality; one theme depicted female indiscriminate availability; and one theme depicted equal sex.

Category definitions used in this study were as follows:

- *Sexually explicit behavior:* Sexual activity that is explicit and mutual without indicating an affectionate personal relationship between the two people ('Equal' was not used with participants.)
- *Availability:* Sexual activity showing that the woman is available to anyone who wants her. She is nondiscriminating.
- *Unreciprocated sex:* Sexual activity that is one-sided. The woman is used to satisfy the man's needs. Her gratification is not important.
- *Status reduction:* Sexual activity that incorporates the idea that a high-status woman can be reduced to a purely sexual being.
- *Status inequality:* Sexual activity and the accompanying scenario that indicates inequality. The woman appears to have less power than the man; she may be younger, less educated, less intelligent, etc.

- *Submission:* Sexual activity that begins with the woman's unwillingness to participate and ends with her loving it. In this category, *no* ultimately means *yes*.
- *Penis/semen worship:* Sexual activity that revolves around worship of the penis. The ejaculate (semen) is especially central to the woman's satisfaction.
- *Dominance:* Sexual activity and the related scenario that explicitly shows that the man is dominant. He may command her to do what he wishes or insult her without any regard for her desires.
- *Objectification:* Sexual activity that treats the woman as an object or a plaything.

The study was run in two parts. First, participants were exposed to nine clips, each representing one of the nine themes. These respondents were given a label and definition of each theme, which may have affected the results. Another group was run later using the same videos, but without definitions. Each clip was rated along 13 adjectives on 14-point scales ranging from 'not at all' to 'extremely' sexually arousing, stimulating, boring, educational, realistic, obscene, offensive, aggressive, degrading to women, disgusting, dehumanising, affectionate, and exciting.

Consistent with feminist theory, both men and women who viewed the excerpts rated active subordination more degrading than status inequalities and both types of inequalities more degrading than sexually explicit material with one qualification. Participants found dominance, objectification, and penis worship the three most degrading themes, more so than the themes of status inequalities and availability. These themes most clearly depict active subordination and most blatantly disrespect women.

In dominance and objectification, not only were women subordinate in status, but they were also reduced to objects and sexual subordinates. Although dominance and objectification are the themes that feminist critiques of pornography have identified as most degrading to women (e.g., Dworkin & MacKinnon, 1988), penis worship, the most unifying and ubiquitous theme in pornography (Cowan et al., 1988), explicitly reminded viewers that pornography is male centered.

Themes of status reduction and inequality, the less active and more subtle forms of subordination, were rated less degrading than dominance, objectification, and penis worship, but more degrading than female availability and equal sex. These status inequality themes, along with submission, were rated moderately degrading, with scores around the scale midpoint. Submission, availability and nonreciprocation were rated less as degrading than other themes.

Submission, or the rape myth that 'no' means 'yes,' was not rated as degrading when presented without its definition. When presented with its definition, it was rated as more degrading. It was also a very arousing theme, among both men and women. In the video examples used, however, there was greater focus on the woman's face in the submission clips. Her clearly displayed pleasure was found highly sexually arousing.

Nonreciprocated sex was not viewed as degrading as were other inequalities. Apparently, the belief that one person is being satisfied by the other does not lead to the assumption of inequality.

Differences were found between men and women in comparisons of theme ratings. Both rated objectification and dominance as the most degrading; however, women rated penis worship as degrading as both of these other two themes. Also, women rated equal sex as significantly less degrading than the other eight themes. Women rated all inequalities and availability more degrading than equal sex, whereas men rated active subordination themes and status inequalities more degrading than nonreciprocated sex and female availability.

DOES PORNOGRAPHY AFFECT WOMEN'S SELF-REGARD?

Although women may evaluate certain types of media sex as degrading their own gender, does exposure to such material actually change that way women feel about themselves? Some feminist writers have contended that women learn to become victims. Passivity is the primary conditioned response in sexual relations (Brownmiller, 1975; Gross, 1978). Men may indeed learn to believe that women will respond positively to force in sexual relations, even if they initially refuse sexual advances. Meanwhile, women may learn to expect a certain degree of physical force in sexual relationships as normal. Media scenarios in which men and women respond in stereotyped ways in sexual situations may condition such sexual schema among both genders.

There is a further complicating factor that has to be considered in this context. We saw earlier in this chapter that reactions to sexual content can vary between individuals. Some individuals, whether male or female, are more sensitive to explicit sexual depictions than are others. Research has shown that this is true of the way women respond to pornographic materials. The evidence for this has derived more from studies of print media than film or video media. Here, the effects of reading pornography on women have been found to vary with the sex-role perceptions and self-confidence of the reader. In one study, women high and low in self-role stereotyping read one of three sexually explicit stories portraying different combinations of women's consent or nonconsent and arousal or nonarousal to forceful sexual activity (Mayerson & Taylor, 1987). Compared to not reading a story, reading any of these stories generally led to changes in self-esteem and greater acceptance of rape myths and interpersonal violence. Women readers who had exhibited high sex-role stereotyping in their beliefs about the sexes had lower self-esteem than women who exhibited low sex-role stereotyping. Exposure to reading a story in which a women was depicted as sexually abused resulted in lower self-esteem among low sex-role stereotyped women but higher self-esteem among women who were initially high in sex-role stereotyping. The authors speculated that exposure to a woman receiving abusive treatment could have led female readers of low self-esteem to put their own problems in perspective. Meanwhile, for women high in self-esteem, such exposure may have drawn their attention to the subordination of women by men in sexual relations producing reduced confidence in their own autonomy and power through identification with the victim in the story.

Other research has revealed that both men and women with high sex-role stereotyped beliefs exhibit greater arousal to rape depictions in the media as compared with individuals with weak-self-role stereotyped beliefs (Check & Malamuth, 1983). More generally, women and men who hold more traditional, stereotyped sex-role beliefs are more likely to have misconceptions about rape (Costlin, Kibler, & Crank, 1982; Dietz, Blackwell, Daley, & Bentley, 1982; Klemmack & Klemmack, 1976).

CONCLUSION

Women have long been known to suffer underrepresentation in mainstream entertainment media such as motion pictures and television dramas. In broadcast advertising, likewise, men have traditionally dominated the authoritative roles, although this pattern began to change in the past decade. The sexuality of women has been emphasised in drama and advertising much more so than that of men. This partly stems from the customary stereotyping of the sexes that has depicted women as preoccupied with personal and romantic relations and men as more concerned with professional and occupational success. However, a view has also prevailed that emphasis on the sexual side of women is used to objectify them. This sexual objectification has been regarded by some feminist critics as a degradation of the female sex.

Even in media that depict explicit sexual content, and where women may enjoy greater physical presence (at least equal to that of men), portrayals of women's sexuality continues to subordinate them to men. Although this latter observation may indeed be true of some sexually explicit pornography, it is not universally true. There are plentiful pornographic films and videos in which women are as sexually predatory, dominant, and pleasure seeking as men.

The representation of women in pornography in which sex is combined with violence, however, has given rise to special concern. Here, it is not untypical for women to be shown as almost willing victims of rape. Furthermore, evidence has been obtained that themes of male dominance and female exploitation do occur in many X-rated videos. Although this type of media sex has restricted distribution, there is little doubt that it is viewed at least occasionally by significant numbers of men. There are many men, along with most women, who find such content offensive. Although much media sex is accepted by a majority, it is rejected by a minority. As media sex becomes more explicit, its constituency declines. However, although a majority of the public is likely to reject themes of female degradation, explicit media sex with violent themes continues to attract a profitable market. Not only are pornographic portrayals of sexually available women, dominated by sexually demanding men, perceived as degrading to women, evidence has emerged that women who watch this content may lower their self-esteem, especially if it is low already. The important question is whether such material has even wider, adverse side effects on those who like to consume it. This is the question to which we turn in the next few chapters.

6

Does Media Sex Give Men the Wrong Ideas?

The previous chapter presented evidence that depictions of sexual behavior in films, videos, and television programs can be degrading to women. Scenes in which women are violently sexually assaulted give rise to considerable concern, generating immediate anxiety reactions among female members of the audience and possibly creating a longer term climate of fear. Even nonviolent portrayals or a purely sexual nature may give out the wrong messages about female sexuality by depicting women as having sexually voracious appetites and being nondiscriminating in terms of who they have sex with.

The ultimate concern about media portrayals of sexual behavior rests with the possible impact they might have on the sexual behavior of viewers (and, in the case of some portrayals, the aggressive behavior of viewers). An initial consideration, however, is whether such portrayals implant certain ideas in the minds of viewers about what could be deemed appropriate sexual conduct, what are healthy ways of expressing one's own sexual urges, and about the sexuality of women. Before turning to evidence that deals with the behavioral effects of sexual material in films, videos, and television programs, we should examine the potential influences of such material at a cognitive level. Do sexual portrayals in the audiovisual media give men the wrong ideas about female sexuality and sexual relations?

Sexual stereotypes abound in the audiovisual media. They can readily be found in mainstream television and movie entertainment, although often in mild forms. More acute examples of the sexual objectification of women occur in pornographic films and videos. Among the most problematic of media stereotypes are those concerning sexual violence, particularly certain images found in adult videos and slasher films.

Research has shown that exposure to media depictions of rape in which the woman appears to be responsible for her own victimisation or appears to enjoy the assault can result in several changes in men's cognitive appraisal of sexual violence (Donnerstein, Linz, & Penrod, 1987). For example, exposure to a sexually explicit rape scene in which the victim shows 'positive' reactions produces a lessened sensitivity to rape (e.g., Malamuth & Check, 1983), an increased acceptance of rape myths and interpersonal violence against women (e.g., Malamuth & Check, 1981a), and an increase in sexual arousal to rape (e.g., Malamuth, 1981). Furthermore, sexual arousal to rape stimuli, a desire to hurt women, and a belief that rape would be a sexually arousing experience for the rapist are all correlated with self-reported possibility of committing rape (Malamuth & Donnerstein, 1982).

The research evidence can be divided under a number of headings. Early indications that exposure to sexual media content might be associated with men's ideas about women's sexuality derived from correlational surveys. These surveys explored the degree of association between men's reported exposure to sexually explicit media and their thoughts and feelings about women, sex, and in particular violent sexual behavior. Of course, such surveys do not demonstrate causal relations between media exposure and ideas about sexual conduct, they merely indicate where the two may be correlated. To understand more about the possible causal connection between exposure to sexual media content and subsequent thought processes, some researchers have conducted experimental studies in which the conditions of exposure are manipulated in advance along with the nature of the material that is shown to individuals.

The research in this area can be further divided in terms of the types of cognitive processes that are measured. Interest has centered on the potential impact of sexual media content on aggressive fantasies and thoughts, especially when directed by men at women; on antifemale attitudes; and on wider opinions and beliefs about female sexuality. Much of this research has, of course, been primarily concerned with demonstrating effects of pornographic content. There is also a body of work that suggests that depictions of sexual behavior in mainstream media can cultivate distorted sets of beliefs and values concerning relationships, marriage, sexual promiscuity, procreation, and sexual performance (Zillmann, 1994).

INSTIGATION OF AGGRESSIVE FANTASIES
AND THOUGHTS

One view about the effects of violent pornography is that it may teach men how to perform antiwoman acts, relax their inhibitions about doing so, and condition them to experience sexual arousal in relation to such acts (Check & Malamuth, 1980; Malamuth & Check, 1985). A body of experimental research emerged during the 1980s to complement the survey findings. A number of studies were conducted that showed that controlled laboratory exposure to sexually violent media content could give rise to aggressive thoughts and feelings as an immediate response.

One particular body of research examined the impact of 'positive' versus 'negative' rape portrayals mostly in pornographic films. One series of studies assessed how either victim arousal or abhorrence at the end of a rape depiction changed the way in which the assault was perceived when the rape itself remained identical in the two versions. When the rape victim became aroused, male participants labelled the assault more as a sexual act. They also perceived greater justification for it, reported a greater likelihood that they and other men would commit such an act, and saw the victim as more responsible for what had occurred (Donnerstein, 1984; R. Rapaport, 1984). These effects have been particularly pronounced for more sexually active men. These experiments showed that changing the outcome of a rape affects the way it is perceived. They did not show that these perceptions carry over to perceptions of rape in general.

In another series of studies, the carry-over effects of perceptions of and attitudes towards rape were directly examined. These studies assessed whether rapes depicting victim arousal changed male viewers' perceptions of other rapes, altered their beliefs about women's reactions to sexual assaults, and increased their acceptance of violence against women.

In two experiments, male participants were shown either film depictions of mutually consenting sex between a male and female couple, rape in which the female victim eventually became aroused, or rape abhorred by the victim. Afterward, the participants were shown a rape depiction and asked about their perceptions of the act and the victim. In one of these studies, those participants exposed to the 'positive' rape portrayal in which the woman became sexually aroused perceived the second rape as less negative than those who initially saw a rape depiction in which the woman victim showed extreme distress (Malamuth & Check, 1980b). Some evidence also emerged that watching a rape victim on film displaying arousal may have led men to perceive rape as a more normal act.

In a second experiment, male participants were asked how women in general would react to being victimised by sexual violence (Malamuth &

Check, 1985a). Those shown a film depiction of a rape with a positive outcome believed that a higher percentage of women would derive pleasure from being sexually assaulted.

Explaining Aggressive Cognitive Reactions

One of the ways in which the psychological processes that generate such effects get underway is through the instigation of aggressive fantasies and thoughts about women. This hypothesis has been criticised as overly simplistic and as failing to acknowledge the influences of life-long learning experiences concerning actions that are socially permitted and those that are socially proscribed. Critics have doubted that brief and transitory exposure to violent sexual images can move men to antiwomen thoughts, attitudes and acts that are at profound variance with the remainder of their learning history (Fisher & Barak, 1989, 1991).

In a replication of earlier research experiments conducted by behavioral psychologists such as Malamuth, and using the same general procedure and similar kinds of film materials, Fisher and Grenier (1994) presented young men with scenes that depicted rape with the victim's sexual arousal, rape without sexual arousal, or nonviolent male–female sexual intercourse. Afterwards, respondents were asked to take a few moments and write down an arousing sexual fantasy of their own. They then completed a projective psychological test also designed to measure sexual fantasies. Although earlier work had indicated that brief exposure to rape scenes led more than one third of male participants to fantasise about rape (Malamuth, 1981), that result was not repeated in this later study, where not a single man displayed such fantasies.

CULTIVATION OF ANTIFEMALE ATTITUDES

A number of surveys and studies carried out in a laboratory setting have indicated that exposure to violent sex scenes may alter male attitudes towards women and more especially towards rape. Evidence from survey studies has generally comprised an analysis of the degree of correlation between self-reports on the part of male respondents of exposure to different kinds of pornographic material (e.g., magazine or film; violent and nonviolent) and their responses to scales designed to measure their attitudes towards women. From this type of analysis, evidence has been reported that more frequent exposure to sexually explicit magazines is linked to beliefs that women enjoy forced sex (Malamuth & Check, 1985; Koss & Dinero, 1988). Further, greater reported exposure to sexually explicit films correlated with higher acceptance of rape myth beliefs (i.e., that all women secretly desire to be raped) and with generally callous attitudes towards sexual relations with women (Check, 1984; Briere, Corne, Rintz, & Malamuth, 1984).

These survey findings have been reinforced by experimental evidence in which male college students were shown films that depicted sex scenes with and without violence and tested for any changes in their attitudes towards women. Experimental research concerning the effects of exposure to sexually explicit material began with investigations of still photographs and literary passages. It moved on to consider the effects of sexually explicit films and videos that portrayed consensual sex scenes (Fisher & Byrne, 1978a, 1978b; Schmidt & Sigusch, 1970) and coercive sex scenes (Check & Guloien, 1989; Malamuth & Ceniti, 1986). Over time, a body of empirical evidence accumulated that indicated that men who are exposed to sexually explicit materials in which women are portrayed as sexual objects who are receptive to any male (or female) sexual advances or in which violence against women in a sexual context is endorsed, develop negative attitudes toward women (Check & Guloien, 1989; Malamuth & Check, 1981a; Zillmann, 1989; Zillmann & Bryant, 1989).

In a typical study, the participants would be tested for their attitudes to a variety of topics (including attitudes to women) in an initial phase of the research. Several days later they would be invited to take part in an apparently unrelated exercise. This involved listening to audiotape recordings of a man and a woman engaging in sexual intercourse. In one version, the woman was a willing participant, whereas in another version she was not. In other versions, the woman displayed pain and suffering or became aroused or upset by the experience. Male listeners who exhibited more callous attitudes to women at the outset were more likely to enjoy scenes in which the woman was forced to have sex, especially if she eventually became sexually aroused (Malamuth & Check, 1983). Such individuals were also less likely to perceive the woman as distressed or the rape as a negative and undesirable behavior (Malamuth & Check, 1980a).

Malamuth (1984) reported three experiments in which participants were presented first with either pornographic rape scenes in which the aggressor perceived that the assault resulted in the female victim's sexual arousal (i.e., a 'positive' outcome) or with other depictions (e.g., a rape with victim abhorrence or a mutually consenting sex scene). Afterwards, all of these participants were given a different depiction of rape and asked to indicate their perceptions of the experiences of the victim. In two of these experiments, those exposed to the positive outcome version of the aggressive scenes in comparison to other subjects thought the rape victim in the second portrayal had suffered less (Malamuth & Check, 1980a; Malamuth, Haber, & Feshbach, 1980).

The third experiment revealed effects on general perceptions about women. In this experiment, male undergraduates were first classified as low versus high in terms of likelihood of raping (LR) on the basis of their responses to a questionnaire administered in a preliminary session (Malamuth & Check, 1981b). A laboratory session was held at a later date. In this session, participants were randomly assigned to listen to audiotapes that were systematically manipulated in their content along the dimensions of consent (women's consent vs. nonconsent) and outcome (women's arousal vs. disgust). Later, participants completed a questionnaire about their beliefs regarding the percentage of women, if any, that would 'enjoy' being raped. The use of such questions raises an ethical issue, inasmuch as their use may perpetuate or strengthen existing beliefs in rape myths. The deployment of a debriefing session, however, was found to be effective as counteracting such false beliefs (Malamuth, 1984).

The results indicated a main effect of LR reports, with high LR participants estimating much higher percentages of women enjoying being raped in comparison with low LR participants. Within consenting portrayals, the nature of the women's reaction had no significant impact on participants' perceptions of women's reactions to rape. However, outcome did make a difference within nonconsenting (rape) depictions. Here, high LR participants were affected by nonconsenting women's arousal. For low LR participants, manipulation of outcome within nonconsenting portrayals had no impact.

Garcia (1986) investigated the relationship between exposure to sexually explicit material and attitudes towards rape among male students age 18 to 38. They were questioned about exposure to pornographic magazines, books and films, and about exposure within these media to specific sexual themes (coercive sex, oral sex, consenting sex between a man and woman, a nude woman). They were also administered the Attitudes Toward Women Scale (Spence & Helmreich, 1972) and the Attitudes Toward Rape Scale (Feild, 1978).

No overall relationships of significance emerged between reported exposure to pornography and attitudes towards women. A distinction was then made between their level of exposure to violent and nonviolent sexual themes. This revealed a set of relationships between exposure to violent themes and traditional attitudes towards women. In addition, exposure to violent themes in pornography was also correlated with a number of attitudes to rape (e.g., stronger agreement that women are responsible for prevention of rape and that rape and that rapists are normal, and disagreement that rapists should be punished or that women should resist). In sum, this study indicated that greater reported exposure to pornography was correlated with less liberal attitudes towards women and a more cynical attitude towards rape.

In a further investigation of links between exposure to pornography and attitudes towards women, Davies (1997) examined a sample of nearly 200 men who voluntarily watched sexually explicit videos of their own choosing. The main focus of this study was on the relationship between the men's renting of porn videos and their attitudes towards feminism and rape. The purpose was to find out if the men who rented the greater number of X-rated videos displayed more negative attitudes towards feminism and if they were more likely to condone violence towards women as compared with men who rented relatively few videos of this type.

The study paid particular attention to a specific category of violent behavior aimed at women—'marital rape.' In this case, a man uses physical force or the threat of force in his sexual relations with his wife. Respondents were asked whether or not they considered such behavior a crime and, if so, what degree of punishment would they proscribe. Options varied from 'do nothing because it is a private matter' through recommendation of counselling, to short- or long-term prison sentences.

The results failed to reveal any significant connections between number of X-rated self-chosen sex videos rented and opinions about feminism or rape. Of course, with survey data of this kind, even in the event of significant correlations emerging between key variables, it would be difficult to determine whether the pattern of video rental caused the development of certain attitudes or whether pre-existing attitudes determined video preferences. On this occasion, no evidence emerged to support either hypothesis.

Effects of Heavy Dosage Exposure

In most of the correlational surveys that have explored relationships between reported exposure to explicit sexual material in the media and attitudes towards women, the principal media measure is weight of exposure to specified types of media content. Thus, heavier reported exposure to sexually explicit media content has been positively correlated with reactions more supportive of violence against women. One consistent finding, for example, was that higher readership of sexually explicit magazines was correlated with firmer beliefs that women enjoyed forced sex (Malamuth & Check, 1985; Koss & Dinero, 1988).

One study of Canadian men, for instance, found that those who turned out to be the heaviest users of sexually explicit media also exhibited the highest acceptance of rape myths and acceptance of violence against women, and displayed the most callous attitudes about sex (Check, 1984). Another study with young college men in the United States found a similar pattern of results (Briere et al., 1984).

Not all the research evidence has been consistent, however. Another American survey did not find any significant degree of association between attitudes supporting violence against women and the extent to which they reported consuming violent or nonviolent pornography. Nevertheless, evidence did emerge of a link between watching films depicting women being violently sexually attacked and reports among male viewers that there was a likelihood they would commit sexual aggression themselves if they could be assured that they would not be punished for such acts (Demare et al., 1988).

Another study that produced nonsupporting results used a combination of survey and experimental approaches (Padgett, Brislin-Slutz, & Neal, 1989). An initial survey administered questionnaires to a sample of nearly 120 college students, around two thirds of whom were female. Self-reported exposure to pornography did not predict attitudes to women for male or female respondents. A follow-up survey was carried out among a small sample of patrons (all except one were male) at an 'adult' movie theatre. These individuals reported significantly greater exposure to pornography than the college students. Once again, the quantity of pornography exposure did not predict attitudes towards women. Finally, an experiment was conducted among male and female college students who were randomly assigned to watch either an hour of erotic film material or of nonerotic film material every day for 5 days. No evidence emerged that exposure to erotica resulted in less favorable attitudes towards women. The erotica in this study, however, comprised soft pornography only, and it is unclear how seriously degrading to women such material may have been.

It would appear that the degree to which claimed viewing of pornographic films is linked to attitudes towards women is mediated by the level of dependence men show on sexually explicit media content as a source of information about female sexuality. Although a general association between reported exposure to explicit material and attitudes concerning sexual violence may not necessarily emerge, there is firmer evidence that for those men who depend on pornography, heavier use of sexually explicit materials is connected to holding attitudes more supportive of violence against women (Malamuth, 1988b). Furthermore, people raised with little education about sexuality, or in families where sex is treated as taboo, may be more susceptible to the influences of explicit media than those reared with more education about such things (Malamuth & Billings, 1985).

EXPERIMENTAL RESEARCH

In survey studies, researchers are dependent on respondents to provide accurate information about their exposure to explicit sexual content in the media. Experimental studies can actually manipulate this factor and make more precise comparisons between the effects on male attitudes of carefully controlled amounts of exposure to film material that depicts sexual or violently sexual behaviors. This approach has yielded the worrying finding that repeated viewing of explicitly sexual or sexually violent films could produce more lasting attitude changes among male viewers.

A program of research conducted by Donnerstein, Linz, and their colleagues during the 1980s systematically investigated the impact of violent erotica on male viewers' attitudes towards women and more specifically towards rape (Linz, 1985; Linz, Donnerstein, & Adams, 1989; Linz, Donnerstein, & Penrod, 1984, 1988). The initial study caused controversy over aspects of its methodology and discrepancies in the details included in different published accounts (Christenson, 1987; Weaver, 1987; Zillmann & Bryant, 1987). This led to subsequent close scrutiny of the series of studies as a whole and the emergence of replication studies that raised further questions about the findings of this work (Weaver, 1987, 1991).

In a typical study, young male participants were exposed to a relatively large 'dose' (approximately 2 hours per day for 5 days) of feature-length sexually violent films. During the week of film exposure, those young men who were shown violent sexual films exhibited signs of desensitisation to them. They gradually came to perceive these films as less violent, less offensive, and less degrading to women across the 5-day viewing period. These effects carried over for another week to a setting in which the male 'guinea pigs' viewed a videotape of a simulated rape trial and were assessed for their attitudes towards the rape offence, the victim, and the accused in this case. Young men who had been fed a week-long diet of sexually violent films exhibited significantly more lenient attitudes towards the accused and less sympathy for the victim as compared with counterparts who had seen a diet of nonviolent, sexual films or nonviolent, nonsexual films. In addition, these same individuals rated the victim in this videotaped simulation as less injured than did a control of males who had not been shown such films (Linz, 1985; Linz, Donnerstein, & Penrod, 1984).

Linz (1985) studied the effects of repeated exposure to X- and R-rated feature-length films portraying sexual violence with primarily negative consequences to victims. He found that these movies had desensitizing effects on viewers. In one experiment, male college students who viewed five such movies had fewer negative emotional reactions to such films over successive viewing sessions. There was even a tendency for the participants' 'desensitization' to carry over to their judgments of a rape victim in a simulated trial presented following their exposure to the films. In a second experiment, Linz again found that males exposed to several R-rated, sexually violent films became less sympathetic to a rape victim in a simulated trial and were less able to empathise with rape victims in general.

Linz, Donnerstein, and Penrod (1988) conducted a further investigation of the emotional desensitization of films of violence against women and the effects of sexually degrading explicit and nonexplicit films on beliefs about rape and the sexual objectification of women. Male participants viewed either two or five R-rated violent 'slasher,' X-rated nonviolent 'pornographic,' or R-rated nonviolent teenage-oriented ('teen sex') films. Emotional reactions and cognitive perceptions were measured after each exposure. Later these men and no-exposure control participants completed a voir dire questionnaire (as mock jurors), viewed a re-enacted acquaintance or nonacquaintance sexual assault trial, and judged the defendant and alleged rape victim.

Participants in the violent condition became less anxious and depressed and were also less sympathetic to the victim and less empathetic towards rape victims in general. However, longer film exposure was necessary to affect general empathy. There were no differences in response between the R-rated teen sex film and the X-rated sexually explicit nonviolent film, and the no-exposure control conditions on the objectification or rape trial variables.

In a later study (Linz, Donnerstein, & Adams, 1989) the original procedure was shortened and no control group was used. Following the usual extensive pre-testing, a sample of male respondents was selected and randomly allocated to one of two experimental conditions. In one condition, participants were shown a 90-minute montage of extracts from various films, some of which depicted sexual violence with nude women being brutally tortured or murdered. In the second condition, a montage was shown comprising clips from films depicting nonviolent sexual and nonsexual scenes. Immediately after viewing, participants were questioned about their mood and evaluations of the film montage they had watched. Next, participants were shown two film clips that showed men verbally and physically abusing women. They were then asked about their perceptions of the perpetrator and victim in each instance. As found before, men who had been pre-classified as holding stronger rape-myth beliefs were less sympathetic towards the victim and perceived the perpetrator's actions as more acceptable and responsible. However, it was men who had seen nonviolent, sexual clips beforehand who attributed more responsibility for the attacks to female victims and less responsibility to male perpetrators. Men who had seen the sexual violence perceived victims as less injured by their experiences.

During the period in which the Donnerstein–Linz studies were being carried out, further studies were carried out by other researchers using similar methodologies. As noted earlier, a debate ensued among these rival groups about the veracity of their findings. One of the key areas of this debate centered on the question of whether shifts in rape myth beliefs, attitudes towards women, and behavioral intentions or responses towards women were influenced specifically by the sexual content of erotica or whether violence was a necessary ingredient as well.

Other research by Zillmann and Bryant (1982, 1984) suggested that long-term exposure (4 hours and 48 minutes over a 6-week period) to non-violent but degrading pornography that depicts women in sexually submissive roles may cause male and female viewers to (a) become more tolerant of bizarre forms of pornography, (b) become less supportive of statements about sexual equality, and (c) become more lenient in assigning punishment to a rapist whose crime is described in a newspaper account.

During the same period, another researcher conducted a study with female participants who, after pretesting, were randomly assigned to watch standard sex scenes, sex scenes involving violence, and violent scenes that had sexual overtones. Other participants who served as controls watched nothing (Krafka, 1985). After 5 film-exposure days, during each of which immediate postviewing evaluations of films were obtained, participants provided further self-ratings and then watched a videotaped enactment of a rape trial. Although the researcher had originally queried the significance of the data on rape myth acceptance, reanalysis of the original results by Weaver (1991) indicated that exposure to violence with sexual overtones produced rape myth acceptance levels significantly above those of control participants. Exposure to violent sexually explicit materials produced no such effect. Interestingly, women who had watched a diet of violence with sexual elements associated with it also felt more confident about themselves and their abilities to fend off unwanted sexual advances, including violent sexual assaults.

This body of research raised certain concerns in that it appeared to show that violent depictions may influence male viewers' attitudes, perceptions and, under certain circumstances, behavior towards women. It falls short of predicting to what extent an individual's viewing of violent pornography might translate into a propensity to rape or commit other forms of sexual violence. In this regard, Malamuth and Briere (1986) hypothesised an 'indirect' model of pornography effects. Specifically, sexually violent media and other social stimuli, in combination with person-specific variables (e.g., childhood experiences), are thought to produce rape-supportive cognitions and perceptions that, in the context of other phenomena (e.g., peer support), may generate sexually aggressive behaviors or proclivities. From this perspective, exposure to certain types of media stimuli may be viewed as a contributory, but perhaps not sufficient, condition in the development of sexual aggression.

Weaver (1991) challenged the work of Linz and Donnerstein on methodological grounds. The failure of some studies to apply adequate control groups or any control group at all represented one problem. Compounded with this was a possibility that demand characteristics—arising from repeated administration of film-evaluation measures that asked questions about sexual abuse and the degradation of women—may have served as prompts to participants who were able to second-guess what the experiment was about. A further problem was that some of the independent variables—that is, allocation of participants to watch different types of film—produced fairly weak effects on attitudes towards women and rape. One possible reason for this may reside in the nature of the video rape trial used by Linz and Donnerstein. The way the evidence was presented in this simulation could have created ambiguity about the accused and victim. Some details about events that led up to the alleged assault were unclear about extenuating circumstances, such as how intoxicated the accused and victim had been when they met, whether the female victim was in any case sexually promiscuous or even a prostitute. The punitive recommendations of observers of this case may have been tempered by such factors and may have been much less equivocal if the trial had recounted an offence in which the woman was clearly an innocent victim who was violently assaulted for no good reason.

Weaver (1991) reported a replication study in which some of these ambiguities were tackled head-on. Different experimental conditions were created for not only the type of film (sexual violence, neutral) but also the presence or absence of cues concerning the degree of suffering and degradation experienced by the victim. During the postviewing evaluation tests, some participants were asked to say how degrading to women they felt the scene had been, while others were asked simply to rate the film sequence for production quality.

Afterwards, participants were invited to read summaries of three legal proceedings in which men were said to have been convicted of physical or sexual assault against women, in an apparently unrelated research exercise. Two cases concerned instances of domestic violence in which the perpetrators were unambiguously inexcusable, whereas in the third case, there were mitigating circumstances that could have excused the perpetrator's actions to some degree. Male and female participants were used in this study, and both gave evaluations of the male accused and female victim in these three cases.

Weaver found that the nature of the evaluations of films, as well as the films themselves, seemed to contribute to subsequent attitudes towards rape victims and their accused. Film evaluation measures that invited respondents to think about the degrading nature of film scenes for women produced increased disparagement of rape victims and greater understanding of the actions of the male accused in rape cases. There was an interaction effect with gender here. Female participants who had had their attention drawn through film evaluations to the degrading nature of sexually violent film clips for women, were less punitive towards the accused rapist in the more ambiguous cases where he allegedly assaulted a female cohabitant. Male participants showed the opposite tendency, although differences between experimental groups were no significant. Women in conditions where female degradation was emphasised in ratings of film violence with sexual overtones, however, were less sympathetic and more punitive towards the perpetrator in the unambiguous case of rape. Punitive judgments were unaffected by exposure to film sequences of sexualised violence in cases where it was unclear whether the accused was guilty of an assault or not.

Check and Guloien (1989) found significant differences in the impact of sexually explicit depictions of rape, standard sexual, and idealised sexual themes (sex depicted in a romantic context). Male participants, drawn from student and nonstudent populations, viewed and evaluated 30-minute montage sequences of excerpts from films exemplifying the three themes. They participated in three sessions over a period lasting between 1 and 2 weeks. Five days after the last session, participants in the three film theme conditions, and a control group who had been shown no film clips, completed a questionnaire measuring their attitudes towards aggressive sexual behavior and women. Participants exposed to film clips of rape or erotic, hedonistic sexual behavior displayed the strongest likelihood of committing rape themselves. Exposure to a diet of erotica in which women were depicted as sexually available and promiscuous enhanced self-reported likelihood among these young men that they would engage in forcible sex acts as compared with the control group. This effect was especially pronounced among men who in pretesting had been shown to score high on a measure of psychoticism.

DO EFFECTS VARY WITH TYPES OF PORTRAYAL?

Much of the research into the effects of sexual portrayals in film, television, and video has used fairly crude typologies of the portrayals themselves (Malamuth, Check, & Briere, 1986). In fact, it is probably not unfair to say that much of the effects research, that stems primarily from concerns about the impact of violent sexual portrayals, has largely failed to distinguish different kinds of depictions, other than to say that some have violence and others do not. Even then, finer distinctions would often have been possible (and relevant) in regard to the nature and degree of violence within a sexual portrayal. After all, in some erotic scenes, the violence takes the form of (usually) a male character physically forcing himself upon a (usually) female victim in scenes depicting rape. Other types of violent sex scene, however, might depict bondage and the use of whips or chains in sadomasochistic scenarios in which participants may or may not be willing.

One study that did discriminate between types of sexually explicit material correlated male university students' exposure to violent and nonviolent pornography with their attitudes towards women and rape (Garcia, 1986). Although consumption of nonviolent pornography did not correlate with such attitudes, there was a small association between violent pornography use and both traditional attitudes regarding women and greater 'pro-rape' beliefs. This research utilised a simple correlational design and did not relate pornography use to any measure of sexually violent proclivities or behaviours.

A subsequent study followed a similar procedure in differentiating between young male college students' reported use of violent and nonviolent pornographic films (Demare, Briere, & Lips, 1988). Claimed use of pornography was then correlated with self-reported likelihood or rape and use of sexual force measures. Because sexually violent pornography can involve both themes that contain explicitly sexual content (e.g., rape and forced sexual acts) and themes that are more overtly aggressive and 'sadistic' (e.g., bondage, whipping, or torture), and given the potentially different impacts of each type of depiction, an attempt was made to differentiate between use of predominantly violent versus sexually violent pornographic materials.

The researchers hypothesised that sexually violent pornography use would be associated with self-reported likelihood of sexual violence, whereas use of nonviolent pornography would not. Among a sample of more than 200 American college students, the great majority (81%) had reportedly watched nonviolent pornographic films in the past 12 months, whereas well under half had watched either violent (41%) or sexually violent pornography (35%). Just over one in four of these men (27%) indicated that they would rape or use sexual force against a woman if they thought they could do so without being found out.

Further analysis of the survey data revealed that claimed viewing of sexually violent films and pre-existing attitudes indicating general acceptance of using violence against women were uniquely associated with the probability of use of force in sexual relations with women. Among the different types of film about which viewing was asked, only reported use of sexually violent films was significantly linked to the probability of use of force against women. One explanation of this relationship could be that such films contain sexual themes and examples of sexual conduct that emphasise the use of violence. Ultimately, though, the evidence that derived from this survey was based on statistical correlations that do not represent a demonstration of a causal connection between viewing of certain brands of pornography and propensity to sexual aggression.

Experimental research has also indicated that sexually explicit depictions of women in distress have been found to give rise to mixed reactions among young male viewers. Much of the experimental research on this topic was carried out with male college students as participants. Some researchers have used still photographic materials of sadism and bondage from pornographic magazines as stimulus materials (Heilbrun & Seif, 1988), some have used verbal descriptions of rape scenes (Malamuth &

Check, 1980a), and others have used audiotaped portrayals of rape or nonsexual aggression (Barbaree, Marshall, & Lanthier, 1979).

The observation of pain being inflicted on others can generate sexual excitement in essentially nondeviant populations under appropriate cueing conditions (see Cline, 1994). Even so, male college students have been found to display no sexual arousal to audio depictions of a woman being raped or attacked in a nonsexual way (Barbaree et al., 1979). A key factor in the context of coercive sexual depictions, however, is whether the female victim is depicted as upset and disgusted by the attack on her person or actually appears to enjoy it. If the woman is apparently sexually aroused by her attacker, young male witnesses may then display sexual excitement themselves (Malamuth & Check, 1980b).

In the study of sexual sadism, it has been argued that erotic gratification may be dependent on the emotional distress of the female victim without real physical harm. For middle-class males conditioned to abhor aggression against women, real physical harm might be expected to reduce the sexually stimulating properties of a sadistic portrayal (Heilbrun & Loftus, 1986). Nevertheless, sadistic sexual gratification remains dependent on at least an illusion of distress among female victims of coercive male sexual advances. Although evidence has shown that exposure to pornography may stimulate aggressive behavior (Sapolsky, 1984; Silbert & Pines, 1984) or encourage the development of callous attitudes about women (Malamuth, 1984), there remains a question as to whether sexual sadism plays a part in determining the erotic value of sexually explicit pictures.

Research conducted with male college students again has indicated that males may respond to distress registered by females in photographs depicting bondage and other sadistic sexual situations with increased sexual arousal (Heilbrun & Seif, 1988). Women depicted with distraught facial expressions in sexual scenes in which they were chained or tied up and seminaked had a powerful effect on some male observers. Pictures of distressed women were more likely to be found erotic than were those of women portraying pleasurable reactions.

EFFECTS OF INTERACTIVE EROTICA

The growth of computer-based erotica has created a new medium for investigation. Computer-based sexually explicit materials of varying levels of user-program interactivity are becoming extremely popular in the electronic and erotic marketplaces (Harmon, 1993). Three of the top ten computer bulletin boards on international computer networks are sexual in nature (Furniss, 1993). An interactive, explicitly sexual CD-ROM has already taken its place among the top ten interactive CD-ROMs in the history of this technology. *Penthouse* magazine and a multiplicity of others have begun efforts to market interactive erotica and have found that the production of such materials is exceedingly lucrative (Harmon, 1993).

Penetration of sexually explicit materials into cyberspace has already been pronounced enough to provoke U.S. congressional hearings aimed at legislation to control computer pornography and court challenges to such legislation (Jones, 1995; Wallace & Mangan, 1996). It has also prompted women's magazines to warn mothers to limit their children's access to such materials (Farrell, 1994), and to lead some 30% of institutions that are connected to the information highway to ban access to such material through their computer networks (Furniss, 1993; Swan, 1994).

Interactive erotica is different from traditional sexually explicit material in that interactive erotica permits the user to manipulate and modify the sexual stimulation that he or she receives. From a theoretical perspective which holds that personality characteristics determine an individual's choice of stimulation, including the individual's choice of erotic stimulation (Bogaert, 1993; Eysenck, 1978; Snyder & Ickes, 1985), the case can be made that the user of interactive erotica will create sexual stimuli that are consistent with his or her preferences. According to this view, interactive erotic stimuli manufactured by an individual reinforces his or her pre-existing inclinations, including prosocial, benign, or antisocial tendencies, and produces stronger effects than would be true of relatively passive exposure to traditional types of sexually explicit material that have not been tailor-made to fit the user's personality (Byrne & Lamberth, 1971; Mosher, 1988a).

Interactive erotica may also increase the viewer's depth of involvement in the erotic stimulus and magnify its impact (Mosher, 1980) by facilitating role enactment (the imagined playing out of a sexual script of the viewer's choice and creation) and by encouraging the development of a sexual trance (in which interactive erotic involvement becomes the viewer's reality and the constraints of objective reality fade away). There is, thus, a theoretical basis for suspecting that the effects of interactive erotic stimulation may be considerably more potent than the effects of traditional erotic fare, particularly when an antisocially inclined individual utilises interactive erotica to construct stimuli that reinforce the individual's dispositions and free the individual from perceptions of reality-based constraints on action.

Barak and Fisher (1997) examined antifemale attitudes and behaviors in men as a function of the use of interactive erotica. A sample of 100 university males were exposed to (a) neutral, noninteractive stimuli (control condition); (b) erotic, noninteractive stimuli; (c) erotic, moderately interactive stimuli; or (d) erotic, highly interactive stimuli on a personal computer. Participants' levels of erotophobia–erotophilia were also assessed.

After exposure to the conditions, participants' attitudes towards women and rape myth acceptance were the cognitive variables measured in this study. In addition, participants' keyboard activity and self-reported sexual arousal to the erotica were also recorded. Results showed that the erotic stimuli resulted in much interactive activity and in significant amounts of sexual arousal, but use of computer pornography by participants did not affect any of the attitudinal measures.

Two theoretical perspectives were considered in attempting to explain these findings. On the one hand, theory has been advanced to suggest that exposure to sexually explicit stimuli that portray women as sexual objects, as sexually receptive and nondiscriminating, or as enjoying sexual assault, strongly reinforces widely held misogynistic views and reliably encourages the development of antifemale attitudes and accompanying actions in men who are exposed to such material (Donnerstein, Linz, & Penrod, 1987; Malamuth & Donnerstein, 1982; Zillman & Bryant, 1989).

On the other hand, theory has also been advanced to suggest that sexually explicit stimuli that portray women as sexual objects, as sexually receptive and nondiscriminating, or as enjoying sexual victimisation, are so profoundly at variance with most men's lifetime learning histories and expectancies for reinforcement that such stimuli should have little or no impact on men who are not predisposed to antifemale thoughts or actions in the first place. Barak and Fisher (1997) presented findings consistent with the position that it is not easy to promote the development of antifemale attitudes or to perform antifemale behaviors.

Individual Differences in Cognitive Responses to Erotica

The effects of sexually explicit media content can vary across viewers in accordance with pre-existing personality characteristics or attitudinal profiles. McKenzie-Mohr and Zanna (1990) demonstrated that exposure to pornography can prime men to view women as sexual objects, but this effect does bot occur in all men. Men classified as *sex-typical* (as measured by the Sex Role Inventory; Bem, 1981), who have gender schemas about men and women that emphasise traditional sex roles, are more likely to be influenced by pornography than are men classified as androgynous or less likely to rely on sex-typical schemas for processing social information.

McKenzie-Mohr and Zanna first classified men whose views were considered sex-typical and then showed them pornography. Afterwards, the men were asked to participate in an interview with a female assistant of the experimenter. Men who were classified as sex-typical and who viewed pornography were judged to be more sexually motivated towards the interviewer, stood closer to the female assistant during the interview, and recalled more information about the interviewer's physical appearance and less of what she said, compared to androgynous men and compared to other sex-typical men who had not viewed pornography.

Stimulation of Attitudes Beyond the Laboratory

Beyond the laboratory, relatively little experimental research has been carried out on the effects of naturally occurring sexually violent content. Experimental studies conducted in the laboratory use conditions divorced from the usual viewing environment of the participants. What we also need to know is whether similar effects can be observed for the viewing of films containing violent sex scenes when viewing takes place under more natural conditions. In a study by Malamuth and Check (1981a), male and female undergraduates were randomly assigned to one of two film watching conditions. In one condition, participants were given free tickets to view feature-length films on two evenings in a local cinema. These films included portrayals of women as victims of aggression in sexual and nonsexual scenes. These films suggested that the aggression was justified and had positive consequences. On the same evenings, the participants in a second (control) condition were given tickets to other films that did not contain any sexual violence. The movies shown in both conditions had also been aired with some editing on network television. Participants viewed these films with moviegoers who were not part of the research. Classmates of the recruited participants who did not see the films were also studied as an 'untreated' control group. Several days after the films were viewed, a 'Sexual Attitude Survey' was administered to the entire class by an independent polling agency, not connected with the experiment as far as the participants were concerned.

Participant responses were assessed by scales developed in earlier research (Burt, 1980). These scales included Acceptance of Interpersonal Violence (AIV) against women (e.g., acceptance of sexual aggression and wife battering), Rape Myth Acceptance (RMA; e.g., the belief that women secretly desire to be raped), and Adversarial Sexual Beliefs (ASB; e.g., the notion that women are sly and manipulating when out to attract a man). Exposure to the films portraying scenes of coercive sex in which the woman eventually became aroused produced significantly increased scores on the AIV scale among male, but not among female participants. A similar pattern was observed on the RMA scale, although the effect was only marginally significant. A similar study, several years later, replicated these results (Demare, 1985). These findings suggest that films that depict rape scenes or scenes of sexual aggression can produce changes in attitude among young adult male viewers of above-average intelligence, even when the films are viewed in natural surroundings. This kind of effect is not confined to laboratory environments. Any restrictions on the nature of effects seem to be determined more by the type of portrayal. The key factor to emerge in these field studies, as well as in laboratory studies, is that male attitudes are most likely to be affected by film portrayals of sexual aggression in which the woman victim eventually becomes sexually aroused. Attitudes towards women and female sexuality are not usually affected when scenes depicting rape show the victim suffering extreme distress throughout.

This study, therefore, demonstrated that male attitudes towards women can be changed outside the laboratory following exposure to movies that depict coercive sex scenes. Another significant point to note about these findings was that the movies in question were not X-rated pornographic films. Instead they comprised two films (*Swept Away* and *The Getaway*) that were eventually shown on broadcast television as well as in movie theatres. Such movies may project more subtle messages, nevertheless false, about women's sexuality as compared with explicit pornographic films. Such messages may break through male viewers' defenses against accepting such information uncritically.

Another study conducted by Wilson, Linz, Donnerstein, and Stipp (1992) evaluated the impact of a television movie about acquaintance rape on subsequent attitudes about rape. This programme, entitled *She Said No*, was aired during peak-time by the NBC network. For the study, more than 1,000 male and female respondents were randomly allocated to view or not to view the movie that was shown via a closed circuit channel, prior to network transmission. This meant that none of the respondents could have seen the program before. Respondents were divided into three age groups: 18–34, 35–49, and 50+. Afterwards, their attitudes towards women and rape were measured.

Three categories of rape attitudes emerged: (a) Blame Woman, defined by items indicating support for the idea that a woman is to blame in rape cases; (b) Wrongful Coercion, defined by ideas that coerced sex is wrong; and (c) Societal Concern, indicating a concern for the societal problems associated with date rape (legal system biased against women, etc).

The movie increased awareness of date rape as a social problem across all those who viewed it. The movie also encouraged older women to be less likely to blame women in a date rape situation. Males viewers, however, were generally more likely to blame the woman in such situations. In fact, older males who watched this movie became even more likely to blame the woman. Viewers of the movie were more likely than nonviewers, however, to perceive date rape as an important societal problem. Personal knowledge of a rape victim made a difference to viewers' reactions to this film. Those individuals who did not personally know a rape victim were more likely to blame the woman than were those who did know a rape victim.

The results of this study were interpreted as showing that a dramatic movie on television can be a useful tool in educational efforts aimed at altering perceptions about a social issue such as date rape. More research of this kind is needed at this stage. The impact of movies like this one are tempered by pre-existing attitudes of viewers about female sexuality and about rape. It was also clear that women in this study were more involved in the movie than were men. The elaboration likelihood model would predict that such involvement would result in deeper processing of the messages contained within the movie. The events depicted in *She Said No* were presented primarily from the female victim's perspective. This may have accounted for the difference in reaction of older women and men. Older women may have been more involved and thought about the implications of the movie more deeply, whereas older men relied on more superficial processing strategies, based on stereotypes.

Perse (1994) tested two different models of the effects of sexually explicit material among college students. The first model, based on a liberal view of sexually explicit materials, argues that they have positive and potentially beneficial functions. They can be conceived as being harmless fantasy and provide viewers with a source of sexual stimulation (Linz & Malamuth, 1993). The second model is drawn from a feminist social responsibility view that holds that sexually explicit material objectifies and demeans women and leads those who use erotica to internalise those themes (Linz & Malamuth, 1993).

Perse conducted a study to test different connections between reasons for using sexually explicit material, exposure to erotica, and three types of hostile beliefs about women that reflect a cultural background that oppresses women (Burt, 1980). This syndrome of female oppression is reflected in gender-role stereotyping that emphasises traditional gender roles, sexual conservatism that rejects failure to conform with traditional sexual orientations, and finally rape myth beliefs that comprise a cluster of prejudicial and incorrect beliefs about rape, rape victims, and rapists.

Under the liberal view of the effects of sexually explicit materials, laboratory research that suggests that watching erotica produces harmful effects is dismissed as lacking external validity. Adverse reactions to erotica are accounted for in terms of individual characteristics. There is no conclusive evidence, for instance, that making sexually explicit materials more widely available causes violent sex crimes or sexually deviant behavior to increase in society (Kutchinsky, 1991).

In contrast, the feminist social responsibility model argues that sexually explicit material conveys an anti-female ideology. Erotica is seen as objectifying and dehumanising women, portraying women as servants to men's sexual desires, denying female sexuality, and promoting sexual and social subordination of and violence towards women (Brownmiller, 1975;

Lederer, 1980). Male beliefs and attitudes that justify male dominance and female submissiveness may be rape supportive and may also be associated with broader acceptance of violence across a range of situations—sexual and nonsexual (Linz & Malamuth, 1993).

Perse (1994) ran a survey with more than 500 college students of both sexes in which she investigated their reported use of erotic material (e.g., magazines or films), their motives for doing so, and their beliefs and attitudes about female sexuality and gender roles. Four principal categories of viewing motive emerged for reading or watching erotic material. These factors were labelled *Sexual Enhancement, Diversion, Sexual Release, and Substitution*. In the case of Sexual Enhancement, erotica was used to get in the right mood for sex, for information about sexual technique, and during foreplay. Diversion signalled the use of erotica for escape, relaxation, entertainment, and reduction of boredom. Sexual Release referred to the use of erotica for sexual fantasy and release. Finally, Substitution referred to the use of erotica as a replacement for a sexual partner.

Males and females differed on two of the four motives for consuming sexually explicit material. Males were more likely to report using erotica for sexual release and as a substitute for a sexual partner than were females.

Exposure to erotica was predicted by all four motivational factors, together with higher rape myth acceptance scores and gender (being male). In a multivariate analysis, gender was linked to Sexual Enhancement (being female) and to Sexual Release (being male). Hence, for the college women sampled, erotica was a source of information about sex or a means of enhancing their own sex life. For the male college students, erotica was used as a substitute for a sex life. Being male and using erotica for Sexual Release were negatively linked to rape myth acceptance, whereas use of erotica as a sexual substitute, greater overall exposure to erotica, stronger gender stereotyping, and holding more conservative sexual attitudes were positively linked to acceptance of rape myths about women. Thus, being sexually aroused by erotica does not appear to contribute to development of rape myth beliefs, but dependency on erotica as a replacement for an active sex life with a real sexual partner seems to make a difference to the kinds of messages that might be absorbed from such material. If the same erotica-dependent individual already holds gender stereotyped beliefs and is sexually conservative, this further enhances the likelihood of a pattern of beliefs about female sexuality that endorse rape.

THE EFFECTIVENESS OF INTERVENTION SESSIONS

The evidence that emerged from studies of sexually explicit media content, especially when the sex is violent in nature, has understandably given rise to concerns about the possible effects such material might have on consumers.

There are important ethical considerations to be borne in mind when undertaking research into which deception is used to disguise the true purpose of the investigation and when the experimental manipulations are intended to produce a shift in participants' attitudes in a socially undesirable direction. Taking these ethical concerns into account, researchers who work in this field have developed educational procedures designed expose the experimental manipulation to participants and draw their attention to the potentially harmful ingredients of explicit pornographic content and the side effects that can result from exposure to them.

In addition to having a potentially valuable social function, debriefing procedures were used by researchers who conducted experimental research in which deliberate attempts were made to manipulate participants' perceptions, attitudes and behavior. Such educational or counselling procedures represented a counteractive process designed to eliminate the possibility of experimentally observed audience reactions developing into permanent, antisocial dispositions (see Intons-Peterson & Roskos-Ewoldsen, 1989; Intons-Peterson, Roskos-Ewoldsen, Thomas, Shirley, & Blut, 1989; Linz, Donnerstein, Bross, & Chapin, 1986; Linz, Fuson, & Donnerstein, 1990). The research done so far has found that pre-exposure treatments can lessen the effects of exposure to explicit sexual materials on some measures, though not others. Desensitization effects, for example, have been reduced by drawing viewers' attention to certain facts about female sexuality designed to run counter to rape myth acceptance.

Several researchers have attempted to correct the negative effects of exposure to stereotypic media depictions of sex and sexual violence. Some of these educational efforts were designed as debriefings for individuals who had participated in experiments involving sexually violent media content. Malamuth and Check (1983) conducted a study in which male and female participants were exposed to sexually explicit stories depicting either rape or mutually consenting sexual intercourse. Afterward, those exposed to the rape version were given statements emphasising that the depiction of rape in the stories was fallacious and that, in reality, rape is a terrible crime. Participants were also given specific examples of rape myths and assurance that these commonly held beliefs are fictitious. Those who were exposed to the rape stories and then debriefed were less inclined to perceive women as wanting to be raped and less likely to see victims' behavior as a cause of rape than were those who read the consenting story and received no debriefing.

In a follow-up study, Check and Malamuth (1984) randomly assigned male and female college students to read either a 'stranger rape' story, an 'acquaintance rape' story, or a mutually consenting sex story. In the 'stranger rape' story, a man secretly followed a woman home, broke into her apartment and forcibly raped her. In the 'acquaintance rape' story, a sexually experienced women was drinking in a bar with a man. She then went back to the man's apartment, where they started kissing. When she refused to go any further than that, the man raped her. The mutually consenting sex story was the same as the acquaintance rape story except that after kissing the man, the women consented to have sex with him.

After reading the stories, all rape story participants and half the mutual sex story participants were administered a rape debriefing. This debriefing advised the participants that no woman enjoys being raped and that exposure to violent pornography can be sexually arousing, even though it depicts behavior that women generally abhor. The rape debriefing statement used by Check and Malamuth (1984) was worded as follows:

> Although rape is a terrible crime, rape themes are frequently found in erotic magazines. In pornographic magazines and books, writers will often present sexual violence (e.g., rape) with other highly explicit and arousing materials .... Over time, people may tend to ignore the violence of rape because there are other sexually pleasing aspects to the stories. We do not want you to feel, however, that your responses were in any way wrong or deviant, because these stories were designed to be highly sexually arousing and do *not* in any way reflect the true horror of real rape. (pp. 21–22)

After the debriefing, the participants were given a number of newspaper articles to read, including one that reported a rape case. The results showed, once again, that the rape debriefing generally increased participants' perceptions of pornography as a cause of rape. Those participants who had been debriefed also gave a more severe prison sentence to the rapist in the newspaper story.

Other small-scale educational efforts have attempted to sensitise participants to the issue of acquaintance rape *prior* to exposure to stereotypic images. Intons-Peterson and Roskow-Ewoldsen (1989; Intons-Peterson, Roskos-Ewoldsen, Thomas, Shirley, & Blut, 1989) administered to college-age men a prefilm briefing dealing with rape and sexual violence towards women. The briefing contained current information about rape drawn from the Uniform Crime Statistics described common effects on victims, and debunked some general myths about rape by citing relevant statistics. The participants, along with a control group who had not seen the briefing, then viewed either a segment from an R-rated slasher film, a segment from an X-rated film that depicted sexual intercourse between two consenting adults, or a segment from a G-rated film. Following the film, participants viewed a videotaped reenactment of a rape trial (Linz, Donnerstein, & Penrod, 1988) and answered additional questions concerning their empathy for the accused rapist and the alleged victim. The prefilm briefing group showed a statistically significant decrease in rape myth acceptance following exposure to the slasher film segments compared to the nonbriefed control group. Further, the briefed persons were more likely to think that the accused rapist in the video-tape trial had caused injury to the victim than were those in the nonbriefed group. Interestingly, the briefing group's increased rejection of rape myths carried over to a session 2 weeks later.

Linz, Arluk, and Donnerstein (1990) compared three types of pre-exposure briefings designed to mitigate the effects of portrayals of violence against women. Male college students were shown two rape education films and a documentary on the psychological impact of slasher films and then were assigned to one of three conditions involving writing essays about the myths of sexual violence or about a neutral topic. Two additional control groups that did not watch the educational films were also included. Later, the men watched clips from sexually violent slasher films and saw a video-taped reenactment of an acquaintance rape trial. Rape myth acceptance was marginally lower for those men in all three intervention conditions. These men also showed significantly higher levels of depression in response to the slasher films, and assigned less responsibility to the defendant than did participants in the control conditions.

The interventions just described are only practical with relatively small groups of people in a controlled setting. In contrast, there have been a few large-scale educational efforts that were targeted towards mass audi-ences. These efforts involved documentaries on rape (e.g., *Cry Rape, Why Men Rape, A Scream of Silence*) and on pornography (e.g., *Not a Love Story*) that were created expressly to increase awareness of such issues among the general public.

A preliminary investigation of the impact of one of these documentaries, *Not a Love Story*, suggests that viewers may benefit from exposure to this type of content (Bart, Freeman, & Kimball, 1984). Bart and colleagues sur-veyed a group of 332 males and 318 females after they had viewed this docu-mentary in an art film house in the Chicago area. The findings indicated that exposure to the film resulted in changes in beliefs and attitudes about pornography (e.g., 'I didn't know pornography was that violent' and 'The film made me angrier about pornography'). Unfortunately, because the film audience was a naturally occurring group, only self-reported attitude change was measured (i.e., respondents were asked if their attitudes about pornography had changed after viewing the film). No attempt was made to assess prefilm viewing attitudes or to compare the viewers' attitudes with a matched control group.

Problems With Intervention Studies

There are various reasons why programs or films aimed at changing atti-tudes towards rape may run into difficulty. It is important in the first place that such programs are viewed by large numbers of people. This means they need to be scheduled favorably. The belief that females deserve or secretly desire sexual assault may be especially difficult to modify. These beliefs can provide males with a socially sanctioned justification for forced sexual access to unwilling females. A survey of a random sample of adults in Minnesota reported fairly high levels of agreement with such statements as 'A woman who goes into the home or apartment of a man on a first date implies she is willing to have sex' and other beliefs measured by the Rape Myth Acceptance Scale (Burt, 1980).

Another study, although preliminary and based on a nonrandom sample, found that college females sometimes engage in token resistance—saying no but meaning yes—in response to sexual double standards in society (Muehlenhard & Hollabaugh, 1988). Moreover, there are strong individual differences in beliefs about male–female power relations, sex-role stereotyping, and hostility towards women (Malamuth, 1986). Thus there are many societal and personal factors, including sex-role socialisation, miscommunication between the sexes, and individual differences that can foster rape myths (Koss & Leonard, 1984; Malamuth, Haber, & Feshbach, 1980). Programs designed to modify attitudes about rape may make only a small dent in belief structures that are reinforced by these other factors.

Ethical issues have been raised about studies of the effects of exposure to violent pornography. Because such studies attempt to change participants' attitudes, beliefs, or behavioral dispositions in potentially negative ways, it is an ethical requirement that researchers conducting such investigations implement procedures designed to reduce to a minimum the possibility that participants leave the study permanently changed in this way (Gross, 1983; Sherif, 1980). These same concerns have also been linked to attempts to counteract the experimental effects reported in some of these investigations. Debriefing sessions work only if all experimental participants attend such treatments. Some critics have asked for more detailed accounts that such sessions were fully attended. Another serious point about intervention treatments is that they are determined by the researchers' interpretations of the psychological effects they have measured among experimental participants. It is important that all the factors that may play a part in mediating participants' reactions to erotica, or subsequent attitudinal shifts contingent on such exposure, are taken into account and effectively counteracted by intervention sessions (Sherif, 1980).

A comprehensive meta-analysis of the results of published intervention studies during the 1980s attempted to assess the treatment effects of debriefings used in studies of the effects of violent pornography (Allen, D'Alessio, Emmers, & Gebhardt, 1996). The typical educational debriefings used in the studies under review comprised a short audiotape or written hand-out pointing out that the material consumed in the experiment was fictional. The participants were reminded that women do not enjoy forced sexual relations, that rape is a crime that violates and dehumanizes the person, and that sexually explicit material depicts an unreal fantasy about sexual relations.

Allen et al. (1996) examined 10 studies and sought to isolate the conditions under which educational efforts were effective. For all conditions, the impact of educational briefings was to negate, to some degree, the impact of exposure to sexually explicit material. The average effect of educational materials was higher for males than for females. The debriefs were also found to be more effective in experiments with control groups than in studies using within-subjects designs. Some studies used prebriefings and others used debriefings. Whether the educational intervention occurred in the early or late stages of a study, a countering effect occurred. The effectiveness of prebriefing suggests the potential value of innoculation effects. The impact of educational materials was correlated with the size of the impact of the erotic material. The greater the impact of the pornographic stimulus materials, the greater also was the effect of the educational intervention. According to Allen et al. (1996):

> The underlying logic of the educational material illustrates to the consumer that the media images are false, created representations of reality. All too often the consumer seems to forget that a media experience assumes a suspension of critical disbelief to permit a person to enjoy the entertainment experience provided. However, the viewer should remain aware that the material displays fictional ideas not necessarily representative of actual experiences. (p. 139)

CONCLUSION

Research into media sex has indicated that one adverse side effect of regular consumption of certain types of explicit sexual portrayal is that it can influence male attitudes towards women and beliefs about female sexuality. Pornographic films, videos, and stories with violent sex themes in which women are raped may give rise to increased male beliefs that women enjoy being raped. This reaction is especially likely to occur among young men exposed to film or video portrayals of rape where the woman becomes sexually aroused by the experience. However, this reaction is by no means universal.

Although research with American college students has indicated that an increased callousness towards women and victims of rape can be produced among young men with otherwise stable psychological profiles following exposure to films that depict rape themes, evidence from research with interactive erotica has shown that this effect does not invariably occur. The reactions of men to such content may depend on the attitudes they hold before hand. For some men, media depictions of women's apparent enjoyment of rape may be so at odds with their own value system and beliefs about women that such depictions are rejected outright. Whether or not young men exhibit shifts in their propensity to believe that women enjoy being raped may depend not simply on their viewing of violent pornography, but on their reasons for viewing such material in the first place. Those men who watch violent pornography as a sexual substitute may be more prone to develop rape myth beliefs than other men who watch the same material for a different reasons such as diversion or personal sexual release.

Research in this area is fraught with ethical problems. Social scientists must be cautious not to condition psychological changes in experimental participants that may render them more likely to offend or to behave in antisocial ways beyond the research situation. Concern has been raised within the research psychology community about such side effects emanating from experimental investigations of pornography. In response to this legitimate concern, several pornography researchers have developed and tested debriefing procedures. These procedures have been found to offset any research effects and effectively serve to raise awareness of the potential harmful influences of violent pornography.

7

Is Media Sex the Cause
of Sexual Deviance?

Perhaps the greatest concern linked to the potential effects of sexually violent films is that they might cause viewers to emulate the behaviors portrayed or use such portrayals to justify their own actions in acting on aggressive sexual fantasies or attitudes. The role played by the media in relation to the development of deviant sexual practices has been investigated over more than 30 years. The focus of this research has concentrated on the potential influence of pornography as a socialising agent or trigger in regard to sexual deviance.

Indications that exposure to explicit sexual material is connected with criminal behavior has derived from law enforcement data. A study of serial murderers in the United States found that the great majority of perpetrators (81%) reported significant consumption of pornography (Hazelwood, 1985). Another American police survey of crime statistics found that a significant proportion (42%) of all sex crimes involved pornography either prior to or during commission of the act (Pope, 1987).

The scientific research can be divided into studies of two broad types. The first type of study was conducted with clinically diagnosed or convicted criminal populations in which the role of exposure to explicit sexual material is examined in relation to the original onset of their deviant behaviors or as a trigger mechanism that activates their impulses before offending. The second type of study generally entailed the analysis of aggregate statistical evidence on relationships between the distribution of pornography in specified geographical areas and the occurrence of sex offences.

Much of the research among known sex offenders used survey techniques to compare them with nonoffenders in terms of their exposure to pornography. A few laboratory-based studies have also been carried out to find out if sex offenders exhibit different reactions from nonoffenders to erotic film material, especially to scenes that depict violent sexual behavior.

EARLY STUDIES WITH OFFENDERS

The earliest research on the effects of pornography focused on sex offenders. Evidence was obtained through interviews with known offenders and their psychiatrists. Gebhard, Gagnon, Pomeroy, and Christenson (1965) set out to discover the ways in which the sexual histories and social backgrounds of sex offenders, who were divided into 14 categories such as incest and peeping, differed from those of nonoffenders. Compared with controls, sex offenders reported somewhat greater exposure and similar reactions to pornography. However, rapists were more likely than controls to report being aroused by sadistic themes. Of all the groups of sexual offenders interviewed, rapists reported the greatest level of exposure to pornography. The data were self-reports of responses to the question, 'Does it arouse you sexually to see photographs or drawings of people engaged in sexual activity?' Another question was, 'Do stories of rape, torture, or violence arouse you sexually?' Although most of the men surveyed said 'no' to this question, the highest responders were 'heterosexual aggressors,' with 16% admitting at least moderate arousal.

Comparisons were also made between known sex offenders, other (nonsex) offenders, and men from the general population on possession of pornography and reactions to it. No significant differences emerged between these samples in terms of reported sexual arousal to pornographic photographs. One weakness of this research, however, was that it failed to explore in any detail the possibility of links between tastes in specific types of pornography and specific categories of offence. For example, did sadomasochistic imagery hold special appeal for rapists? Did depictions of child pornography prove to be distinctly arousing for child sex offenders (Eysenck & Nias, 1978)?

Studies of this kind, that depend on self-report data and explore links between pornography exposure and offending retrospectively, are unable to demonstrate causal links. Despite this weakness, much of the early research into the effects of explicit sexual material took this form. The 1970 U.S. Commission on Obscenity and Pornography, for instance, sponsored six surveys of offenders (Cook & Fosen, 1971; K. E. Davis & Braucht, 1971a; Goldstein, Kant, Judd, Rice, & Green, 1971; Johnson, Kupperstein, & Peters, 1971; Propper, 1972; Walker, 1971).

Walker (1971) compared sex offenders in hospital with other patients, and sex offenders in prison with other inmates. There was a nonsignificant trend for the sex offenders to report less exposure to pornography than the controls, but the sex offenders claimed a greater increase in sexual activity after viewing pornography. Johnson, Kupperstein, and Peters (1971) conducted interviews with sex offenders and a comparison sample from the general population. Both groups revealed similar past experiences with pornography.

Cook, Fosen, and Pacht (1971) examined the patterns of exposure to pornography among sex offenders and found that, if anything, they were generally less likely to consume such materials than were other (nonsex) offenders. Unfortunately, no distinctions were made between different types of erotic stimuli for which different offending groups may have had a preference, nor were any detailed distinctions made among different offending groups in terms of type of offence.

Cook and Fosen (1971) had participants rate their degree of sexual arousal to erotic slides and interviewed them about previous exposure to pornography. Respondents comprised sex offenders and other inmates in a state prison. The two groups were similar in their reactions to erotic slides, but the sex offenders reported less frequent and milder exposure to pornography.

Some of this early research conducted as part of the 1970 U.S. Pornography Commission's enquiry found a positive relationship between exposure to pornography and sexual deviance. K. E. Davis and Braucht (1971a) reported a study conducted with male students and prisoners in which questions were asked designed to measure sexual deviance and moral character, as well as exposure to pornographic material. Signs of sexual deviance were found to be associated with amount of claimed exposure to pornography.

Propper (1972) studied prisoners who were classified as having high or low exposure to pornography. Prisoners with high exposure to pornography were found to have had earlier experience with sex, and to have engaged more often in group and oral sex. They were also more likely to have friends involved in sexual deviance and antisocial behavior (unlike the findings of K. E. Davis & Braucht, 1971a). It was concluded that pornography may have played a role in the development of sexual deviance in these cases.

Goldstein et al. (1971) conducted a retrospective study based on interviews. Compared with poorly matched controls, sex offenders were found to have less experience with pornography, especially in adolescence. However, many people claimed to have 'tried out' sexual activities depicted in pornography. The sex offenders here included rapists and boy and girl molesters. There are problems with claims made here by sex offenders. There is no way of knowing, for example, whether controls who volunteered for these studies had more experience with pornography than did people who refused to take part.

Goldstein (1973) reported a further survey of convicted male rapists, pedophiles, homosexuals, transsexuals, heavy pornography users, and a community control group. These groups were all interviewed to assess their experience with erotic materials in photographs, films, and books during adolescence and adulthood. Adolescent exposure to erotica was significantly less for all nonheterosexual and offender groups, compared with controls. During adulthood, the sex offenders and transsexuals continued to report less exposure to erotic stimuli than controls. The homosexuals and users of pornography, however, both reported greater exposure during adulthood. Respondents were asked whether anything had been seen in erotica materials that they wished they had tried at a later time. Fewer than one in four respondents in any group reportedly imitated sexual behavior experienced through erotic material immediately or shortly after its consumption.

Goldstein had initially hypothesised that extent of exposure to erotica during adolescence would be positively related to the emergence of sexual pathology in later life. This hypothesis was not borne out by the findings of this survey. Indeed, the control groups who were surveyed here, comprising individuals with no known record of sexual offence, exhibited greater levels of exposure to erotic material during their adolescent years than did known offenders.

When asked about their reactions following exposure to erotic materials, sex offenders and other sexually deviant groups reported a higher incidence of masturbation than did nonoffenders. The rate of reported masturbation declined slightly from adolescence to adulthood for all groups, except homosexuals. When asked whether thoughts or feelings stimulated by erotica led to sexual activity, around half of all groups reported than they did. Nonoffenders differed from offenders in this context, however, in being more likely to mention the stimulation of sexual behavior with a partner, rather than masturbation.

The low exposure to erotica reported by institutionalised sex offenders was compatible with many aspects of their sexual history and attitudes. For the rapists, a very repressive family background regarding sexuality was indicated. Rapists uniformly reported that sex was never a topic of discussion in their homes, and that when family members were aware of their interest in erotica, they were highly punitive. The pattern of inhibition was consistent with the rapists' report that pornography in adult years did not stimulate them to desire sexual activity or to actually engage in sexual activity. The high percentage of rapists reporting frequent homosexual activity suggested the possibility that the aggressive sexual act can at times represent an attempt at covering homosexual tendencies.

Cline (1974) pointed out inconsistencies between Goldstein et al. (1971) and Goldstein, Kant, and Harman (1974). Whereas the offenders claimed only rarely to act out their pornographic desires, a majority of people in general claimed to have 'tried out' activities depicted in pornography. More needs to be known about what these imitative practices entail. One problem with all these studies was that measures of exposure to pornography and of sexual deviance were nondiscriminatory. No attempts were made to differentiate between serious and less serious sexual offences. Participants in these surveys were assessed for reactions to nudity, sex play, and intercourse, but not to rape or child sex abuse. There was no attempt to distinguish between different types of sex crime or how they might relate to exposure to different types of pornography.

LONGITUDINAL EFFECTS OF PORNOGRAPHY

Field research has been used to try to establish whether there are links between exposure to pornography and sexual deviance over time. The studies reviewed in the first part of this chapter all used cross-sectional surveys to obtain data from respondents at one point in time, although one survey (Goldstein et al., 1971) did use a retrospective approach to try to ascertain over-time links. An alternative approach is to examine broad trends in society based on analysis of available statistics. Some studies have used aggregate statistical data to assess the relationship between the circulation of pornography in society and the occurrence of sexual violence against women. These studies often compare the circulation rates of various magazines or the number of adult theatres with rates of rape and other sex crimes. According to one writer, the effects of exposure to violent pornography may represent a 'ripple effect' on behavior. Laboratory studies try to identify direct linkages between exposure to such material and attitudes or simulated behavior. Social trends identify more general influences of pornography by tracing any changes in the volume of categories of offence that follow on from changes in the prevalence and availability of pornography.

One approach has been to assess the changing extent to which pornography is available in a society and shifts in the incidence of sexually deviant behavior. Two initial studies of this sort were carried out in Denmark during the 1960s and 1970s (Ben-Veniste, 1971; Kutchinsky, 1971a, 1977). Another examined U.S. statistics (Kupperstein & Wilson, 1971).

Ben-Veniste (1971) conducted a survey of police statistics on reported sex crimes in Copenhagen for a 12-year period. Results indicated a decline in various sex offences from 1965, with the exception of rape which remained constant at around 20 cases a year for the period of study. This study is often quoted as showing that pornography led to a decrease in sexual deviance. However, this conclusion may not be warranted. First, the data were examined only up to 1969 and the impact of changes in law regarding pornography, which took place in Denmark in the mid-1960s, may have not been truly felt for a few more years. Another factor is that both the police and victims had become more tolerant of sex crimes, with the result of less reporting of such crimes (Eysenck & Nias, 1978).

Research in Denmark revealed a negative association between the availability of sexually explicit materials and the incidence of sexual offences reported to the police (Kutchinsky, 1973). Increased circulation of pornographic materials, following the legalisation of pornography, was apparently linked to a significant drop in reported sexual offences, particularly rape and child molestation. This finding could be interpreted as suggesting that unrestricted distribution of sexually explicit materials served as a safety valve for deviant sexual behaviors. Other factors were also likely to have been important at this time, including greater political and social participation for women and a generally increasingly liberal social policy perspective.

Kutchinsky (1971a) designed a survey to find out whether the decline in reported sex crimes in Denmark was due to changes in public attitudes. He interviewed people in Copenhagen about their likelihood of reporting sex crimes. They were also questioned about how seriously they regarded various types of sex crimes and whether their attitudes had shifted over time. The possibility of changes in police attitudes or to the law was also investigated. It was found that the law and police enforcement practices had not changed, but that people had become more permissive with regard to certain categories of sex offence, such as peeping, exhibitionism, and indecent interference. These results did not shed any light on whether availability of pornography is linked in any way to the incidence of sex crimes such as rape. Indeed, the incidence of reported rape increased in Denmark from the mid-1960s to early 1970s, although levels remained low.

Kutchinsky (1971a) noted a decrease in rates of occurrence of four different types of sex crimes registered by the police in Copenhagen. For three types of offence—exhibitionism, peeping, and (physical) indecency towards girls—the availability of pornography was identified as a key factor. This conclusion was underlined as tentative only, however. More serious types of sex offence such as rape, rape with robbery, attempted rape, and intercourse on threat of violence did not show evidence of decline over the same period. Indeed, the Danish study's focus on less serious forms of sexual offence meant that it revealed little of relevance to the subject of causality of serious sex offences (Court, 1984).

This Danish research was challenged by other writers (e.g., Cline, 1974; Court, 1984). Later investigations showed a positive relationship between the incidence of sexual offences and the availability of sexually explicit materials. Data from several other countries indicated that variations in the availability of pornography corresponds positively with changes in reported occurrences of rape (e.g., L. Baron & Straus, 1984, 1989; Jaffee & Straus, 1987; Scott & Schwalm, 1988a).

Cline (1974) noted that violent sex crimes remained at around 220 per year from 1960 to 1970. Thus, the findings for Denmark actually indicated a reduction, over the period of increased relaxation of pornography restrictions, in less serious sex offences, but not in more serious offences. Public attitudes also showed increased leniency towards less serious sex offences.

Kupperstein and Wilson (1971) conducted research on the relationship with availability of pornography and occurrence of sex offences in the United States. During the 1960–1969 period, when pornography became increasingly available, arrests for sexual offences increased by 18% with rape showing the greatest increase at about 50%. However, the rape figure was less ominous when set against the general increase in crime. Cline (1974) extended this survey by 2 years and found that the increase in rape had accelerated after 1970. He also found a similar trend for divorce rates, a more general index of sexual morality. Kupperstein and Wilson again failed to distinguish between serious and less serious sex offences. Yet such distinctions are highly relevant when considering the impact that pornography might have on sexual offending (Court, 1977; Williams Committee Report, 1979). Trends in minor sex offences have not always run parallel to those in major sex offences such as rape (Court, 1980; Geis & Geis, 1979). There are also issues surrounding the types of statistics utilised by researchers to operationally define sex crime trends. Some researchers have used arrest data, others police reports data, or others victimisation study data. Police reports have come to be regarded as most reliable (Court, 1984; Fox, 1976).

A cross-national survey of sex crimes and availability of pornography conducted in several countries was made by Court (1977). Results indicated that reports to the police of rape and attempted rape showed further signs of increase in the mid-1970s.

Eysenck and Nias (1978) pointed out, however, that changes in rates of serious sexual offence could have been influenced by a variety of other factors, including the emergence of the women's liberation movement, population mobility (from urban to rural), and the impact of specific campaigns or media events designed to change public attitudes

In the United States again, Scott and Schwalm (1988b) reported no relationship between rape rates and the number of adult theatres or bookstores. However, they found a significant positive relationship between rape incidence and per capita sales of sexually explicit magazines (e.g., *Playboy, Penthouse*), after controlling for demographic factors and the general circulation of nonerotic magazines. Similar data were examined in the mid 1980s by other American researchers. L. Baron and Straus (1984) found a high correlation between circulation rates of certain soft-core pornographic magazines (e.g., *Playboy, Penthouse, Hustler, Gallery*, etc.) and rape rates. This relationship survived statistical controls for other demographic and psychological variables believed to be linked to the incidence of rape (L. Baron &

Straus, 1984). Later research also found a positive correlation between rape rates and sales of *Playgirl* (L. Baron & Straus, 1989).

Baron also later reported positive correlations between rape rate and gender inequality, social disorganisation, urbanisation, economic inequality and unemployment. The presumed relationship between magazine circulation and rape rates vanishes statistically when a measure of cultural support for violence is added, which has been interpreted to indicate that 'a macho culture pattern independently influences men to purchase more pornography and commit more rapes' (L. Baron, 1990, p. 364). Thus, magazine consumption and rape are both the outcomes of a target pattern of traditional masculine attitudes.

Kutchinsky (1991) revisited the subject and examined the incidence of rape in several different societies where pornography had become readily available. He included 20 years of crime data in his study and assumed that a substantial number of people had been exposed to aggressive pornography due to a general trend towards greater public availability of sexually explicit materials of all forms. He then counted the number of cases of rape and aggravated assault in Denmark, Sweden, Germany, and the United States from 1964 to 1984. The results showed that in no country did rape increase more than nonsexual violent crimes despite the large increase in pornography in each country during that period. In fact, in three countries—Denmark, Sweden, and Germany—rape increased less than other nonsexual assaults. In the United States, rape and nonsexual assault followed about the same pattern over time. The lack of a relationship between the availability of pornography and rape rates in four Western societies, including the United States, suggested that the widespread availability of pornography had not increased rape rates.

The conclusion that pornography has no impact on rape rates from such data has been disputed (Lahey, 1991). Research conducted in the United States revealed a relatively strong correlation between pornography availability and rape rates (L. Baron, 1990; L. Baron & Straus, 1984). Baron and Straus tried to account for differences in reported rapes across the 50 states in the United States. They developed indices to measure state-by-state differences in rape rates. One of these measures was the number of copies of sex-oriented magazines sold per capita in each state. This index was calculated by looking at sales (subscription and news stand) of eight magazines: *Chic, Club, Galley, Genesis, Hustler, Oui, Penthouse,* and *Playboy.*

In 1979, there was a highly significant correlation of .63 between sex magazine circulation and rape rates. The correlation between rape rates and magazine circulation in 1980 was .55. A later analysis of rape rates between 1980 and 1982 showed a correlation with sex magazine circulation of .64. This evidence showed only that there was a strong association between sex magazine readership and incidence of rape, not that one causes the other. It was also suggested that there might be a third variable explanation. Hypermasculine sex role orientation might vary from state to state. Baron and Straus found that a Violence Approval measure for each state cancelled out the relationship between magazine circulation and rape rates. Men predisposed to hypermasculinity may engage in acts of sexual aggression to validate their masculinity, and they may buy sexually oriented magazines for the same reason.

Kimmel and Linders (1996) conducted an aggregated statistics study linking the availability of pornography to sex crime rates in six American cities. Two of the cities had laws that outlawed pornography within city limits, whereas the others did not have or enforce such laws. The researchers examined the empirical relationship between magazine circulation and rape rates. Rape rates increased dramatically during the 1970s, nearly doubling from 1970 to 1980, remained stable during the first half of the 1980s, and increased slightly during the second half. Changes in rates for aggravated assault followed closely the changes in rape rates. The circulation of pornographic magazines in the United States dropped sharply from 1979. The correlation between circulation rates and rape rates for 1979–1989 was strongly negative ($r = -.79$). State and city data also failed to reveal a positive relationship between changes in rape rates and changes in pornography circulation.

One reason there was a lack of relationship between pornography and rape might be to do with the measurement of pornographic consumption solely in terms of magazine circulation. Pornographic material is available in video form and there was an increase in rentals of explicit videos in the United States between 1980 and 1989. The question is whether an 11% increase in video rentals compensates for a reduction of almost 50% in the circulation of pornographic magazines. There is one view that the technological shift from pornographic magazines to X-rated videos has been accompanied by a gender democratisation of pornography consumption. One survey of 500 video stores in 1989 found that only 40% of renters of X-rated videos were individual men, whereas 29% were men with women renting together, and 15% were women renting tapes alone (Kimmel & Linders, 1996).

OFFENDERS AND VIOLENT PORNOGRAPHY

Research has been carried out with known sex offenders to find out whether their reactions to violent sex scenes differ from those of nonoffenders. Evidence referred to earlier in this chapter indicated that surveys of offenders had largely failed to establish significantly distinct patterns of exposure to pornography for this group. Even so, when they are exposed to certain types of erotic scene, the reactions of known rapists are different from those of most nonoffenders. More direct evidence of the significance of pornography to sex offending was gathered from clinical settings and obtained through experiments. Such research examined more directly the specific part that pornography can play in the genesis of sex offending, and the distinctive reactions to pornography displayed by offenders.

Clinical Evidence

Evidence has emerged from clinical diagnostic settings that known sex offenders report the use of pornography as a facilitator not only in relation to the acquisition of their deviation, but also as a device to break down resistance and inhibitions of their victims or targets of molestation, especially where these are children (Burgess, 1984; Carnes, 1984).

According to Reed (1994), addiction to pornography is an identifiable illness that can be linked, clinically, to the development of compulsive, dependent, and addictive sexual behavior. In clinical cases of addiction, the use of pornography is prevalent (Donovan, 1988). Pornography addiction is a complex, self-induced pathological relationship. Viewing pornography, masturbating, promiscuity, and even sexual assault have been identified as forms of addictive behavior (Colman, 1988; Herman, 1990; Robertson, 1990). In cases of sexual problem behavior, pornography use has generally featured as part of an overall syndrome (Carnes, 1989). Pornography can be used to establish a desired mood state, but do so by altering neurotransmission patterns (Milkman & Sunderwirth, 1987). Pornography can therefore facilitate changes in behavioral dispositions by altering brain neurochemistry.

A category of compulsive–addictive mental illnesses related to sexual deviance has been identified called *paraphilias*. These are characterised by recurrent, intense sexual urges. There are eight of these disorders: pedophilia, fetishism, sexual masochism, sexual sadism, transvestite fetishism, voyeurism, and exhibitionism. Most sex offenders who manifest these disorders report the onset of such tendencies before the age of 18 (Abel & Rouleau, 1990). This is also about the time when adolescents report more frequent exposure to pornography (Reed, 1990). Overall, data concerning paraphilias have indicated that pornography does play a part in their development and maintenance (Reed, 1994). A table produced by Reed (1994) summarised the role of pornography in the lives of incarcerated sex offenders (see Table 7.1).

Some writers have argued that sex offenders should be amongst those who are influenced by sexually explicit materials and that the influence of such materials will be manifest in various ways at different points in their life (Marshall & Barbaree, 1984). A social learning theory of rape has been pro-

TABLE 7.1

Role of Pornography in the Lives of Incarcerated Sex Offenders

1. Compared to nonoffenders, adult masturbatory activity in response to pornography is more common in sex offenders (Murrin & Laws, 1990, p. 88).
2. Compared to nonoffenders, sex offenders show a greater desire to own pornography; and report owning more; and reported a greater desire to procure pornography for themselves in adolescence (Murrin & Laws, 1990, p. 88).
3. Compared to normals, rapists are 15 times as likely to have been exposed to explicit pornography during ages 6–10 (Goldstein, Kant, & Harman, 1974).
4. One-third of the rapists and nonfamilial child molesters reported exposure to explicit pornography during pubescence (Marshall, 1989, p. 206).
5. High-frequency masturbation behavior patterns predict general pornography use. More paedophiles than rapists are high frequency masturbators. When they masturbate, they fantasize about raping or child molesting (Marshall, 1989, p. 207).
6. Sex offenders with high-frequency rates of masturbation are more likely to be current users of pornography. It plays a more important role in the life of pedophiles than rapists (Marshall, 1988).
7. More than one third of the rapists and child molesters had been incited by the use of hard-core sexual stimuli (depicting both aggressive and consenting sex) to commit an offense (Marshall, 1989, p. 207).
8. Exposure to pornography prior to age 14 years predicted greater involvement in deviant sexual practices (Davis & Braucht, 1971a, p. 7).
9. Chronic offenders are more likely to be pornography users (Abel, Mittelman, & Becker, 1985; cited, in Marshall, 1989).
10. Over half the rapists who were current users of consenting sex pornography claimed they used it to stimulate fantasies of rape (Marshall, 1989, p. 207). Explicit material elicits a greater arousal in rapists than does nonexplicit pornography (Marshall, 1989, p. 190).
11. Child molesters and rapists reported use of pornography prior to and during their offenses (Marshall, 1989, p. 205).
12. Rapists and child molesters deliberately use pornography as part of their preoffense preparation to commit an offense, after incitement. The extensive use of pornography serves as an escalating factor in their rape and assault cycles (Blanchard, 1989, p. 54; Marshall, 1989).
13. Rapists justify their deviant actions by viewing pornography that appears to sanction the behavior (Silbert, 1989); so do child molesters (DSM-III-R).

Note. Source: Reed, 1994. Reproduced with permission of Lawrence Erlbaum Associates.

posed in which it is argued that certain men, as a result of their experience, would be prepared to respond to pornography in a negative way, whereas others, by virtue of their experience, would be protected from displaying such antisocial urges. It was suggested that certain early experiences (exposure to traditional views of women's roles associated with exposure to a powerful and forceful male who modelled aggression toward females; poor training in social skills; parenting that was either neglectful or in other ways failed to instil self-confidence and a concern for others) would make young males search for information that would bolster their sense of their own manliness. Certain forms of pornography (e.g., those depicting rape or sex with children), although interpretable by others in quite different ways, might reinforce views that serve this need.

Those men whose experiences have shaped their perceptions of sexuality in the ways described should be particularly receptive to information that they take to confirm their beliefs. These beliefs might include the notion that women enjoy being raped and that masculinity is reflected in coercing someone to have sex and in humiliating and degrading that person. These are just the types of view presented in those examples of pornography that depict a man forcing a woman to have sex with him. For some of these men, the thought of struggling to overpower a woman is too threatening, so they look to other sources of power and prestige in a sexual context. These men are ready to believe that children want to have sex with adults, that child pornography clearly suggests this and also clearly demonstrates that the man in the scenario is in control of the sexual interaction.

A poll of U.S. mental health professionals found that 254 psychotherapists reported that they had come across cases in their clinical practices where pornography was found to be an instigator or contributor to a sex crime, personality disturbance, or antisocial act. Another 324 psychotherapists suspected such a link. Many others reported no such relationships, but the total of 578 who had either evidence or suspicions about pornography represented a significant number (Lipkin & Carnes, 1970).

Working with a sample of sex offenders in a voluntary outpatient environment, Marshall (1988) found that child molesters and rapists frequently used sexually explicit materials incitefully both immediately prior to and during sexual assault. In addition, Marshall discovered that, when compared with two different control groups, offenders reported substantially greater use of sexually explicit materials, and that such use was significantly related to the chronicity of sexual offenders' assaults. These findings indicate a direct link between exposure to sexually explicit materials and the occurrence of criminal sexual offences. Despite the recurrent pattern of results, the limitations inherent to correlational data must be recognised and the findings interpreted with appropriate caution.

Of course, not all men with these unfortunate formative experiences become sexual offenders, but, according to the social learning perspective, most sexual offenders come from this type of background and entertain views consistent with those outlined previously. Regular exposure to sexually explicit materials is not essential to the etiology and maintenance of sexual offending; but should a man with the right kind of personality profile or background be exposed to such stimuli, they could have a stronger impact on him than on others.

Offenders and nonoffenders alike have been found to experience sexual arousal, as measured through self-reports and physiological measures (e.g., penile tumescence), in response to nonviolent sex scenes. Rapists are more likely to be aroused, however, by rape scenes, with more violent rapists being aroused most of all by particularly violent sex scenes (Abel, Barlow, Blanchard, & Guild, 1977; Abel, Blanchard, & Becker, 1976, 1978). Abel and his colleagues developed a 'rape index,' which is a ratio of sexual arousal to rape portrayals compared with arousal to consenting sex portrayals. With this index, a man whose sexual arousal towards rape is similar to or greater than his arousal to consenting sex would be considered to have an inclination towards rape. In a similar vein, child molesters are characteristically more aroused by scenes involving children (Freund, 1967; Quinsey, 1977).

Little research has been devoted to understanding the effects of exposure to sexually explicit material on males who later become sexual offenders. Such investigations rarely distinguish differing content (e.g., consenting versus forceful sex; sex involving children; depictions of violence and humiliation, etc.), nor do they define the stimuli along dimensions of explicitness, even though these are issues relevant to the effects of exposure to such materials.

Research carried out in Australia in the late 1980s found that sex offenders guilty of rape or child molesting acknowledged frequent use of pornographic films and videotapes while preparing themselves to commit an offence and were more likely to engage in deviant fantasies during masturbation. This research distinguished between a number of types of sex offender whose use of pornography was compared with that of nonoffenders. Child molesters (heterosexual and homosexual) and rapists reported more frequent exposure to erotic pornographic materials during adolescent years than did other sex offenders. However, neither of the first two offending groups provided evidence of greater exposure to pornography than nonoffenders during this critical period of psychological development. As adults, the child molesters and rapists made more use of pornographic materials than did either the nonoffenders or incest offenders (Marshall, 1988).

In clinical interviews, such offenders were found to attribute some influence of deviant pornographic material in the offences they committed. Child molesters and rapists were more likely than any other groups to entertain deviant fantasies during masturbatory activities and during nonmasturbatory daydreams. The most disturbing finding, however, was the reported use of explicit materials by sex offenders in relation to committing their illegal behaviors. Slightly more than one in three of the child molesters and rapists claimed to have been incited to commit an offence following exposure to certain erotic materials. For some offenders interviewed, the role of erotica as an instigator to offend was accidental, or at least the stimuli were not deliberately sought out to excite them to offend.

However, among the child molesters who were incited to offend, more than half (53%) claimed that they deliberately used erotica in their typical planned preparation for offending, as did one in three (33%) of the rapists who claimed to have been incited to offend by these materials. The demonstration of relationships between the use of sexual stimuli as instigators to offend, the strength of deviant sexual interest, and the rates of masturbatory activities, strengthened the conviction that child molesters (in particular) are preoccupied with deviant thoughts that unfortunately appear to mediate a high rate of sexual offending.

On a cautionary note, however, such data were derived from retrospective recall accounts, and such accounts are subject to error. Moreover, there was the additional possibility, acknowledged by the researcher, that sexual offenders may be eager to attribute responsibility for their misbehaviors to some external source (Marshall, 1988).

Cline (1994) believed that pornography could play a significant part in the development of sex offending across such behaviors as child molestation, exhibitionism, voyeurism, sadomasochism, fetishism, and rape. Offenders might first become addicted to pornography. It might serve as a sexual release to begin with, but then also provide a powerful source of fantasies that might be recalled later. Following initial addiction, there may follow an 'escalation effect.' Over time, the porn addict's appetite changes, requiring more and more explicit material to achieve a turn-on. If transferred into their own sex lives, they may begin to require their sexual partners to engage in increasingly bizarre, even deviant sexual practices. A further response is desensitization. Material originally perceived as shocking or repulsive, although sexually arousing, may come to be seen as acceptable. A final response is an increasing tendency to act out sexually the behaviors viewed in the pornography to which they had been repeatedly exposed. It was during this stage that deviant sexual behavior would begin to appear in its fully developed form.

There is a need to go beyond considering the media in a vacuum. Individuals respond to media—including to their sexual content—in different ways according to their own psychological make-up. Individuals who have been inadequately socialised, for example, may be susceptible to effects of pornography (Fisher & Barak, 1991). An early study by Goldstein (1973) reported, in relation to the individuals studied, that 'the sex deviates had less exposure to what we would define as erotica (e.g., heterosexual acts) as well as less exposure to what we would define as violent pornography (e.g., sadistic and masochistic material)' (p. 300). A careful reading of a more detailed version of this same study, however, indicates that although rapists reported less exposure to pornography in adolescence than did control groups, various aspects of the data suggested that the type of pornography to which rapists were exposed and the degree to which they were affected by it may have been idiosyncratic to the offending group (Goldstein, Kant, & Harman, 1974). For example, rapists reported an earlier age of peak experience with pornography. In addition, they were far more likely to have encountered pornographic photographs displaying explicit sexual acts (rather than nudes) at an early age and to have expressed a desire to imitate the activity portrayed in pornography (although they said they were less likely to have actually done so). Rapists were more likely to relate daily masturbation to thoughts of pornography, to have developed a stronger interest in pornography early in life, to have become repeatedly aroused by a particular theme, and to have more feelings of frustration and guilt related to their exposure to pornography than control respondents.

Although Goldstein et al. (1974) did not specifically inquire about pornography involving coercive sex themes, depictions involving sexual violence (e.g., motorcycle films depicting 'gang bangs') frequently became part of rapists' daydreams and fantasies. These researchers reported that 55% of rapists, compared with 9% of controls, used scenes from pornography in their fantasies and daydreams. How can we account for the data suggesting that rapists had less exposure to pornography in childhood but may have been more affected by such exposure? Goldstein's study, as well as other research, suggests that rapists were more likely to come from home environments where education about sexuality was highly restricted and sex in general was treated as a taboo subject. With such a background, exposure to pornography might be expected to exert a relatively more powerful influence on rapists' responses because it would be more of a primary source of information and stimulation.

Such a conclusion is consistent with other research. In one study, university students indicated how much information about sexuality they obtained in their childhood from various sources, such as peers, parents, church, educational media, educational courses, sexually explicit media, and doctors (reported in Malamuth, 1993). Sexually explicit media were ranked second only to peers as the most important source of information. Respondents who reported obtaining more information from explicit media also held attitudes more supportive of violence against women. Such a correlation was not found with respondents who named other sources of information as primary. Information from sources such as educational courses actually correlated with lower levels of attitudes supportive of violence against women. In fact, the link of sexually explicit media to antisocial attitudes tended to be stronger when compared with other sources of sexual information than when measured alone.

Similarly, Tjaden (1988) asked college students to indicate all sources from which they may have received information about various sexual topics as they were growing up. Sources included school, church, parents, peers, mass media, and nonpornographic books and magazines as well as pornographic magazines and films. In general, pornography was relatively unimportant for females. For males, it was also unimportant for some topics, such as venereal diseases, pregnancy, and childbirth. For other topics such as masturbation, arousal and orgasm, and oral and anal intercourse, however, men reported pornographic materials as an important primary or secondary information source.

The impact of a particular variable may have synergistic effects when interacting with other factors (Malamuth, 1986). Using a nationally representative sample of post-high school students in the United States, Malamuth, Sockloskie, and Koss (1991) examined whether respondents who consumed relatively high levels of pornography were more likely to be sexually aggressive. Their findings showed that, for the population as a whole, information about pornography usage did not add a great deal of predictive value. Significant predictive value, however, was found for those men who had earlier been identified as at highest risk for committing sexual aggression. Although these data do not allow inferences about cause and effect, they illustrate the importance of not relying on simple models of the potential impact of pornography or any other factor; instead, the potential interactive effects of various factors must be probed carefully, particularly for some individuals.

Experimental Evidence

Clinical evidence is dependent on post hoc gathering of information about offenders after they have committed offences and requires the identification of factors that characterise offenders and their backgrounds which may have a causal role in relation to their deviant behavior. Experimental evidence is built on studies in which interventionist procedures are adopted enabling the measurement of offenders' (as compared to nonoffenders') responses to pornographic material.

In laboratory experiments, researchers have attempted to test causal hypotheses by controlling the pornographic material to which participating sex offenders and nonoffenders are exposed. The aim of these studies is to find out if convicted sex offenders exhibit different patterns of response to specific categories of explicit sexual material from comparison samples of nonoffenders. The responses that are measured in these studies comprised physiological indicators of sexual arousal as well as verbal, attitudinal responses.

The mechanisms underpinning the conditioning of deviant sex-related practices have been demonstrated through experimental procedures. For instance, research demonstrated that deviant sexual behavior could be created among hitherto nonoffending individuals, in a laboratory setting. In this case, a classical conditioning procedure was adopted through which a sexual arousal response to highly erotic pictures was transferred onto a rubber boot. A fetish was created whereby a nonsexual stimulus item came to acquire properties through close association with a sexual stimulus that enabled the item to produce a sexual response in conditioned male participants (Rachman, 1966).

Another writer conducted research that suggested that exposure to special sexual experiences (including the consumption of pornography) and then masturbating to the fantasy of the experience could sometimes lead to participation in deviant sexual acts. Orgasm experienced during enjoyment of pornography provided reinforcement of the experience. Such experiences could be powerful enough that memories of them get locked into the brain and are difficult to erase (McGaugh, 1983). Through this type of mechanism, pornography can acquire significant appeal for potential offenders and comes to represent a key source of information that is used to feed their deviancy.

Evidence has emerged that known sex offenders, guilty of crimes such as rape, are more strongly aroused by media depictions of rape than of mutually consenting sex between two sexual partners. Nonoffender comparison groups, in contrast, have usually been found to respond more positively towards depictions of mutually consenting sex. It has been suggested that certain men commit acts of violent sex because they are turned on by depictions of coercive, nonconsenting sex (Baxter, Barbaree, & Marshall, 1986). Not all the evidence has been consistent on this point, however.

In one set of studies, rapists were found, under controlled laboratory conditions, to show greater sexual arousal to rape depictions than to scenes of consenting sex. Nonrape offenders, in comparison, were more likely to exhibit arousal to scenes in which women consented to sex (Quinsey & Chaplin, 1984; Quinsey, Chaplin, & Upfold, 1984; Quinsey, Chaplin, & Varney, 1981). Elsewhere, though, a different pattern of responses was found to depictions of rape and consenting sex. When rapists were presented with audiotaped vignettes in which a woman was either clearly being raped or engaging in consenting sex, convicted rapists exhibited physiologically measured sexual arousal to both types of content, whereas nonrapists were aroused only by the consenting sex portrayal (Abel, Barlow, Blanchard, & Guild, 1977). Moreover, rapists did not show a preference for the rape scenes. Yet further evidence has emerged that rapists showed similar or even less arousal to rape depictions than did nonrapists (Baxter, Barbaree, & Marshall, 1986; Wydra, Marshall, Earls, & Barbaree, 1983). Interestingly, both rapists and nonrapists were equally able to discern the inappropriateness of the coercive sex scenes (Wydra et al., 1983).

Further research indicated that males with no prior history or record of sex offending could be aroused by media depictions of rape where the female victim eventually became sexually aroused (Malamuth, Heim, &

Feshbach, 1980). Thus, sexual arousal to rape depictions is not the preserve of violent sex offenders.

Taking this line of enquiry a stage further, Malamuth (1981) identified that nonoffender samples of college men could be differentiated into those who were 'force oriented' in their own lives and those who were not. Such force orientation could also be reflected in their sex lives. Two groups of college males, one 'force oriented' and the other not, were presented with a film that depicted a man who stopped his car on a deserted road to pick up a female hitchhiker. Later, the man and woman have sex. In one version, the sex is mutually consenting, whereas in another version the man forces the women to have sexual intercourse, and she eventually ends up enjoying the assault. The men were then invited to create their own sexual fantasies to achieve a high level of sexual arousal. Whereas the non-force-oriented men were more aroused by the consenting sex scene than by the rape scene, for the force-oriented men the reverse was true. This finding was further corroborated by a later experiment in which young men were exposed to audio tapes depicting scenes of consenting sex between a man and women, nonconsenting sex where the woman showed sexual arousal, and nonconsenting sex where the women showed disgust. Again, force-oriented males were more sexually aroused than non-force-oriented males by rape scenes. On this occasion, however, even non-force-oriented males were aroused by the rape scene in which the woman became sexually aroused (Malamuth & Check, 1983). It is clear from this evidence that it is important to consider the potential impact of pornography, especially violent sexual content, on nonoffenders as well as offenders.

Furthermore, it is not only the limited release, extreme media sex content, sought out by rapists and other sex offenders, that show scenes of violent and degrading sexual behavior that is of concern. There are sexually explicit films and television programs and other forms of media that contain images of explicit sex. To what extent are such themes sexually arousing to media consumers in general? This is the topic to which we turn in the next chapter.

8

Can Media Sex Portrayals Influence Nonoffenders?

Leaving aside the possible role it might play in shaping the conduct of individuals with deviant personalities, is media sex a good thing or a bad thing? For ordinary people with stable personality profiles and a socially conditioned sense of moral responsibility, is exposure to media sex necessarily a problem? Opposing schools of thought have emerged on this question. For some people, the depiction of sex in the media is a matter of taste and decency. It is deemed to be either acceptable or unacceptable as a matter of personal preference. Another line of thought focuses on the empirical evidence that even among ordinary media consumers, regular exposure to sexual portrayals may have social or psychological side effects that may not always be welcome.

In the end, however, this is not a black-or-white issue. Much depends on the type of media sex content under consideration and the nature of the sexual depictions it presents. More extreme and unusual forms of sexual behavior can cause discomfort among many members of the public (Millward-Hargrave, 1992). Although sexual depictions that typify the mainstream media may be accepted by most people, the more explicit materials that can be found on the fringes of publicly available entertainment command a different reaction. Among this type of material is the range of entertainment labelled as 'pornography.'

One view is that pornography is simply a form of entertainment that people consume for their own amusement (Malamuth & Billings, 1986). In some cases, it might serve educational or therapeutic functions, helping individuals to enhance their own sex lives through learning new sexual techniques or by fuelling their fantasies (Goldstein, 1984). Following this line of thinking, the only pornography about which there really needs to be concern is that which depicts sexually violent imagery with women as victims. Evidence has emerged that repeated consumption of such material may foster negative attitudes about women, female sexuality, and rape among young men (Donnerstein, Linz, & Penrod, 1987). One might also add material that depicts degrading and illegal portrayals of child sex abuse, bestiality, and certain forms of sadomasochism in which participants are coerced.

A different school of thought with primarily feminist origins has voiced concerns about a wider array of erotic portrayals than those just mentioned. The concern here centers on demeaning portrayals of women in which they are depicted as sex objects whose sole purpose is to cater to male sexual gratification (Brownmiller, 1984; Diamond, 1985). Such depictions have been accused of cultivating a climate of loss of respect for women generally (Lederer, 1980; Russell, 1988).

Despite the equivocal evidence on whether or not sexual material in film, television, video, or other media plays a part in the causation of sexual offending, a substantial body of evidence has accumulated on the influences of such material on nonoffending populations. This research effort has concentrated on the impact of violent sexual material more than any other, although a handful of studies have investigated the effects of nonviolent sexual content.

The key distinctions that can be drawn among studies in this area are based on the nature of the stimulus material, the nature of the effects being measured, and whether the study is conducted in the laboratory or in the field. Content distinctions are centered on whether the stimulus material is of a purely erotic and sexual nature or whether it contains violence. Similarly, the effects measures can be distinguished between those that focus on a purely sexual response and those that focus on aggressive responding. Much of the research has been conducted under controlled laboratory conditions in which the investigator determines the kind of material to which participants will be exposed and the nature of the response they will be given an opportunity to make. Some researchers have explored the possible effects of erotic material in the field using subtle interventionist methodologies or post hoc reporting. In this case, the researcher either manipulates sets of circumstances or systematically measures the effects of naturally occurring changes of circumstances. In contrast to studies of potentially adverse effects of media sex, this chapter also considers the usefulness of erotica in a therapeutic context. Clinical evidence has emerged that sexual media portrayals can be used to treat sexual dysfunction among nonoffending individuals.

In giving consideration, initially, to the potential impact of sexual portrayals on nondeviant populations, evidence exists for effects that operate at a number of distinct (though possibly interrelated) psychological levels. Media portrayals of sex (and violent sex) may influence consumers at cognitive, attitudinal, and behavioral levels. Cognitively, such material may give rise, in the short term, to sex-related thoughts and fantasies. In the longer term, such content may affect the way individuals think about sexual practices and male and female sexuality. Continued exposure to explicit depictions of women engaged in sexual activity, for instance, may activate thoughts about female promiscuity in viewers (Zillmann & Bryant, 1982, 1984). Repeated exposure to scenes of sexual violence may play a significant part in shaping public perceptions about the prevalence of such behaviors in real life. Such thought patterns may, in turn, increase the likelihood that nonoffending individuals will come to accept such behavior in their own lives (Malamuth, Sockloskie, & Koss, 1991).

Attitudinally, regular viewing of sexual scenes in which casual sex is depicted, where women are shown as being promiscuous, or in which women are portrayed as obtaining pleasure from being raped, may create a psychological climate in which such behaviors are classified as acceptable (Malamuth & Check, 1985; Malamuth, Haber, & Feshbach, 1980). Effects that operate at the level of the ideas that people, and especially men, hold about sexual relations and female sexuality were discussed in chapter 6. This chapter focuses on behavioral-level effects that media sex could have on nonoffending populations.

EXPERIMENTAL STUDIES OF THE IMPACT OF EROTICA ON SEXUAL BEHAVIOR

Relatively little research has been conducted on the impact of portrayals of sexual behavior on mainstream television on audience behavior—whether sexual or otherwise. Focus has instead been placed upon more extreme forms of sexual portrayal than would ordinarily be found on the major television channels, which would generally be classified as pornographic. This material is available either on videotape or through adult-only subscription television channels where consumers must purchase decoding equipment to be able to receive a scrambled television signal.

Concern about the impact of this kind of material has been fuelled by research indicating that exposure to particular forms of erotic imagery can result in an increase in aggressive sexual fantasies, cynical attitudes towards women, and aggressive behavior towards male or female targets, depending on the circumstances surrounding the aggression (Malamuth & Donnerstein, 1982). In extreme instances, the fusion of sex and violence is such that sexual arousal is achieved only through images that depict violent and coercive sexual intercourse (Abel, Barlow, Blanchard, & Guild, 1977). As we saw in chapter 7, this sort of material can be found especially arousing by convicted rapists. The current chapter, however, is concerned with the impact of different types of sexual portrayal on individuals, especially men, with no history of sex offending.

Sexual Reactions to Erotic Imagery

In Germany, Schmidt, Sigusch, and Meyberg (1969) found that orgasms, usually through masturbation, were more frequent among male students in the 24 hours following exposure to erotic slides, as compared with the day before the slides were shown. Intercourse, spontaneous erections, and petting also increased, but not significantly. There was also a tendency for the increase in sexual activity to apply more to radical than to conservative students. None of the students admitted to practising any new or perverse forms of sexual activity.

This study was repeated several times, with the addition of female participants and erotic films and stories. The results were similar each time (Schmidt et al., 1969; Schmidt & Sigusch, 1970). Fantasizing about scenes of erotica was reported more often by those who had been exposed to the pornographic material. The increase in sexual activity applied to both men and women, with women being more affected by erotic stories (Schmidt, Sigusch, & Schafer, 1973).

This form of experiment was also conducted in research carried out for the 1970 U.S. Pornography Commission. In one such experiment, male students were assessed for the week before and week after exposure to erotic slides. Although there was a large increase in masturbation on the day of viewing, reported sexual activity over the rest of the week was similar to that of the previous week (Amoroso, M. Brown, Pruesse, Ware, & Pilkey, 1971).

In another experiment, married couples were recruited to participate instead of college students. Obviously, they would have more opportunity to indulge in sexual activities. Byrne and Lamberth (1971) assessed the effects of erotica on married couples. The erotic stimuli comprised slides, short passages from erotic books, or erotic scenes that participants were asked to imagine for themselves. One week after this intervention, the couples were assessed for any changes in their usual pattern of sexual activity for that week. Very few reported any changes.

In yet another 1970 U.S. Commission experimental study, K. E. Davis and Braucht (1971b) showed male college students films portraying couples undressing each other, petting and then engaging in oral sex and coitus. Questionnaires were used to assess the thoughts and actions of the students during the 24 hours before and after the study. The main effect of exposure to this pornographic material was to produce an increase in daydreaming and talking about sex. There was also evidence of an increase in tension, desire for sex, masturbation, and thinking about the films to provide a source of added stimulation while engaging in sex.

Further evidence has emerged of the ability of pornography to increase sexual fantasies, although not necessarily to produce any changes in sexual behavior (Mosher, 1971). There were more relaxed attitudes towards premarital sex for the sexually experienced, and for male respondents, indications emerged of increased sexual tension, sometimes manifest behaviorally in aggression where satisfactory sexual outlets were unavailable for its release. Early evidence also emerged from this study that exposure to erotica could shift male attitudes towards women in a more cynical direction, with greater approval of the use of tactics or even force to get a girl to have sex.

Kutchinsky (1971b) also conducted an experimental study to investigate the effects on students of exposure to pornographic material that approached hard-core types. Films were presented that contained scenes of three-in-a-bed sex and lesbianism, or colored pornographic magazines and a 15-minute recording of pornographic literature by a poet. The participants in this study were mature graduate students, most of whom were married. After exposure to this material, sexual intercourse (rather than masturbation) increased in the 24 hours afterwards. This increase applied mainly to those participants who were most aroused when viewing the pornography, and was also more likely to occur if both partners watched the pornography together. The impact of pornography on sexual behavior was short-term only however. No longer term changes in sexual practices were reported.

One of the key limitations to all of this early experimental research was that participants were for the most part individuals with a prior history of exposure to the kind of pornography to which they were exposed in the experimental sessions. It therefore remained an open question as to just how people not familiar with such material would respond to it. Another factor is that in all these experimental studies, just one session of exposure to erotica was employed. What happens when participants are given repeated sessions of exposure to pornography?

In one study, participants had four sessions of watching erotic films, held once a week for a month. The films depicted heterosexual and homosexual sex scenes and group sex as well as more standard forms of sexual activity. Control participants saw either neutral films or no films at all during this period. The participants were all middle-class couples who had been married for at least 10 years. They made daily reports of their sexual activity for the month before, during, and after the film sessions.

On the night after the films, there was usually an increase in sexual activity, but it was only the couples' usual sexual habits that were activated. No evidence emerged of imitation of the sex scenes in these films. There was no evidence, either, of disinhibition effects as indicated by an increased tendency to engage in sex with partners other their spouses (although there is an issue about whether such practices would be admitted anyway). There was a tendency for the couples to become more open in talking about sex and to become more permissive in their attitudes towards pornography (Mann et al., 1971). A later analysis of the same data indicated a satiation effect with repeated exposure to the erotic films (Mann et al., 1974). The increase in sexual activity on the film-viewing nights tended to decline over the four sessions, although it remained higher than for other nights of the week.

One study investigated the effects of prolonged exposure to erotica. Male college students at an American state university were provided with a range of erotic materials for 90 minutes a day for 15 days (Howard et al., 1971; Reifler et al., 1971). They had access to erotic films, photographs, magazines and novels as well as to nonerotic materials. During the first session, the students spent nearly all the time looking at the erotic materials, but for subsequent sessions the amount of time spent looking at them gradually declined. Satiation was specific to the erotica and not to their sex life; the frequency of sexual intercourse and other activities remained stable over the course of the study. Satiation with pornography was evidenced in terms of reduced sexual arousal to pornographic films and also by an increasingly bored attitude towards all forms of pornography. Participants largely moved towards more permissive attitudes towards pornography and no longer saw it as an important social issue. Regular exposure to pornography did lead to an increased desire to be promiscuous in their own lives, but this wish was seldom translated into action.

Laws and Rubin (1969) established that four of seven men responded to an erotic film with erections. They then found that the men could produce an erection by relaxing and having sexual fantasies. They were also able to inhibit erections while watching the erotic film by thinking of other things. What this experiment showed was that fantasy may play as significant a role in men's responses to erotica as the erotic stimuli themselves. Thus, in examining the effects of sex scenes per se, it is necessary to control for the effect of sexual fantasising among viewers.

Laboratory Studies of Violent Media Sex and Sexual Arousal

It is not only the kinds of graphic depictions that appear in pornographic films and videos that have been studied. There are sexually explicit films and programs shown on television in which erotic portrayals are featured, some of which may also contain violence. Distinct patterns of results have emerged from studies conducted with nonoffenders, as compared with those observed for offenders. However, even with nonoffenders, there are certain types of erotic portrayal that may cause sexual arousal, even when a female is depicted as being raped (Malamuth, Heim, & Feshbach, 1980). What seems to be significant is whether a rape portrayal is depicted with the female victim eventually displaying sexual arousal. Male viewers find this kind of depiction especially pleasurable to watch.

Schmidt (1975) reported that both males and females rate themselves as feeling more aggressive after seeing films of sadomasochism and group rape than after seeing a film depicting romantic (nonaggressive) sex. In an important series of studies, Malamuth and his colleagues examined the way people respond to sexual violence and its association with rape-related attitudes and behaviors. These researchers showed that, for males, sexual responses to descriptions of sexual violence are associated with the propensity to rape, callous attitudes towards rape and victims of rape, and the simulation of sexually violent fantasies (Malamuth, 1981; Malamuth & Check, 1981a; Malamuth, Haber, & Feshbach, 1980).

Experiments conducted with nonoffenders found that rape depictions produced very little sexual arousal in male viewers when the victim was portrayed as being distressed. In contrast, scenes in which the rape victim became involuntarily aroused sexually produced sexual arousal among male viewers and were even slightly higher in the arousal they produced than scenes depicting mutually consenting sex (Malamuth & Check, 1980a, 1983). The reactions of the rape victim are not the only factor that may be at play here. Other features such as the extent to which scenes contain extreme, vicious violence with blood and gore can also make a difference to the level of audience sexual arousal (Quinsey & Chaplin, 1984; Quinsey, Chaplin, & Upfold, 1984).

IMPACT OF VIOLENT EROTICA
ON AGGRESSIVE BEHAVIOR

One oversight of the early research into the effects of erotica, particularly that work conducted for the 1970 U.S. Pornography Commission, was the link between sex and violence. This was surprising given work by therapists that had already shown the possibility that exposure to pornography was linked to the occurrence of sex crimes or other antisocial acts. Furthermore, the early German experiments had indicated that exposure to erotic stimuli could produce changes in mood in the direction of increased aggressiveness and decreased friendliness (Schmidt & Sigusch, 1970; Schmidt et al., 1973). Even studies conducted for the 1970 Commission revealed an increase in feeling angry for men relative to women after reading erotic stories (Byrne & Lamberth, 1971). Two other studies dealt specifically with the link between sexual arousal and aggression (Mosher & Katz, 1971; Tannenbaum, 1971).

Mosher and Katz (1971) found that the desire for sexual stimulation can override conscience and guilt by allowing verbal aggression to be expressed against a female. hey showed male students examples of aggressive and derogatory comments and accusations (e.g., 'You really are a dumb ___') and then asked them to be as verbally aggressive as possible against a female assistant. After being shown a film, the students were asked to repeat their attack against the female, being told that they had to achieve an increase in their level of aggression if they wanted to see an exciting sex film. Aggression did increase when made instrumental to seeing this sex film. A more interesting finding was that even males with a severe conscience and guilt about aggression increased the severity of their attack.

Tannenbaum (1971) also provided evidence that censorship of an erotic scene in a film can increase aggression. A romantic setting, involving ocean waves crashing onto rocks and dappled sunlight streaming through leaves, was artistically portrayed with two lovers engaged in sex play and intercourse complete with a symbolic representation of its aftermath. Male students were shown one of three versions: the original with or without the intercourse scene, or a 'scenario' version in which the intercourse was replaced by a written description of it. The students had earlier been angered by the experimenter's assistant and then were given a chance at revenge, by being asked to administer electric shocks to him as part of another study. A significantly higher level of shock was applied by those students who had seen the scenario version of the film. It appeared that their feelings of aggression had been intensified by the frustration of having their sexual appetite whetted and then having their attention drawn to the nature of the censored scene.

This evidence suggests that regular exposure to pornography will gradually lead to a decline in interest in it. This effect may be restricted, however, to certain categories of individual and may be less likely to occur among others. Studies of individuals who routinely consume erotica in their own lives indicate that boredom with pornography per se does not occur. Instead, if a porn consumer gets bored with one type of material, he switches to something different (Winick, 1971).

Laboratory Research

The research evidence for behavioral effects of violent erotica derives mostly from laboratory studies. Although such studies enable the testing of cause–effect relationships, they do so in artificial settings in which the nature of the viewing experience and the way aggressive behavior is enacted are different from everyday reality. In a typical experiment, the participant is placed in a position where he interacts with another person in the laboratory, who may be male or female, and who is also a confederate of the experimenter's. In one condition, the other person attempts to antagonise or annoy the participant, whereas in a control condition, he or she behaves in a personable and friendly manner. Later on in the experiment, the participant is given an opportunity to retaliate against this person, either by being critical of his or her performance on a task, or more usually by being given an opportunity to deliver electric shocks to that person every time he or she makes a mistake on a task. The number of shocks given and the strength of the shocks delivered are the measures of aggressiveness. Before the retaliatory phase, however, the experimental participant is invited to watch a film that, for some participants, contains a scene of a woman being raped, whereas for others it may depict nonsexual violence, nonviolent sex, or scenes containing neither sex nor violence.

Much of the research using this basic design has produced results that have been interpreted as showing effects of exposure to violent pornography on subsequent aggressiveness. Although one researcher reported that exposure to nonviolent, erotic stimuli (in the form of still pictures of young women in various states of undress or nudes taken from *Playboy* magazine) could serve as a distraction that could reduce angered males' inclination to respond aggressively (R. A. Baron, 1974b), most research using film or video pornography has indicated that aggression is stimulated by such material in a laboratory situation.

Male Laboratory Aggression on Males

The main distinguishing feature of laboratory experiments has been the manipulation of the sex of the attacker and target. Some studies have investigated the impact of erotic materials on male aggression against other males; others have studied effects on male aggression directed against a female target. The latter is probably more important to the present review. Nevertheless, it is probably worth noting that in experiments in which males are invited to attack other males, aggressive retaliation against a male target (who earlier annoyed the participant) can apparently be increased by exposure to violent or nonviolent sex scenes. Thus, in a situation in which a young male was annoyed by another male, the level of retaliatory aggression displayed by the former was aroused to an equal extent by watching either pure sex scenes or violent sex scenes. Aggression can be enhanced not just by hostile material, but also by unpleasant material. In this case, a scene that depicted violent behavior (a man being whipped by a female) and one that depicted nonviolent, but degrading sexual activity (bestial sex) both invoked arousal that led to subsequent aggression (Zillmann, Bryant, & Carveth, 1981).

Elsewhere, though, rape scenes were found to produce greater laboratory aggression among men on other men than scenes of sexual intercourse with no violence (Donnerstein, 1980). One explanation for varying behavioral reactions could be that they are affected by how much male viewers enjoy the film extracts they are shown. For example, some sex scenes were found to generate greater laboratory aggression among men on other men when those scenes were disliked. Other equally arousing but liked scenes did not have such an effect. Rape scenes depicting female sexual arousal can stimulate subsequent aggression against male targets in a laboratory, provided the male viewers under observation were previously angered. Less enjoyable depictions of female distress-causing rape, sadomasochism, and bondage did not promote aggressiveness against other males to anything like the same degree (Sapolsky & Zillmann, 1981; Zillmann, Bryant, Comisky, & Medoff, 1981). The importance of enjoyment in combination with excitement to postviewing behavioral effects is examined again later in the section that deals with psychological explanations of such effects.

Female Laboratory Aggression on Females

It is not exclusively men who have been found to feel or respond more aggressively after viewing material of a violent or deviant sexual nature. Schmidt (1975) reported that both males and females rated themselves as feeling more aggressive after seeing films of sadomasochism and group rape than after seeing a film of nonaggressive sex.

Female laboratory aggression on female targets has also been shown to be differentially sensitive to different types of sex scene. In the prototypical laboratory design, female participants displayed stronger retaliatory aggression against a female annoyer after they had watched a scene of explicit sexual intercourse and oral sex (hard core) than after watching a sex scene with nudity, but no genitalia showing (soft core). One explanation offered for this difference was the finding that female viewers regarded the hard core scene as more disturbing and displeasing (Saplosky & Zillmann, 1981).

Male Laboratory Aggression Against Females

Most laboratory research into the behavioral effects of violent sex scenes has investigated male aggression aimed at females. Initial findings showed that in the typical laboratory experiment of this kind, males appeared to be reluctant to display aggression against a female target. However, such restraint could be readily dissolved when repeated opportunities were presented for a male experimental participant to retaliate against a female who repeatedly antagonised him. Indeed, if the male participant was also shown a film sequence that depicted nonviolent sex, this could produce enhanced aggressiveness against the experimenter's female assistant (Donnerstein & Barrett, 1978; Donnerstein & Hallam, 1978). When, in subsequent experiments, male participants in this situation were shown film clips depicting rape scenes, their aggression against a female target became even more pronounced. Indeed, exposure to a sexually violent film clip with a female victim increased male viewers' own aggressive responding in a laboratory setting to a greater level against a female target than a male target (Donnerstein, 1980). A further study found that angered males' heightened aggression against a female target was in evidence whether the scenes of violent sexual behavior shown to them caused distress or sexual arousal in the female victim (Donnerstein & Berkowitz, 1981). The conclusion reached at this time was that violent pornography was a potent stimulator of male (nonsexual) aggression against females.

In another experimental study, male participants were paired with female confederates of the experimenter and exposed to a slide presentation featuring actors engaged in explicitly depicted precoital and coital heterosexual behaviors or nonsexual, neutral behaviors (control condition; Leonard & Taylor, 1983). Of equal importance, three different manipulations of the social situation were enacted by the female confederates during the presentation of the sexually explicit slides. In what was termed the *permissive cues* condition, the female made apparently spontaneous positive comments such as, 'That looks fun' and 'I'd like to try that.' In a *nonpermissive cues* condition, she made negative, disapproving comments such as 'This is disgusting' and 'Oh, that's awful.' In a *no cues* condition, the female made no comments. Following the exposure treatment, the participants were presented with a multiple-trial reaction-time task. On first trial, the participants chose a level of shock without knowledge of the confederate's intentions (i.e., no provocation). Then, in subsequent trials, the participants responded to inappropriately intense electrical shocks they received at the hands of the female confederates (i.e., provocation). For all trials, the shock intensity selected by the participant served as the measure of aggression.

Leonard and Taylor found that men in the *permissive cues* condition—where the female displayed sexual openness—had a significantly more aggressive response than their counterparts in the other two conditions. The researchers speculated that because of her sexually permissive and promiscuous behavior, participants formed callous perceptions of the female confederate that disinhibited aggressive responsiveness.

Aggressive Cues Perspective

Donnerstein observed that erotic films equated for arousal but varying in aggressive content led to differing levels of male–female aggression

(Donnerstein, 1980, 1983). The arousal capacity of the stimuli, while contributing to an enhancement of aggressive behavior, is not seen as a necessary component. Rather, an explanation of the differential effects is based on the proposal that an individual can assume aggressive cue value when he or she is associated with film-mediated violence (Berkowitz, 1984).

Specifically, when a male views a film depiction of rape and is then given an opportunity to aggress against a female annoyer, he inflicts more harm because of the female target's aggressive cue value—her association with the victim in the film. A nonaggressive erotic film, in contrast, lacks aggressive cues that would lower the male's inhibitions for inflicting harm against women and, therefore, male aggression against the female target is lower.

The aggressive cues perspective appears to account for heightened male aggression against a female target subsequent to exposure to pornography featuring violence against women, in particular the portrayal of rape. There is also evidence to suggest that *nonerotic* stimuli featuring aggression against a female can facilitate male–female aggression (Donnerstein, 1983).

In a further elaboration on this point, it emerged that young men who had not been angered by their female target, nevertheless responded in an aggressive manner towards her after they had been shown a rape scene in which the female victim became sexually aroused (Donnerstein & Berkowitz, 1981). When they witnessed a rape scene in which the victim appeared to suffer extreme distress throughout, this aggressive response was much more subdued. Thus, a pleasurable outcome in a rape scene may be especially likely to stimulate male viewers' subsequent aggressive tendencies towards females (Malamuth, Heim, & Feshbach, 1980).

A more recent attempt to replicate Malamuth and Donnerstein's (1982) results, using the same procedure and similar film materials, found that the extent to which a male participant will aggress against a female who has annoyed him, in a laboratory setting, depends on the options that are provided for the male response. In the early experiments, the male participants were permitted to respond only in an aggressive manner. In a more recent replication, the researchers gave their male participants opportunities either to respond in kind (i.e., aggressively) to the woman who had annoyed them, or to engage her in a nonaggressive way. When this other option was provided, few men chose the aggressive response option, even though they may have viewed violent sex scenes in the interim period (Fisher & Grenier, 1994).

INDIVIDUAL DIFFERENCES IN RESPONDING

Although differences in behavioral responding to violent and nonviolent erotic material have been observed to occur among males and females, are there other individual differences, perhaps linked to personality or attitudinal predispositions, that mediate such responding? Evidence was discussed in earlier chapters that changes in attitude towards women contingent upon exposure to film portrayals of rape can be mediated by pre-exposure attitudinal sets. The difficulty with demonstrating such varying behavioral effects, whether they are manipulated in a laboratory or field context, is that it may be ethically unsound to attempt to enhance an individual's antisocial behavioral dispositions. Researchers have therefore tended to use 'safer' simulations or substitute responses for overt behavior.

In a study conducted by Malamuth and Check (1983), a preliminary session was run in which male subjects were administered questionnaires concerning their sexual attitudes and behaviors. One item enquired about the likelihood that the subject himself would rape if he could be assured of not being caught and punished (i.e., the likelihood of raping or LR item). On the basis of this item, 62 participants were classified as low LR (a rating of 1—'not at all likely' on the 5-point scale) and a further 42 subjects were classified as high LR (a rating of 2 or higher).

Several days later, these subjects listened to one of eight audiotapes of an interaction involving sexual intercourse between a man and a woman. The content of these depictions was systematically manipulated along the dimensions of consent (woman's consent vs. nonconsent), pain (woman's pain vs. no pain), and outcome (woman's arousal vs. disgust). The findings indicated the importance of the interaction between individual differences among subjects and variations in the depicted content. On both self-report and tumescence measures, when the woman was portrayed as experiencing disgust, both low and high LR participants were less aroused sexually by the nonconsenting as compared with consenting depictions. However, when the woman was perceived as becoming sexually aroused, a very different pattern emerged. Low LR participants were equally aroused to the consenting and nonconsenting depictions, whereas high LR participants showed greater arousal to the nonconsenting scenes.

In a further analysis of individual differences, Malamuth and his colleagues in a later study asked subjects to indicate how sexually aroused they thought they would be by forcing a woman to do something against her will (Malamuth, Check, & Briere, 1986). They then analysed whether reported arousal from this measure was predictive of sexual arousal from rape and nonsexual aggression. In addition, they analysed whether differences in sexual arousal to force were associated with four general areas: (a) *ideological attitudes* concerning areas such as adversarial male–female relations, rape, and male dominance; (b) *aggressive attitudes* about interpersonal and international aggression; (c) *sexual responses* such as attitudes, inhibitions, experiences, and knowledge; and (d) *self-ratings* regarding whether the subject himself might engage in sexually aggressive acts and how attractive he found such acts, as well as his reactions to mutually consenting intercourse.

Results indicated that aggression may be a sexual stimulant for some individuals. Men's reported arousal from forcing a woman is predictive of their actual sexual arousal to media depictions of violent sex (as measured by self-reports and penile tumescence). For those who reported no arousal or moderate arousal for force (c70%), the presence of aggression inhibited sexual arousal. In contrast, for those who reported a relatively high level of arousal from force (c30%), aggression was indeed found to enhance sexual arousal, particularly when assessed via penile tumescence. Those who were more highly aroused by rape depictions were more accepting of an ideology that justifies male aggression against and dominance over women. In contrast, arousal from force did not relate to noncoercive sexual responses, including attitudes, inhibitions, or sexual experience and knowledge. The data were supportive of theoretical approaches, such as a feminist one (Brownmiller, 1975), that implicate cultural attitudes and roles as causes of aggression against women, but they are not supportive of theoretical approaches that implicate sexual causes.

NATURALISTIC STUDIES

One of the critical issues of debate about the largely laboratory-based studies that have been used to test the potential behavioral effects of media depictions of sex or sexual violence is that measurements take place under artificial conditions that fail to match real world viewing situations and social interactions. The impact of films featuring sexual and sexually violent themes on viewers' attitudes towards female sexuality, rape and coercive sexual relations has been investigated in a field setting. Malamuth and Check (1981b) randomly assigned male and female college students to watch films with sexual, sexually violent and nonsexual themes in a standard movie theatre with other members of the public. Classmates of the selected participants, who did not watch these films, were used as controls. Those male students who attended a movie with a sexually violent theme showed the most positive attitude towards the use of violence in a sexual context and greatest acceptance of rape myth. Female college students who watched this type of movie did not exhibit the same opinion profile. This study was restricted to changes in participants' perceptions, beliefs, and attitudes. Is there any evidence, from a nonlaboratory setting, that exposure to such media content can produce negative changes in behavior?

Of course, it would be ethically problematic, in a completely satisfactory way, to test the proposition that certain thought patterns contribute causally to the occurrence of rape or other forms of serious sexual aggression. To do so would require some experimental manipulation that would intentionally increase such thought patterns, particularly among those most likely to commit sexual aggression. To conduct such research for real would be potentially hazardous and ethically unsound. Nevertheless, a number of studies have attempted to cast light on possible links between exposure to sexual content in the media and real-world sexual aggression among nonoffending populations.

Ageton (1983) gauged the extent to which a variety of measures predicted levels of sexual aggression. In this study, 11- to 17-year-old participants were drawn from a representative national sample and were interviewed in several consecutive years in the late 1970s. The sexual aggression focus was added to a study primarily designed to focus on other issues, creating some limitations in the extent to which longitudinal predictions concerning sexual aggression could be properly assessed. However, the study's design allowed predictor measures (e.g., attitudes, involvement with peers, etc.) to be obtained before the occurrence of sexual aggression, which was assessed by self-reports. Analyses were conducted by identifying 'offenders' and comparing them to a variety of variables discriminated between the two groups, but in a discriminant analysis, it was found that involvement with delinquent peers at a young age was the best single predictor of sexual aggression in later life. Another predictor, those less significant than peer group experiences, was the attitude factor. Ageton did not specifically assess acceptance of sexual aggression or attitudes regarding violence against women. These attitudes are likely to be associated with sexually aggressive behavior rather than the type of attitudes assigned by Ageton (i.e., sex-role stereotyping, beliefs in rape myths, and attitudes about aggression in general).

Malamuth (1989) challenged the definition of sexual aggression used by Ageton to classify offenders versus nonoffenders. It included 'all forced sexual behavior involving contact with the sexual parts of the body' including rape, incest, sodomy, forced fondling, and attempted sexual coercion where the force component was as mild as verbal pressure or as severe as a physical beating or injury from a weapon. It may be inappropriate to group together such diverse acts.

In a cross-sectional study, Alder (1985) used a subsample from a larger representative sample of men from a county in Oregon to assess variables potentially predictive of sexual aggression. These included family background, social class, educational attainment, war experience, peer behavior, and personal attitudes towards sexual aggression. The findings suggested that the most important factor relating to sexual aggression was having sexually aggressive friends. The other two factors found likely to contribute to sexual aggression were attitudes legitimizing such aggression and military service in the Vietnam war.

Several studies using samples of college men also reported significant links between attitudes and actual sexual aggressiveness (Briere et al., 1984; Koss, Leonard, Beezley, & Oros, 1985; Mosher & Anderson, 1986; K.

K. Rapaport & Buckhart, 1984). These studies measured self-reported sexual aggression on a continuum of behaviors ranging from psychological pressure on women to rape. Similar results were reported by Kannin (1985), who compared the attitudes of 71 university students who admitted committing rape with a control group of nonaggressive college males. He found that a much higher percentage of rapists justified rape in general than did control participants. Moreover, he found that rapists were far more likely to believe their reputations would be enhanced among their peers by sexually aggressive behavior toward women, particularly those perceived as 'pick-ups,' 'loose,' 'teasers,' or 'economic exploiters.'

Using a sample of 155 men, Malamuth (1986) divided the variables that might contribute to sexual aggression into three classes : (a) motivation for sexual aggression included sexual arousal to aggression (measured by penile tumescence), hostility toward women, and dominance as a motive for sex; (b) disinhibition to commit sexual aggression included attitudes supporting aggression and antisocial personality characteristics, measured by Eysenck's psychoticism scale; and (c) opportunity to aggress sexually was assessed by sexual experience. These predictors were then correlated with self-reports of sexual aggression. All the predictors except psychoticism were significantly related to naturalistic aggression, with psychoticism showing a marginally significant relationship.

BENEFICIAL EFFECTS OF EROTICA

The discussion so far has centered on the hypothesis that exposure to explicit media sex, especially when it is combined with violence, has negative effects. To what extent, though, can the same kinds of materials be used to produce more positive and beneficial outcomes? Two categories of evidence have emerged on this question. In one case, sexual materials have been used as educational interventions to counteract the potentially harmful reactions that may follow from untutored viewing of explicit media sex. In the second case, erotic materials have been used in psychotherapeutic contexts as part of a course of clinical treatment of sexual dysfunction among otherwise normal (i.e., nonoffending) individuals.

Erotic Material as Education

There have been a number of active advocates of the use of educational programs to counteract the potentially harmful psychological side effects of watching pornography (Check & Malamuth, 1984; Linz, Malamuth, & Beckett, 1992; Malalmuth & Check, 1985). These programs can be effective, although not everyone who participates in them responds in the desired way.

Erotic Material as Therapy

Some experts have promoted the use of erotic video material in a psychotherapeutic context. Sex counselling clinics have made use of explicit sexual materials—including pictures, films, magazines, and books—to change individuals' or couples' sexual behavior, beliefs, and attitudes. The value of such material in an educational or therapeutic context has been disputed. According to some writers, it is not clear whether this use of pornography counts as education or miseducation (Cline, 1994). Certainly individuals who lead sexually promiscuous lives have reported finding that pornographic films provide a stimulus or model that has been linked, for example, with behavior such as men pushing their wives or girlfriends into partner swapping or lesbian sex scenarios (Bartell, 1971). It is understood, even in psychotherapeutic contexts, that the use of erotic materials needs care and skill. There is often no guarantee that exposure to sexually explicit materials will have positive benefits for those with whom they are used. There is a likelihood that the achieved effects will be the opposite of the ones desired.

Despite such caveats, there is a supportive body of professional opinion about using erotic materials in therapy. One survey of American and Czech/Slovak mental health professionals indicated that the use of soft-core and certain hard-core sexually explicit materials was favorably received in the context of sex therapy. Materials featuring violent sexual behavior or bizarre and degrading sexual depictions were roundly rejected for such application (Robinson, Scheltema, Koznar, & Mantheir, 1996).

Visual sexual stimulation (VSS) has been used for many years in the investigation of sexual dysfunction (Wagner, 1985; Yaffe, 1982). VSS is regarded by its users as a noninvasive and useful first line of analysis in relation to the diagnosis and treatment of erectile dysfunction. Although this general view about the therapeutic value of explicit sexual material has some support, there remain further questions about which types of material work best and the need to attain a balance between the effectiveness of the material and not causing embarrassment or offence to individuals being counselled (Buvat et al., 1990).

The effectiveness of erotic material in a therapeutic context depends in part on the continued ability of specific depictions of explicit sex to facilitate sexual arousal in individuals followed repeated exposures. Men have been found to show habituation to specific sexual stimuli more quickly with repeated exposure than do women (Laan & Everard, 1995). This means that sexual stimuli may lose their capacity to produce sexual arousal in men after they have been used with the same individuals a number of times. This habituation effect is likely to occur more readily to print stimuli than to film or video stimuli. The speed with which this reaction occurs, especially among men, also depends on the degree to which viewers become involved with the sexual stimulus. Greater involvement in an erotic depiction renders it more arousing (O'Donogue & Geer, 1985).

It has been observed in Britain, for example, that many pornographic films are available on video, but many have been imported or are 'homemade' and, as such, have not been subject to review by the British Board of Film Classification. Without classification, they are, in principle, not legally distributable to the general public, though they can be used in restricted clinical settings (Riley, 1992). There is a real concern, however, about the use of poor quality productions because they may be perceived by patients as confirmation that this form of therapy is itself a sleazy procedure (Wylie, 1996).

CONCLUSION

This chapter considered the effects of media sex on nonoffending populations. It was concerned primarily with the impact of explicit media sex of the kind that might be found in soft-core or hard-core pornography. Previous chapters had considered the effects of media sex on consumers' thoughts, perceptions, beliefs, and attitudes. Here, attention was shifted to behavioral effects. Two broad types of effect were examined: effects on sexual behavior and effects on aggressive behavior. One might expect to find a discussion of effects of media sex on sexual behavior, however, as much scholarly attention has been devoted to the question of how people respond to depictions of violent sexual behavior.

This chapter also distinguished between methodologies that have been applied to investigate these media sex issues. Researchers have used experimental manipulations and field surveys to explore the cause–effect relationships, if any, between explicit media sex and the subsequent behavior of those who consume it. With such a sensitive subject as this, researchers have often found themselves restricted in the approaches they can take by either ethical constraints or the willingness of people to participate in such studies. When exploring questions of personal sexual behavior, research often runs into problems linked to what people are prepared to divulge about their sex lives and how honestly they are likely to respond to probing questions about it. Sexual behavior is not something that can be readily studied within an experimental framework. Hence research on individuals' sexual reactions to erotic imagery is usually confined to surveys that yield self-report evidence. In contrast, studies of the impact of sexual violence have turned to the use of experiments in which exposure to media sex scenes and the subsequent behavioral responses of viewers can be tightly controlled. It would be ethically questionable to try to manipulate individuals to perform real aggression towards others in a naturalistic setting.

Exposure to erotic material does seem to be able to generate sexual thoughts and fantasies that, on the basis of self-report evidence, may in turn be linked to individuals' subsequent sexual activity. Some people use pornography as a sexual stimulant to spice up their own sex lives. There is no consistent evidence, however, that viewers imitate sex scenes witnessed in erotic films or that they necessarily increase the level of their own sexual activity as a result of exposure to such material. Pornography may be used to fuel fantasies and assist with achieving sexual arousal shortly before usual sexual activity.

Exposure to sexual violence in a laboratory setting has been found to increase aggressiveness in immediate postviewing situations in which aggressive responding towards another person is encouraged to take place. This enhanced aggressiveness has been found to occur among young adult males whether the target of their controlled aggression is male or female. Limited evidence has also emerged that even female viewers may be enticed into responding more aggressively towards another female in the laboratory after they have been shown explicit (nonviolent) sex scenes. Not everyone responds in this way, however, even in the laboratory. Personality characteristics and pre-existing attitudes towards rape and coercive sex can mediate aggressive responding following exposure to sexual violence in laboratory settings.

Going beyond the laboratory, ethical constraints have generally prevented or restricted the investigation of the impact of explicit sexual materials in natural settings. Self-report data and multivariate statistical analysis techniques have been used to assess the correlates of sexually aggressive orientations. Although these studies have identified a number of psychological and social background characteristics of individuals who exhibit sexually aggressive tendencies, they have produced less clear evidence on the role that media depictions of sex might play in the causation of such tendencies.

Finishing on a more positive note, explicit media sex can be used as an educational and therapeutic tool. Pornography has been used in interventions designed to draw attention to the distortions of female sexuality that frequently characterise such material. Explicit sex scenes from films and videos have also been used under controlled clinical conditions to treat individuals with sexual dysfunction. Although such material needs to be carefully chosen and used in combination with other clinical techniques by skilled therapists, it can prove to be successful in some cases.

9

Can Media Sex Sell Commodities?

The use of sexually attractive imagery in advertising has been widespread practice for many years. Sex has been used to sell many different products, but has traditionally been most often associated with clothing, cosmetics, toiletries, and certain foodstuffs (e.g., savory snacks, coffee, ice cream). Sexually attractive females have also been used to sell more expensive items such as cameras, cars, carpets, and furniture.

The use of sex in advertising is based on an assumption that sex can help to sell the advertised product by rendering a commercial message more attention-grabbing and memorable to consumers, by creating a more attractive brand image that people want to buy through association of the product with attractive models or actors, and by making the product itself more desirable because it linked to a certain sexual lifestyle. Sexual messages in advertising may be aimed at men or women. Traditionally, the sexual imagery in advertising is created through the use of alluring female models or actors. These models may be scantily clad or even nude and featured in suggestive poses.

The use of sex in advertising has a long history (Trachtenberg, 1986). Over time, the use of sex in magazine advertising has become much more widespread and graphic (Schorin & Vanden Bergh, 1985; Soley & Kurzbard, 1986; Sullivan & O'Connor, 1988). With television, however, indecency restrictions are more stringent, meaning that there is much less latitude for using sex to sell in televised advertising (Lin, 1997). One of the major concerns about the use of sex in advertising is the observation that advertisements routinely portray women as objects—most commonly as

194

sexual objects. Women are presented as decoration without personalities—often with sexual symbolism (Courtney & Whipple, 1983).

Psychological evidence on the importance of physical attractiveness in relation to communication effectiveness and attitude change would, in principle, support the potential commercial value of using sexy models to promote advertised products (Chaiken, 1979). Attractive people are usually rated as more desirable, respectable and influential than less attractive people (Berscheid & Walster, 1974; Debevec, Madden, & Kernan, 1986). A physically attractive communicator can also be more persuasive (Patzer, 1985).

Despite the evidence on the power of physical attractiveness, the impact of physically attractive models on consumer purchase behavior is not so clear cut (Joseph, 1982). Nudity and erotic content can increase consumer attention to an advertisement, but not necessarily enhance recall or positive attitudes toward a brand (Alexander & Judd, 1978). Other concerns stem from the presentation of women as sex objects.

Critics believe portraying females as sex objects and decoration strips them of identity and symbolises them as 'things' to be owned, desired, rejected and replaced rather than as people (Bem, 1993). Media convey this by presenting pieces, or parts, of female bodies (Kilbourne & Lazarus, 1987; Kilbourne & Wunderlich, 1979). Advertising features female body parts more than their faces (Archer, Iritani, Kimes, & Barrios, 1983). Male faces appear more often than bodies, and males appear twice as much as females (Sullivan & O'Connor, 1988; Hall & Crum, 1994). Sexy body shots are used for such products as undergarments, cologne, and clothing as well as cars and power tools (Kilbourne & Wunderlich, 1979).

The traditional woman-as-sex-object representation is accused by critics of reinforcing stereotypical male fantasies about women and promoting a wider ideology of masculine dominance in society (Dow, 1990; Gitlin, 1994). The conventional form of advertising in which young, slim, beautiful female models attribute their physical attractiveness to the product has been labelled as exploitative (Kilbourne, 1989). Such advertising is believed to encourage female consumers to model themselves on these media icons. Some susceptible consumers may go to extreme lengths to achieve an ideal look or shape (Downs & Harrison, 1985). The attractiveness stereotypes of advertising can make women feel less adequate about their own physical appearance (Kamins, 1990; Lafky, Duffy, & Berkowitz, 1996).

In considering the use of sex in advertising, there are three broad issues that need to be examined. The first consideration is the way sex is presented in advertising. How has the use of sex in media advertising evolved over the years? A second consideration is to investigate the impact that sex in advertising has on the impact of commercial messages upon consumers. There are many ways in which advertising impact can be measured. Ultimately, advertisers judge the performance of advertisements on the basis of impact on product sales and market share. However, before this type of impact can be felt, advertising campaigns have to make a mark, psychologically, among consumers. Consumers must pay attention to an advertisement, learn and remember its message, and develop a favorable impression about the product so that it becomes a desirable commodity that they would wish to purchase. Third, there is the question of what consumers think about the use of sex in advertising. Is sex in advertising regarded as acceptable or offensive? Are certain types of sexual image or depiction more acceptable than others? What differences of opinion exist among consumers and are such differences associated with specific consumer characteristics?

REPRESENTATION OF SEXUAL IMAGERY IN ADVERTISING

Research conducted between the 1950s and 1970s repeatedly found that television advertisements portrayed women as decorative, domestic, dependent on men, and primarily concerned with personal beauty (Caballero, Lumpkin, & Madden, 1989; Ferrante, Haynes, & Kingsley, 1988; Knill, Persch, Pursey, Gilpin, & Perloff, 1981; Lovdal, 1989). Women were more likely to appear as sex objects than were men (Rak & McMullen, 1987; Sullivan & O'Conner, 1988). These gender differences were found to persist into the 1990s, but the gap between the sexes had narrowed over time (Bretl & Cantor, 1988).

Three types of implicit sex appeals were found to occur on television: double entendre, sexual attractiveness, and nudity (Cohen, 1981; LaTour, Pitts, & Snook-Luther, 1991). As with sex in programs, sex in advertisements can be depicted in an overt fashion or appear in more subtle forms such as innuendo and other forms of talk. In consequence, some advertising can be classified as 'sexually oriented' in its appeals, whereas other commercial messages use 'sex' as a selling point. Although this book is concerned with sex and the audiovisual media, some reference is made here to studies of sex in printed media. One reason for doing this is that many trend studies tracking the presence of sex in advertising over the years focused on magazines. Another reason is that at least one such study investigated the use of sex in print advertising for television programs.

One content analysis of television commercials used a cross-cultural sample of Clio award-winning advertisements to determine the similarities and differences in the use of sex in American and international television advertisements. This investigation found that less than 7.7% of advertisements for the American market contained anything other than fully dressed models, and only 0.5% depicted partially clad models. Overall, nudity was more common in the advertisements aimed at international markets (Reid, Salmon, & Soley, 1984). The same authors conducted another study that showed that more than one in three (35%) print advertisements for television programs used sexual content (Reid & Soley, 1985). Between the mid-1960s and mid-1980s, a marked increase in the use of provocatively dressed models, male and female, in magazine advertising was found to occur (Soley & Reid, 1988). This trend was observed to continue for a further 10 years into the mid-1990s, with the percentage of advertisements containing a woman and man involved in sexually suggestive behavior more than doubling from one in five to more than one in two (Reichert, Lambiase, Morgan, Carstarphen, & Zavoina, 1999).

Comparing publications from 1964 and 1984, Soley and Kurzbard (1986) found an increase in and more overt use of sexually oriented appeals in advertising in a content analysis of visual and verbal sexual portrayals in magazine advertisements. Degree of nudity could be classified along a scale that indicated the presence of progressively less clothing, from demure, through suggestive, to partially revealing and finally, nude. These varying degrees of nudity generally applied to female models. *Suggestive dress* was represented by open shirts that exposed cleavage, tight-fitting clothing that accentuates the body, or mini skirts. *Partially clad* would include males with their shirts off or female models in their underwear or bathing suits. *Nudity* ranged from either the implication that the model was not wearing any clothing to displays of full-frontal nudity.

Soley and Kurzbard (1986) concluded that visual sexual portrayals increased, along with more frequent, explicit sexual appeals, nudity, and more implicit sexual acts. In addition, the amount of female–male contact depicted in the advertisements they studied tripled between 1964 and 1984, with females more likely to be sexually clad or nude, compared to males.

Advertisers increasingly rely on overt sexual messages, but research has not necessarily supported sex's success in all cases. Although highly suggestive poses and semidressed models are found to attract attention, consumers have evaluated advertisements with nudes as more offensive than other advertisements. This finding was more pronounced with females than males.

Despite the wider use of sex in print advertising, research on advertising on television has indicated that sex is not a common feature. Sex appeals remain an important element that advertisers can deploy, but they do not account for the great majority of broadcast advertisements. Lin (1998) reported that around 12% of advertisements from a sample of over 500 commercials recorded from one week of network American television contained less than fully dressed models (an increase of 5% on10 years earlier; Reid, Salmon, & Soley, 1984). In this analysis, advertisements were coded for three dimensions of sexually oriented conduct: physical innuendo (flirting, dressing, undressing, bathing or swimming); verbal innuendo (verbal expressions of sexual desire), and physical contact (hand-holding, fondling, embracing, kissing or implied sexual activity). One per cent of the advertisements contained verbal references to sex, 7% contained physical references, and 8% contained physical contact of a sexual nature. Despite the relative rarity of sexual content in network television advertising, the customary gender difference survived. Women remained more likely than men to be cast in sexually appealing roles.

Use of Bodies

Perceiving women as sex objects strips women of their individual identities. They are viewed as 'things,' objects of male sexual desire, or as part of the advertised merchandise rather than as people (Bem, 1993). This nonhuman image of women can be conveyed by reducing women to 'body parts' instead of a whole person (Kilbourne & Lazarus, 1987; Kilbourne & Wunderlich, 1979). For example, women's body parts are featured more than women's faces in print advertising (Archer, Iritani, Kimes, & Barrios, 1983; Dodd, Harcar, Foerch, & Anderson, 1989). Men's faces, on the other hand, appear more often than men's bodies in print advertising; men also appear twice as often as women (Sullivan & O'Connor, 1988).

A subtle message is conveyed to the audience through these differences in body and facial images. Intelligence and personality are communicated through pictures of faces, but only attractiveness is communicated through pictures of bodies (Dodd et al., 1989). The number of 'face-isms' (Archer, Kimes, & Barrios, 1978)—degree to which a camera shot focuses on the face versus the body—shows that women largely remain stereotyped as unintelligent, attractive bodies with no personality.

The type and number of female body shots in print advertising does not seem to differ with the type of product advertised. For example, sexy body shots are used for such products as undergarments, cologne/perfume, and clothing, as well as cars and power tools (Boddewyn & Kunz, 1991; Kilbourne & Wunderlich, 1979).

The use of provocative female models in commercials advertising boots or cigarettes or other products propagates the unintelligent/decorative image of women, but the use of these women in alcohol commercials adds an additional dimension to these ads. Tying these dehumanised female characters with stereotypical aggressive male images and alcohol may be a volatile combination. Combining beer and sexy female images may be dangerous considering the increasing alcoholism in society, the increasing connection between alcohol and domestic violence, and the promoting of male aggression (Lang & Sibrel, 1989; Miller, Downs, & Gondoli, 1989).

Male aggression is displayed during such sporting events as football, boxing, and wrestling. Marketing research has discovered a strong link between sports viewing and beer drinking; thus beer commercials air frequently during sports events ('Alcohol and Sports,' 1992; Postman, Nystrom, Strate, &

Weingartner, 1988). Research has also shown that sports viewing and violence are highly correlated (Horn, 1985).

Hall and Crum (1994) conducted research on women in TV advertisements to assess the way in which men's and women's bodies are used. They focused on pictures in ads and the appearance of bodies and body parts ('body-isms'), and of faces ('face-isms'). They addressed the issue of women as sex objects and decoration in TV ads as determined through observation of the number and type of body camera shots used in TV beer commercials.

Hall and Crum (1994) analysed a sample of 59 TV beer commercials covering 23 different brands of beer. They identified the number of male and female characters in these commercials and further analysed gender representation in terms of body-isms. In other words, to what extent were male and female characters shown in chest shots, buttock shots, leg shots, and crotch shots. Of 34 commercials containing at least one body camera shot, the average number of shots per ad of males was 1.15 and of females was 2.18. This was a statistically significant difference. Overall then, men appeared more often than women in these advertisements. However, female bodily exposure was greater. There was, for instance, a 49% chance that a commercial in this sample contained at least one camera shot focusing on the woman's chest, but for men it was only 24%.

AUDIENCE IMPACT

Analysis of the representation of sexual imagery in advertisements can reveal potential messages about sex, the sexuality of women and of men, and about sexual relations in society, but does not demonstrate that any such messages are apprehended by consumers who are then subsequently influenced by them either in relation to their disposition towards the advertised product or in terms of broader social beliefs and perceptions about sex and sexuality. In examining evidence for the impact of sex in advertising, therefore, research can be divided into those studies interested in measuring the direct or indirect effects of sex on the commercial impact of advertising and those that have investigated a wider social impact of sex in advertising.

The Commercial Impact of Sex

Sex in advertising is designed to draw consumers' attention to an advertisement. This is the first stage of advertising influence and is increasingly important in media markets that have become more crowded. Any single advertising message on television, for example, may have to compete for the attention of the audience with other advertisements in the same advertising break, with adjacent program content, and with advertisements that appear subsequently for competing products in ad-breaks elsewhere in the schedule.

Sexual content may also make an advertising message and the product being advertised more memorable. Not only are members of the audience more likely to pay attention to an advertisement featuring an attractive scantily clad model, they are also more likely to remember the advertisement subsequently. In addition, if the advertisement creates an association between a desired sexual lifestyle or the attainment of personal, sexual attractiveness and the advertised product, that product's image may be enhanced as a result. So what is the evidence for each of these kinds of impact following from the use of sex in advertising?

Sexual imagery in advertising may grab audience attention, improve memory for the commercial message, and affect consumer attitudes towards the product. However, these effects do not always occur together, nor do they necessarily occur in a consistent direction. Hence nudity in advertising might increase consumers' attention, but may be less effective than nonsexual illustrations in leading to brand recall (Baker, 1961). This result has been replicated. Courtney and Whipple (1983) found sexual imagery in advertisements, although attracting attention, led to lower levels of recall and appeal evaluations as well as poorer manufacturer and product perceptions.

With print media, such as magazines, advertising researchers have shown higher brand recall with nonsexual print illustrations as opposed to sexual ones (Alexander & Judd, 1978; Steadman, 1969). In this type of case, it has been argued that the presence of sexual material, in the form of female models depicted in various stages of undress, could have distracted readers' attention from the brand-related information in the advertisement (Steadman, 1969). However, greater exposure of the naked female form from head and bare shoulders to full frontal nudity did not produce progressively worse brand recall of magazine advertisements presented to experimental participants as slides (Alexander & Judd, 1978).

The use of sexual themes in advertisements could also have a potential impact on consumer attitudes towards the advertisement, the advertised product, or both. The evidence that has emerged on this issue so far, however, has been inconsistent. Smith and Engel (1968) found that sexual attractiveness in advertisements influenced emotional and objective evaluations of the product in a magazine advertisement for a car. This effect was observed to occur among both male and female participants. Baker and Churchill (1977) found that physically attractive models produced more favorable evaluations than did unattractive models for fabricated advertisements for hypothetical brands of coffee and perfume. Alexander and Judd (1978) found no effect of female nudity in advertisements on consumers' attitudes towards the advertisement.

Further evidence has indicated that, as the levels of nudity or sexiness rise, the intended communication effects either dissipate or turn unfavorable (LaTour et al., 1991). Consumers' opinions about advertisements with nude female models were linked to demographics, with male responses tending to be more favorable (LaTour et al., 1991). Using a physically attractive spokesperson is no guarantee of commercial success in the form of decision to purchase the advertised product (Caballero, Lumpkin, & Madden, 1989). Yet, in contrast, physically attractive celebrity endorsers did elicit better brand recall than unattractive celebrity endorsers (Kahle & Homer, 1983). This effect has been confirmed. Attractive celebrity endorsers can create a more positive attitude towards advertisements featuring a desired product (Kamins, 1990).

Elsewhere, Peterson and Kerin (1977) found experimental subjects did not rate print advertisements with varying degrees of nudity as favorably as they rated advertisements with partially clothed models. They found that a female model was more effective for a body oil product than a ratchet wrench set, and argued that audience members see the model's role as a more titillating function; thus, the degree of congruency between product and sexual image may be critical.

Although the research has thrown out some inconsistent findings (Joseph, 1982), these can be reconciled to some extent by considering more closely the different kinds of sexual appeal that have positive or negative results in terms of commercially relevant consumer responses. The use of nude models was found on a number of separate occasions to reduce the effectiveness of advertisements (Alexander & Judd, 1978; Smith & Engel, 1968; Steadman, 1969), but using physically attractive models can enhance certain aspects of an advertisement's communication effectiveness (Baker & Churchill, 1977).

Steadman (1969) suggested that when a logical relationship exists between a sexual image—for example, a sexy model—and a product, the sexual appeal may increase recall. Baker and Churchill (1977) offered support for this view in that perception theory would argue physically attractive models increase source credibility of a product, if congruent. More appropriate sexual appeals, where the consumer infers some congruency between sexual appeal and uses of the product, are more highly evaluated (Courtney & Whipple, 1983; Richmond & Hartman, 1982; Tinkham & Reid, 1988).

One type of sexual appeal in advertising depends primarily on the use of decorative models. They are nonfunctional in that they play no part in demonstrating the effectiveness of the product or how to use it, nor do they offer any explanation of the products special attributes or advantages over other competing products. Decorative models are merely an attractive stimulus designed to attract consumers' attention (Reid & Soley, 1983). In the case of decorative appeals, however, there is seldom any obvious, logical connection between such 'sexual' elements and the product itself. Even so, the

presence of an attractive female model has been found to influence consumers' reactions to the product in positive ways (Smith & Engel, 1968).
Advertisements with a sexy, female model present have been found to attract greater attention (Reid & Soley, 1981). Furthermore, this type of sexual appeal can enhance advertisement recognition, though this effect does
not generalise to enhanced brand recognition (Chestnut, La-Chance, &
Lubitz, 1977).

The overt use of sexual appeals has been found less successful than
nonsexual appeals with respect to recall (Severn, Belch, & Belch, 1990).
Although sexual advertisements were rated as more entertaining, more interesting, and more original than advertisements with no sexual content,
this positive evaluative response did not transfer over to better commercial
information processing. Consumers generated more thoughts associated
with the advertised product following exposure to advertisements without
sexual content. The presence of a sexually alluring model distracted attention from other informational ingredients on the commercial message. The
use of explicit sexual imagery in a magazine advertisement yielded a negative effect on copy-point recall (Severn et al., 1990). Researchers argue that
the use of sexual imagery 'interferes' with message comprehension, with
more product-related thinking occurring in response to the non-sexual
than the explicitly sexual appeal (Severn et al., 1990).

Although they used a cognitive listing procedure to measure their subjects' thought processes while evaluating an advertisement, Severn et al.
(1990) noted limitations to their study that showed sexual imagery less successful than nonsexual imagery on recall of an advertisement's copy. They
used 180 college students, who might have somewhat liberal views on sexuality in advertising, compared to other individuals their age or in the larger
population; they manipulated a single magazine advertisement to be high
and low in sexual imagery; the study took place in a college classroom, with
the magazine print ad stimulus projected on a slide screen, creating both an
artificial environment for consuming a magazine ad, as well as an artificial
print ad stimulus. Even so, this was one of the few studies to use a cognitive
listing procedure in this context, a higher order cognitive response measure
that is more sophisticated than mere recall or recognition.

Another factor that has been investigated in relation to the effectiveness
of sex in television advertisements is the presence or absence of sexual content in the surrounding program. There is ample evidence that program environment can affect recall of advertising (see Bryant & Comisky, 1978;
Furnham, Gunter, & Walsh, 1998; Kennedy, 1971; Norris & Colman, 1992,
1993; Schumann, 1986; Soldow & Principe, 1981). Bushman (1998) reported that placement of advertisements in a violent program environment
could impede recall of the commercial information as compared to a nonviolent program environment.

Bello, Pitts, and Etzel (1983) tested the impact of sexual and nonsexual versions of an advertisement for Calvin Klein clothing when placed within a sexual or nonsexual program environment. The sexual program sequence preceded the critical advertisement. The sexual version of the advertisement was found more interesting by male participants than the nonsexual version, but this factor made no difference to how much the advertised product was liked or likely to be purchased. Female observers found the sexual version of the advertisement more interesting and it also enhanced their intention to purchase the advertised product. Among male participants only, sexual content in the program preceding the advertisement had no effect on interest in the advertisement, but reduced product liking and intention to purchase, when the nonsexual advertisement was shown. With the sexual advertisement, the presence or absence of sex in the preceding program had no effect on its communication effectiveness.

These results are interesting in their demonstration not only of an effect on the commercial effectiveness of television advertising of sexual content within the advertising itself, but also of sexual material within the adjacent programming. The nonsexual version of the criterion advertisement was less effective on following sexual program content. One explanation offered for this effect is that the advertisement may have been perceived as an interruption when following the sexual scenes in the program. By disrupting a drive for closure, the processing of the advertisement may have been impaired (Kennedy, 1971). When the nonsexual version of the advertisement followed the nonsexual program, the advertisement may not have been perceived as disruptive and was processed without interference. Females and males were clearly influenced in different ways by the presence of sexual material. According to Bello et al. (1983), the female participants were angered by the sexy program more than by the nonsexual program. However, the degree to which this emotional reaction occurred was apparently not sufficient to interfere with the processing of the advertisement. This finding contrasted with results obtained by Axelrod (1963) and much later by Bushman (1998).

One summing up of the literature on the effectiveness of using sexual imagery in advertising concluded that the impact of sex in this context depends on the type of product advertised, the gender of the receiver and the kinds of measures used to determine commercial effectiveness (Belch, Belch, & Villareal, 1987).

The Social Impact of Sex in Advertising

Sex in advertising can have incidental effects on observers in addition to any commercial impact. The ways in which women or men are depicted in advertising can convey implicit messages about male and female sexuality.

Advertisements have the potential, then, to influence beliefs about sex, sexual relations, and the sexual mores of men and women. In addition to these influences directly related to sex, there are other subtle influences of advertising that depict physically attractive actors or models. One of the most significant areas of concern is that the focus that advertising places on a slim physique as attractive may influence the body self-esteem of certain consumer subgroups.

Idealised body images in advertising may contribute to lower levels of self-esteem, especially in relation to their own body shape, among some individuals. These effects most commonly occur among young women. Young men also make comparisons between themselves and male models seen in advertising. While the concern of young women emphasises the need to remain slim, for young men the body ideal emphasises the need to maintain a muscular upper torso, slim waist, and small buttocks (Pearson, 1992; Richins, 1991).

A number of experimental studies have indicated that exposure to advertisements containing images of alluring models with slim physiques can result in lowered body self-esteem and greater overestimation of own body size and weight, especially among young women (Heinberg & Thompson, 1992; Ogden & Mundray, 1996; Stice & Shaw, 1994). Although the effects of such images on female observers' body image perceptions have not always been confirmed, further evidence has emerged that exposure to pictures of attractive and slender female models does cause women to think more about their own weight (Champion & Furnham, 1999). A combination of advertising with slim, sexually attractive actors and programs with similar body role models can have an immediate impact on viewers estimations of their own body size whereby chest, waist, and hip measurements become overestimated compared with pre-exposure levels (Myers & Biocca, 1992). These effects were found to be even more pronounced among non-clinically diagnosed women who exhibited attitudes consistent with disordered eating orientations, and even more so among woman who have been clinically diagnosed as suffering from eating disorders such as anorexia nervosa and bulimia nervosa (Hamilton & Waller, 1993; Waller, Hamilton, & Shaw, 1992).

Noncommercial influences of sexual content in advertising can extend to the maintenance of certain gender stereotypes relating to occupational, professional, and even political aspirations. The presentation of women as sex objects in magazine ads resulted in men reporting less interest in politics subsequent to exposure. Women were not influenced by such portrayals in this way. However, women exhibited less interest in politics subsequent to exposure to ads depicting women in domestic or homemaker roles (Schwarz, Wagner, Bannert, & Mathes, 1987). The results were explained in terms of the cognitive accessibility of sex role concepts influenced by exposure to certain types of ad portrayal of men and women. Exposure to domestic female portrayals reminds women of this traditional role and suppresses thoughts conducive to political aspirations. It was argued that depictions of women as sex objects affected men's aspirations because such images reminded men of playboy lifestyles not conducive to a serious political career. In contrast, one would therefore expect to find that exposure to ads depicting women in career roles ought to have the opposite effect to exposure to domestic role portrayals, but this was not tested.

Rouner, Domenech-Rodriguez, and Slater (1998) investigated the impact of sexual content in beer TV ads on adolescents' cognitive responses to advertising. They used 72 ads in total—24 beer ads, 24 beer ads with sports content, and 24 non-beer ads. Although not clearly explained, it appears that respondents were invited to express their thoughts and feelings about each ad immediately after it was shown. The authors are not clear whether respondents saw every ad (72!). This would have been an overpowering workload. If they saw a subset of the ads, it is not explained how many or how these were selected, nor is it clear how much programming surrounded the ads.

According to the researchers, the findings indicated that there were many negative stereotypic images regarding females. Most of the advertisements were aimed at males. Beer advertisements were targeted at young and old people, but beer advertisements with sports content were targeted at younger people. Unfortunately, the research was discussed in insufficient detail to demonstrate these findings.

Adolescent respondents freely made comments about male images in advertising that were relatively neutral in gender-role presentations. Most comments about females tended to be critical with regard to gender roles and sexuality. Ward (1995) argued that prime-time TV contained common themes of sexuality in the shows adolescents view most. These societal constructed scripts from adults establish norms and expectations about how to be sexual, why to have sex, with whom to have it, and so on. Ward added that the youth who watch these shows are eager to consume this information, particularly if they do not get it from other, perhaps more realistic, trusting reliable sources.

CONSUMER OPINION ABOUT SEX IN ADVERTISEMENTS

Interest in the way the public reacts to sex in advertising stems from concerns about social policy and commercial effectiveness. Media regulations place restrictions on the treatments advertisers may use to promote their products. The principal concerns in this context are that consumers should not be mislead or offended. Even advertisers recognise that commercials that cause offence may be detrimental to the attractiveness of their products. In the context of advertising on television, although audiences can be quite open-minded about the use of treatments with sexual overtones, their judgements about what is or is not acceptable are tempered by the perceived appropriateness of the style of advertisement for the product in question, the time it is transmitted and the type of channel on which it is shown.

Research in the United States has shown that consumers have rated advertisements showing a member of the opposite sex higher than those showing a member of their own sex (Baker & Churchill, 1977). This research also showed attractiveness as an important attention-getting characteristic, but this failed to be related to cognitive acceptance of the ad's message. When some portion of a presentation has sexual overtones, only certain consumer segments object; others either fail to make the interpretation or do not find it offensive. For example, older women have been found to be more offended than younger women by overt sexual material in advertising, whereas younger women were more concerned about sexual inneundo, especially when it could also be considered sexist (Johnson & Satow, 1978).

American consumers have shown distaste for television advertisements for acceptable products, like jeans and pantyhose, that had too much sex orientation (Warwick, Walsh, & Miller, 1981). Males and females are likely to view sexually controversial advertisements as more entertaining and interesting (Severn et al., 1990).

A significant body of public opinion research was conducted in the United Kingdom during the 1980s that tracked general principles relating to what the public found acceptable in advertising on television. This work was concerned, in particular, with the public's acceptance not just of sexual treatments in advertising, but with the advertising of products that were associated directly or indirectly with sexual matters (Independent Broadcasting Authority [IBA], 1988; Wober, 1980). One of the key issues of controversy was the proposal by the beginning of the 1980s to introduce televised advertising of sanitary protection products. With the emergence of health scares during that decade linked to AIDS, attention focused also on the need to permit advertising on television for condoms as part of a wider campaign to promote safe sex (Shaw, 1999).

A national survey of UK viewers in 1980 laid down benchmark opinion data on sources of embarrassment to the public in television advertising. Despite concerns among regulators and critics writing in the national press that most people would find advertisements that featured sexual matters or promoted products for personal hygiene deeply offensive, a systematic analysis of public opinion indicated that it was only a minority of viewers who voiced real concerns. Only a modest proportion of UK television viewers (16%) admitted to having experienced embarrassment or upset by an advertisement. Among these individuals, the greatest sources of embarrassment were advertisements (mentioned by 41%) for feminine wear depicting nudity or scenes deemed to be 'sexy.' Three in ten of these individuals

(30%) also said they would find advertisements for sanitary protection products embarrassing (Wober, 1980). To put these results into further perspective, however, individuals who expressed concern about advertisements with sex or nudity in them comprised fewer than 7% of all viewers.

The same survey also asked respondents whether they found any advertisements on television annoying. Over one in four (28%) respondents expressed some annoyance at television advertising, but it was the treatment of women as sex symbols rather than sex per se that was mentioned as a source of such annoyance (by 3% of all viewers). This attribute was by no means the most often mentioned source of annoyance.

A later survey on public opinion towards advertising shifted the question focus from embarrassment and annoyance to offensiveness. A nationally representative UK sample of more than 1,100 UK television viewers were asked if they had ever been caused offence by television advertisements. They were further asked to distinguish between advertising on the main commercial television channel of that time (ITV) and advertising on the second commercial channel (Channel 4). Fewer than one in ten (8%) said that they had been offended by advertising on ITV, and half that number (4%) said the same of Channel 4 advertising. These individuals were then asked to say what it was that had caused them offence. The most nominated types of advertisement that caused offence were for sanitary protection products (ITV—2% of all viewers; Channel 4—1% of all viewers); AIDS (1% of all viewers); and contraceptives or condoms (less than 1%; IBA, 1988). Proportionately speaking, viewers aged 55 and over were much more likely than younger viewers to be offended by advertisements for sanitary protection products and contraceptive products.

A series of surveys conducted among British viewers in the 1980s tracked opinions about the acceptability of different types of advertising on television. The range of products and services upon which focus was placed in these polls included many connected with sexual behavior. In response to a question about whether these different forms of advertising should be allowed, the results are summarised in Table 9.1.

It can be seen that there was widespread support for advertisements for family planning clinics and pregnancy advice services at this time. A majority of British viewers were prepared to accept televised advertising for contraceptives, with support for this advertising showing marked growth from the mid- to late 1980s. There was much less acceptance of advertising for homosexual advice services and little acceptance of the proposal for advertising on television of homosexual magazines. It should be noted that none of these products or services were advertised on television in Britain when these surveys were undertaken (Gunter & Wober, 1990).

One of the reasons people objected to televised advertising for some of these products and services was because they believed that watching such

TABLE 9.1

Acceptance of Different Types of Advertising
on Television in Britain

	% Saying TV Advertising Should Be Allowed			
	1984	1986	1987	1988
	%	%	%	%
Deodorants	95	94	93	96
Underwear	87	85	85	90
Family planning clinics	78	80	81	82
Pregnancy advice services	77	80	81	80
Syringes for diabetics	63	65	65	60
Contraceptives[1]	56	67	70	78/70
Sanitary napkins/tampons	55	62	63	66
Undertakers/funeral services	41	42	40	46
Marriage/dating agencies[2]	–	–	–	44
Homosexual advice services	36	37	38	34
Homosexual magazines	13	11	13	9

Note. Source: Gunter and Wober, 1990. Reproduced with permission of authors.
[1]In 1988 two questions were asked, with a distinction made between 'condoms' and 'other contraceptives';
   the first % refers to 'condoms.'
[2]Question asked in 1988 only.

advertising would make them feel uncomfortable. With advertising for family planning clinics, pregnancy advice services, and marriage or dating agencies, around 10% to 15% of British viewers surveyed through the mid-1980s expressed this feeling, whereas for contraceptives advertising, 20% to 30% said they would find such advertisements uncomfortable to watch. Around one in two viewers said they would be made uncomfortable by advertising for homosexual advice services, and a majority (60% to 75% would experience the same feeling when faced by advertisements for homosexual magazines (see Gunter & Wober, 1990).

Research conducted in the 1990s in Britain turned its attention to some more specific aspects of television advertising including the appearance of nude or partially nude models and actors in commercials. This research was triggered by the appearance in early 1994 of an advertisement for *Neutralia* shower gel that became the first on British television to feature a woman's nipple. The campaign was accepted by the television broadcasters for transmission after 9 p.m. (the end of Family Viewing Time) and represented an experiment to assess whether such an advertisement would be acceptable to viewers. As it turned out, the advertisement generated the second highest number of complaints (199) from viewers to the commercial television regulator, the Independent Television Commission (ITC), for that year. In consequence, the ITC launched its own investigation. This comprised a nationwide attitude survey and focus group research. The survey measured public attitudes towards nudity in television advertising and the qualitative research explored reactions of smaller groups of people to specific advertisements containing varying degrees of female and male nudity. Because frontal nudity in British television advertising was nonexistent before the *Neutralia* commercial, the study used advertisements from overseas markets where such treatments were more accepted (ITC, 1995).

The research found that nudity was not uppermost in British viewers' minds when discussing television advertising, but that they nevertheless expressed some strong opinions when pressed on the subject. It was difficult and, to a large degree, meaningless to attempt to establish universal views because opinions varied with the personalities of viewers, the circumstances under which viewing occurred, and the nature of the production treatment featuring nudity in the advertising itself. The qualitative research, for instance, distinguished between individuals who were embarrassed about nudity ('Puritans'), those who felt it should not be allowed ('Moralists'), those who believed it would encourage people to be less prudish ('Crusadors'), and those who wanted to see as much nudity as possible ('Libertines').

The social circumstances of viewing were linked to the perceived acceptability of advertising with nudity, in part because, as observed earlier, viewers can be made to feel uncomfortable by certain kinds of advertising. Furthermore, their discomfort can be exacerbated by the company with whom they are watching. Hence, for viewers who did not adopt the extreme high moral ground that preferred an outright ban on all nudity, there were many who found nudity in advertising acceptable only within limits. Often this meant that such advertising should be restricted to late night viewing or those channels that are available on a subscription basis only. This would help to reduce the likelihood of embarrassment that would be caused by the unexpected appearance of such advertisements when watching in the company of children or much older people, or even, for some viewers, when viewing with members of the opposite sex (ITC, 1995).

The nature of the advertising itself and the production treatment given to the nudity were factors that mediated public perceptions of its acceptability. Nudity was regarded as more acceptable when it was relevant to the product. Thus, nudity in an advertisement for a bath product, for which the user would normally be unclothed when applying it, would be acceptable. Nudity in relation to advertising a car, however, would be less acceptable.

Nudity became more problematic when there was a sexual side to it. For many viewers, this was a dangerous combination. There were also strong feelings about which parts of the body should be exposed. The exposure of naked female breasts caused some concern, but side views were regarded as less problematic than full frontal exposure. The rear view of a male was also problematic for some viewers. Exposure of genitals was generally considered as unacceptable for either sex. Other factors, such as the duration of the nudity, how much of the advertisement it occupies, the degree of contact between nude people on screen, and the degree of movement also affected viewers' judgements. Excessive lingering of the camera on the naked body invoked some criticism, as did significant amounts of physical contact between nudes in the camera shot. Still images were less controversial than moving images. Table 9.2 summarises the types of advertisements featuring nudity that emerged as acceptable at any time, acceptable only late in the evening or not acceptable from this study (ITC, 1995).

TABLE 9.2

Types of TV Advertising in Which Nudity Is Acceptable

Acceptable Any Time

Cellnet (mobile phone, UK)
Nude man standing on globe throws net over UK. Frontal from a distance (crotch detail airbrushed out).

Isotoner (women's underwear, USA)
Woman clad in underwear moves in balletic/athletic manner. Product's supporting benefits explained.

Danepak (bacon, UK)
Family of naturists (young and old, bodies not perfect) having barbecue, who are clearly naked but all 'danger areas' cleverly hidden by props.

Pearl (soap, UK)
Brief pan of nude carved figurehead, including bare breasts; shots of naked woman showering using product.

Evian (mineral water, UK)
Pan across snowy mountain range morphs into side view of naked woman (breast concealed).

Brylcream (mini toiletries, UK)
Man showering (waist up), shaving (using product range). Puts on raincoat and goes out. Women gather, man arrives and drops raincoat (camera pans very quickly down front). Female heavy breathing starts on soundtrack. Becomes apparent that he is a model for women's art class.

Cleopatra (soap, French)

Epic production in which Cleopatra prepares to bathe, leading to a brief glimpse of topless Cleopatra bathing in asses' milk (view from side, using product on arm).

Acceptable After 9 p.m. Watershed

Davidoff Cool Water (aftershave, English language)

Shots of man clothed, then diving into sea. Close shots of swimming, not full-frontal. Shots of man, now fully dressed walking.

XS (perfume, UK)

Dark imagery, including pan up body of shadowed nude perspiring woman, in which light falls on her breast as the camera passes.

Vittel (mineral water, UK)

Nude couple entwined under stream of water. No full frontals.

Tahiti (threesome) (shower gel, French)

Woman and two men are trekking through tropical jungle. It rains, and all use product on (bared) chests. Fully dressed again, they all frolic in a waterfall.

Tahiti (group) (shower gel, French)

Young men, women, and children in tropical jungle village, waiting for rain. Starts to rain and many strip topless and use product.

Acceptable After Later Watershed

Neutralia (shower gel, UK)

Product's benefits described on voice-over followed by shots of topless girl pleasurably applying product. Girl, now clothed, caresses chest.

Fa (body spray, French)

Nude female on a beach applies product, runs along shore waving diaphanous veil. Involves repeated close-ups topless. Filmed in black and white.

Perrier Zest (lemon drink, French)

Girl in bikini by pool side pours drink over T-shirt, puts on T-shirt and takes bikini top off. Walks over to seated man and holds bottle to his lips.

Dim (men's underwear, French)

Nude man frolics and swims in sea, including almost full frontal. Close-up view of rear whilst towelling back. Puts on underwear and runs along shore (close up of crotch).

Unacceptable

Bio (yoghurt, Spanish)

Camera pans slowly in close-up from nude girl's face (eating yoghurt) to chest and around to bottom.

(table continues)

TABLE 9.2   *(continued)*

MR (coffee, English language)

Man arrives home, embraces woman, leading to love-making. Sex scenes intercut with shots of coffee percolating. Couple have postcoital cup of coffee. No full nudity. Strapline is 'real pleasure can't come in an 'instant."

Chilly (feminine douche, Italian)

Nude woman paddles and jumps up and down on sea-shore. Full-frontal nudity throughout.

Davidoff Relax (aftershave, English language)

Full rear and side topless views of man and woman both individually and embracing, caressing in and out of water. Black-and-white.

Old Nick (rum, French)

Nude girl giggling suggestively on beach, fondling rum bottle. She goes for a swim then returns to lie beside the rum bottle, involving close-up topless and full-frontal nudity from a distance.

Note. Source: ITC, 1995.

THE FUTURE OF SEX IN ADVERTISING

Increased use of sex in advertising across the 1970s and 1980s was explained in terms of a growth in sexual freedom and liberalism (Reichert et al., 1999; Soley & Kurzbard, 1986; Soley & Reid, 1988). In later years, a shift in the cultural value system associated with the onset of more conservative politics and growing concern about the spread of sexually transmitted diseases, especially AIDS, produced a transformation from a climate of sexual openness and freedom to one of sexual selectiveness, monogamy, and even celibacy (Hall, 1990; West, 1994). Where sexuality became linked to politically incorrect 'sexism,' pressures were applied to the advertising industry to clean up its act (Miller, 1992). Indeed, much as the sensitivities about political correctness, the inappropriate or excessive use of nude or semiclad models may have a counterproductive effect on advertising's effectiveness (Belch, Belch, & Villareal, 1987; Percy & Rossiter, 1992). Even though overt sexual portrayals can attract attention to advertisements (Alvaro, Reichert, & Ahern, 1997; Belch, Holgerson, Belch, & Koppman, 1981; Reid & Soley, 1981), sexual material can interfere with effective cognitive processing of brand information (Grazer & Keesling, 1995; Judd & Alexander, 1983; Severn, Belch, & Belch, 1990). Further evidence has indicated that overt sexual appeals may have negative effects on attitudes towards the advertisement and the brand (Simpson, Horton, & G. Brown, 1996) and purchase intention (LaTour & Henthorne, 1994).

Despite concerns about sexually transmitted disease, unwanted teenage pregnancies, and political correctness, sex continues to be a regular promotional feature in many advertising campaigns. Sex is used to attract consumer attention and promote a brand through its association with sexual satisfaction or certain lifestyles in which sex is a prominent element (Frazier, 1994).

CONCLUSION

Sex is frequently used as a selling device in advertising. Physically (and hence sexually) attractive female and male models and actors are used to endorse products. Women appear in sexually alluring roles with advertising more often than men, leading to accusations of sexual objectification of women by advertisers. Over the years, there has been an increasing trend in the use of sex to sell, although without any empirical justification for doing so. The accusation of sexual objectification of women in advertising has received some support from research showing that female body parts are used more frequently than male body parts in association with advertised brands. Hence, it is not the identity or personality of the model that is emphasised in relation to the brand, but simply the attractiveness of the body parts revealed.

There is evidence that sexual imagery can draw increased attention to advertising, may make the advertising message more memorable, and may even influence attitudes towards the product. These effects do not always occur together, however. Furthermore, they may not all change in a consistent direction. Thus, attention to an ad may be increased by the use of sexual imagery, but recall of the brand may not. Whether or not the use of sex has a positive impact on attitudes towards the brand can depend on how appropriate that selling tactic is perceived by consumers to be. Sex in the program adjacent to an advertising break may also affect ad recall. Sex in a program has been found to reduce product liking among some consumers, although this effect may be counteracted in some degree by the use of sex in the ad.

Apart from the commercial benefits of sex in advertising, there may be social side effects. One of these concerns the use of female actors and models with slender body shapes. Research has indicated that exposure to such imagery can adversely influence the body self-esteem of young female consumers, especially if they already suffer from low self-esteem.

Essentially, the use of sex in advertising is broadly accepted by the public, although within limits. It is important that sex is deemed as an appropriate technique given the nature of the product. The use of nudity in advertisements for bath products would be regarded as acceptable because people generally take a bath or shower without any clothes on. In contrast, the use of nudity to sell a car may be regarded with more suspicion. The acceptability of sex and nudity in advertising, however, is culturally linked with some countries being more accepting of it than others.

10

How Are Effects of Media Sex to Be Explained?

Psychologists who investigated the effects of media portrayals of sexual scenes from films, videos, television programs, and other media, with or without violence, have produced a number of explanations for the effects they have on viewers. Some theories attempt to explain immediate reactions, whereas others focus on longer term effects. As we saw in chapter 8, research has indicated relationships between exposure to sexual stimuli and aggression among males, aggression among females, and aggression perpetrated by males on females. Most of this evidence derived from studies carried out in controlled laboratory environments. Some research was conducted under more natural conditions and suggested that exposure to films that contain certain kinds of explicit sexual material can cause attitudinal shifts, but was unable to establish whether these led to behavioral effects.

An initial body of work that emerged during the 1970s found contrasting results. One group of studies found an aggression-enhancing effect for erotic media content (Jaffe, Malamuth, Feingold, & Feshbach, 1974; Meyer, 1972; Sapolsky, 1984; Zillmann, Hoyt, & Day, 1974). Another group established an aggression- or annoyance-reducing effect (Baron, 1974a, 1974b; R. A. Baron & Bell, 1977; Donnerstein, Donnerstein, & Evans, 1975; White, 1979; Zillmann & Sapolsky, 1977). In studies of interfemale aggression, both a facilitatory (Cantor, Zillmann, & Einsiedel, 1978; Jaffe et al., 1974; Sapolsky & Zillmann, 1981) and an inhibitory (R. A. Baron, 1979) effect for erotica were again observed. To try to explain these discrepant findings, it is important to consider various theoretical explanations for media effects that apply in this context and to examine the methodologies deployed by researchers to investigate the effects of media erotica. This chapter focuses on an analysis of theoretical perspectives and explanations, whereas chapter 11 turns attention towards methodological issues.

AROUSAL

Exposure to sex in the media can cause consumers to become aroused. Explicit sexual content especially, whether it occurs in print media or audiovisual media, can give rise to sexual arousal in readers and viewers. This arousal can be measured by verbal self-reports of individuals or by physiological measures such as penile tumescence (Eccles, Marshall, & Barbaree, 1988; Malamuth & Check, 1980a; Schaefer & Colgan, 1977), vaginal changes (Sintchak & Geer, 1975), and thermography (Abramson, Perry, Seeley, Seeley, & Rothblatt, 1981).

Sexual arousal to stimuli not naturally evoking such response may be learned through classical conditioning. In one conditioning exercise, researchers classically conditioned men to be sexually aroused by women's boots by pairing the boots with nude photographs, thus providing a model for how fetishes could be learned (Rachman, 1966; Rachman & Hodgson, 1968). The degree of arousal is not necessarily highly correlated with the degree of explicitness of the media content. Sometimes less explicit sexual content can be more arousing than more explicit content (Bancroft & Mathews, 1971).

The arousal hypothesis has been invoked in particular to explain audience reactions, mostly among male viewers, to violent sexual content. The interest here centres not simply on whether viewers become sexually aroused, but also whether they become aggressively aroused. According to the arousal hypothesis, the aggression-eliciting effect of a violent sex scene is a function of its ability to excite viewers (Zillmann, 1982). Once aroused in this way, if a person is then subsequesntly annoyed or angered, the arousal from the erotic material becomes compounded with their anger to enhance it still further. This reaction, in turn, increases the likelihood that that person will openly display anger in the form of aggression.

One explanation of discrepant findings might therefore be found in the choice of experimental stimuli. Whereas an increase in aggression occurred following exposure to highly arousing, explicit films, a decrease in aggression was found subsequent to viewing mildly arousing, less explicit still photographs. In light of evidence that motion pictures induce greater sexual arousal than still photographs (Adamson, Romano, Burdeck, Corman, &

Chebib, 1972; McConaghy, 1974; Sanford, 1974), it would seem that an explanation for the divergent findings resides in the differential arousal capacities of erotica.

According to the arousal perspective, the aggression-moderating effect of a communication is a function of its excitatory potential (Zillmann et al., 1974). Specifically, following exposure to highly arousing erotica, residues of excitation intensify feelings of anger and aggressive behavior. In contrast, after exposure to less arousing, mild erotica, minimal residues of excitation are available to intensify subsequent aggression. An important element in aggression facilitation is the emotional state of the aroused individual: An aggressive disposition is first established (through provocation) and then later reinstated. Aggression enhancement would not be expected (and, generally, has not been observe) for individuals not predisposed to behave in an aggressive fashion. More simply, the excitation transfer paradigm suggests that individuals would be expected to behave more aggressively when (a) they are angered, (b) they are then exposed to arousing erotica, and (c) residues of arousal are available to energize the motivated aggression when they are again confronted with an annoyer.

According to Zillmann (1978, 1979, 1982), exposure to erotica fosters increased sympathetic activity as an accompaniment to more specific genital responses and, after sexual stimulation, residues of the slowly dissipating nonspecific sympathetic excitation from sexual arousal are likely to intensify these experiences and to energize the hostile and aggressive actions incited by them.

On the other hand, researchers have suggested that the aggression-reducing effect of nonarousing but usually pleasant erotic fare results from incompatible affective stimulation (R. A. Baron, 1974a, 1977; Zillmann & Sapolsky, 1977). They have argued that the elicitation of hedonically opposite responses interferes with the maintenance of a particular state. The affective-arousal hypothesis is examined in more detail later.

EMOTIONAL INCOMPATIBILITY

This hypothesis offers an explanation for aggression-reducing effects of mild sex scenes (Bandura, 1973, 1986). Such scenes are usually experienced as pleasurable and create a positive mood among viewers that is usually incompatible with being angry (R. A. Baron, 1974b; Zillmann & Sapolsky, 1977). In the presence of a positive, sexy feeling, anger tends to dissipate.

Once an annoyed person is immersed in pleasant erotica, his anger dissipates, thus making it less likely that he will be driven to respond aggressively. In theory, the stronger the erotic stimulus, the greater should be the emotional incompatibility that is created. Unfortunately, this hypothesis fails to account adequately for research findings that have shown that aggression can be enhanced after exposure to nonviolent erotica (Zillmann et al., 1974).

AROUSAL-AFFECT MODEL

As a means of reconciling the apparent contradictory findings, a model has been proposed that integrates the arousal capacity and affect-eliciting qualities ascribed to erotica (Sapolsky & Zillmann, 1981; Zillmann, Bryant, Comisky, & Medoff, 1981). Specifically, the excitation-transfer paradigm has been modified through the recognition that affective response to an erotica stimulus may interfere with the aggression-facilitating effect of residual excitation. Likewise, the emotional incompatibility rationale (R. A. Baron, 1974b) has been modified through the consideration of affective responses to erotica emotionally *compatible* with annoyance and anger (e.g., disgust and disturbance). Taken together, the components of excitation and affective response are viewed as contributing *additively* to the level of motivated aggressive behavior.

According to this explanation, then, the amount of excitement caused by watching sex scenes needs to be added to how much such scenes are liked to determine how the viewer will subsequently behave. The enjoyment a viewer experiences while viewing a sex scene modifies the effect of any arousal that is also caused by it. A sex scene that is both highly arousing and found to be unpleasant can generate a higher level of aggression in a person who has already been annoyed. In contrast, a highly arousing sex scene that is found to be pleasant can have the opposite effect on an angry person, helping to dissipate their anger.

The arousal-affect model provides a number of predictions for the aggression-moderating effects of erotica based on a consideration of the combined impact of the stimulus' excitatory potential and its ability to create a positive or negative affective state:

1. Highly arousing erotica inducing negative affective reactions would lead to the higher level of aggression through the summation of the aggression-facilitating effects of residual excitation and of compatible unpleasant emotions.

2. Highly arousing erotica inducing positive reactions would facilitate aggression but to a level below that of Condition 1 due to the aggression-reducing effect of pleasant emotions counteracting the aggression-enhancing effect of high arousal.

3. Moderately arousing erotica inducing negative affective reactions would lead to an increment in aggression below that of Condition 1 due

to a reduced level of residual excitation combining with compatible unpleasant emotions.

4. Moderately arousing erotica inducing positive affective reactions would maintain the level of aggression (relative to a control condition) due to the aggression-reducing effect of pleasant emotions cancelling out the aggression-enhancing effect of moderate arousal.

5. Nonarousing erotica inducing negative affective reactions would create an increment in aggression solely on the basis of the aggression-enhancing effect of negative emotions.

6. Nonarousing erotica inducing positive affective reactions would, in the absence of residues of excitation, lead to a reduction in aggression due to the incompatibility of pleasant emotion with anger and aggression.

Evidence supporting the arousal-affect model can be found in a study by Zillmann and Sapolsky (1977). Direct measures of excitation and affective response were obtained. Mildly erotic stimuli (pictures of nudes) and highly erotic stimuli (pictures of intercourse, fellatio, and cunnilingus) were found to be no more arousing than nonerotica, and the erotica were judged to be equally pleasing and nondisturbing. The erotic stimuli thus possessed qualities that, according to the two-component model, would lead to a lowering of aggressive inclinations. Exposure to the mildly and highly erotic stimuli reduced males' expression of annoyance. The erotica did not, however, affect retaliatory behavior, suggesting a lack of strength of the behavior-modifying impact of exposure to mild erotica.

Elsewhere, studies found a reduction in retaliatory behavior after exposure to mild erotica (R. A. Baron, 1974a, 1974b; R. A. Baron & Bell, 1977; Donnerstein et al., 1975). One exception to this pattern is worth noting, however. Following exposure to pictures of sexual acts (intercourse and oral sex), Donnerstein et al. (1975) did not observe a reduction in aggressive behavior. This discrepancy may have resulted from Donnerstein using stimuli that evoked a less positive affective state.

Sapolsky and Zillmann (1981) exposed males to erotic motion pictures that ranged from suggestive to explicitly sexual (nudity, precoitus, R-coitus [without genitalia showing], and X-coitus [explicit intercourse and oral sex]). The precoitus and coitus films were found to be arousing. Males reported positive affective reactions to the nudity and coitus films but not to the film depicting precoital behavior. Nonarousing erotica eliciting positive affective response (nudity) did not reduce retaliatory behavior, nor did arousing erotica associated with positive affective response (R- and X-coitus) facilitate such behavior. Rather, the retaliatory actions of provoked males were enhanced by arousing and disturbing erotica: a film of precoital behavior. Although the latter finding is projected by the arousal-affect

model, the level of retaliatory behavior subsequent to exposure to the remaining erotic films fails to conform to expectations. One explanation for
the coitus films' failure to produce an increase in hostile behavior may derive from the males' habituation to strong erotica.

Zillman, Bryant, Comisky, and Medoff (1981) also demonstrated an aggression-enhancing effect for arousing, negatively valenced stimuli. This
facility effect was in evidence regardless of whether the stimulus was erotic
or nonerotic: nonarousing and pleasing erotica (such as photographs of attractive nude females in sexually enticing poses), nonarousing and displeasing erotica (such as photographs of masturbating, highly pregnant women,
and unattractive women smeared with menstrual blood), arousing and pleasing erotica (such as films depicting fellatio, cunnilingus, and coition), or
arousing and displeasing erotica (such as films depicting women fellating and
masturbating animals, heterosexual flagellation, and the painful deformation
of genitals in sadomasochistic activities). The arousal and unpleasant aspects
of these stimuli had an additive effect on aggressiveness of viewers, assuming
they had been aroused to behave aggressively in the first place.

Pleasing and nonarousing stimuli reduced aggression because of the affective incompatibility between pleasantness and aggressiveness. Displeasing, nonarousing erotica increased aggressiveness because of the
displeasing affective quality of the stimulus. Displeasing and arousing erotica increased aggressiveness because of the negative affective tone of the
material and its excitatory capacity, which further motivates aggression.
With pleasing and arousing erotica, the net effect on aggression depends on
whether the arousing nature or pleasing nature of the material is dominant.

Zillmann et al. (1981) did not find an increase in males' retaliatory behavior following exposure to arousing erotica eliciting positive affective reactions, nor following nonarousing, negatively valenced erotica. Also,
contrary to expectations, nonarousing pleasing erotica were not shown to
reduce the level of retaliatory behavior. The erotic stimuli were chosen to be
not very pleasing, so as to match the nonerotic stimuli.

The studies by Sapolsky and Zillman (1981) and by Zillmann et al.
(1981) are consistent in finding (a) an increase in aggression after exposure
to arousing-negative erotica but not after arousing-positive erotica (coital
behavior), and (b) no decrease in aggression following the viewing of
nonarousing-positive stimuli (nudity).

One study is particularly relevant to the issue of affective response. A film
of rape with the raped female becoming sexually aroused by her attacker led
to a greater level of retaliatory behavior by nonangered males towards a female target in a laboratory setting than did a film of rape culminating in the
victim's extreme distress (Donnerstein & Berkowitz, 1981). The rape versions were found to be equally arousing, but no measure of affective response
were obtained. It is presumed that observing a rape victim's suffering elicits an

adverse emotional response among viewers, whereas witnessing her experiencing sexual arousal invokes a pleasurable response in viewers. Other research corroborated this point. The depiction of rape with a pleasurable outcome was observed to foster more positive emotions among the audience than a rape portrayal that concluded with the victim experiencing disgust (Malamuth, Heim, & Feshbach, 1980). In line with the arousal-affect model, the greater negative affect associated with the suffering outcome should prompt more aggressive behavior from male viewers.

An additional explanation for the differential effects of exposure to erotica on aggressive behavior is that of *cognitive labelling* (R. A. Baron, 1979; White, 1979). According to this notion, the label applied to experienced arousal is derived from the affective reaction to a specific stimulus. The cognitive labelling process, in turn, determines whether the source of arousal will foster or impede aggression. If the affective response is positive, arousal will be labelled in a positive manner, leading to a decrement in later aggression. If the affective response is negative, arousal will more likely be labelled as anger, and the resulting aggressive behavior will be intensified.

CATHARSIS

The catharsis hypothesis posits that emotional arousal can be purged through vicarious experiences. This hypothesis has been discussed most usually in relation to aggression. A strong form of the hypothesis has been discussed most usually in relation to aggression. A strong form of the hypothesis has argued that individuals can release their aggressive impulses by observing mediated aggression. If true, this means that angered viewers watching a violent movie can obtain harmless release of their aggressive urges through vicarious involvement with the action on screen.

Experimental tests for cathartic reactions among viewers in the context of aggression discharge provided only equivocal evidence for type of reasons. Laboratory and field experiments conducted by Feshbach and his colleagues yielded findings that were interpreted as providing evidence for aggression catharsis (Feshbach, 1955, 1961; Feshback & Singer, 1971), but these results have not been universally accepted, and attempts at replication have failed to support the catharsis hypothesis (Wells, 1973).

A weaker form of the hypothesis has suggested that this vicarious release of hostile urges is not possible for everyone, and that certain personality types may be better equipped to achieve this effect than others (Gunter, 1980). Hence, catharsis became regarded as a form of skill or competence. In particular, it was believed to be associated with an individual's imaginative capacity (Biblow, 1973; Copeland & Slater, 1985). This capacity may be manifest as skills in creativity, daydreaming, or fantasy play behavior. Although the necessary cognitive apparatus for these processes is available in all human beings, it may not be equally developed throughout all groups of individuals (Singer, 1966). The practised daydreamer can turn to fantasy activity to work out or resolve anger-arousing problem situations, whereas the inexperienced daydreamer is more limited to the direct behavioral expression of his or her urges. High fantasizers have been observed to show greater control over their emotions and behaviors, which is, in turn, reflected in lower levels of overt activity in general than in low fantasizers (Singer, 1961; Singer, Wilensky, & McGraven, 1956). Individuals with highly developed imaginations tend to exhibit less overt behavioral aggression than individuals with lower imaginative competencies (Pytkowicz, Wagner, & Sarason, 1967; Townsend, 1968).

These mental faculties are not equally well developed in all individuals. A person who is skilled at using his or her imagination, for instance, may also be better at entering into the drama of an exciting media sequence, better at identifying with the characters, and more likely, therefore, to become vicariously involved with the action. Indeed, highly skilled fantasizers are adept at utilising a fantasy experience to help in changing any negative mood states they might be feeling to more positive moods (Biblow, 1973).

The notion of catharsis has been considered in relation to audiences' responses to sexual media stimuli. In this context, the catharsis notion argues that consuming media sex can relieve sexual urges. Magazine or video content, for instance, can serve (in conjunction with masturbation) as an imperfect substitute for real sexual intercourse. The catharsis argument has been used to support the lessening of restrictions on availability of sexually explicit material in countries such as Denmark (Kutchinsky, 1973, 1985).

DISINHIBITION

This hypothesis derives from behavioral research into media violence effects. It also applies to the more specific form of violence in a sexual context. According to the disinhibition hypothesis, viewing violence on screen inhibits ingrained social constraints against behaving violently. Attractive exemplars of the use of violence on screen serve to justify the use of violence by members of the audience. In the short term, at least, witnessing the use of violence justified by a film character may legitimise its use in real life as well for some viewers.

In the present context, the possibility that disinhibition effects occur following exposure to erotic media content, especially when accompanied by violence, derives from evidence that repeated viewing of films that depict scenes of women being raped can change men's verbally reported, behavioral intentions towards performing similar acts themselves (Malamuth &

Check, 1981a; Malamuth, Haber, & Feshbach, 1980; Check, 1984). Watching a scene in which a woman is raped and appears to become sexually aroused and experiences pleasure may reduce male inhibitions against committing such behavior themselves (Check, 1984; Malamuth, Haber, & Feshbach, 1980).

AGGRESSIVE CUE MODEL

With this model, aspects of the sex scene, most especially the types of actors involved, are regarded as being as significant as its capacity to excite the audience in influencing the way viewers behave afterwards. The arousal capacity of the stimuli, while contributing to an enhancement of aggressive behavior, is not seen as a necessary component. Rather, an explanation of the differential effects is based on the proposal that an individual can assume aggressive cue value when he or she is associated with film-mediated violence (Berkowitz, 1984).

In a situation in which an individual has been angered by another person, his or her subsequent retaliatory aggression against that person may be enhanced by watching a film clip in which an actor who resembles that person in critical respects is depicted as a victim of violence. For example, when a man views a film depiction of rape and is then given an opportunity to aggress against a woman who had earlier annoyed him, he may inflict more harm because of the female target's aggressive cue value—her association with the victim in the film. In contrast, if the laboratory target is another man, the aggression may be less pronounced because no immediate connection would be made between the film violence and the laboratory situation (Donnerstein, 1980, 1983). A nonviolent erotic film, in contrast, lacks aggressive cues that would lower the male's inhibitions for inflicting harm against women and, therefore, male aggression against the female target is lower.

The aggressive cue perspective appears to account for heightened male exposure to pornography featuring violence against women, in particular the portrayal of rape. There is also evidence to suggest that nonerotic stimuli featuring aggression against a female can facilitate male-on-female aggression (Donnerstein, 1983). The presence of aggressive cues and the sex of the target of aggression are central factors in this interacting rationale. Arousal is also important in this context in that it can facilitate the retaliatory response and is therefore seen as interacting with the content of an erotic communication.

DESENSITISATION

According to this explanation of media effects, repeated exposure to certain types of media content results in the audience becoming habituated to it.

Any strong emotional or behavioral reactions that it may have caused initially become gradually weakened with repeated exposure.

Does repeated exposure to sexually violent media content change people's arousal by such stimuli? One study looked at this question. Ceniti and Malamuth (1984) classified 69 adult males into force-oriented, non-force-oriented, and unclassifiable categories based on their penile tumescence when presented with portrayals of rape and consensual sex during a pre-exposure session. Those classified as force-oriented had shown relatively high levels of sexual arousal to rape depictions. Those classified as non-force-oriented had shown relatively little arousal to rape depictions, but they had become aroused to consensual sex portrayals. Experimental participants labelled as unclassifiable had shown little arousal to either type of portrayal.

Following this classification, participants were randomly assigned to one of three exposure groups: sexually violent, sexually nonviolent, or control. Those assigned to the sexually violent condition were exposed to 10 sexually violent stimuli (including feature-length films, and written and pictorial depictions) over a period of 4 weeks. Participants in the sexually nonviolent condition were exposed to 10 presentations of sexually nonviolent activities only. Participants in the control condition were not exposed to any stimuli. Soon after their exposure, participants returned to the laboratory and were presented with depictions similar to the pre-exposure session. Penile tumescence and self-reported sexual arousal were measured again.

Force-oriented participants, whether exposed to sexually violent or nonviolent media, became *less* aroused to the rape depictions in the postexposure session than those in the control condition. They also tended to be less aroused by the postexposure nonviolent depictions, although this effect was considerably less pronounced. Both non-force-oriented and unclassifiable participants, however, showed no significant effects of exposure. The reduced arousal of force-oriented participants appears similar to the temporary habituation effects frequently found in studies using nonviolent sexual material (Mann, Berkowitz, Sidman, Starr, & West, 1974; Zillmann & Bryant, 1984).

Mann, Sidman, and Starr (1971; also Mann, Berkowitz, et al., 1974) exposed married couples in four consecutive weekly sessions to sexually explicit films or, in a control condition, to nonerotic films. During the treatment period, participants recorded their sexual activities in diaries. Attitudes about pornography were assessed initially and after treatment. Exposure to erotica was found to stimulate sexual behavior only shortly. Sexual activities were more frequent on exposure days than on the days thereafter. More important to this discussion was the finding that the transitory, sex-stimulating effect grew weaker over the weeks and became negligible in the fourth week.

Mann et al. (1971) emphasised that the stimulating effect was rather nonspecific, manifesting itself in a variety of sexual activities with which the couples were familiar. The couples did not readily adopt depicted sexual practices that were not already a part of their behavioral repertoire. Many dormant practices were revived, however. This finding, together with the fact that all couples were married for at least 10 years, would seem to suggest that exposure to erotica failed to exhibit sexual novelties for the participants of this particular investigation and that the lack of specific emulation might not generalise to more sexually naïve persons. The sexual maturity of the participants might also explain the finding of no appreciable attitudinal change.

An investigation conducted by Howard, Reifler, and Liptzin (1971; see also Reifler, Howard, Lipton, Liptzin, & Widmann, 1971) addressed the dissipation of sexual arousal more directly. On 15 days distributed over a 3-week period, male college students were given access to pornographic films, photographs, and readings or were not given such access in a control condition. The experimental participants were free to choose from among these materials and from among nonerotic ones in the first 10 sessions. In the following three sessions, the original pornographic materials were replaced by new ones, and in the last two sessions, the nonerotic materials were removed. Each session lasted 90 minutes, and during this time the participants recorded their activities in regular intervals. Both experimental and control participants were shown an explicitly erotic film. Numerous measures of sexual arousal were taken during and after exposure to these films, and a battery of self-perception and attitudinal measures was recorded following exposure.

The findings showed that the young men initially had a strong interest in erotic films. This interest, however, faded rapidly with repeated exposure. Erotic photographs and readings received continued attention, but such attention was at comparatively low levels. After unrestricted exposure to pornography, even the introduction of novel materials failed to revive initial levels of interest. In fact, such unrestricted exposure to pornography led participants to appraise their reaction to explicit erotica as boredom. Analysis of physiological data confirmed these results. There was decreased interest and increased boredom in erotic materials over time. Compared with responses to the pre-treatment film, exposure to an explicitly sexual film immediately after the conclusion of the longitudinal treatment produced diminished reactions of sexual excitedness.

The findings by Howard et al. (1971) and Reifler et al. (1971) are highly suggestive of habituation of sexual and autonomic arousal to erotica as the result of massive and continued exposure. However, because in their investigation the longitudinal treatment was both an independent and a dependent variable (i.e., exposure was both a measured effect and a potential cause for later effects), amount of exposure varied across individuals and was by no means massive throughout.

Zillmann and Bryant (1984) presented a study to examine habituation to erotica. It also examined the extent to which habituation to erotica generalises to less explicit depictions of sexual behavior and to portrayals of less common forms of sexual practices to which respondents are relatively unaccustomed. They assigned 80 male and 80 female students to four experimental groups. Three of the groups participated in weekly sessions over about 9 weeks. The remaining group was a no-treatment control. Participants in experimental groups met in six consecutive weekly sessions. They watched six films of about 8 minutes duration and evaluated aesthetic aspects of each movie. In the massive exposure condition, participants saw six explicitly sexual films per session. Over the 6-week period, they saw 36 erotic films. In the intermediate exposure condition, participants saw three erotic films and three nonerotic films. They saw a total of 18 erotic films in all. In the no-exposure condition, all 36 films were nonerotic.

Participants in all three treatment groups returned to the laboratory one week after their final session. At that time, all participants were exposed to three films in the following order: (a) a sexually suggestive film depicting heterosexual petting and precoital behavior; (b) a sexually explicit film depicting fellatio, cunnilingus, and heterosexual intercourse; and (c) a film depicting both bestiality and sadomasochistic activities (such as a woman fellating and having intercourse with a dog and a man being whipped by a woman during cunnilingus). All films were of 8 minutes duration. Participants reported their emotional reactions immediately after exposure to each film.

The participants returned to the laboratory 2 weeks after their final session of prior exposure treatment. All participants were provoked by a same gender confederate, exposed or not exposed to erotica, and then provided with an opportunity to retaliate against their annoyer. The confederate treatment participants rudely and seemingly deliberately caused them pain when, in violation of instructions, he or she overinflated a blood pressure cuff and did not deflate it properly. Participants were later given the opportunity to retaliate in the same way.

During the third week following the completion of the initial exposure treatment, participants who had received one of three treatments and the participants who had not received any prior treatment participated in a final session. They first estimated, as a percentage, the portion of American adults performing particular sex acts, common ones as well as uncommon ones. Among other things they estimated the portion of sexually active adults, of adults employing oral-genital stimulation techniques, and of adults practicing anal intercourse, group sex, sadomasochism, and bestiality.

The participants were then introduced to a rape case simulation. They read the newspaper coverage of a hitchhiking that resulted in the sexual offence. The rapist's jury conviction was reported, but a sentence was not stated. Participants were asked to recommended a prison term for the particular offence. The length of the term was considered to indicate disapproval or condemnation of rape. Sexual callousness towards women was expected to find expression in minimal prison sentences.

Physiological measures revealed signs of habituation to erotica over the duration of the study in the massive and intermediate exposure conditions. There was no indication, however, that generalisation occurred from one type of sexual content to another. Massive exposure to erotica produced diminished affective reactions to it over time. Moderate exposure had a similar effect. The effects of massive exposure to explicit erotica on repulsion and enjoyment were still in evidence 2 weeks after the termination of the initial treatment. Indeed, both massively and moderately exposed participants reported being less offended by pornography, and even considered pornography less pornographic, up to 3 weeks after the end of the treatment.

There were some aggression modifying effects of exposure to explicit erotica. Habituation to erotica also resulted in reduced aggressiveness. Massive and moderate exposure produced a trend toward decreased motivated aggression. There was a close correspondence between decreased arousal, decreased repulsion, and reduced aggressiveness.

More generally, however, exposure to erotic films featuring less common sexual activities produced more aggressive behavior than did the control condition, and more also than the standard erotica condition. It should also be noted that films depicting sadomasochism or bestiality produced much higher repulsion scores as well and were much less enjoyed. Interestingly, there were no gender effects or interactions in the mediation of aggression.

CULTIVATION EFFECTS

The notion of cultivation posits that the mass media, and especially television and films, have a tendency to present a stereotyped view of the world in which certain social groups and patterns of behavior are emphasised at the expense of others. The media offer disproportionate overrepresentations of some groups and behaviors and underrepresentations of others relative to their statistically established rates of occurrence in the real world. Individuals who are, for example, heavy users of television, become exposed to this distorted 'television world' more often than light users of the medium. As a result, heavy users may exhibit perceptions of the real world that are consistent with the television world. Hence, those viewers exposed to a regular diet of prime-time television drama programs that frequently depict portrayals of crime and violence may come to see the world as a violent, crime-ridden place, relative to light viewers (Gerbner & Gross, 1976; Gerbner, Gross, Morgan, & Signorielli, 1986).

The cultivation effect has been observed to occur in relation to gender-role perceptions and beliefs. The cultivation argument here is that women and men tend to be depicted by television in stereotyped ways. Men and women are differentially represented in particular dramatic roles and tend to be further stereotyped in terms of dominant personality traits. Men have traditionally been depicted in successful professional roles, in positions of authority, as independent, assertive, and commanding, whereas women have been placed more often in limited domestic roles, subservient occupational roles, and shown as dependent on men, submissive, and pre-occupied by romantic and personal matters (see Gunter, 1995). According to some observers, television has also emphasised women's physical attractiveness and tended to use them as sex objects in its advertising and its programming (Atwood, Zahn, & Webber, 1986; Venkatesan & Losco, 1975).

A key feature of the cultivation hypothesis is that media influences are felt at a cognitive level rather than primarily at a behavioral level. Furthermore, media influences are not tied to short-term or immediate reactions to individual portrayals of a specific character. Instead, the emphasis is placed on long-term effects that arise from regular and repeated exposure to stereotyped patterns of behavior on screen. In relation to the way certain social groups are displayed, as much weight is attached to messages that are learned from the recipients of actions as from the perpetrators of actions. In connection with depictions of violence, for example, researchers have been concerned with the effects of exposure to patterns of victimisation. This emphasis is to be contrasted with traditional behavioral effects research that focused on the influences on viewers of the behavior of the perpetrator of violence.

In relation to sexual portrayals, certain stereotypes have been identified that may have cultivation effects on viewers. Most concern has been reserved for cultivation effects associated with portrayals of sexual violence in which women are the usual victims. Exposure to portrayals of this kind may, according to some writers, create distorted beliefs among men about female sexuality (Malamuth, 1986). Another form of cultivation effect that may stem from prolonged exposure to erotic entertainment is one that have implications for family values (Zillmann, 1994). Pornography depicts many sexual interactions among actors who have just met. The sex takes place outside of any kind of established interpersonal or romantic relationship. The actors may have sexual engagements with many partners, and sometimes with multiple partners in the same scene. Sex is depicted as an activity designed to deliver physical pleasure and little or nothing else. Women are depicted as eager to deliver sexual gratification to any man who happens along (see Brosius, Weaver, & Staab, 1991; Palys, 1984; Prince, 1990).

Cultivation of Sexual Values and Conduct

It has been argued that repeated exposure to such material may influence values relating to faithfulness and sexual promiscuity, beliefs about marriage, divorce, and child-raising, and perceptions regarding the prevalence of rampant sexuality and own sexual performance (Zillmann, 1994). In studies of young males' and females' reactions to repeated exposure to pornographic films, Zillmann and Bryant (1982, 1984) measured values and attitudes relating to marriage and personal happiness to investigate such cultivation effects.

Prolonged exposure to pornography under controlled experimental conditions, lasting about a week, resulted in increased acceptance of male and female promiscuity. In particular, such exposure was linked to increased acceptance of sexual relationships prior to marriage and with partners outside marriage. Nonexclusive sexual intimacy was accepted to a greater degree by those young adults who viewed a diet of pornographic films in which casual sexual liaisons were thematically central to the action. Prolonged pornography exposure was associated with the perception that an unrestrained sex life is healthy.

Young adults exposed to the pornography diet were much less likely than a matched group who viewed nonpornographic films to be supportive of the institution of marriage. The breakdown of marriage on grounds of sexual disinterest on the part of one partner was regarded as acceptable by a greater proportion of those individuals exposed to the diet of pornography than of those who viewed other material, whereas the continuation of a marriage despite either partner's sexual unfaithfulness received greater support among the pornography group. Exposure to pornography also apparently weakened the desire to have children.

It cannot be concluded that the beliefs and attitudes that were observed by Zillmann and Bryant among young adults exposed to a week-long diet of pornographic films were conditioned solely by their experimental viewing experiences. Indeed, the researchers noted that one must not discount the attraction that pornography, outside the laboratory, may have for certain classes of individual who already hold cynical attitudes and beliefs about family values. This research does provide evidence nonetheless that pornographic films that depict sex as a casual, pleasure-driven activity divorced from any emotional involvement between sexual partners may reinforce antifamily beliefs.

Further support for the cultivation of sexual issues through viewing of soap operas on mainstream television emerged from several other studies conducted during the 1980s and 1990s. Carveth and Alexander (1985) showed soap cultivation effects among college students in relation to estimates of the number of illegitimate children and number of divorced men and women. Burekel-Rothfuss and Mayes (1981) identified a cultivation effect for an overestimate in the number of women who have had abortions and in the number of men and women who have had affairs and, again, in estimates of the number of illegitimate children.

Olson (1994) provided further evidence of the potential of television soaps to cultivate distorted perceptions of reality in relation to sexual issues. Content analysis of television soaps had indicated little, if any, portrayal of safe sex practices and contraception, but many pregnancy stories (Greenberg & Busselle, 1996). College students who reported regular viewing of soaps differed from those who were nonviewers in expressing less need for contraceptives, higher rates of pregnancy, higher rates of adultery and higher estimates of sexually transmitted diseases in everyday reality.

Cultivation of Sexual Dissatisfaction

Using the same methodology as their earlier studies (i.e., Zillmann & Bryant,1982, 1984), Zillmann and Bryant conducted further experimental studies to explore cultivation effects of exposure to media sex on individuals' degree of satisfaction with their own sex lives. Participants were recruited from student and nonstudent populations. Exposing some respondents to a diet of sexually explicit films resulted in lower reported satisfaction with the affection received from, the physical appearance, and the sexual performance of their real life partners, as compared to a control group who did not see these films. Participants exposed to the sex material also regarded sex without emotional involvement as being relatively more important than did the control group. The viewers of explicit media sex exhibited greater acceptance of premarital and extramarital sex and gave lower ratings for marriage and monogamy. The explicit sex viewers showed less desire to have children and greater acceptance of male dominance and female submission (Zillmann & Bryant, 1988a, 1988b).

This particular type of cultivation effect, however, may depend on the nature of the sexual material presented to individuals and the way they are invited to become involved with it. Evidence emerged from an earlier experimental study that participants who were told to think about their sexual partners before reading explicit passages about a woman's sexual fantasies later rated their own partner *more* sexually attractive (Dermer & Pyszczynski, 1978). This contrasting result may indicate that different types of sexual content, presented through different media, may give rise to different levels of sexual fantasizing among consumers. In some instance, the sexual fantasies that are facilitated may produce a positive view of one's own sexual partner, whereas on other occasions the reverse reaction occurs.

These 'cultivation' influences may reflect the cognitive heuristic of *availability*, whereby we judge the frequency of occurrence of various activities by the ease with which we can generate examples (Taylor, 1982; Tversky & Kahneman, 1973, 1974). Recent vivid media instances can lead to an overestimation of such occurrences in the real world.

Further explanations of these effects derives from social comparison theory. Here, it is suggested that media consumers make comparisons between role models seen on screen with people in their own lives. In a sexual context, individuals may compare their sexual partners, in terms of appearance and performance, with actors seen in sexually explicit sequences in films or videos. Men, in particular, seem prone to make these comparisons between their wives or girlfriends and beautiful female models engaged in promiscuous sexual activity in explicit pornography. In consequence, they may rate their own partners as less physically endowed, although this does not invariably produce lowered satisfaction with their own sex lives (Weaver, Masland, & Zillmann, 1984). It may, however, affect the perceived depth of their feelings for their partner (Kenrick, Gutierres, & Goldberg, 1989). Further, in the short term, exposure of young men to sexually explicit videos can cause them to respond in a more overt sexual manner towards a female with whom they subsequently interact in the context of an interview, although this effect appears to be most pronounced among men who already hold stereotyped opinions about women (McKenzie-Mohr & Zanna, 1990).

Cultivation of Anti-Female Values and Beliefs

Some theories have explored the longer term effects of pornography on the public. A viewpoint put forward by antipornography feminists is that sex scenes in erotic films tend to promote a sexist ideology and discriminatory practices against women (Brownmiller, 1975). Advocates of this model argue that sexually explicit material conveys an antifemale ideology. Erotica is seen as objectifying and dehumanising women, portraying women as servants to men's sexual desires, denying female sexuality, and promoting sexual and social subordination of and violence towards women (Brownmiller, 1975; Lederer, 1980).

This theory has been substantiated by empirical research findings from laboratory studies that found that repeated exposure of young males to films depicting violent and nonviolent degrading portrayals of women can shift male attitudes to women and rape in a more sexist and callous direction (Linz, 1989; Linz & Malamuth, 1993; Zillmann & Bryant, 1982). Furthermore, reported consumption of pornography in which women are shown in subordinate sex object roles is associated with greater acceptance of rape myths and cynical attitudes towards women (Check & Guloien, 1989).

Studies of media violence of a sexual nature suggest three conclusions according to Malamuth, Check, and Briere (1986): (a) Males act against female targets in the majority of the depictions (D. G. Smith, 1976); (b) although media sexual aggression has increased in the last 15 years, it is considerably lower than media nonsexual violence (Malamuth, 1986; Malamuth & Spinner, 1980; Palys, 1986; Slade, 1984; Winick, 1985); and (c) sexual aggression is often depicted quite differently from nonsexual aggression (Malamuth et al., 1986).

Experimental research has observed connections between exposure to erotica and several adversarial beliefs about women. Exposure to sexually explicit materials has been linked to perceptions that one's mate is less sexually attractive (Weaver, Masland, & Zillmann, 1984) and to less satisfaction with one's partner's affection, physical appearance and sexual performance (Zillmann & Bryant, 1988).

Experiments have also observed that exposure to erotica leads men to be more accepting of violence towards women and less sympathetic towards women's viewpoints and feelings in the sexual and nonsexual arena (Zillmann & Weaver, 1989). Prolonged experimental exposure to sexually explicit materials is associated with increased acceptance of violence against women (Malamuth & Check, 1981b), increased aggressive behavior against women (Donnerstein & Berkowitz, 1981), increased acceptance of rape myths in both men and women (Malamuth & Check, 1985), and less compassion for rape victims and recommendations of lighter sentences for rapists (Zillmann & Bryant, 1982). Advocates of the feminist social responsibility model argue that these beliefs and attitudes may 'justify male dominance and female submissiveness,' may be 'rape supportive,' and may be associated with a 'broader acceptance of violence in nonsexual situations' (Linz & Malamuth, 1993, p. 47).

Survey research provides some limited support for this model. Malamuth and Check (1985) reported that reading men's magazines such as *Penthouse* and *Playboy* was positively related to beliefs that women enjoy being raped. Burt (1980) noted that exposure to media treatment of sexual assault was linked to acceptance of rape myths. Preston (1990) found that exposure to mainstream soft-porn magazines and X-rated videos was related to male college students holding more sex-role stereotypes. Other research, however, located no connections between exposure to sexually explicit material and several adversarial attitudes towards or beliefs about women (Demare et al., 1988; Padgett, Brislin-Slutz, & Neal, 1989).

Researchers have offered theoretical explanations for the connection between exposure to sexually explicit material and hostile views about women and rape myth acceptance. Zillmann and Bryant (1989), for example, suggested that negative depictions of women in sexually explicit media content may become the basis for schemata or scripts about women and sexuality that direct thoughts and behavior (Fiske & Taylor, 1984).

Social learning theory suggests that the rewards inherent in exposure to erotica make the content more likely to be learned and imitated. Malamuth et al. (1986) suggested that erotica's effects on sexual aggression are indirect. According to their model, exposure to sexually explicit media content affects how people think about women and rape, which then influences behavior. Experimental research on sexual violence has demonstrated that college men's frequency of reading sexually explicit material correlated positively with their beliefs that women enjoy forced sex (Brier, Corne, Rintz, & Malamuth, 1984; Malamuth & Check, 1985).

In another experiment, subjects exposed to a 'positive rape portrayal' were less negative in their responses to a second rape portrayal (Malamuth & Check, 1980a, 1981a; Malamuth, Haber, & Feshbach, 1980). In a similar vein, Linz (1985) found that males exposed to sexually violent films were less sympathetic to a rape victim in a simulated trial (see also Linz, Donnerstein, & Penrod, 1984).

Viewing Motives as Mediating Variables

Evidence has emerged that the cultivation effects of mass media can be mediated by the motives underpinning media consumption. Much of this work has been conducted in relation to soap opera viewing and is therefore of relevance to any discussion of media cultivation effects in relation to beliefs about sex and sexuality. Other work has been conducted with explicit erotic materials. The uses and gratifications perspective holds that exposure to media content provides only part of the explanation for media effects. According to this perspective, people are active because they select media content for specific reasons. People's reasons for using media content influence attention levels, how they interpret content, how actively they use the content, and attitudinal and cognitive effects (Katz, Blumler, & Gurevitch, 1973; Levy & Windahl, 1985; Rubin & Perse, 1987).

Regular soap opera viewers have been found to watch primarily for excitement, to relax, to pass time, and for companionship (Greenberg, Neuendorf, Buerkel-Rothfuss, & Henderson, 1982). In addition to these motives, soap operas have been regarded as sources of advice on social issues and as having social utility by giving viewers something to talk about with others (Compesi, 1980). Adolescent girls have reported using soaps to cheer themselves up, forget about problems, and get away from their families (Woods, 1998). Evidence has emerged that the sex in soaps is a key aspect of their appeal for some viewers. Babrow (1987) asked survey respondents to give their reasons for viewing television in general and more especially for watching or avoiding soaps. Many of the reasons for watching soap operas were common to those mentioned for television in general. Three reasons unique to soaps viewing were the serial format, with never-ending or unpredictable story lines; character development over time; and the sex and romance.

Motives for viewing have been discriminated in broader terms between ritualised and instrumental reasons for watching. Viewing as ritual reflects nondirectional, habitual forms of viewing for no specific reason. Viewing for instrumental purposes means that media consumers are goal directed and have specific reasons for watching specific programs (Rubin, 1985). Research conducted by Rubin on consumption of television soaps revealed four viewing factors: orientation, avoidance, diversion, and social utility. Orientation referred to the use of soaps to explore aspects of reality and to learn lessons or strategies in how to deal with other people, situations, or problems. Avoidance referred to watching soaps for escapism and filling time. Diversion referred to the entertainment value of soaps. Social utility meant the use of soaps to acquire things to talk about with others. These four categories of gratification were highly and positively correlated with affinity with soaps and, to a lesser degree, with involvement with them. There was no indication, however, that use of soaps for any of these reasons, and in particular for social utility purposes, was linked to actual levels of social interaction among viewers.

Loneliness has been found to relate closely to soap opera viewing. Perse and Rubin (1990) found that chronically lonely people among regular soap viewers perceived soaps as more realistic. Such individuals viewed soaps mainly to kill time, rather than to stimulate social interaction with others. Whereas people who are alone temporarily in a particular situation may turn to soaps for distraction and entertainment, the chronically lonely tend to obtain fewer satisfactory escapism experiences from their soaps viewing (Canary & Spitzberg, 1993).

Elsewhere, more direct attempts have been made to assess the significance of soap-related gratifications as mediators of cultivation effects arising from these programs. The cultivation hypothesis predicts that heavy television viewers will make estimates as to the frequency of specific groups and behaviors that are more in accord with the frequency of television portrayals than their real-life frequencies. Such cultivation effects were found in relation to amount of soap opera viewing, but in a more pronounced way for viewers who watched soaps for ritualistic reasons rather than instrumental ones (Carveth & Alexander, 1985).

A subsequent study added the variable of *involvement* with or perceived importance of watching television soaps among adolescent females. The prevalence of different relational problems and the perceived usefulness of soaps were correlated not only with overall reported soap viewing, but more significantly with adolescent girls' perceived involvement with soap operas (Woods, 1998).

Further research in this vein has examined how viewing motives might mediate cultivation effects of more restricted circulation and explicit sexual materials. Perse (1994) surveyed college undergraduates (two-thirds female) about their use of erotic or pornographic material—magazines or X-rated videos. She established respondents' principal reasons for using such material and related usage data to measures of gender-role stereotyping and rape myth beliefs concerning women. From the outset, males exhibited more stereotyped gender role beliefs than did females. To what extent, however, were these beliefs linked with reported usage of pornographic media content and the reasons for using such material?

Four categories of pornography usage motivation emerged. These were labelled *sexual enhancement* (using erotica to enhance mood or for information about sexual technique); *diversion* (escape, relaxation, relief of boredom); *sexual release* (sexual fantasy and release); and *substitution* (as a replacement for a sexual partner). Males and females differed on two of the four motives for consuming sexually explicit material. Males were more likely to report using erotica for sexual release than were females. Males also scored higher on substitution than did females.

One of the objectives of Perse's study was to explore the feminist social responsibility model that holds that exposure to sexually explicit materials is linked to adversarial views about women. These might take the form of extreme sex-role stereotyping or hostile beliefs about women, particularly in relation to rape. Perse found considerable support for the feminist social responsibility model. Two of the 'functional' uses of sexually explicit materials were linked to negative beliefs about women. Sexual enhancement was directly linked to holding adversarial views about women. Males who used erotica for sexual stimulation and foreplay with their partners were more likely to report more traditional and conservative beliefs about women and sex. It was reasoned that because erotica depicted a sexist view of women (Brownmiller, 1975; Smith, 1976), use of these materials to stimulate one's female partner might cause, reinforce, or grow out of views that dehumanize women and see them as objects that need to be 'turned on.' According to Perse, although advocates of the liberal model often argue that sexual enhancement is a beneficial use of sexually oriented content, sexual enhancement had a significant indirect influence on rape myth acceptance through its connection to gender role stereotypes, sexual conservatism, and exposure, all significant predictors of rape myth acceptance.

The use of erotica for substitution was significantly and positively related to rape myth acceptance. Although this motive was not strongly endorsed by the students in this study, using erotica as a replacement for a sexual partner was associated with greater acceptance of rape myths. Sexual release was a significant negative predictor of rape myth acceptance, adding support for the liberal model. Using erotica for solitary fantasy and sexual release was related to lower levels of rape myth acceptance. 'If this motive reflects one 'safe' approach to sex, this use of sexually explicit media content may not pose a risk for women or society' (p. 507).

EVOLUTIONARY THEORY OF GENDER ORIENTATIONS TO MEDIA SEX

Malamuth (1996b) offered a theoretical model within which to consider the impact of explicit sexual material based on evolutionary psychology. An evolutionary model can be used to explain differences between genders in their consumption of media sex. The type of sexually explicit media content preferred by each gender reflects their wider sexuality strategies. Males prefer erotica that reflect the short-termism of the male sexual strategy. Females prefer erotica that emphasise the long-term orientation of their mating strategy.

According to its protagonists, evolutionary psychology provides a framework for the analysis of gender differences (Buss, 1995). In some respects, males and females can be expected to have common psychological mechanisms, such as '... in domains where natural selection has focused the same solutions to adaptive problems for all humans regardless of their gender' (Malamuth, 1996b, p. 13). In other domains, where males and females have had to contend with different problems over time, different psychological mechanisms have emerged. Sociobiological models that incorporate ingredients from psychology, sociology, genetics, and evolution acknowledge the importance of environmental factors in the development of the character not just of individuals, but of entire species. Such models place much emphasis on the notion that individuals are 'hard wired' biologically and psychologically to display certain dominant characteristics or behavioral orientations. Although these attributes are endowed to a degree by genetic inheritance, their intrinsic nature is determined by the environment experiences of earlier generations (Cosmides & Tooby, 1987). The genetic codes that are handed down from one generation to the next, therefore, contain a kind of 'memory imprint' of the experiences and knowledge of past generations that predetermines individual members of later generations of the species to prefer certain behavioral options over others in different environmental circumstances. Where different roles have been adopted by each gender in past generations, resulting in different kinds of environmental experiences, there may be differences in the genetic codes that result in each case. These distinct, gender-specific codes may produce different psychological mechanisms that orient each gender somewhat differently in they way they approach and respond to different classes of environmental stimuli (Tooby & Cosmides, 1990). These psychological mechanisms include cognitive associative networks that are believed to represent connections between perceptions, ideas, emotions, and behavioral orientations (Berkowitz, 1993). For example, across generations, men may establish cognitive networks that predispose them to process information differently and to adopt different behavioral strategies from women (Malamuth, 1996b).

One area where a difference in evolutionary development can be expected is sexuality. Differing natural selection processes for males and females have resulted in 'sexual dimorphism' in relevant psychological mechanisms. Thus, men and women adopt differing sexual strategies, underpinned by distinct psychological mechanisms. One of the core elements of this gender difference is the degree of investment required of males and females in the production of offspring. The act of conception, usually initiated by the male, requires only a few minutes to achieve, whereas pregnancy lasts for many months. For females, it is more adaptive to invest in each offspring by carefully selecting a mate with successful characteristics who will participate in raising the offspring. For males, having intercourse with a large number of fertile females was more conducive to reproductive success. Females are able to bear a limited number of children, whereas males can sire literally thousands of offspring should they wish to. For males, therefore, a sexual strategy that emphasises quantity of reproduction is uppermost, while for females, one that emphasises quality is more important.

In ancestral environments, a man's reproductive success would have increased (other things being equal) if he had been able to (a) gain sexual access to a larger number of women, particularly women who were highly fertile, and (b) minimise commitment and investment in any single woman, so as to enable access to other fertile women (Buss & Schmidt, 1993). Female ancestors did not face such issues. They adopted a different sexual strategy—one that was more advantageous for them. Partly because men's reproductive ability is less highly correlated with a particular age, a strategy that emphasised short-term mating with many young men could actually have been quite disadvantageous. This may have been particularly the case if men's sexual strategy had been inclined to monopolise female sexuality and might have resulted in aggression against promiscuous females (Malamuth, 1996a; Smuts, 1995, Wilson & Daly, 1992). Instead, females' adaptive problems included identifying men who had the ability and willingness to successfully invest in them and their offspring. It was also important that such men provide physical protection, particularly during the period of increased vulnerability associated with pregnancy and child rearing. At the same time, it was important to mate with a man who possessed such attributes as sensitivity and kindness, which suggest potential parental abilities and the skills to help nurture offspring.

Table 10.1 shows similarities between major adaptive problems and contents of sexually explicit media. The types of content preferred by males shows casual sex with numerous accessible women who display fertility cues through their age, body shape, and so on. Research on body shape has found that the type of 'waist-to-hip' ratio featured regularly in male-oriented sexually explicit magazines such as *Playboy* (i.e., a 0.70 ratio) corresponds exactly to the ratio found most attractive by men of various ethnic and cultural backgrounds (Singh, 1995; Singh & Luis, 1995; Singh & Young, 1995). Moreover, such a ratio is the most reproductively optimal across the range of female body weight and size.

Many survey and laboratory studies focusing on various media, including magazines, movies, and the Internet, find that, in comparison to women, men are more likely to seek out (even when alone or with a same-sex friend), to consume more regularly, to be more sexually aroused by, to have

TABLE 10.1

Similarity Between Evolutionary Adaptive Problems
and Content of Sexually Explicit Media

Males' Short-Term Mating Problems		Content, Male-Targeted Sexually Explicit Media
(1) Partner number problem	→	(1) Numerous women depicted
(2) Sexual access to women problem	→	(2) Women eager to 'service' men sexually
(3) Identifying fertile women problem	→	(3) Youthful women with 'shapely' bodies (cues associated with fertility)
(4) Minimizing investment problem	→	(4) Casual sex without investment

Females' Long-Term Mating Problems		Content, Female-Targeted Sexually Explicit Media
(1) Problem of identifying man who is able and willing to invest in her	→	(1) High status man who desires and eventually loves only her
(2) Physical protection problem	→	(2) Man is powerful, often 'brutish' towards others
(3) Problem of identifying man with good parental abilities and skills	→	(3) Man becomes kind and gentle with her by end of story

Note: Arrows show correspondence between adaptive problems and media content.

more favorable attitudes towards, and to react with less negative affect to portrayals featuring nudity of the opposite sex or sexual acts devoid of relationship context (Abelson, Cohen, Heaton, & Suder, 1971; Bryant & D. Brown, 1989; Hsu, Kling, Kessler, Knape, Diefenbach, & Elias, 1994; Kinsey, Pomeroy, Martin, & Gebhard, 1953; Laumann, Gagnon, Michael, & Michaels, 1994; Mann, Sidman, & Starr, 1971; Rimm, 1995; Stauffer & Frost, 1976). Another observation that confirms the different sexual orientations of the genders is that women are less likely to volunteer for studies involving sexually explicit media, regardless of whether the materials to be used in such studies are described as hard- or soft-core. This does not mean that women universally dislike consuming erotic or sexually explicit materials. They do exhibit different thematic tastes and preferences from men. Women show a preference more often than men for viewing erotic films with 'loving' themes as compared to purely lustful hard-core sequences (Kenrick, Stringfield, Wagenhals, Dahl, & Ransdell, 1986). Indeed, research has shown that films with erotic scenes that were contextualised within a romantic story line, in which emphasis was placed on the emotional relationship of a man and a woman, are more likely to arouse female members of the audience (Mosher & MacIan, 1994).

CONCLUSION

Social scientists who have investigated media sex offer a variety of explanations for its impact on media audiences. In considering the theory of media sex effects, it is apparent that the effects themselves are not invariably sexual in nature. Exposure to media sex has also been linked to nonsexual audience responses, such as aggression.

Thus, sexual scenes in the media may excite and arouse media consumers in sexual and nonsexual ways. This nonspecific physiological response can be psychologically interpreted in more ways than one and hence gives rise to a variety of subsequent behaviors among observers. The link between media sex and audience aggression is not too surprising given that explicit sex scenes are combined with violence in some media sex output. Indeed, other psychological models of behavior, originally developed to explain the effects of media violence, may be applied in the context of depictions of sex and more especially, sexual aggression. Hence, certain categories of media sex (e.g., scenes involving coercive victimisation) can be conceived to influence viewers through such psychological mechanisms as disinhibition, triggering, and desensitisation. Individuals who watch this sort of material may experience a weakening of social inhibitions against behaving similarly, may be stimulated to follow a media actor's lead, and may experience a reduction of concern about the consequences of such conduct.

The effects of media sex may occur not just at a behavioral level, but also at a cognitive level. A regular diet of explicit media sex may condition inaccurate beliefs about female sexuality, shift moral codes and values towards greater acceptance of sexual promiscuity, and create distorted impressions about the 'normality' of unusual or exaggerated sexual practices.

The reactions of media consumers to media sex and the degree to which their social attitudes, beliefs, and perceptions are influenced by such content are mediated by other factors. Thus, not everyone responds in the same way to sexually explicit portrayals. The nature and instrumentality of individuals' consumption of media sex are closely linked to whether explicitly sexual media content is used for purely entertainment purposes and whether it performs some other deeper-seated psychological function. For some individuals media sex is a diversion, whereas for others it is a substitute for the real thing.

As with anything sexual, there are gender-related distinctions to be drawn between the nature and explanation of media consumers' responses to media sex. Evolutionary psychological theory points to long-established differences between males and females in the nature of their inherent sexuality, that have become imprinted as distinct genetic codes. There are biological reasons why women are stereotypically selective in choosing a sexual partner and men are less discriminating, associated with the degree of investment each gender makes in the process of procreation. Such biological differences are manifest in different sexual behavior patterns among men and women and may, in turn, explain differences in their preferences for and enjoyment of media sex portrayals.

Although theories provide a crucial organising framework for any empirical research, knowledge enhancement does not proceed through the acceptance or rejection of hypotheses on which theories are built. There must also be trust in the veracity, reliability, and validity of the research itself. Methodologies must truthfully measure what they set out to measure. The findings that are produced in any study must be judged in terms of their internal coherence and external relevance. Research on media sex has not been accepted uncritically. The principal methodologies of surveys and experiments have widely established limitations. In the specific context of their application in the field of media sex, a number of prominent programs of research have faced serious challenges from critics who questioned their validity. The debate that has ensued on this subject is examined in the next chapter.

11

Can We Trust the Research on Media Sex?

Do depictions of sexual behavior in the media really affect sexual values, attitudes, or behaviors in society? Television has been accused of becoming increasingly obsessed with sex. Movies have been criticised for regarding graphic sexual portrayals as an essential ingredient of box office success. Videos have been identified as a source of immoral influence by depicting, in vivid detail, scenes of explicit sexual behavior that can be degrading to women and deeply offensive to the great majority of the public. In the latter case, the blending of violence with sex has been identified, socially and psychologically, as a particularly damaging form of entertainment. Even with movies and some television programs, violent sexual themes emerge that, though much milder than those found in pornographic videos, have nevertheless been thought by some experts to be capable of cultivating the wrong ideas about women in a sexual context.

In this chapter, we consider whether the results of research carried out to date on media sex can be accepted at face value. It is important to consider the methodological limitations of any research before findings can be confidently used in the context of determining policy guidelines or codes of practice for television producers, film makers, or censors. The evidence for the impact of sex on television has so far been fairly thin. This is probably because it has been overshadowed by concerns about the effects of televised violence, a topic that has achieved a far higher public profile. Sex in the movies and, more especially, in videos, has received more attention than sex on television as an area for investigation by media effects researchers. The reason for this may partly be explained by the fact that sexual portrayals in films made originally for theatre showings or video distribution have tended to be more explicit than those usually shown on mainstream television and also because of the blending of violence with sex in those two media. Hence, the research into the effects of sexual violence has represented an extension of earlier research into the effects of violence in the media.

Although evidence has emerged that exposure to violent sex scenes can cause men to fantasize about rape (Malamuth, 1981), enhance men's acceptance of rape myths (Linz, 1989), and increase men's direct physical aggression against a woman in a laboratory setting (Donnerstein & Berkowitz, 1981), the evidence for these apparently dramatic effects can be challenged on methodological grounds. Furthermore, not all the evidence that has emerged so far has been consistent either in the strength or direction of media effects that have purportedly been demonstrated.

In considering the efficacy of research evidence to date about the representation of sex in the audiovisual media and its effects on audiences, it is necessary to consider the validity and reliability of the methodologies that have been used. Counting procedures have been adopted to quantify and classify the occurrence of sex in films, television broadcasts, and videos. These have derived from content analysis methodology. Public opinion about sex in the media has been measured primarily through surveys. The impact of sex in the media has been measured either with surveys or experimental methodologies. In each case, there are important issues that need to be closely examined about the way data were collected in order to establish the robustness of the research and its findings and recommendations.

REPRESENTATION OF SEX

The analysis of sexual representations in the media has depended primarily on content analysis in which sexual behavior has been defined according to an a priori analytical framework. This type of framework specifies the unit of analysis (i.e., what is to be counted on screen) and the attributes according to which on-screen events are further classified. Thus, content analysis studies of sex on television, for example, have distinguished between different types of sexual behavior largely in terms of degree of intimacy displayed. Sexual behaviors may, therefore, range from embracing and hugging, through kissing and intimate touching, to oral sex or sexual intercourse (Franzblau et al., 1977; Kunkel, Cope, & Colvin, 1996; Sprafkin & Silverman, 1981). Distinctions have also been made between physical sexual displays and verbal references to sex (Fernandez-Collado et al., 1978;

Greenberg, Stanley, et al., 1993; Kunkel et al., 1999). Sex as depicted in specific categories of programs, such as soap operas, has been emphasised by other work (Greenberg et al., 1986; Lowry & Towles, 1988). Researchers have also catalogued occurrences of sex offending and sexual violence (Sapolsky & Tabarlet, 1991; Kunkel et al., 1999).

These content analyses of the occurrence of sex in films, videos, and television programs have provided useful evidence of the prevalence and nature of sex in these media. On their own, they represent purely descriptive accounts that cannot demonstrate anything about the impact or acceptability of media sex. To be really useful, content coding frames need to be informed either by public opinion or media effects evidence. Public opinion data can give some indication as to the kinds of portrayals ordinary people find acceptable or offensive. Media effects evidence can indicate how viewers might respond subsequently after exposure to a diet of media sex. In the latter case, interest may center on the impact of sheer volume of exposure to sex in the media. More usually, however, emphasis is given to the kinds of sexual depictions to which individuals are exposed, and their impact on values, attitudes, perceptions, and behavior.

Public opinion seldom remains stable over time. People exhibit shifting attitudes towards the media and their contents. This observation is especially true of public opinion towards the representation of sex in the media. Although significant numbers of people may personally find offence in explicit pornographic materials, equally one might find a relaxation of feelings about less explicit depictions of sex in mainstream media. Over the past two decades, for example, people have become more tolerant nudity and simulated sex scenes in cinema films and television programs. Evidence for this observation derives from findings that showed increases in the levels of sex on television (Greenberg, J. D. Brown, & Buerkel-Rothfuss, 1993; Kunkel et al., 1999), increased availability and consumption of sexually explicit videos (Showers, 1994), and tolerant public opinion concerning sex channels on television (Gunter, Sancho-Aldridge, & Winstone, 1994). In part, public opinion is probably responsive to media producers who push back taste barriers and test public tolerance for more and more explicit sexual depictions. In the context of investigating the representation of sex in the audiovisual media, it is important that such analyses are informed by the latest public opinion evidence.

As we saw in chapter 3, however, the measurement of public opinion about media sex can be influenced by methodological artifacts. The form of question wording that is used to explore attitudes towards the representation of different kinds of sexual content on television, for example, can make a marked difference to the profile of opinion obtained. The more directly a form of questioning addresses an issue relating to the depiction of sexual content in the media, the more extreme is the nature of the audience's response. Although members of the public may indicate personal offence in response to certain categories of sexual depiction on screen, for example, they may be less likely to call for an outright ban of that content.

While individuals may display varying tastes and preferences for media sex, the question of its impact on them is a separate one. Where evidence exists that specific types of portrayal may produce a particularly adverse audience reaction, such data need to be taken into account by descriptive analyses of media sex. This argument has been made with some conviction in relation to the debate about media violence. Research evidence has shown here not only that violent portrayals can be differentiated in terms of how they are perceptually rated by people (Gunter, 1985; Van der Voort, 1986), but also according to the different cognitive, emotional, and behavioral reactions they can trigger (Wilson et al., 1996). Although not investigated to the same extent, this last point is probably just as pertinent in relation to the analysis of media sex. Research has shown that depictions of rape may increase men's acceptance of rape myths (Linz, 1989) and cause them to fantasize about rape (Malamuth, 1981). Depictions of violent sex in laboratory session can apparently cause young men to show increased propensity to display hostile actions against a female target (Donnerstein & Berkowitz, 1981). Further research has indicated that repeated exposure to a diet of media sex in which marital infidelity and sexual promiscuity are emphasised may cultivate the view that such behaviors are far more prevalent and more acceptable than would otherwise be the case (Zillmann & Bryant, 1982, 1984). This evidence therefore provides pointers towards the kinds of attributes of sexual portrayals media content analysts should be examining.

THE IMPACT OF MEDIA SEX

As earlier chapters have already shown, the impact of media sex can be defined in many different ways. Sexual representations in the media may shape public values, perceptions, beliefs, and attitudes about sexual behavior, sexual relationships, and sexuality orientations and preferences across the genders. There has been concern that certain types of explicit sexual depictions can act to loosen public morals and challenge established institutions such as marriage and the family. Even more concern has been reserved for the possibility that explicit media sex (especially certain kinds of pornography) can influence sexual behavior. Although some research has considered whether exposure to sexually explicit material renders viewers more sexually active, much more attention has been paid to the links between exposure to extreme forms of pornography and sex offending.

Three types of impact methodology can be distinguished: (a) surveys of offending and nonoffending groups; (b) correlational analysis of aggregated statistical data from archival sources; and (c) experimental studies. The choice of methodology rests in part on the nature of the research question being investigated and in part on whatever data may be available or obtainable of relevance to that question.

Survey and Archival Studies

Although not equipped to demonstrate causal connections between variables, surveys and archival analyses may provide broad indications about where causal connections could lie or suggest the possibility that causal links may exist. Furthermore, such methodologies are appropriate where the researcher is interested in examining the historical links, if any, between variables. In some cases, also, researchers may be interested in examining questions with special groups among whom experiments are not possible. Hence, surveys have been used to explore possible connections between exposure to explicit sexual materials (i.e., pornography) and the onset of offending among convicted sex offenders (L. Baron & Straus, 1989; Kutchinsky, 1991; Scott & Schwalm, 1988a). One would need to observe extreme caution about conducting manipulative experimental research with such potentially dangerous individuals. This would be particularly so where one might be interested in finding out if such individuals' offending could be triggered by pornography.

One a wider, societal level, there are concerns not just that sex offenders may be susceptible to antisocial influences of media sex, but that the general availability of mediated sexual materials—especially those of an explicit nature—could be linked to overall changes in sexual mores (Zillmann, 1994) and overall levels of criminal offending (Cline, 1994). If such links exist, then an obvious policy recommendation would be to control or restrict the production and distribution of media sex. Given the knowledge that certain geographical areas have observed more controls than others over the distribution of explicit media sex, it should be possible to compare these areas in terms of levels of relevant offending over time. If the availability of pornography does cause sex offending, then one would expect to find higher rates of such crimes in regions where pornography is more readily available. The problem with this type of research is that such studies seldom collect data on rates of exposure to pornography. Varying rates of availability of explicit sexual material does not guarantee varying rates of pornography consumption. Furthermore, such databases do not show whether sex offenders in the regions being compared exhibited different rates of pornography consumption. The fact that pornography is legally banned from a region does not mean that it is not available or that it is not being consumed.

Experimental Evidence

To investigate cause–effect relationships, it is generally acknowledged that experimental methodologies are best because they enable researchers to manipulate potential causal variables in advance. Thus, if we are interested in establishing whether a diet of erotica leads to a shift in male attitudes or behavior towards women, an experiment could be set up in which different groups of men are fed varying diets of films or videos—some erotic and others not. The men could also be tested beforehand for their attitudes and compared afterwards on attitudes and behavior. The behavior would involve a laboratory simulation rather than real world behavior (e.g., Donnerstein, 1980; Donnerstein & Barrett, 1978; Zillmann, Bryant, & Carveth, 1981). One of the problems with experiments in this area is that researchers must avoid contravening ethical guidelines and principles that place restrictions on the manipulation of participants' psychological condition that may carry over into the real world with unfortunate and undesirable side effects. Almost inevitably, therefore, experiments take place under artificial conditions that do not generally match those that exist in the real world. For some, this is a critical weakness of experiments (Harre & Secord, 1972). Much of the criticism of media sex research has centered on the application of experimental methods to investigate the impact of explicit sexual materials, including violent pornography.

How Consistent Is the Experimental Evidence?

There are now numerous published studies that have indicated that exposure to violent sexual material presented on film or video is associated with undesirable changes in young men's attitudes towards women and rape and is apparently linked to actual displays of violence against women in a laboratory setting. Not all the findings to date have been in a consistent direction (Fisher & Grenier, 1994).

To convey the level of inconsistency seen in research on effects of exposure to violent pornography, consider the following results. In one research line, several investigators showed that even very brief exposure to violent pornography is sufficient to cause men to fantasize about rape (Malamuth, 1981), to increase men's acceptance of rape myths (Donnerstein, Berkowitz, & Linz, 1986, cited in Linz, 1989), and to increase men's direct physical aggression against a woman in a laboratory setting (Donnerstein & Berkowitz, 1981). These fairly dramatic effects of exposure to violent pornography were produced by experimental contact with such material which in no case exceeded 5 minutes' duration. In complete contrast, other investigators have shown that even repeated exposures to full-length sexually violent films had no effect on men's rape myth acceptance, endorsement of the use of force in sexual relations, simulated rape trial verdicts (Donnerstein, 1984; Linz et al., 1988), self-reported likelihood of raping a woman, or physical aggression against a woman in a laboratory setting (Malamuth & Ceniti, 1986). These failures to find effects of violent pornography occurred despite repeated exposures to two or more full-length feature films involving sexual violence.

Another problem with research into sexually violent media content involves the co-variation between respondents' endorsements of rape-supportive beliefs and their reported use of pornography. In the presence of a significant association between these two variables, it is unclear whether a pornographic effect may, in actuality, constitute a pre-existing attitude effect (e.g., Briere et al., 1984; Garcia, 1986). Pre-existing attitudes towards sexual violence could create interest in pornography and in sexually violent behavior—any relationship found between pornography use and sexual violence would then be spurious.

Critique of Experiments.   It is widely accepted among media researchers that experimental studies based on random assignment of participants to experimental conditions provide the best methodology for assessing cause and effect relationships in the laboratory (see Neuman, 1994; Wimmer & Dominick, 1994). Yet, the results of this work on the question of the impact of media depictions of sex are empirically mixed and ambiguous.

One approach to understanding inconsistencies in the research findings involves identifying methodological and conceptual problems in the research. A number of such limitations have been identified (Fisher & Barak, 1989, 1991). In relation to research that has adopted experimental methodologies in which participants are placed in a researcher-controlled environment for exposure to specific portrayals of sexual behavior, there are problems that may, in some instances, call into question the validity of the findings.

In particular, experimental studies are significantly limited in their external validity. Experimental conditions do not reproduce real-world conditions; in fact, they significantly distort the experience of real life media consumption and thus make generalisations to the world beyond the laboratory difficult. With explicit sexual materials, depictions of sex are decontextualised, removed from their original context and detached from their function (sexual arousal, masturbation). Some studies used only those scenes that were sexually explicit, thus removing any semblance of narrative or character development. Controlled laboratory experiments may provide opportunities for an artificial range of available responses to media sex, forcing participants to react in ways they would not have chosen in more 'natural' settings.

Participant Awareness. Many of the laboratory-based studies that have served as a basis for concluding that violent sexual scenes in films and videos can cause anti-female thoughts, attitudes, and actions appear to be highly vulnerable to participant awareness problems. Doubts have been cast on laboratory studies because participants may be given sufficient clues as to what the study is intended to achieve, for them to give the experimenter the results he or she is looking for (Fisher & Grenier, 1994; Orne, 1962).

These so-called 'demand characteristics' may, in part, arise from the limitations or confinement of responses imposed by the experimental procedure. In the typical pornography experiment, for instance, the only response usually allowed is the administration of electric shock to an experimental confederate or the display of aggressive attitudes. Clearly, where behavioral measures are concerned, researchers have ethical responsibilities to ensure that they do not unwittingly encourage or cause realistic aggressive impulses to be acted on by experimental participants. Nevertheless, the use of the electric shock measure offers participants a rather narrow range of response. Furthermore, participants are drawn into this behavior by being angered first by the experimenter's assistant. In the real world, of course, consumers of pornography may not be angry at the time they see such material. Any effects of pornography may, therefore, be expressed quite differently in the real world, with modes of behavior adopted by viewers that are quite different from the kind of behavior encouraged in a laboratory setting.

In Malamuth's (1981) research, for example, in which brief exposure to violent pornography caused men to fantasize about rape, participants were exposed to rape themes or scenes of heterosexual consenting sex and were asked a short time later to generate an arousing sexual fantasy. In Donnerstein and Berkowitz's (1981) research, participants were exposed to violent pornography and were then instructed by the experimenter to choose a level of electric shock to deliver to a female target. Participants may have perceived the experimenter's purpose in each of these studies, and what appear to be effects of violent pornography may have been effects of participant awareness and compliance with the experimenter's perceived purpose.

Berkowitz and Donnerstein (1982) disputed the notion that experimental participants spend their time trying to guess what the study is about or succeed in doing so. Despite the high likelihood that these fairly obvious experimental procedures would result in considerable participant awareness, however, there was no report of the identification of even a single suspicious participant in the Malamuth (1981), Check and Guloien (1989), or Donnerstein and Berkowitz (1981) studies. Laboratory experiments often provide evidence of a link between violent pornography and anti-female aggression, but survey research on the association of the two in natural settings has rarely indicated a link (e.g., Goldstein, 1973; Langevin et al., 1988; Marshall, 1988).

An associated concern about experiments is 'evaluation apprehension.' Although few participants may actually have much interest in trying to guess the experimenter's hypothesis, they may nevertheless want to look good to the researcher. At the very least, they may not wish to look bad. They may therefore try to impress the experimenter because they believe they are being tested for their competence or morality in some way. There is evidence that this desire of experimental participants to please does occur (Weber & Cook, 1972).

Selective Attrition. Another problem with experiments of this sort is that selective attrition of experimental participants may have created effects that appeared, at first glance, to derive from exposure to violent pornography. In one analysis of this problem, researchers found that when young males were allocated either to watch violent pornographic films across a number of sessions or to a condition where they watched nothing, only the men in the pornography exposure condition exhibited increased self-reported likelihood of raping a woman across the duration of the experiment. However, the pornography exposure group also suffered a 14% attrition rate across experimental sessions as participants dropped out through their distaste for such films. It is possible, therefore, that in the end, the men who were left (and among whom the major 'effects' of violent pornography were measured) were individuals who were in any case highly tolerant of violent sex scenes and callous towards women, and whose opinions may not have been shaped in the first place by the violent pornography per se (Check & Guloien, 1989).

Nonrandom Samples. Most experimental studies have used nonrandom samples of college students. In typical social psychology and media experiments, participants are selected from a roster of students, usually in introductory psychology or communications classes. Although participants may be randomly allocated to experimental conditions, they are originally extracted from a nonprobability sample that is not representative of the wider population either in terms of demographics or in terms of relevant psychological profiles (Brannigan & Goldenberg, 1987a).

Chance Findings. Linz (1989) pointed out that research on effects of pornography often involves the administration of a large number of dependent variables and the detection of a few significant effects. Consequently, there is reason for concern that some reported effects of violent pornography may be chance findings among a preponderance of null effects.

Malamuth and Check's (1980a) findings for 'undesirable cognitive–perceptual changes' following exposure to 5 minutes of violent pornography rests on a multivariate analysis of variance main effect with a single significant univariate effect among four dependent variables and a further such analysis with *no* significant main effects that was nonetheless followed up to disclose a single significant univariate effect for six dependent variables. If such effects of exposure to violent pornography are simply chance findings, the literature may overestimate the impact of violent pornography, and findings for effects of such material may be unreliable.

Preference for Rejection of Null Hypothesis.   Related to the problem of chance findings, there is also considerable prejudice against publication of null findings. Moreover, prejudice against publication of null findings may be especially pronounced in the current instance, in which failures to confirm effects of violent pornography may contradict strongly held moral, political, and philosophical views. Taken together, the reporting of chance findings and the prejudice against publication of null findings would make even the considerable inconsistencies that appear in the literature underestimates of the actual degree of unreliability in effects of violent pornography.

Ecological Validity.   Perhaps the most serious problem for most of the experiments that have been carried out on media sex is that laboratory procedures for studying effects of explicit sexual materials are not representative of conditions in natural settings. Experiments conducted in a laboratory do not represent the natural, everyday surroundings in which people behave. Critics argue that any findings that emerge from such artificial conditions are unlikely to be generalizable to the real world. Even in such experiment-driven disciplines as psychology, the widespread reliance on experiments has been regarded as a serious shortcoming (Gilmour & Duck, 1980; Strickland, Aboud, & Gergen, 1976). The standard laboratory method for studying effects of violent pornography on aggression against women, for example, involves artificial behavioral constraints that usually require male research participants to engage in some level of antifemale aggression.

Several researchers have pointed out that laboratory procedures for studying the effects of the media are so unrepresentative of conditions in natural settings that they reveal little or nothing about relationships between media and behavior in the real world (Brannigan & Goldenberg, 1987a, 1987b; Fisher & Barak, 1989, 1991). The measurement of aggressive behavior in a laboratory context has always occurred in highly contrived circumstances. In every case, reactions were measured to very brief scenes and in an artificial setting where the usual societal rules of conduct were suspended. For example, the standard laboratory method for studying effects of violent pornography on aggression against women has tended to involve artificial behavioral constraints that require male research partici-pants to engage in some level of antifemale aggression (Donnerstein & Berkowitz, 1981).

In the standard laboratory method, male research participants are an-gered by a female confederate who delivers hostile verbal feedback and painful electrical shock to them, or they are treated equitably by her. Male research participants are then shown violent pornography or comparison stimuli and are told by the experimenter to send some level of electric shock to the woman each time she errs in a subsequent experimental task. Men who have been angered and shocked by a woman, and who have seen violent pornography, generally send higher levels of electric shocks to her than do men who have seen comparison stimuli or who have been equita-bly treated.

These findings, however, tell us little about how men might respond in natural settings where nonaggressive response options, such as speaking to the woman or simply walking away, are open to them. The ecologically in-valid constraints of the laboratory methodology in question guarantee that some level of antiwoman aggression will occur, and it is not at all clear that even provoked men who have seen violent pornography would aggress at any level if they had the opportunity simply to escape the situation or to re-spond to the female provoker nonaggressively.

The ecological unrepresentativeness of laboratory procedures for study-ing pornography and aggression may help explain why laboratory findings for a pornography–aggression link (e.g., Donnerstein & Berkowitz, 1981) are not always replicated in research on the use of violent pornography and the commission of sexual aggression in natural settings (Abramson & Hayashi, 1984; Goldstein, 1973; Langevin et al., 1988; Marshall, 1988). Even on this count, however, there is conflicting evidence. In the context of aggression measurement, laboratory measures have been found to correlate with aggression measures taken beyond the laboratory (Williams, Meyerson, & Eron, 1967). In this case, 8-year-old boys and girls were pro-vided with an opportunity to punish a peer for mistakes made on a joint task, using a slightly modified version of the Buss Aggression Machine. These laboratory aggression were then related to an independently vali-dated index of each child's customary aggressiveness as rated by the chil-dren's classmates. The youngsters of both sexes who were seen by their peers as being most aggressive in their daily social encounters adminis-tered significantly more intense punishment on the laboratory apparatus, for longer durations, and with greater frequency than did their less aggres-sive counterparts. This result was replicated elsewhere (Shemberg, Leventhal & Allman, 1968).

Do these criticisms totally invalidate experimental research? Can experiments have real value even though they tend to be conducted under artificial conditions? Some defenders of the method have argued that they can (Berkowitz & Donnerstein, 1982). It is not the case, as many of its critics would claim, that the experimental method treats participants as if they were unthinking automatons. The fact is that experimental research has placed great emphasis on the active cognitive nature of participants and the varying interpretations they may place on situations and experiences.

According to Berkowitz and Donnerstein (1982), the issue of generalisablity needs to be put into perspective. Should a researcher wish to make broad claims about the status of relationships between variables in the wider population, then a large scale survey with a representative sample of individuals should be adopted. However, if the main interest and aim is the testing of a specific causal hypothesis, then an experimental methodology is more appropriate. A distinction needs to be made between two different research objectives: tests of the accuracy of statements about specific instances and tests of the universality of findings across a range of different types of people and situations (Kruglanski, 1975). Reviews of large numbers of laboratory experiments and field studies have concluded that there may be little difference of any social significance between the two types of study in the external validity of their findings (Dipboye & Flanagan, 1979). It is important to recognise that nonrepresentativeness of sampling does not mean that the results are nongeneralizable. A single study as such could not demonstrate or prove the extent of generalizability of its findings, but they may be shown to have wider applicability with subsequent tests (Bass & Firestone, 1980).

Methodological Critiques of Violent Pornography Work. The work of Donnerstein, Linz, Malamuth, Bryant, and Zillmann came under fierce attack in the late 1980s by critics who offered challenges to the veracity of their findings on methodological grounds (Gross, 1983). While focusing on methodological issues, some of these critiques also conveyed a more serious, and unwarranted undertone that the researchers had been selective in the way they reported their findings because of a political agenda (Christensen, 1987; Mould, 1988).

Gross (1983) challenged the findings of Zillmann and Bryant (1982). In this study, 80 male and 80 female undergraduates from a large eastern university were randomly assigned to four conditions. In three of these, participants took part in experimental sessions of about 1 hour each, during which they saw films. For one group all the films seen were nonerotic, for a second group half of the films were erotic and half nonerotic, and the 'massive exposure' group saw only erotic films (a total of 4 hours and 48 minutes of heterosexual activities, mainly fellatio, cunnilingus, coition, and anal intercourse). It was noted that none of the erotic activities entailed coercion or the deliberate infliction or reception of pain.

The dependent variables in the study were derived from responses to questionnaires administered several weeks after the exposure treatment, including the widely reported question of what prison sentence the participants would recommend for a convicted rapist. The results indicated that the 'massive exposure' participants recommended lighter sentences than did subjects in the 'mixed' and 'nonerotic' film groups and in the control group that saw no films at all.

Gross (1983) was unconvinced by the findings. He felt that experimental participants could have guessed what the study was about and obliged the experimenters by giving them the results they wanted to obtain. Participants may also have talked to each other about the films and experiment outside the experimental sessions. He also raised ethical concerns about attempts to manipulate participants' attitudes and questioned whether adequate debriefing sessions had been run to ensure that any attitude, belief, or behavioral disposition changes could be undone.

Zillmann and Bryant (1983) responded. They confirmed that an ethical committee had been consulted in advance and had deliberated about their study. The debriefing procedure was rigorous. Participants were fully informed about the study immediately afterwards. The purpose of the research was elaborated fully. Participants also were apprised of likely effects of exposure to erotic materials.

Zillmann and Bryant felt it was unlikely from the conditions of the experiment that any participants could have second-guessed what questions would be asked of them afterwards. Indeed, it seems entirely reasonable to argue that there was no reason to believe that exposure to pornographic films per se would have led viewers to expect questions about recommended sentences for rapists and other sex offenders. The criticism that participants may have talked to each other outside the experiment and that this may have contaminated the results was also dismissed. Zillmann and Bryant argued that in real life situations, one might expect individuals to talk to others about explicitly sexual films they have seen, particularly if, as young people, they often watched such films in the company of others anyway. Thus, any conversations experimental participants in this case might have held about the films they saw in the study merely reflected what one would expect under more natural viewing conditions. Once again, though, it is difficult to see how this phenomenon could invalidate the results.

Mould (1988) wrote a painstakingly detailed critique of experimental studies by Malamuth and Check (1980a) and Donnerstein and Berkowitz (1981). Malamuth and Check's work attempted to demonstrate that sexually explicit rape depictions portraying the victim experiencing sexual arousal have an antisocial effect by changing the perception of an actual rape experience to one in which the victim is seen as being minimally damaged, as well as helping maintain the rape myth that women secretly desire to be raped. Penile tumescence measures were linked to self-reported arousal. A significant correlation was reported by Malamuth and Check (1980a), but this was disputed by Mould. He claimed they shared about 9% variance only—a weak association.

Mean levels of arousal within each experimental group for the rape-criterion tape were substantially higher than arousal to the pre-exposure tapes. (Experimental participants heard audio tapes depicting three types of scene: victim becoming aroused through rape; victim abhorring rape; mutually consenting sex). Arousal among participants in the mutually desired sexual intercourse condition was not significantly different from those in the rape depiction group. According to Mould, the main experimental effect from the rape abhorrence tape was suppression of participants' subsequent arousal rather than the rape arousal facilitating it.

The proportions of men who would rape if placed in the same circumstances as the perpetrator in the rape tape were greater after exposure to the rape arousal tape as compared to exposure to the rape abhorrence story or the mutually desired story. Post hoc analyses, however, showed no significant differences between rape arousal and rape abhorrence conditions on this measure.

In the same study, Malamuth and Check compared the reactions of men high and low in rape proclivity as measured by a technique developed by Abel et al. (1977). The research question in this case was: Are those men high in rape proclivity more like rapists than those low in rape proclivity? Mould suggested that an alternative question might be better: Are those high in rape proclivity more like rapists than they are like those low in rape proclivity? Mould argued that no research up to that point had demonstrated that men high in rape proclivity held attitudes towards women as callous as those of actual rapists, even though high proclivity male attitudes towards women were generally more callous than those of low rape proclivity men.

Mould went on to challenge experiments reported by Donnerstein and Berkowitz (1981). The latter investigated whether the behavior exhibited by the women characters in erotic films differentially affects subsequent aggression against male or female targets by angered male participants and what sorts of differential effects could be elicited by varying anger as well as film content in subjects' aggression against female targets. Donnerstein and Berkowitz made a number of predictions: (a) a nonaggressive erotic movie would elicit a stronger attack on the male target than on the female target; (b) a violent erotic film with a positive ending and a female target would elicit more aggression than the nonviolent erotic film with a female target, and the violent erotic film with a positive ending and female target would draw more aggression than the same film condition with a male target; (c) with female targets, the violent erotic film with the negative ending and the violent erotic film with the negative ending and a female target would elicit more aggression than the same film with a male target.

There were significant effects for film and an interaction between gender of target and film type. The first hypothesis was validated. However, the erotic condition did not facilitate aggression against the male target (or female target) compared to the neutral condition. The authors attributed this finding to unusually high shock levels in the neutral film, male target group. Mould disputed this explanation on the grounds that other studies had found similar shock levels under similar conditions.

Donnerstein and Berkowitz's rationale for predicting higher aggression against the female target in the positive-ending violent condition than either the female target in the erotic condition or a male target in the positive-ending aggressive condition was that '(a) the aggressive content of the sex film would evoke strong aggressive reactions from the angry viewers, (b) the positive outcome would lower their inhibitions against attacking women, and (c) the female target's sex-linked association with the victim of the assault on the screen would facilitate attacks on her' (p. 712). Of these, the last two are sex specific, whereas the first is sex neutral. Furthermore, inasmuch as the experimental participants were angry, they were disposed or predisposed toward aggression. Consequently, it would be expected that in the positive ending, violent condition with a male target, they would evidence greater aggression than in either of the erotic or neutral conditions with a male target. Whether this difference is significant or not is not reported. There is, therefore, little clarity as to the factors producing the experimental effects, and there are no significant effects for the rewarding behavior of the participants, constituting a failure at convergent validation.

A second experiment showed that violent erotica in which the woman enjoys being raped would produce more pronounced reactions against a female target. This reaction would be especially strong among angered males in the audience. The increase in aggression in the violent erotic positive outcome condition was attributed to participants believing that somehow behaving aggressively towards female targets would have a payoff. It was also suggested that exposure to such behavior could elicit similar behavior among participants. Mould disputed this as well. In doing so, he pointed to findings from Mann et al. (1974) that although married couples were more likely to have sex after watching erotic movies, this did not facilitate greater amounts of sexual behavior more generally. Couples shifted their sex behavior to those occasions when they watched the erotica.

The researchers whose work Mould challenged mounted a vociferous defence. Malamuth (1988c) responded by pointing out many inaccuracies in Mould's arguments and his representation of earlier research. The inhibition of sexual arousal by rape abhorrence, for instance, was consistent with experimental hypotheses. Contrary to Mould's claim, there was no point at which significant differences were reported between variables that did not actually exhibit such differences. The reinterpretation by Mould of the rape proclivity data was dismissed as unhelpful. Whereas Mould argued that one should examine whether those high in rape likelihood are more like rapists than those low in rape likelihood, Malamuth pointed out that convicted rapists often exhibited wide variance in responding on many measures and in some instances show profiles similar to those on nonrapists (Feild, 1978).

Mould minimised the fact that in the Malamuth and Check (1980a) study, several items showed correlations between likelihood of rape ratings and reactions to the rape and the rapist. He argued that the fact that significant correlations were not found with perceptions of the victim's pain and trauma seriously weakens the findings. Mould regarded these as the two most important items reflecting a callous attitude. But why was this the case?

Rather questionable arguments were then made that construct validity would require that, on an absolute scale, the rape-related attitudes of those high in likelihood of rape should be below the midpoint. This appears to be based on the presumption that convicted rapists would score below the midpoint. Studies with convicted rapists had not shown this to be true (Burt, 1980; Feild, 1978). Mould attempted to argue that likelihood of rape ratings had not been shown to relate to sexual arousal to aggression. He emphasised that the correlations with penile tumescence did not reach statistical significance in the Malamuth and Check (1980a) study. He failed to note that in other studies by the same authors (Malamuth & Check, 1983) and in those of other investigators (Murphy, Coleman, & Haynes, 1986), significant relationships were found with penile tumescence.

Donnerstein and Linz (1988) challenged the suggestion that they designed their research to fit with certain public policy requirements. They stated that no evidence existed to support any such claim. Although their work had been involved in political debates, Linz and Donnerstein reported that they had openly challenged some of the interpretations placed by politicians on their own work and similar work by others. Indeed, they had warned policymakers to beware of the shortcomings of experimental research in terms of sampling, external validity, and demand characteristics. They reiterated the findings of Donnerstein and Berkowitz (1981) and roundly rejected Mould's critique. Male participants exposed to violent pornography acted more aggressively towards a female target than a male target, and did so more vigorously than males shown an erotic or neutral film. The lack of difference between the erotic and neutral conditions was explained by high aggression levels among participants in the neutral condition. This reason was not readily accepted by Mould, but his attempt to discredit it by averaging shock intensity scores across both sexes was dismissed as questionable. It was misleading because shock intensity scores against female targets were low in the neural condition. Mould did not like the use of cognitive processing to explain the results, but had failed to notice that in the literature, media theory during the 1980s had moved on to embrace this form of explanation.

In another scathing attack on pornography research, Christensen (1987) argued that a claim made by Zillmann and Bryant (1986) that pornography has been shown to cause callousness toward women is flatly false (p. 186). He further accused the authors of presenting misleading evidence to back up this claim, in which data from experimental conditions involving violent pornography when nonviolent pornography had been used. This point centered on a debate that had raged during the 1980s about whether violence in media sexual displays was necessary to facilitate subsequent aggressive responding among male viewers. Donnerstein and Linz were also drawn into the dispute with Christensen as a consequence of a reference to their work (i.e., Linz, Donnerstein, & Penrod, 1984) by Zillmann and Bryant (1986). According to Christensen, the Linz et al. study involved portrayals of violent sexual acts, whereas Zillmann and Bryant's study used nonviolent sexual stimuli. Thus, there was no unequivocal evidence from these studies that sexual material alone, in the absence of any violence, could produce subsequent aggressive responding. Christensen challenged the claim that pornography in general had been shown to cause increased callousness towards women. He further hinted that the reason for these authors making such a claim may have been politically motivated.

Zillmann and Bryant (1987) responded to these criticisms by arguing that their research has been misrepresented along with that of Linz and his colleagues. In defending their own position, they also indicated an inconsistency in the reporting of their findings by the Linz–Donnerstein group. A summary of Linz's results by Donnerstein (1984) showed in no uncertain terms that the effects of R-rated slasher films, violent X-rated films, and nonviolent X-rated films were parallel. Exposure to all those materials produced reduced sympathy for rape victims compared to a control group. However, there was confusion because the findings on the effects of nonviolent pornography had been omitted from subsequent publications (e.g., Linz, Donnerstein, & Penrod, 1984). Indeed, the findings in question were not found in Linz's (1985) doctoral dissertation either. Further, Zillmann and Bryant (1987) noted that Check (1984) reported that men's self-acknowledged proclivity to commit rape increased after consumption of nonviolent pornography just as significantly as after consumption of violent pornography.

Linz and Donnerstein (1988) joined this particular dispute by offering further clarification on some of the points discussed about their research. They indicated that results from two different experiments of theirs produced varying results. In one study, prolonged exposure to R-rated slasher films, X-rated violent pornography, and X-rated pornography that was not overtly violent, but may have been demeaning to women, resulted in participants judging a victim later portrayed in a videotaped re-enactment of a rape trial as less physically and emotionally injured as compared with control participants. There was no indication that participants in any of the experimental conditions felt less sympathy for the rape victim, however.

A second experiment found that participants' empathy or sympathy were affected by exposure to slasher films that combined sex and violence, but not by prolonged exposure to pornographic films (with no violence). They also failed to find significant effects on scales designed to measure endorsement of force in sexual relations, belief in conservative sex roles, and the tendency to view women as sexual objects. Further, there was no evidence for the assignment of greater accountability to the rape victim, no sign of participants' willingness to excuse the defendant in the rape trial, nor any change in verdict or defendant sentence following prolonged exposure to degrading pornography.

Exposure to nonviolent pornography could hypothetically be expected to produce a change in men's perceptions of women on certain dimensions, given the tendency of such films to depict women as sexually insatiable and the willing receptacles for any male sexual urge. Such ideas may in turn create a psychological mindset about women more accepting of the use of force in sexual relations. On this issue, Bryant and Zillmann were in broad agreement with Linz and Donnerstein. These researchers exhibited less agreement about the interpretation of results from a study by Check (1984). The latter's study assigned student and nonstudent participants to three conditions in which they watched either nonviolent dehumanising pornography, nonviolent erotica, or nothing. Results showed that exposure to pornography affected participants' later self-reports about certain antisocial behaviors. Compared to control participants, those exposed to the dehumanising materials were more likely to report that they might commit a rape if assured that no one would know and that they would not be punished.

Linz and Donnerstein (1988) identified three problems with this study. First, participants were recruited through newspaper advertisements and hence represented a self-selected sample. Second, participants were told that their evaluations of pornography would be used by their government (in Canada) so that their responses may have been influenced by social desirability factors. Third, the time periods during which participants viewed the stimulus materials and the interval between the last film viewing session and completion of postviewing tests varied across participants. There was no assurance that these varying time periods varied randomly across participants. These criticisms were not totally convincing, though (Zillmann & Bryant, 1988c). The Check study was not unique in using newspapers advertisements to obtain participants (see Malamuth & Ceniti, 1986). The knowledge that the results would be reported to government may have encouraged some participants to be extra critical of the pornographic material if they personally found such material offensive, believing that on this occasion such views would carry more weight. Equally, others who enjoyed pornography may have been inclined to offer more liberal views to argue against the introduction of strict censorship. Hence, the opinions of these participants could have balanced out in the end.

Zillmann and Bryant (1988c) argued for clarification regarding dependent variables in pornography experiments. It is clear that various dependent measures have been used to show that exposure to pornography can change male attitudes or behavior. There is no inherent inconsistency in failing to find an effect on laboratory-based aggression effects (e.g., Malamuth & Ceniti, 1986) and changes in attitudes towards rape. Even in the context of rape myth effects, however, male viewers' reactions may depend upon intrinsic factors within the re-enactment videotape itself. In some of the rape re-enactments, it was unambiguous as to the responsibility of the perpetrator, whereas in others the attribution of responsibility was far less clear. Where doubts existed as to whether, for example, a rape had been committed, this could clearly have an important mediating influence on male viewers' judgments about the defendant and plaintiff.

Another challenge to the veracity of research findings on the effects of pornography was launched by Christensen (1990). On this occasion he focused more on the work of Donnerstein, Linz, and their colleagues. He argued that value judgments had entered the debate about pornography and should not be allowed to cloud objectivity in reaching conclusions about whether pornography is socially harmful or not. Feminists had argued that pornography was degrading and therefore offensive to women; it should, in consequence, be banned. Christensen focused in particular on the conclusions reached by Donnerstein, Linz, and Penrod (1987). Although the latter based their conclusions on scientific research evidence, largely derived through experimental research, Christensen (1990) argued that there were subtle biases in their interpretations of the scientific evidence.

In making his case, Christensen highlighted a number of specific results that derived from experimental research on pornography for which more than one interpretation was, in his view, usually available. The sexual cynicism supposedly cultivated by exposure to pornography was operationally defined in terms of verbal measures of attitudes and perceptions concerning rape and rapists and the severity with which sexual offences against women should be penalised. Young men exposed to pornography characterised by purportedly degrading depictions of women were found to recommend more lenient sentences for rapists, as compared to those recommended by similar young men not exposed to pornography (e.g., Zillmann & Bryant,

1982). Christensen argued that such a result might be explained other than simply as a manifestation of a pornography effect on male attitudes about the seriousness of rape. Instead, the sexual component of a rape crime may come to have less significance for individuals' judgments about the crime: "... the metaphysical loss of "virtue" ... [may come to be seen] ... as not such a tragedy after all" (Christensen, 1990, p. 354). The difference of opinion among young men exposed or not exposed to pornography may be explained by rape being perceived as more comparable to other crimes, rather than by some loss of compassion for women. In addition, if sexual anxieties are reduced, the degree of harm suffered by a rape victim may also be viewed differently. For one thing, the victim may be regarded as having suffered less. However, this would not necessarily mean the same as a loss of compassion for serious crimes. Instead, the amount of compassion felt for a victim would be linked to the degree of suffering they apparently experienced. The solution to this problem would be education whereby individuals are taught that rape remains a serious offence, even if anxieties about sex are desensitised through exposure to pornographic portrayals, that compassion for their victim is warranted, and that offenders should be severely punished.

Christensen (1990) also disputed the way a decrease in respect for women, contingent upon a regular diet of pornography, was explained. The explanation offered here rested on the assumption that regular consumers of pornography come to regard women as naturally highly sexed and easy conquests, because that is the way they are often shown in pornographic films. Christensen argued that the root of the opinions about female sexuality should feature more prominently in any explanation of supposed pornography effects here. A pre-existing aversion to the idea of sexually liberated women lies at the root of the opinions measured in these experiments. Hostility towards uninhibited female sexuality is a pre-set value that encourages contempt towards women who enjoy an active and open sex life. One should therefore not rush to conclude that pornography is a primary cause of such changed beliefs or opinions. The impact that pornography may have on perceptions of female sexuality must be examined in the wider context of existing social and moral values that establish what is 'good' or 'bad' conduct.

Christensen (1990) went on to question the view, implicit in so much of the literature, that the balance of power between males and females in pornographic films is inequitably distributed. He questioned the view that female sexual subordination is the norm in pornographic materials. Rather, men and women are more usually portrayed as sexual equals—both being likely to instigate sex and both enjoying the experience. Both sexes are depicted as equally sexually uninhibited. Christensen challenged the reasoning that observing women engaged readily in a variety of sex acts with a multitude of partners would lead viewers to believe that such women might not mind being raped. He argued that we should not lump together various types of pleasurable, consensual behavior with rape.

Another finding on which Christensen focused was the increased likelihood that men exposed to pornographic materials would commit coercive sexual acts if they thought they would not get caught (Check, 1984). The experimental evidence underlying this finding was questioned. The participants had been found to consume pornography fairly regularly anyway. Among those who did, therefore, could the further limited exposure offered by the experiment really be expected to make much difference to their beliefs? Christensen noted that only the highest consumers of pornography showed an increase on the likelihood-to-rape scale.

Findings from pornography research were further criticised for mixing up descriptive and evaluative measures (see Linz, 1985). According to Christensen (1990) '... beliefs about things like other people's attitudes and behavior are taken as claims about what is good or bad, what ought or ought not to be felt or done' (p. 361). Weaver (1987) reported that after viewing sexually explicit materials, his students perceived women in general to be a bit more sexually permissive. However, Christensen argued that not all Weaver's measures produced results in the same direction. Once again, a loss of respect for women should not be equated with increased perceptions of women as sexually disinhibited (such as the way they are often shown in pornographic films). Perceptual changes on relevant measures did not occur in the same direction or to the same extent for different categories of women in Weaver's studies (differentiated in terms of their perceived assertiveness or promiscuity).

According to Christensen, scientists have an obligation to speak out on moral issues. But they must do so in a responsible fashion and be sure of their facts before doing so. In this context, the measure of the recommended length of prison sentence for a convicted rapist was discussed. Hence, comparisons are usually made between experimental and control groups, who have respectively been exposed or not exposed to pornographic materials. A 'pornographic effect' is operationally defined as the significance of the difference in recommended sentences of the two groups, with experimental treatment participants suggesting sentences of shorter duration. Christensen argued, however, that it was a moot point as to whether the sentence typically awarded by the experimental group (usually between 5 and 6 years) can be regarded as trivial or lenient, despite being less than the sentence typically awarded by controls (10+ years). Perhaps comparisons should be made of the perceived seriousness of rape with other crimes. Is there a pre-exposure to post-exposure shift in the sentencing recommended, for example, for rapists or offenders found guilty of non-sexual crimes?

Conceptual Limitations in Pornography Research.   There are problems of definition relating to different types of pornographic portrayal. Although references are made in the research and by social commentators to depictions that are classified as debasing or demeaning to women, among such portrayals can be found a wide range of different types of sexual conduct. In some cases, scenes of violent rape may indeed be justifiably regarded as debasing to women. But can the same be said of scenes in which women are shown as willing and enthusiastic participants in sex driven by purely hedonistic motives? There is clearly a need to derive a more comprehensive taxonomy of sex scenes, defined by the form of the behavior, the nature of the participants and their motives and relationships with one another.

The conceptual basis for expecting effects of violent pornography on men's attitudes and behaviors towards women has itself been questioned (Brannigan & Goldenberg, 1986, 1987a, 1987b; Fisher & Barak, 1989, 1991; Mould, 1988). For example, Malamuth, Check, and Briere (1986) theorised that exposure to violent pornography may teach men how to perform antiwoman acts, relax their inhibitions about doing so, and condition them to experience sexual arousal in relation to such acts.

Fisher and Barak (1989, 1991) criticised this conceptualisation as an implicit 'monkey see, monkey do' theory of media effects and pointed out that human behavior is not the simple equivalent of all the models that human beings may have observed. They argued, in contrast, that the human observer of violent pornography is a cognitively active person who interprets incoming stimuli and who has a lifetime of learning experiences concerning acts that are socially permitted and those that are socially proscribed (Rotter, Chance, & Phares, 1977; Skinner, 1953, 1974). The notion that brief and transitory exposure to violent pornography can move men to antiwoman thoughts, attitudes, and acts that are at profound variance with the remainder of their learning history is regarded as highly oversimplified and naïve (Fisher & Barak, 1989, 1991).

Certainly, as exposure to violent pornography accumulates across time, its effects can gain increasing power (Check & Malamuth, 1986). Equally, it must be recognised that reinforcement for self-restraint and behaving decently can also accumulate across time and may do so with greater strength and consistency than is true for vicarious or actual performance of sexually violent acts (Fisher & Barak, 1989, 1991). It has been argued that violent pornography may have particularly strong effects because it reinforces antiwoman values that are pervasive in our society (Check & Malamuth, 1986). It must be emphasised, however, that violent pornography so obviously offends so many fundamental social values—concerning decency, violence, and the 'unmanly' act of harming women—that it may prove to be a particularly weak influence on behavior (Fisher & Barak, 1989, 1991).

Finally, it has been proposed that violent pornography may have especially strong effects on some individuals, such as those who have pre-existing tendencies to aggress against women or those who possess few internal restraints against antisocial behavior (Check & Guloien, 1989; Check & Malamuth, 1986). Although such individuals certainly exist, they would seem to be vulnerable to effects of such a diversity of media—ranging from violent pornography to evening news broadcasts—that it would be impossible to keep such individuals from contact with harmful media messages. Empirically, however, it must be emphasised that researchers have generally not found that exposure to violent pornography is a correlate of sexual aggression against women in natural settings (Becker & Stein, 1991; Goldstein, 1973; Langevin et al., 1988; Marshall, 1988).

Fisher and Grenier (1994) tested the unreliability of effects of violent pornography by exposing men to violent pornographic stimuli of the type and duration often employed in this research area (e.g., Donnerstein & Berkowitz, 1981; Donnerstein, Berkowitz, & Linz, 1987; Malamuth, 1981). This was done to create conditions that should produce antiwoman thoughts, antiwoman attitudes, and antiwoman acts, if violent pornography indeed reliably produces such effects.

In an initial experiment, male participants were exposed to violent pornography or to comparison stimuli, and methodological checks were employed to ensure that the stimuli had the desired impact and were perceived as intended. Effects of these stimuli were then assessed on dependent measures of fantasies and attitudes toward women. Fisher and Grenier argued that transient exposure to violent pornography is unlikely to produce changes in a direction that is at profound variance with important and well-learned values to the contrary. They used a 9-minute sexually explicit violent film clip as master tape, then produced different versions of this in which there was (a) a violent male–female sexual interaction that ended with an ostensible positive outcome for the female; (b) an violent sexual interaction with a negative outcome for the female; or (c) a nonviolent male–female sexual interaction.

Measures of sexual arousal to the experimental stimuli included the Sexual Arousal Self-Report Grid (Fisher & Byrne, 1978b), which assessed self-rated sexual arousal on a five-point scale, and the Self-Report of Sexual-Physiological Reactions (Fisher & Byrne, 1978a), which assessed self-rated physical excitement on a five-point scale. The film clip itself was rated in each on 13 five-point Likert type scales, including ratings of how well the woman participant was perceived as being, and how much she appeared to enjoy the activity. Measures of postexposure sexual fantasy included direct and indirect assessments. Respondents were asked to take a few moments and write down an arousing sexual fantasy. They also answered questions to a Thematic Apperception Test. Measures of postexposure attitudes towards women included the Attitudes Towards Women Scale, the Women as Managers Scale, Acceptance of Interpersonal Violence Scale, and Rape Myth Acceptance Scale.

The violent pornographic stimuli was similar in content and duration to stimuli that in previous research appeared to increase men's fantasies about raping a woman (Malamuth, 1981), men's acceptance of rape myths (Donnerstein et al., 1987) and men's physical aggression against women in a laboratory (Donnerstein & Berkowitz, 1981).

The stimuli were significantly sexually arousing and they were perceived as differentially coercive in the manner intended. However, these different stimuli produced no effects on attitudes towards women or rape. Although Malamuth (1981) reported that exposure to 4 minutes and 20 seconds of violent pornography was sufficient to cause nearly 36% of his male subjects to fantasize about rape, not a single man in the Fisher and Grenier experiment created such a fantasy following exposure to similar stimulus materials. Donnerstein and Berkowitz (1981) found that exposure to roughly 4 minutes of violent pornography was sufficient to cause men to increase their endorsement of rape myths or to engage in physically aggressive behavior against a woman. A similar level exposure to such material in the Fisher and Grenier study produced no such effects on any of the measures of attitudes towards women, including acceptance of rape myths and acceptance of interpersonal violence against women.

In a second experiment, male participants were provoked by a woman, exposed to violent pornography, and given an opportunity to aggress against the woman or to engage in nonaggressive responses to her. This design followed that of Donnerstein and Berkowitz (1981). After male participants were angered by the female confederate, they viewed a violent pornographic stimulus that portrayed a woman who has been sexually assaulted but who eventually appears to be aroused by the assault. At this point, experimental procedures diverged from the usual paradigm in that the men were provided with nonaggressive as well as aggressive options for responding to the woman who had provoked them. It was hypothesised that exposure to violent pornography would not be a reliable cause of laboratory aggression against a female target when nonaggressive response options were available to men in the experimental situation.

This study found that even when men are provoked verbally and physically by a woman, and exposed to violent, positive outcome pornography, they chose to engage in little and arguably no laboratory aggression against their female provoker when nonaggressive response options were open to them. These results can be compared to findings from standard laboratory research in this area (e.g., Donnerstein & Berkowitz, 1981) in which, because nonaggressive response options were not available, 100% of men who had seen violent pornography aggressed against a female experimental confederate. In Fisher and Grenier's study, just two participants opted to send electric shock back to the female who had earlier provoked them. Both of these individuals had expressed considerable interest in using the electric shock machine when they were first introduced to it and before they were shown the violent stimulus.

CONCLUSION

This chapter examined the question of how much trust can be placed in research on media sex. The research on this subject can be divided into studies of the representation of media sex, public opinion about media sex, and the impact of media sex. The representation of sex in the media has been investigated through content analysis. As with most research of this type, the content definitions and categories are produced by researchers. The meaningfulness of content analysis data, however, needs to be defined in relation to audience response. The reasons for conducting content analysis research go beyond the objective of producing a description of the way the media depict things. It is important to know whether the media emphasise themes or images that are likely to produce a specified audience response. This point has long been recognised in relation to studies of media violence (e.g., Gunter, 1985; Wilson et al., 1996). It applies equally to the study of media sex.

Research into public opinion about media sex can indicate the status of public feeling about sexual themes as entertainment at particular points in time. Opinions as such are linked to public values and mores, but are likely to shift over time. Opinion profiles concerning media sex (as with media violence) may vary at one point in time with the type of questioning that is used. Questions that ask media consumers to indicate their views about media sex with minimal prompting may lead to an apparently lower level of concern than questions that take the form of sweeping generalisations about the media. Furthermore, although individuals may take personal offence at certain kinds of sexual depiction in the media, they may not necessarily also demand a total ban on that offensive material.

Most of the methodological debate about media sex research has focused on research into media effects. Experimental methodologies has been closely scrutinised and the validity of their findings have been challenged for lacking external validity and leading participants to respond in narrowly defined ways. The debate about experimental research into pornography has, at times, been unnecessarily vitriolic. Scholarly debate should be conducted in a civilised manner and focus on objective, impersonal analysis of the scientific evidence. Veiled and unfounded accusations of researchers being driven by political agendas are irrelevant and unhelpful.

Defenders of laboratory experiments have pointed out that some experimental findings have been externally validated through survey research. Furthermore, laboratory behavior does not take on the same form as real-life behavior for sound ethical reasons. Even an artificial aggressive response within a laboratory setting may indicate an intention to commit harm. Despite these claims, more problematic evidence for experimentalists has derived from a modified form of the classic design that offers participants an expanded choice of behavioral responding beyond a specific aggressive response. In this situation, even previously antagonised participants may be much more likely to choose a nonaggressive response option over an aggressive one, even if the target person had previously annoyed them.

Evidence for physiological arousal to sexual materials in a laboratory setting may come closer to real-life responding, because of the autonomic nature of that type of response. Furthermore, attitudinal shifts following a controlled diet of media sex may also represent a real response, albeit a temporary one. Shifts in behavioral response tendencies, however, may be much more difficult to demonstrate through experimental research conducted under highly artificial conditions.

In previous research on violent pornography and antiwoman aggression (e.g., Donnerstein & Berkowitz, 1981) men were provoked by a woman, exposed to violent pornography or to comparison stimuli, and then told by the experimenter to send electric shock to the woman, ostensibly to evaluate her performance. Men were not permitted to make nonaggressive responses to the woman who had provoked them. Generally, men who had been provoked by a woman and who had seen violent, positive outcome pornography sent the highest level of electric shock to her (Donnerstein & Berkowitz, 1981). Fisher and Grenier (1994) argued that these results may have been shaped by the experimental constraints placed on the participants. In the event of experimental participants being offered nonaggressive response options as well as aggressive ones, there is a strong tendency to choose the former over the latter, even among those individuals who earlier have been made angry. While one might be persuaded by the argument that even artificial laboratory measures of overt aggression may indicate real underlying hostility, the suggestion that aggressive responding in the lab context may not be the response of choice places a much more significant question mark over the veracity of laboratory-based research evidence.

Taking a wider view of the scientific research on the impact of exposure to the most explicit forms of media sex, some reviewers have identified limitations that embrace not so much specific methodological techniques, but the failure to consider the circumstances under which serious real life effects are likely to occur (Lyons & Larsen, 1990; Showers, 1994). Although some of the empirical research has indicated that ostensibly normal males may experience attitude shifts following exposure to pornography, there are certain subgroups of the population who may be especially vulnerable to such effects. Teenagers and sexually deviant personality types may, for varying reasons, utilise pornography in the service of specific needs and gratifications. Furthermore, many types of media sex may be enjoyed as harmless fun, but certain categories of hard-core pornography display highly disturbing scenes and may be most likely to produce adverse side effects. In addition, the effects of highly explicit media sex may build up gradually over a long period of time. Regular exposure to pornography in the long term and use of it as a sexual stimulant may cultivate strongly conditioned deviant sexual attitudes and practices. For various ethical and practical reasons, these are difficult phenomena to investigate. Nevertheless, these are the areas where the most severe and socially unwelcome effects of exposure to media sex are likely to be found.

12

How Effective Are Controls Over Media Sex?

This book has addressed a number of important questions regarding the representation of sex in media such as films, television, and video. These ubiquitous audiovisual media provide major sources of entertainment for millions of people. The growth of electronic communications and information technologies in the past 10 years has brought vastly increased choice for media consumers and greater control over what and when to consume. Indeed, although such developments are regarded as largely welcome by most people, there are concerns about the handing over of control to the marketplace. These concerns become especially acute when attention turns to the provision of material of a salacious nature. With the establishment of multichannel television environments in which content is beamed directly to homes from sources beyond a country's own national boundaries and with the rapidly growing popularity of the Internet through which consumers can access material from international sources, there are increased opportunities for reaching individuals with material that would once have been banned or at least centrally controlled in terms of its nature and distribution.

These communications technology developments have given rise to specific concern about the distribution of erotic or pornographic material. Compounded with this concern is the criticism of mainstream movies and television for joining in a trend towards the depiction of increasingly graphic and realistic erotic portrayals. As the boundaries of what is apparently deemed by the media industries to be tasteful and appropriate for mass consumption are pushed back further, some observers have questioned the freedom that is given to producers of such material (Dunkley, 2000). Much of this critical argument stems not from any assessment of public opinion, but from the conclusion that ample scientific evidence now exists to demonstrate that salacious, pornographic materials are not just offensive but harmful. The case of harm being caused by pornography or, indeed, by mainstream media portrayals of sexual behavior and the kinds of relationships associated with that behavior, has experienced a mixed reception, however. The review of research evidence provided by this book has indicated that, whereas some studies appear to offer convincing evidence of harmful effects caused by exposure to pornography, especially violent pornography, other studies cast doubt on the veracity of this relationship.

The question of whether more controls are needed over the availability and accessibility of sex in the media does not have a simple answer. Consideration must be given to public opinion and the veracity of research evidence concerned with the harms that sexual depictions in the media might have. The need for regulation, control, and censorship must be balanced against the entitlement of most people to choose for themselves the kinds of entertainment to which they wish to be exposed. Consideration must then be given to the different forms of sexual representation in the media and the different channels of communication through which such material can be accessed. There is an important distinction to be made, for example, between a medium, such as open broadcast television, to which everyone has free access, and encrypted television services, videos obtained from specialised stores, and films shown in art house theaters. In each case, different standards may need to operate. Even with productions that are put on restricted release and explicitly labelled as suitable for certain markets only, it would be unwise to allow a free-for-all; certain legal standards must be observed, and clinical evidence regarding the possible role of extreme forms of sexual representation in the genesis of psychological disorders that are associated with the commitment of sexual offences must be given appropriate weight.

In examining the issue of control over sex in the media, it is important to draw a broad distinction between the representation of sex in mainstream media such as television and the production of pornographic material for film or video release on a more restricted basis. A further area that can be included in this discussion is the potential value of educational and therapeutic applications of sexual material. Explicit sexual depictions have been used to draw attention to adverse sexual practices and representations that may give rise to distorted or inaccurate perceptions of male and female sexuality, especially the latter. Such materials have also been used as visual sexual stimuli in the context of the treatment of sexual dysfunction, such as impotency (Robinson, Scheltema, Koznar, & Mantheir, 1996; Wagner, 1985).

Sex is part of life. It would be unrealistic to expect the mass media to ignore it. Whether it causes offence or harm to the public depends critically on how it is portrayed, and on how it is used by individuals. Blanket controls or restrictions may appease some political or religious lobbies, but may not be welcomed by many other people and will not necessarily result in a diminution of society's ills. The types of controls applied and the way they are applied must be sensitive to the type of medium being considered. Controls also reflect a particular school of thought about the influence of sex in the media. Conservative, liberal, and feminist theories about the impact of pornography, for example, represent different perspectives that would endorse different forms of regulation and control over media depictions of sex. All three theoretical orientations, however, are based on values and assumptions that cannot always be empirically tested (Linz & Malamuth, 1993). Hence, any system of control will ultimately be steered by prominent value systems about the kinds of sexual depictions that a society regards as socially acceptable.

Feminist groups have argued that it is not the depiction of sex per se that is offensive in the media, but rather the way women are objectified in sexual contexts. Controls of particular forms of media sex are called for, rather than a blanket banning of erotic entertainment. Indeed, it may not be unreasonable to state that such critics might be more accepting of explicit material in which sexual relations are depicted from a feminine perspective than of less explicit material in which women are shown as sex objects. Equally, concerns have been raised about dangers inherent in any moves towards more restrictive regulation over the publication and distribution of sexually explicit media content. Any such censorship could be conceived of as the thin end of a wedge that might eventually lead to a dangerous degree of constriction of freedom of speech. Commenting on this tension, Cowan (1992) observed:

> Censorship and the growth of conservative forces within society have become increasingly salient. Liberal feminists, along with liberals in general, are concerned about the proliferation of censorship as the solution to media. Along with censorship of media that oppress women, conservative forces are attempting to censor material that is only distasteful to some and material that presents nontraditional orientations. Anticontrol liberal feminists' legitimate fears of the oppression inherent in the right wing antiwoman, anti-sexuality agenda in pornography control must be addressed' (p. 176).

MEDIA SEX: IS THERE A NEED
FOR TIGHTER REGULATION?

A distinction can be made between sex content in mainstream media such as films on general theatre or video release, open broadcast television, and the more explicit materials available on video through specialist outlets or on subscription cable and satellite television channels. This may be regarded by some as a distinction of convenience. In reality, some critics argue that such a distinction is artificial as increasingly explicit sexual images appear even in mainstream media (Dunkley, 2000). There are, of course, plentiful examples of explicit sexual depictions in cinema films on general release and in films, plays, and drama series made specifically for television. Moreover, sex channels can also be found on encrypted satellite and cable television services containing material that might reasonably be classified as soft pornography. Such channels are openly offered at premium rates within the channel portfolios provided by many cable or satellite television operators. In some of these cases, scenes of real sexual intercourse are depicted, although not in the same degree of detail that one would find in pornographic films and videos available only through video stores or sex mail order services.

There are three important areas of media regulation and control to be considered in this context. First, are current regulations very clear and explicit? This question is, in part, concerned with whether those bodies responsible for regulating films and television have detailed and practicable guidelines that are implemented to ensure that adequate and appropriate standards for a particular medium are maintained. There is a further consideration of whether existing legislation is adequate. This has been a subject of some debate and enquiry in relation to controls over pornography.

Second, is the public satisfied that enough is being done to protect its interests through the nature and implementation of adequate media regulations? Public opinion about media sex was examined in chapter 3. Whereas that chapter was concerned with the measurement of the boundaries of acceptability of media sex to ordinary people, in this chapter, evidence will be considered on what views the public holds about the way media sex is regulated. Such opinions have been measured in respect of sex on mainstream media and in pornography.

Third, how much is done to help media consumers decide what to watch? Are comprehensible and effective systems in place not only to classify film and program content, but to ensure that the public knows what these classifications are and what they mean? Linked to this second question is a concern about whether content classifications really work in the way they are supposed to.

THE NATURE OF REGULATION

It is convenient to consider the regulation and control of sex in mainstream media and sex made available through more restricted circulation channels under separate subheadings. Well-established systems exist for the control of cinema films, videos and broadcast television material. Most developed nations have bodies with the responsibility for the vetting of new films prior to their general release and systems in place to control, in varying degrees, broadcasters who operate within their national boundaries. The amount and type of regulation varies across different countries, reflecting the different political, religious and cultural value systems that exist around the world. Whereas Muslim cultures have zero tolerance for nudity in films, television broadcasts, or advertising, in most Western nations, restrictions are relatively light. Having made that broad distinction, however, even within the European region, varying degrees of national tolerance can be found, for example, for the use of nudity in advertising (ITC, 1995).

Regulation of Mainstream Media

In the United States, regulation of media content must tread a fine line between protecting the interests of media consumers and not breaking constitutional rights of freedom of speech. Under this legislative system, media producers must be free to publish whatever they wish, provided that by doing so they do not break criminal law, for example, by inciting members of the audience to commit offences. Equally, media consumers should be free to consume whatever they wish. To assist consumers, however, media content ratings systems exist for films, television, video games, and the Internet. These ratings systems supply advance information to the public about media content in terms of what kinds of material are featured or, more usually, in terms of its suitability for various age groups.

The first rating system was devised by the motion picture industry in the 1960s. In 1966, Jack Valenti was appointed head of the Motion Picture Association of America (MPAA), which comprised a group of film industry professionals, and given responsibility for the development of a voluntary industry code of practice for the classification of films in terms of age appropriateness. The Classification and Ratings Administration (CARA) was created in 1968 to provide the public with advance information about the content of films. Films were initially rated as G (suitable for general audiences), M (suitable for mature audiences), R (restricted under 16, need parent or guardian present), and X (no admission if under 17). The M rating was later changed to GP (general audiences, but parental guidance) and then to PG. A PG-13 (recommend parental guidance under age 13) category was added in 1984, and the X designation was changed to NC-17 in 1990.

Appointees to the CARA board are nonindustry individuals who use a reputedly complex, yet ambiguous set of guidelines in the rating process. The appeals panel, which reviews disputed decisions, is comprised of industry professionals. Obtaining an MPAA rating is voluntary. Attempting to bypass the system and release a film without a rating is unusual, as the members of the National Association of Theatre Owners have agreed not to show films without a rating.

In the United States, new legislation was introduced in 1996 encouraging the television industry to create a voluntary code for rating programs or to have one imposed by the industry regulator (Federal Communications Commission). Although sex, along with violence and bad language, were each considered, the television rating system was specifically designed to be used in conjunction with the V-chip. This technology installed within TV sets enables viewers to block out reception of programs rated as having unsuitable content for children.

MPAA president Jack Valenti headed the commission that developed an initial age-based television program rating system. The ratings devised at this stage were: TV-G (suitable for all children), TV-Y7 (for children over age seven), TV-G (suitable for all audiences), TV-PG (unsuitable for younger children), TV-14 (suitable for children under age 14), and TV-M (unsuitable for children under age 17). Lobbying by parent groups, media experts, and child advocacy groups such as the National Parent–Teacher Association (PTA), the National Education Association, and the American Psychological Association persisted in supporting a content-based system for television ratings (Cantor, Stutman, & Duran, 1996). Proponents of a content-based system believed that differences in backgrounds, individual characteristics such as developmental as opposed to chronological age, and family standards were not addressed in an age-based system. The age-based system's categories were considered to be overly broad because they encompassed significantly different developmental levels. Content proponents also noted that the age-based system could not allow for developmental variability.

The television industry responded to these concerns by agreeing to add content-based descriptors to the age-based advisories. These additional descriptors included S (sexual content), V (violence), FV (fantasy violence for cartoons), L (language), and D (dialogue with sexual innuendo; Salvosa, 1997).

Use of Television Ratings by Broadcasters

Kunkel and his colleagues (1998) explored how effectively the new TV rating system had been applied during its first year in operation, during the 1997–1998 television season. These researchers content-analysed a randomly selected composite week of television programming on 11 channels. In addition, a further sample of prime-time programming on the major broadcast networks was compiled covering a further 3 weeks. While the analysis provided a quantitative count of sexual acts in programs, it also took into account the degree of intensity of the depictions and the context in which they were shown. Sexual behavior and sexual dialogue were analysed and measures were used to evaluate levels and explicitness of such conduct.

The purpose of this exercise was to compare the amount and nature of violent, sexual and bad language content across programs with different age-based classifications. The principle interest in this book is on the findings for sexual content on television. The six ratings were: TV-Y, TV-Y7, TV-G, TV-PG, TV-14, and TV-MA. Programs rated as TV-Y are designed to be appropriate for all children and therefore are expected to contain effectively no sexual content. Programs rated as TV-Y7 are designed for children age 7 and over. Such programs are deemed appropriate for children with adequate developmental skills to distinguish between fantasy and reality. Programs rated as TV-G should be found by most parents to be suitable for all ages, though such programs may not have been produced with a child audience in mind. Again, programs with this rating would be expected to contain little sexual dialogue or behavior. Programs rated TV-PG may contain material that parents could find unsuitable for younger children. This means that some sexual situations and sexually suggestive dialogue are likely to be featured. Programs with a PG-14 rating are likely to contain some material that most parents would find unsuitable for children under 14 years of age. This means that intense sexual situations and intensely suggestive sexual dialogue are likely. Finally, programs rated as TV-MA are designed to be viewed specifically by adult audiences and may therefore be unsuitable for children under 17. Such programs may contain explicit sexual activity and crude or indecent sexual language. The rating system also provided for content descriptors (V for violence, S for sexual behavior, D for sexual dialogue, L for adult language, and FV for fantasy violence in children's programs).

In general, the study found that age-based ratings are being supplied in a way that reasonably reflects the content of those programs. The study also identified programs that received questionable if not inappropriate ratings in regard to sexual depictions and dialogue, but these were the exception rather than the rule. For example, comparing across TV-G, TV-PG, and TV-14 shows, the content of programs with these ratings fell largely within the bounds of the definitions of those ratings as provided in the guidelines.

The TV-G rating is defined as indicating a program with little or no sex. Nine out of ten (91%) TV-G shows contained no sexual behavior. Nine per cent of TV-G shows did contain sexual situations, averaging 1.4 sexual scenes per show, mostly consisting of physical flirting, with some intimate touching or passionate kissing. Almost three quarters (72%) of all TV-G shows had no sexual dialogue at all. Of shows rated TV-G, 28% did contain sexual dialogue, averaging 2.1 scenes per show featuring talk about sex, with a moderate level of emphasis in the scenes.

Among TV-PG shows, 28% contained sexual behavior and 68% contained sexual dialog. These shows averaged 2 scenes of sexual behavior and 3.8 scenes of sexual dialog, but again with only moderate or low levels of explicitness. TV-14 shows were more sexual. Fifty-six per cent contained sexual behavior and 82% contained sexual dialog. These shows averaged 2.4 sexual behavior scenes and 4.9 sexual dialog scenes. The level of explicitness was higher than in the case of the other two classifications.

Although the sexual content found in programs generally matched what would be expected on the basis of their age-based descriptors, content descriptors were not being used in a majority of programs that contained sex. (The same point was true also of violence and language.) Age-based ratings do not indicate the level or degree of explicitness of sexual content in programs. For this, a content-based label is needed. More than nine out of ten (92%) shows with sexual behavior did not receive an S content descriptor. These shows averaged 2.1 scenes of moderate sexual behavior per show. In general, most of the sexual behavior in shows without an S consisted of acts such as passionate kissing, although many contained scenes in which sexual intercourse was depicted or implied. More than eight out of ten (83%) shows with sexual dialog did not receive a D content descriptor. These shows averaged nearly four (3.9) scenes of moderate sexual dialogue per show.

A number of reasons were identified as to why programs may not have received content descriptors. The NBC network declined to use content descriptors at all. In addition, under the rules, TV-G programs are not required to have content descriptors anyway. But also, not all sensitive content in TV-PG and TV-14 shows received a content descriptor. Some TV-PG and TV-14 programs were identified that contained substantial amounts of sex, but did not receive an S rating. In some cases, ratings guidelines deliberately allowed some sex to go through and would only label a program if the depictions were categorised as 'intense.' Another factor was that movies originally made for the cinema and broadcast on TV can be presented with MPAA ratings instead of new TV ratings.

Among children's programs, 11% received a content descriptor. Among general audience programs, 23% received a content descriptor. The most frequently used content descriptor on general audience shows was the rating D (sexual dialog), which was applied to 12% of nonexempt shows, followed by V (violence) at 10%, L (adult language) at 5% and S (sex) at 3%. In prime-time programming on the major networks, V was the most commonly used content descriptor, applied to 18% of nonexempt shows; L was applied to 16%; D to 13%; and S to 4% of nonexempt shows.

According to Kunkel and his colleagues (1998), 'In terms of applying the age-based ratings, the evidence from this study indicates that the television industry is generally differentiating well across the basic levels of the system. For all four areas of content assessed in the study, there is a hierarchical progression with the lowest levels of sensitive material in programs with a TV-G rating, somewhat higher levels found in TV-PG shows, and the greatest level or intensity of sensitive content found in TV-14 programs' (p. 89).

Although there was no problem with the application of age-based ratings, these alone reveal relatively little directly about the nature of sexual content in programs. For this, additional content-based ratings are needed. Public opinion surveys have shown that most parents strongly prefer content-based ratings over age-based advisories (Cantor et al., 1996; Kaiser Family Foundation, 1998; Mifflin, 1997). Unless more effective deployment of content-based ratings occurs, the V-chip technology will offer parents only a modest degree of help in identifying programs that are unsuitable for their children.

Regulation of Media Sex in Britain

The established audiovisual media in Britain—cinema, television, and video—are all regulated to ensure that their contents do not cause offence or harm to consumers. Although Britain does not have freedom of speech legislation as does the United States, there is a recognition in its media regulations and regulatory practices that not everyone has the same maturity or tastes. Some people may find media sex offensive; others do not. Although there is a need to protect the interests of younger viewers, there are many households in Britain that are occupied by adults only. British broadcasters, for example, have employed restrictive scheduling practices for many years. The principles of the Family Viewing Policy and 9 p.m. Watershed centre on the need to achieve a balance between protecting the interests of children and catering to the needs of the adult audience. Before 9 p.m. on the mainstream terrestrial channels in Britain, no programs may be broadcast that are unsuitable for children (under 16 years); after 9 p.m., this rule is gradually relaxed. Most British parents seem to be aware of this regulation (ITC, 1999).

More specific program labelling systems are also used. Ratings have been used for many years to classify cinema films and more recently videos. Broadcasters have also adopted cinema ratings systems or derivatives to classify televised films.

In Britain, the classification of films for theatre distribution and video productions for sale or rent is carried out by the British Board of Film Classification (BBFC). The regulatory picture for broadcast television services is more complicated. The British Broadcasting Corporation (BBC) is self-regulated, with an executive board of senior managers being accountable to a

Board of Governors. Commercial television services, whether transmitted via terrestrial transmitters, satellite, or cable, are licensed and regulated by the Independent Television Commission. However, another body, the Broadcasting Standards Commission (BSC), has also been legally charged with handling viewers' complaints on matters relating to the tastefulness or offensiveness of broadcast television content and with conducting audience research into such matters. The BSC deals with complaints from viewers that concern all television services—BBC and commercial alike.

Within the context of cinema films, many regulators have adopted increasingly liberal views about the control of sexual images in screen entertainment, reasoning that the cinema-going public has become more accepting of such material. In Britain, films for theater showing are classified as 'U' (Universal—suitable for all), 'PG' (parental guidance—general viewing, but some scenes may be unsuitable for young children), '12' (suitable only for persons of 12 years and over), '15' (suitable only for persons of 15 years and over), '18' (suitable only for persons of 18 years and over), and 'R18' (to be supplied only in licensed sex shops to persons of not less than 18 years). Table 12.1 shows what each of these classifications means as far as sex content is concerned.

In Britain, scenes of simulated sex in films rated with an 18 certificate is generally accepted by the public. Indeed, there is tolerance for some sex scenes within films classified as 15. There is greater concern and vigilance, however, over the combination of sex and violence. Gay sex, however, is treated similarly to heterosexual sex. The degree of explicitness of sex scenes permitted depends on the classification of the film. The guidelines adopted by the BBFC in Britain are shown in Table 12.1. In 1997, the BBFC was presented with 382 feature films, 58 short films, and 356 trailers for theatre showing to classify for general release. Cuts were made to 15 (3.9%) features, one short film (1.7%), and 19 trailers (5.1%). No cuts were made to new films offered that year for reasons of sex or sexual violence. In the same year, the BBFC received 3,192 video features, 649 video trailers, and 124 video advertisements for classification. Cuts were made to 224 features (7%), 41 trailers (6.3%), and just one advertisement (0.8%). During 1997, the BBFC made 44 cuts to remove scenes of sexual violence. Most of these were for 18-rated films, and only one was for nonvideo material. The one case of film was for a re-release of the movie, *Pink Flamingos*, by John Waters. This film contained the prolonged sexual abuse and forcible artificial insemination of a woman. Despite its best efforts, however, the BBFC (1998) noted the significant increase in the number of unlicensed sex shops in Britain from which illegal and unclassified material can be obtained.

Turning to broadcast television, in Britain the BBC is self-regulating and commercial television is regulated by the Independent Television Commission (ITC). In addition, the Broadcasting Standards Commission

TABLE 12.1

British Film Classifications and Sex Content

'U' – UNIVERSAL *Suitable for all*

Nudity
There will be little or no nudity.

Sex
There will be no sexual behavior or references.

'PG' – PARENTAL GUIDANCE *General viewing,*
but some scenes may be unsuitable for young children

Nudity
There may be occasional nudity in a non-sexual context, but this should not be nudity for
the sake of it.

Sex
Sex may be suggested, but should be discreet and infrequent.
There may be some mild sexual innuendo.

'12' – *SUITABLE ONLY FOR PERSONS OF 12 YEARS AND OVER*

Nudity
Occasional nudity is acceptable.
Nudity in a sexual context will be brief and discreet.

Sex
Sexual activity may be implied, but without any physical detail.
Sexual references may be stronger and less ambiguous than in 'PG' films and videos, espe-
cially in a comedy context.

'15' – *SUITABLE ONLY FOR PERSONS OF 15 YEARS AND OVER*

Nudity
Full-frontal nudity may be shown, sometimes in a sexual context.
Close-up detail will be avoided.

Sex
Sexual activity may be shown, but will not include intimate physical detail.
Sex scenes will be justified by context and will usually further plot, character or theme.
There may be strong sexual references.
Casual sex scenes will be brief, and sex will mainly illustrate developing relationships.

'18' – *SUITABLE ONLY FOR PERSONS OF 18 YEARS AND OVER*

Nudity
Extensive full frontal nudity is acceptable in a sexual context, as long as there is no undue
focus on genitals.

(table continues)

TABLE 12.1   *(continued)*

Sex
Scenes of simulated sex are allowed, but sex scenes may be limited because of length or strength.
Images of real sex must be brief and justified by context.

'R18' – TO BE SUPPLIED ONLY IN LICENSED SEX SHOPS
TO PERSONS OF NOT LESS THAN 18 YEARS

The 'R18' category is a special and legally restricted classification for videos where the focus is mainly on real sexual activity. Such videos can be supplied to adults only in licensed sex shops, of which there are about 60 in the UK. 'R18' videos may *not* by supplied by mail order.
The sex scenes in all 'R18' videos must be nonviolent and between consenting adults. They must also be legal, both in the acts portrayed and in the degree of explicitness shown. There are no limits on length and strength apart from those of the criminal law. Group sex is allowed, and there is parity as between homosexual and heterosexual sex.
Erections may be shown, as may a broader range of mild fetish material, but no threats or humiliation or realistic depictions of pain are permitted.
There must be no explicit sight of penetration, oral, vaginal, or anal. Ejaculation must not be shown.
Context may justify exceptions.

Note: Source: British Board of Film Classification, 1998.

represents another body to which the public can turn to complain about broadcast standards. The ITC Code permits inclusion of sex and nudity in entertainment and drama programs. It does not allow for indiscriminate or gratuitous inclusion of sex in programs, however. Any such material should be pertinent to the plot. Furthermore, depictions of sexual intercourse are restricted to the post-9 p.m. period (see Table 12.2).

The Broadcasting Standards Commission has a code on the Portrayal of Sexual Conduct for broadcasters, covering television and radio (see Table 12.3). According to the BSC (1998), 'Radio and television have to meet the expectations of wide audiences which will encompass a spectrum of tolerance towards the portrayal of sexual relationships. However, even those unlikely to be offended themselves may be concerned about viewing some programs in the company of others, and are likely to be mindful of the effects on children' (clause 80, p. 35).

The BSC advises against unjustified explicitness and for the depiction of relations between the sexes within a clearly defined moral framework. Broadcasters are further advised to observe sensitivity to scheduling of sexual matters around the Watershed. Even with encrypted channels, there must be limits to what is shown, with channels being bound in their depictions of sex by laws relating to hard-core pornography and obscenity.

The depiction of sexually explicit scenes before the Watershed on television fiction should be a matter of judgment at the most senior levels with the broadcasting organisations concerned. Even in factual programs, stories with sexual aspects should not be presented without due consideration having been given to the scheduling of the program and the likely presence of children in the audience at the time of transmission.

Although it is legitimate to deal with subjects such as sexual relationships between adults and children, the treatment of such topics must be thought through very carefully, being mindful of not just the morality but also the legality of certain kinds of behavior. Explicit sexual acts between adults and children should not be transmitted. The BSC (1998) makes reference to the Protection of Children Act 1978, which makes it an offence to take an indecent photograph, film, or video-recording of a child under the age of 16, or involve a child under 16 in a photograph or recording which is itself indecent—even if the child's role in it is not.

The inclusion in programs of subjects such as incest or child abuse may have a public information role and can be justified on that basis. They may advise children of the dangers of abuse and advise them of the help available. However, realistic, contemporary drama must take account of the ease

TABLE 12.2

ITC Code on Sex and Nudity on Television

1.1 General Requirement

Section 6(1)(a) of the broadcasting Act 1990 requires that the ITC does all it can to secure that every licensed service includes nothing in its programmes which offends against good taste or decency or is likely to encourage or incite to crime or lead to disorder or be offensive to public feeling. [Remainder of this section refers to code giving guidance on the depiction of violence.]

1.3 Sex and Nudity

Popular entertainment and comedy have always relied to some extent on sexual innuendo and ambiguous (or suggestive) gesture and behavior; but this does not justify mere crudity. Much of the world's great drama and fiction has been concerned with love and passion, and it would be wrong (if not impossible) to require writers to renounce all intention to shock or disturb, but the aim should not be to offend.

The portrayal of sexual behavior, and of nudity, needs to be defensible in context and presented with tact and discretion.

Representation of sexual intercourse should be reserved until after 9.00 pm. Exceptions to this rule may be allowed in the case of nature films, programmes with a serious educational purpose, or where the representation is non-graphic, and must be approved by the licensee's most senior programme executive or the designated alternate.

Note: Source: ITC, 1991.

TABLE 12.3

Broadcasting Standards Commission Code
on the Portrayal of Sexual Conduct

Research shows that audiences in Britain have generally become more liberal and relaxed about the portrayal of sex, but broadcasters cannot assume a universal climate of tolerance towards sexually explicit material. Offence may be given by making public and explicit what many people regard as private and exclusive.

Radio and television have to meet the expectations of wide audiences which will encompass a spectrum of tolerance towards the portrayal of sexual relationships. However, even those unlikely to be offended themselves may be concerned about viewing some programmes in the company of others, and are likely to be mindful of the effects on children. Broadcasters have a duty to act responsibly and reflect the fact that relations within and between the sexes normally reflect moral choices. Audiences should not be reduced to voyeurs, nor the participants to objects. The youth and physical attractiveness of the participants are no justification for explicitness.

Sensitive scheduling, especially within the hour around the Watershed, is particularly important for items involving sexual matters. Broadcasters should provide straightforward labelling in clear language and sufficient warnings about programmes containing explicit material.

Encrypted subscription and pay Per View services offering explicit sexual content cater to self-selected adult audiences. But the depiction of sex is bound by the law relating to hard-core pornography and obscenity.

Factual Programmes

Where a news story involves a sexual aspect, it should be presented without undue exploitation. The relative explicitness of such reports must, in any case, be measured by the broadcaster against the time of day at which they are transmitted and the likely presence of children in the audience. Other factual programmes deal with a variety of sexual themes. But producers should ask themselves whether an explicit representation is justified.

Discussion and 'Phone-in' Programmes

There is a wide difference of attitudes, particularly between the generations, towards the open debate of sexual topics. Programmes need to be scheduled with care and labelled to give warning of their likely content.

Fiction

Broadcasters must ensure that actual sexual intercourse is not transmitted. The broadcast of sexually explicit scenes before the Watershed should always be a matter for judgment at the most senior levels within the broadcasting organisations. On radio, broadcasters must take into account the likely composition of the audience before scheduling more explicit portrayals of sexual activity.

When a scene involves rape or indecent assault, careful consideration must always be given to achieving the dramatic purpose while minimising the depiction of the details.

Rape should not be presented in a way which might suggest it was anything other than a tragedy for its victim.

Children

A sexual relationship between an adult and a child or between under-age young people can be a legitimate theme for programmes: it is the treatment which may make it improper, or even unlawful. The treatment should not suggest that such behavior is legal or is to be encouraged.

Explicit sexual acts between adults and children should not be transmitted.

The Protection of Children Act, 1978, makes it an offence to take an indecent photograph, film or video-recording of a child under the age of 16, or involve a child below 16 in a photograph or recording which is itself indecent – even if the child's role in it is not. Even when legal advice judges material to be on the right side of the law, it should be subjected to careful scrutiny at the highest level over the need to include the sequence in the programme. This applies even when the child is played by an older actor or actress.

Incest and Child Abuse

The inclusion of these subjects in well-established serials or single programmes may be justified as public information, even in programmes directed at older children. These programmes may also play a legitimate role in warning children of the dangers of abuse, and advising them of the help available.

Where a play or film takes incest as its theme, there should be particular awareness of the relative ease with which some people, including children, may identify characters or actions with their own circumstances, and may also take them as role models.

In television, material of this kind should be accompanied by clear labelling of the programme's content, while sensitive scheduling and labelling are also called for in radio.

Animals

Explicit sexual conduct between humans and animals should never be shown and should be referred to in programmes only after consultations at a senior level.

Nudity

There is now a greater relaxation about the human body. The appearance of the nude human body can have a justifiable and powerful dramatic effect and be a legitimate element in a programme, provided it does not exploit the nude person. But it can also be disturbing and cause offence, especially where it appears that there is no clear editorial rationale. The justification must come from the intention and the merit of the individual programme itself.

Innuendoes

Sexual humour and innuendo may cause offence especially if broadcast when there are children and young people in the audience. It may pass over the heads of the young, but may nevertheless cause embarrassment to older people watching or listening with them. Care is needed therefore in the scheduling of risque programmes and programmes which would not normally be expected to contain material of this kind.

Note. Source: Broadcasting Standards Commission, 1998.

with which certain viewers may identify with events and characters on screen and may, therefore, take them as role models. The BSC code contains a reminder that explicit sexual conduct between humans and animals is outlawed.

The BSC notes that there is a fairly relaxed attitude towards nudity. There is recognition that the public, too, has more relaxed attitudes about it. Even so, this is not true of everyone and some viewers may still take offence at certain types of portrayal. Finally, the code deals with sexual innuendo and humor that may cause offence when there are children or young people in the audience. It may cause embarrassment to older people viewing with them. Thus, care is needed over when to schedule programs with potentially controversial sex content.

THE UTILITY OF CLASSIFICATION AND RATING SYSTEMS

Media content ratings systems succeed to the extent that media consumers are aware of, understand, and use the ratings and also to the extent that the guidelines are enforced by producers and distributors. Surveys have indicated that parents are aware of and use film ratings to make initial determinations about whether a film is suitable for children (Wilson et al., 1990). Research among American parents indicated that program ratings and advisories lead parents to discourage their children from watching content labelled as age-inappropriate. When discussing programs with their children, warnings about sex (and violence) result in parents making more disparaging remarks about such programs. Furthermore, a rating indicating the age-appropriateness of a program appeared to have more force than a mere verbal warning about sensitive content (Krcmar & Cantor, 1997).

Media ratings have been characterised by controversy and confusion about their purpose ever since the inception of movie ratings in 1969. There is a loose consensus that content that is not appropriate for certain segments of the population, specifically children, is present in today's media. There is little consensus, however, about how to limit access to such content. Opponents to rating systems warn that mandatory systems are a form of censorship, even when their principal goal is ostensibly to be informational. If the ultimate goal of ratings is to provide information that can be used to control access for vulnerable individuals, then it is important to consider both whether control is warranted and whether that stated goal is usually achieved.

There are important issues surrounding the way media content ratings are used by media consumers. If, as a result of their ratings, certain films, for example, are perceived as forbidden fruit by those members of the audience for whom it is deemed to be unsuitable, there may be a boomerang effect whereby the appeal of the restricted film is heightened (Bushman & Stack, 1996; Kunkel, 1997). This may be less problematic with younger children, if their parents already manage their media choices, but may be an important consideration for teenagers, among whom parental control is likely to be more relaxed or even nonexistent (Cantor, Harrison, & Krcmar, 1996; Cantor, Harrison, & Nathanson, 1998).

Media ratings have been more sensitive to sexual content than to violent content. In most cases, explicit sex earns more restrictive ratings than extreme violence, which implies that exposure to explicit sex in media presentations is more harmful than exposure to extreme violence. Research on the influence of explicit sexual portrayals on sexual behavior in children and adolescents has been limited by the lingering taboos about asking children about these topics (Strasburger, 1995). The limited information available suggests that sexual portrayals in the media have limited independent impact in terms of prompting sexual behavior in adolescents (Strasburger, 1995; Wilson et al., 1990). When sex is combined with violence, however, the effects may be different. In particular, the potential influence of violent pornography (defined as depictions of women victims enjoying sexual assault or rape) and sexualised violence (defined as less sexually explicit depictions, but with more violence such as torture) have raised concerns (Wilson et al., 1990). Sexualised violence is prevalent in many films and television programs. Furthermore, as a significant body of research literature reviewed in earlier chapters indicated, depictions of violent sex or rape can shift male attitudes towards female victims of rape, rape offenders, and female sexuality.

REGULATION AND CONTROL OF PORNOGRAPHY

Turning from sex in mainstream media to pornography, several important commissions of enquiry have been launched by governments in countries such as Australia, Britain, Canada, and the United States to review laws on obscenity. These enquiries received evidence from various sections of society, from the legal, medical and education professions, and usually commissioned original research or reviews of existing research literature to inform their deliberations. One of the critical features of these enquiries was the relative weight they attached to evidence concerning public opinion and values about and evidence on the potential harms that might be caused by extreme forms of sexual representation. Although references have been made to research reported under some of these commissions of enquiry earlier in this book, they are considered together collectively at this point because their principal objective was to produce recommendations concerning censorship and control of pornographic publications and productions.

The 1970 U.S. Pornography Commission

The 1970 U.S. Commission on Obscenity and Pornography was established by President Lyndon Johnson to analyse the distribution and effects of consuming sexually explicit material. It also reviewed existing pornography control laws and was charged with producing recommendations of appropriate legislative or administrative action to deal with pornography. The final report (U.S. Commission on Obscenity and Pornography, 1970) recommended stronger controls on distribution to minors, but an abolition of all limits on access by adults. This recommendation was based on the majority conclusion that there was 'no evidence that exposure to or use of explicit sexual materials play a significant role in the causation of social or individual harms such as crime, delinquency, sexual or nonsexual deviancy or severe emotional disturbance' (p. 58). This conclusion was not accepted by everyone. Critics accused the commission of being overloaded with anticensorship civil libertarians (Eysenck & Nias, 1978). In the end, though, its majority conclusions were rejected by the new conservative Nixon administration, which was against relaxing controls over pornography.

Concerns about the conclusions and recommendations of the 1970s Commission did not emanate only from politicians. There were some social scientists who expressed doubts about the credibility and validity of the evidence and the way it had been interpreted (Cline, 1974; Eysenck, 1972). One problem stemmed from the observation that not all the evidence had been given equal weight. There were findings that could be interpreted as providing evidence for negative effects of pornography, but these were played down or ignored. One of the Commission's studies found that exposure to pornography was associated with promiscuity and sexual deviance (K. E. Davis & Braucht, 1971a). Then, other findings that supported a 'no-harm' position were accepted at face value when, in fact, they were based on dubious self-report measures (Cline, 1974). Many of the surveys and other studies commissioned by the 1970 enquiry into pornography suffered from the characteristic shortcomings of such methodologies. Yet, the Commission members chose not to discuss the findings with appropriate caveats in which such limitations were highlighted (Eysenck, 1972). Instead, the Commission's conclusion appeared to be strongly influenced by value judgments on the part of the majority of its members (Cline, 1974).

The Williams Committee in Britain

Over the next decade, further commissions of enquiry were launched into pornography in Britain (Longford, 1972; Williams Committee, 1979) and Canada (Special Committee on Pornography and Prostitution, 1985). The

Williams Committee in Britain was set up to undertake a fundamental review of the laws relating to obscenity. It reached the conclusion that there was no conclusive evidence that exposure to sexually explicit material triggers harmful responses. The Committee recommended the removal of all censorship of pornography inasmuch as it is 'neither immediately offensive nor capable of invoking ... harms' (p. 160).

The major piece of legislation governing obscenity at the time was the 1959 Obscene Publications Act, which employed the statutory test of whether the effect of the material in question was, 'if taken as a whole, such as to deprave and corrupt those who are likely, having regard to all relevant circumstances, to read, see, or hear the material contained or embodied in it.' Despite this presumed test, court interpretations tended to focus on the determination of offensiveness to general community standards, as in North America. Considerable problems in the interpretation of the prevailing standards led to fewer convictions and to some dissatisfaction with lax judicial enforcement, particularly in light of what was perceived to be significant increases in the volume and explicitness of adult material (Wilson, 1972). It was in this context that the Williams Committee began its work.

One of the Committee's major criticisms was that the deprave-and-corrupt test was ambiguous and tended, in fact, to be ignored by jurors in deciding obscenity cases. On a more general level, the Committee came to the conclusion that any new comprehensive legislation should be based on considerations of the harms that could stem from exposure to obscene material. In other words, the Committee felt that unless it could be shown that specific harms arose from exposure to obscene materials, the law had no right to suppress such material. The definition of harm chosen was a very narrow one. Before the law can intervene, the Committee recommended, it must be demonstrated that pornography is likely to have some effect on human behavior, in particular, that it caused the commission of sexual crimes.

Three types of evidence were considered by the Committee in evaluating the potential harms caused by exposure to pornography: (a) evidence from particular court cases; (b) statistical trends in crime as a function of the availability of pornographic materials; and (c) experimental social psychological evidence.

With respect to the first type of evidence, the Committee considered infamous British criminal cases such as the Moors Murders and the Cambridge Rapist, where pornographic materials, supposedly found in the possession of the defendants, were claimed to be instigators to crime. As the Committee noted, it is exceedingly difficult to prove that these crimes would not have been committed had the defendants not been exposed to pornographic material. Consequently, the Committee rejected this type of evidence as inconclusive.

Second, the Committee reviewed conflicting research on the relationship between the availability of pornography in Denmark in the 1970s and reports of rape and attempted rape during the same period. The Committee concluded that the research in this area conducted by Kutchinsky (1973; including some research presented to the U.S. commission) was comprehensive, detailed, and scrupulously careful, and was viewed as indicating no relationship between greater availability of pornography and the commission of sex-related crimes. (See also detailed research by Court, 1980 that was rejected by the Committee.) The Committee also rejected the notion that rising trends in sexual assault in Great Britain in the 1960s and 1970s were the result of greater availability of pornographic materials.

Finally, the Committee considered the experimental research that had been undertaken up to about 1976. They concluded that, since much disagreement existed among experimenters as to the effects of pornography on behavior, the Committee could not recommend further suppression of such material.

The conclusion that there was little empirical evidence to demonstrate that exposure to pornography caused harm was challenged. From the time of the U.S. pornography commission's report in 1970 until the Williams report in 1979, three substantial developments had occurred. First, the nature of pornographic materials themselves had changed. Second, public concern with these materials had increased. Finally, a new body of social science research, particularly experimental social psychological research, on the effects of aggressive, sexually explicit materials had been produced (Penrod & Linz, 1984). Although the Williams Committee commissioned a literature review, this failed to take account of the findings of experimental studies conducted mostly in the United States during the mid to late 1970s. These studies had indicated potential harmful effects of explicit sexual material (R. A. Baron, 1974a, 1974b, 1978; R. A. Baron & Bell, 1977; Cantor, Zillmann, & Einsiedel, 1978; Donnerstein & Barrett, 1978; Donnerstein, Donnerstein, & Evans, 1975; Feshbach & Malamuth, 1978; Zillmann & Sapolsky, 1977). Other clinical work had also demonstrated the sexual arousal of rapists to specific sexual stimuli (Abel, Barlow, Blanchard, & Guild, 1977; Barbaree, Marshall, & Lanthier, 1979).

By the latter part of the 1970s, many people were becoming concerned at what they felt was both an increase in violence and changes in the nature of pornographic materials. Feminists warned that images of male–female relationships were becoming explicitly perverse in the widespread pornography trade. There was a marked trend in the coupling of sex and violence (Malamuth & Spinner, 1980) in men's magazines and also in movies (Penrod & Linz, 1984). In the latter instance, this trend could be witnessed not just in limited distribution art house films or X-rated video releases, but also in some films available on wider general release (e.g., The Getaway and Swept Away).

The Fraser Committee in Canada

Canada's Fraser Committee was created in response to increasing debate over public displays of sexual explicitness. In Canada, as in the United States, there was growing and active opposition to pornography by some feminists, who conceived of it as a harm rather than a moral issue. A committee examining the issue of sexual abuse had completed its investigation only a year before the Fraser Committee ended its work in 1985 (Government of Canada. *Report of the Special Committee on Sexual Offenses Against Children and Youth*. Ottawa: Minister of Supply and Services, 1984).

Incorporation into the Canadian constitution of a Charter of Rights and Freedoms embodied not only freedom of speech rights, but also rights relating to equality of treatment among different sectors of society. Under this legislation, feminists accused pornography of denigrating women. There was also dissatisfaction with regulatory provisions in the Criminal Code with regard to obscenity and the difficulty in applying consistent criteria (Government of Canada, 1985. Special Committee on Pornography and Prostitution. *Pornography and Prostitution in Canada*, Volume 1. Ottawa: Minister of Supply and Services).

The Canadian pornography commission decided not to attempt to define pornography, observing that the terms obscenity, pornography, and erotica all had an elaborate web of various meanings. Instead, the committee decided to concentrate on identifying classes or types of representations and recommending criminal sanctions where these were deemed appropriate. The committee arrived at a three-tier classification system, recommending criminal sanctions for child pornography and sexually violent pornography, and no public display for nonviolent pornography. In adopting this approach, the Canadians recognised the difficulties that the Williams Committee had incurred in specifying intent to arouse as a cornerstone of its definition. Furthermore, the committee clearly adopted the antipornography feminist position that differentiated between erotica and pornography.

The Fraser Committee relied on a research review of the literature to guide its examination of the effects of pornography (McKay & Dolff, 1985). Researchers whose work had been cited were also invited to testify. The committee noted that three distinct points of view—liberal, feminist, and conservative—required different standards for the demonstration of harm. The liberal view saw freedom of speech as the highest value, a perspective that demanded that a clear and definite link be demonstrated between pornography and harm to specific individuals. The feminist view was regarded as arguing for a broader interpretation of harm, in which the mere representation of women as dehumanised and demeaned was sufficient to deny women full equality. This view, the committee felt, made less stringent demands of research findings. The conservative approach espoused a concern for the sanctity of the family as the cornerstone for the larger social whole. The encouraging of sexual relations outside this context—as pornography was perceived to do—was considered an assault on the family unit. The Committee concluded that the available research was of little use in addressing questions of harms to society and to individuals caused by pornography. Problems stemmed from methodological limitations of social scientific studies.

In examining evidence about sexual offenders, the Committee concluded that the importance of pornography as a factor in the commission of sexual crimes had not been established. The research review commissioned by the committee was very harsh, dismissing correlational studies unequivocally and casting doubt also on laboratory studies. Although arguing that the research evidence was inconclusive, the committee nevertheless stated that pornography could impact on the fundamental values of Canadians. The feminist view was accepted, despite reservations about the social science evidence on the harms of pornography. Pornography was regarded as depicting women in a degrading fashion that was contrary to Canadian values. Hence the notion of social harm was accepted, but this view extended beyond the scientific evidence.

The 1986 U.S. Commission on Pornography

From the time of the first U.S. pornography commission in 1970 to the mid-1980s, a number of significant changes were noted in the nature of explicit sexual media. There had been an increase in sadomasochistic themes and the linking of sex and violence—themes that were relatively rare in 1970. Communications technology developments in the form of the penetration of cable and satellite television reception and home ownership of video-recorders made sexually explicit materials available in the home more readily. There had also been a significant increase in the production of pornographic videos and films (Showers, 1994). In addition, new social scientific evidence had emerged during the early 1980s that cast doubt on the conclusions reached by the 1970 Report of the Commission on Obscenity and Pornography. In this context, U.S. Attorney General, Edwin Meese, instigated a new enquiry into pornography (Attorney General's Commission on Pornography, 1986) to 'determine the nature, extent, and impact on society of pornography in the United States.' The enquiry was to produce recommendations for the control of the spread of pornography, consistent with the constitution (Paletz, 1988).

A fairly stringent test of obscenity was put in place in 1973 in *Miller v. California* (413 U.S. 15 [1973]). Material was defined as obscene if it fulfilled all the following criteria: (a) to the average person, applying contemporary community standards, the material, taken as a whole, appealed to prurient interest; (b) the work depicted or described sexual conduct in a particularly offensive manner; and (c) the work, taken as a whole, lacked serious literary, artistic, political, or scientific permit. The material has to fail *all three tests* before it can be found obscene in the eyes of the law and any penalties prescribed. Thus, something could be labelled as 'pornographic' but still not be legally obscene.

In the dozen or so years that the *Miller* standard was in place, the number of obscenity prosecutions declined (32) for reasons that included difficulties in defining what was obscene as well as greater overall public tolerance for sexually explicit materials. Given the growth in production, distribution and availability of pornography in America, however, the conservative Reagan administration called for another examination of pornography 15 years after the first U.S. Commission on Obscenity and Pornography had given pornography a clean bill of health.

The 1986 Commission was financially not as well endowed as the earlier 1970 U.S. Commission. The latter had a mandate to study the effects of pornography and obscenity on the public, analyse obscenity laws, and make recommendations, if deemed necessary to regulate the flow of pornographic materials. This Commission had a budget of $2 million, a staff of 22, and 18 appointed commissioners—plenty of resources to facilitate a large amount of work. The 1986 Commission, in contrast, was less well funded. It had a budget of $400,000 and a staff of nine to complete its mandate. No original research was funded. Few social scientists were called upon as expert witnesses. The major source for social science input came from a Workshop on Pornography and Public Health organised by Surgeon General C. Everett Koop, who separately organised this event to assist the Attorney General's enquiry (Wilcox, 1987). The Surgeon General organised his independent enquiry because he believed that pornography had received insufficient attention as a social issue. Modest funding meant that an economic method had to be adopted to collate relevant evidence. The Workshop invited 19 leading researchers in the field to contribute and present papers based on their own work. This evidence was debated over one weekend and the main conclusions are presented in Table 12.4 (Koop, 1987).

The 1986 Attorney General's Commission on Pornography held public hearings in six major cities around the country. The U.S. Commission avoided the production of a definition of pornography, but it suggested four tiers of sexually explicit materials: sexually violent materials; nonviolent, degrading sexually explicit materials; nonviolent, nondegrading materials; and nudity. Despite being constrained by limited funds, the enquiry nevertheless produced a significant volume of evidence for consideration, some of which derived from its review of empirical research. A significant amount of space was also devoted in its final report to consideration of legal recommendations and descriptions of potentially problematic media imagery and content.

TABLE 12.4

Main Conclusions of Surgeon General's
Workshop on Pornography

Children and adolescents who participate in the production of pornography experience adverse, enduring effects. This activity was regarded as a route to later involvement in child prostitution. *Prolonged use of pornography leads consumers to believe that less common sexual practices are more common than they really are.* In other words, repeated use of pornography can cultivate in users a distorted perception of reality leading them to believe that the behaviors depicted in pornographic materials are actually quite normal.

Pornography that portrays sexual aggression as pleasurable for the victim increases the acceptance of the use of coercion in sexual relations. Films and videos that depict women being forced to have sex against their will, but who then become sexually aroused nevertheless and appear to enjoy themselves, may cultivate the myth that all women enjoy coercive sex. Such a stereotype could encourage some men to believe there is nothing wrong with using violence in sex.

Acceptance of coercive sexuality appears to be related to sexual aggression. Moving forward from stereotyping effects, this observation assumes that changes in beliefs about women's sexuality may produce behavioral effects whereby men introduce violence into sexual relations with women.

In laboratory studies measuring short-term effects, exposure to violent pornography increases punitive behavior towards women. Under controlled conditions, evidence has emerged that men will display more 'aggression' towards a female after being shown a film of sexually violent behavior. For ethical reasons, this kind of research can only be conducted using simulated behavior. It may therefore lack some external validity. Nevertheless, experts attending the workshop believed that this conclusion could be drawn about the results of laboratory-based research, and that it might be indicative of possible effects in the wider sphere (as reinforced by the results of some survey studies).

Note. Source: Koop, 1987.

According to the 1986 Commission, *pornography* was 'material (that) is predominantly sexually explicit and intended primarily for the purpose of sexual arousal' (pp. 228–229). *Obscenity* was defined as 'material that has been or would likely be found to be obscene in the context of a judicial proceeding employing applicable legal and constitutional standards' (p. 230). The Commission covered a wider range of material than would traditionally be subsumed under these headings, however. The Commission considered the issue of pornography and harm and distinguished between harm that may be caused directly to consumers of pornography and spin-off (or secondary) harms that might be caused to others with whom pornography consumers interact. The Commission expressed special concern about sexually violent pornography, which was observed to be on the increase. It was also noted that some research had indicated that exposure to pornography could cause changes to men's attitudes towards women and increases in aggression towards women in a laboratory setting. Some critics of the Commission review of evidence advised caution in the way the existing literature should be interpreted. The evidence was not totally consistent on whether sex alone or sex plus violence was essential to produce attitude shifts or antisocial behaviour. Furthermore, it remained to be demonstrated as to whether the cultivation through viewing pornography of callous attitudes towards women led, in turn, to enhanced propensity to commit rape offences (Linz et al., 1987).

Unlike both the British and Canadian commissions, the U.S. commission made no recommendation to eliminate 'obscenity' from legal use, preferring instead to retain the current definition set forth in *Miller v. California*. The U.S. commission relied to a greater degree than did the other two commissions on social scientific evidence, concluding that the research did show a causal relationship between exposure to sexually violent material and aggressive behavior towards women. It also concluded that exposure to such material could lead to greater acceptance of rape myth beliefs. However, it also recognised that nonviolent sexually explicit materials did not result in the same effects. The limitations of research were noted, but despite these limitations, the Commission was still prepared to accept some of the evidence. The data for sexually violent were less equivocal. One reason for this lay with the greater consistency of material used in such studies. In addition, there were consistent reactions to stimulus materials through self-reports and physiological indices.

According to Einsiedel (1988), the varying evaluations of social science in these three different cultural contexts may indicate differences in the role of research in public policymaking in each case. Differences in research traditions between Britain (or Europe) and North America may account for the more ready dismissal of laboratory-based research in Britain. The European approach tends to regard social problems as stemming from a range of factors indigenous to the culture, compared with which the effects of mass media are trivial. In the United States, the effects of mass media have been studied by experimental social psychological approaches in which the influence of a single factor is magnified. However, the Williams Commission conducted its enquiry before much of the experimental research referred to by the Canadian and U.S. commissions was published.

PUBLIC OPINION AND REGULATION OF MEDIA SEX

The issue of harm that might be caused by sexual content in films, television programs, or videos is a separate consideration from public attitudes towards such material. Regulators and policymakers need to be mindful of public values and public opinion as well as the possibility that genuine harm may be caused by sexually explicit material, especially when mixed with violence.

The public has opinions not just about sex in the media, but also about the way it is controlled or regulated. Surveys in Britain, for example, have indicated broadly liberal attitudes towards the showing of sex on television. This disposition is reflected in opinions about the regulation of such content. During the early 1990s, for instance, the majority of British television viewers (78%) agreed that people should be allowed to watch sex on television if that is what they want. An even bigger majority (88%) agreed that people who do not like watching sex on television can always switch the set off (Millwood-Hargrave, 1992). Reflecting a climate that welcomes greater choice and the need to cater to a variety of tastes, another survey reported a majority of British viewers as endorsing the opinion that if people want to pay extra for pornographic TV channels, they should be allowed to do so (Gunter et al., 1994).

Such apparently liberal attitudes did not mean that the British public was prepared to accept sex on their television screens under any circumstances, nor was there universal acceptance of all forms of sexual behavior being shown in programs on mainstream channels. For example, gratuitous sex was frowned upon. Most viewers (65%) felt it was important that sex scenes should have an important and integral part to play in telling the story in a drama. Although the occasional sex scene might be acceptable, a clear majority of British viewers (61%) felt that it was less acceptable to have sex shown all the way through a program. There was a general perception (among 60%) that the broadcasters operate a clear policy on such matters and do not allow sex to be shown in an uncontrolled fashion. A distinction was made, however, between television and video. Most viewers (83%) agreed that more explicit sex can be shown in videos than on broadcast television (Millwood-Hargrave, 1992).

Perceived Harms and Need for Control

Public opinion about the need for tighter control of media sex has tended to be driven by beliefs that such material can have harmful effects on consumers. This perception is usually linked to more explicit representations of sex and has been especially strongly focused in debates about the depiction of women.

Concerns about harmful effects of media sex have been investigated among American feminist groups. Although feminists regard much pornography as degrading and offensive to women, opinions about what steps to take relating to censorship or control vary. Two opposing positions have become established, distinguishing feminists who support and who oppose greater legislative control of pornography. Some feminists have argued that pornography infringes the civil rights of women by depicting them as powerless and subordinate to men (Mackinnon, 1984). Furthermore, pornography promotes inequality and violence against women (Dworkin & Mackinnon, 1988). Opposing this position, liberal feminists fear that increased censorship of pornography could be disadvantageous to women and could lead to other legislative restrictions on women's rights and freedom in other areas including sexual relations and abortion (Killoran, 1983; Tong, 1987). One group of writers adopted an even more extreme position, opposing antiporn lobbies and arguing that pornography served to release women from a male-dominated culture in which sexual expression among women was repressed. The traditional value system in which female sexuality was tied to monogamy and the family narrowed the range of acceptable options for expression of female sexuality (Russo, 1987; Vance, 1984; Willis, 1983).

National public opinion surveys in the United States (Abelson et al., 1971; Gallup, 1985) have shown that substantial proportions of their respondents believed that pornography has negative effects, such as causing sex crimes or reducing respect for women, or at least, denied that pornography has positive effects, such as improving the sex lives of couples. Some researchers have drawn a distinction for their respondents between depictions of nonviolent and violent sex and found that public opinion is considerably harsher towards depictions of sexual violence (Gallup, 1985; Linz et al., 1991).

In the 1985 Gallup poll, respondents were told that the interviewer was going to read them several descriptions of adult entertainment. Respondents were then invited to give their views on whether they thought laws should totally ban any of these forms of activity, allow them for so long as there is no public display, or impose no restrictions at all for adult audiences. The percentages of respondents willing to ban magazines that show sexual violence (73%), theaters showing movies that depict sexual violence (68%), and sale or rental of video cassettes featuring sexual violence (63%) were much higher than the percentages of respondents willing to ban magazines that show adults having sexual relations (47%), theaters showing X-rated movies (42%), sale or rental of X-rated video cassettes for home viewing (32%), and, even more so, magazines that show nudity (21%).

Further evidence about different political and moral standpoints on the acceptability of explicitly sexual media content emerged from a study with self-identified fundamentalists and feminist women (Cowan et al., 1989). In-depth interviews were used to probe the attitudes of these women towards pornography. The fundamentalists, and anticontrol or procontrol feminists, exhibited uniformly negative attitudes towards pornography and the belief that pornography is related to violence towards women. Fundamentalist women were also uniform in their support of pornography control. Feminist women were split, however, with some opposing pornography control. Anticontrol feminists tended to have a greater concern for individual rights and freedom, whereas procontrol feminists and fundamentalists were more concerned with responsibility for the welfare of others.

Summarising the responses of the 119 recipients of the National Organization for Women (NOW) newsletter, Cowan (1992) concluded that virtually all feminists have negative attitudes towards 'pornography,' but many did not support control of pornography through legislation, because they also were concerned about the harm of censorship, and they associated support for censorship with right-wing groups. In this study, Cowan assessed attitudes towards six classes of pornography: (a) partial female nudity; (b) full female nudity; (c) male nudity; (d) nonviolent, noncoercive, nondegrading explicit sexual activity; (e) highly degrading or dehumanizing explicit sexual activity (e.g., sex in which one partner is depicted as unequal and/or exploited or presented as an object to be used); and (f) violent sexually explicit activity such as rape, use of force, or threat of force.

An overwhelming majority of respondents found degrading material (96%) and violent sexually explicit material (95%) to be pornographic. Around one in three (33%) found other sexually explicit, nondegrading material to be pornographic. Only a few found either full female nudity (13%) or partial female nudity (8%) to be pornographic. Those who labelled more of these materials as pornographic more strongly agreed that pornography should be legislatively controlled. A procontrol orientation was positively correlated with negative feelings towards pornography, beliefs that women are portrayed unfavorably, and that men are adversely affected by exposure to such material. Once again, those in favour of tighter controls of pornography were less concerned about free speech and the costs of censorship to women's rights. They were primarily concerned about the direct harms pornography wrought on women.

The results of the Cowan (1992) study are limited to some extent by her procedure of asking respondents 'to use only degrading or sexually violent material as the[ir] definition of pornography' when responding to questions concerning pornography control (p. 170). Also, sampling only men and women identified as 'feminist' by their membership in NOW did not allow a comparison between the attitudes of feminists and other members of the public.

In another study, Fisher, Cook, and Shirkey (1994) assessed willingness to ban various forms of sexual, violent, and sexually violent media through a random-digit dialling survey of a sample in Florida. Of 1,291 eligible adults contacted, 304 (23.5%) completed the interview. Substantial majorities (71%–77%) supported censoring sexually violent media, about half (47%–54%) supported censoring nonsexual violent media, and about one third supported censoring nonviolent sexually explicit movies (32%) and videotapes (28%; see Table 12.5).

TABLE 12.5

Percentages of Respondents Who Favoured Various Level
of Restriction of Different Forms of Adult Entertainment

Entertainment Forms	Levels of Restriction			
	Total ban	No public display	No restriction	No response
Magazines that show nudity	25	56	18	1
Sexually explicit magazines	47	43	9	1
Sexually violent magazines	77	19	3	1
Sexually explicit movies	32	50	16	2
Sexually violent movies	71	19	8	1
'Slasher' films	54	29	16	1
Graphically violent movies	47	37	15	1
Sexually explicit videos	28	50	20	1
Sexually violent videos	65	24	9	2

Note. From Fisher, Cook, and Shirkey (1994), p. 234.

This study found generally lower levels of support for censorship, but similar levels of support for censorship of sexual and sexually violent materials to a survey conducted by *Newsweek* (cited in Fisher et al., 1994). When violent and nonviolent forms of pornography were distinguished, respondents were much less likely to support censorship of nonviolent sexual media than they were of those depicting sexual violence. Fewer than one third said they would censor nonviolent, sexually explicit films or videotapes, whereas nearly half would censor graphically violent or slasher films. At the same time, more respondents would ban sexually violent media than would ban nonsexual depictions of violence. The combination of sex and violence was critical.

Support for censorship of violent media and support for censorship of sexual media are clearly distinguishable attitudes, although they are also correlated in some degree. Support for the censorship of sexual media showed substantial correlations with age, religiosity, gender, authoritarianism, sexual conservatism, sex role stereotyping, and concern about pornography's effects. Concern about pornography's effects was the best single predictor of support for censorship of sexual and violent media.

Belief that pornography has harmful effects may be one manifestation of 'cultural fundamentalism,' a worldview that favours adherence to traditional norms, respect for family and religious authorities, an ascetic lifestyle, and a moral outlook on life (Wood & Hughes, 1984). Cultural fundamentalism and belief in the harm of pornography results from a set of socialisation processes and represents the expression of strongly held cultural values. Both interpretations are consistent with Fisher et al.'s findings that concern about pornography's harms is greater in older, more religious, more sexually conservative, and female respondents.

Fisher and colleagues also found that feminists were relatively tolerant of sexual media, as compared with religious conservatives. Indeed, Fisher's feminists were more liberal than were Cowan's feminists. However, the latter's respondents were allowed to use their own definition of pornography. The concept of pornography adopted by Cowan's respondents may have been more negative than that adopted by respondents in Fisher's study (Fisher et al., 1994).

Individual Differences and Tolerance for Restrictions

Attitudes to restrictions on the production and distribution of explicit sexual media content are not uniform across all individuals. This fact emerged in studies of the varying opinions about pornography held by different feminist groups. In addition to differences of opinion linked to peer group membership and values system affiliation, personality variables have been linked to liberal versus conservative attitudes concerning sex and media sex. Individual differences in authoritarianism, sexual experience, and anxiety about sexuality may all play a part in influencing an individual's opinions about pornography (Byrne, Fisher, Lamberth, & Mitchell, 1974; Byrne & Kelley, 1981; Kelley, 1985b; Mosher, 1973).

Social Behaviors Sequence Theory offers an explanation for the disgust some individuals experience with sex. According to this theory, repressed attitudes about sex may produce in individuals stronger objections to pornography (Kelley & Byrne, 1983). People who hold negative attitudes about sex have also been found to avoid sexual situations (Gerrard & Gibbons, 1982). People who express positive sexual attitudes are more likely to approach rather than to avoid, and to accept rather than to reject, sexual content (Byrne, 1982). Two specific individual difference variables are connected with attitudes towards erotica. These are level of sex guilt and authoritarianism. High authoritarians are more intolerant of sexual expression and exhibit a stronger desire to control the freedom of others to express themselves in a sexual way (Kelley & Byrne, 1983). Indeed, authoritarians may label erotica as bad per se. In the United States, there is evidence that the most stringent official restrictions on pornography are advocated by individuals who fit the pattern of high sexual authoritarianism and high sex guilt (Kelley, 1985a).

SOCIAL SCIENCE EVIDENCE AND THE LEGAL SYSTEM

Regardless of whatever public calls there may be for tightening regulations relating to the distribution of explicit sexual materials, there has been an uneasy tension observed between the evidence collected by social scientists concerning the harmful effects of pornography and the willingness of the legal system to accept this evidence in a court of law. In the United States, for example, a number of cases have been brought to trial in which the commitment of a sex offence was causally attributed to pornography. Yet the courts have generally refused to find in favor of the plaintiff in such cases. Even where the social scientific evidence has been accepted, courts have been reluctant to endorse greater censorship of erotic materials or tighter restrictions on their distribution because this would conflict with the free speech rights of individuals under the First Amendment (Linz, Donnerstein, & Penrod, 1984).

In the case of *Olivia N. v. National Broadcasting Company, Inc.* (1978), a minor brought a civil suit against NBC claiming that a television drama, *Born Innocent*, had triggered a group of juveniles to inflict injury on her by raping her with a bottle. It was alleged that the perpetrators had viewed a similar incident in the program and that this had caused them to perform a similar act against the girl. The case was eventually dismissed on the grounds that the program was protected speech, under the First Amendment. Inasmuch as the sexual depiction under examination did not set out deliberately to incite others to perform an illegal act, it retained its protection under the freedom of speech law. This 'incitement standard' emerged in other cases in which various kinds of speech, mass mediated and otherwise, have been challenged in court as causes of harmful actions. Such cases have served further to reinforce the need to establish, beyond reasonable doubt, that the speech in question was intended to incite legal or harmful actions (Krattenmaker & Powe, 1978). In the context of media sex, any erotic depictions must be demonstrated to have produced direct, particular, and identifiable harms before they lose the protection afforded to any speech by the First Amendment. Given the methodological limitations of much social science research, it is likely to prove extremely difficult to establish unequivocally that explicit sexual content, even those depictions that include violence, will cause harm.

With the debate that has ranged around the veracity of social–psychological evidence on media effects, and the strengths and weaknesses of survey and experimental research (e.g., Berkowitz & Donnerstein, 1982; Freedman, 1984, 1986; Friedrich-Cofer & Huston, 1986), methodological doubts have undermined the status accorded to the scientific evidence in a court of law.

There is another problem with which legislators must contend, even as-suming that the scientific evidence can unequivocally prove a causal link between exposure to media content and antisocial behavior. Serious crimi-nal acts tend to be limited to small numbers of individuals. The introduc-tion of legislation and accompanying regulations designed to prevent exposure to such stimulus material among those small, but 'high-risk' groups would also affect the great majority of law-abiding citizens whose First Amendment rights would be limited by any bans placed on that mate-rial. In this instance, any benefits in terms of decreased crime from a legal endorsement of increased censorship would need to be weighed against the concomitant reduction in the free speech rights of the majority.

Within the United States, therefore, the First Amendment rights of indi-viduals have been treated as paramount. This can be contrasted with the position adopted by legislators in Canada, who have shown greater willing-ness to regulate pornography more stringently, despite the lingering doubts about the social scientific evidence on harmful effects. In Canada, however, the law has exhibited concerns about pornography that go beyond the need to protect the public against harmful effects. There is additional concern about causing offence to social values (Government of Canada Special Committee on Pornography and Prostitution, 1985).

Although material that is libelous, insulting, inciting to crime, or that features under-age performers would cease to enjoy First Amendment pro-tection, explicit material that does not break the law in any of those ways is unlikely to be censored by the U.S. courts, no matter how graphic it may be or how much some individuals find it personally offensive. One of the rea-sons for the courts' reluctance to adopt a more active role in restricting por-nography has stemmed from an anxiety that this would be the thin end of the wedge. If restrictions were placed on these forms of free speech, cases would be brought elsewhere to restrict other forms of free speech. The con-sequence would be the effective loss of free speech. This effect would have far more severe and wide-reaching implications for society than inconclu-sively proven harms of pornography. Even if the methodological problems associated with social scientific findings are put to one side or are overcome, the implementation of tighter censorship rules by policy makers would re-main a difficult decision to take, given its implications for free speech rights. As Linz and his colleagues (1984) noted:

> If regulatory laws are designed to prevent criminal acts and if the base rate of criminal acts among regulated groups is low, then prediction models based on social psycho-logical variables will tend to 'overpredict' the number of individuals who will commit an illegal violent act. The question that policy makers must then ask is, Are we pre-pared as a society to deprive all persons, or even some persons, of their right to view forms of violent material if only a very small percentage of these individual will be-come criminally violent? (p. 133)

References

Abeel, E. (1987, October). Bedroom eyes: Erotic movies come home. *Mademoiselle*, 194–195, 234, 238.

Abel, G. C., Barlow, D. H., Blanchard, E. B., & Guild, D. (1977). The components of rapists' sexual arousal. *Archives of General Psychiatry, 34*, 895–903.

Abel, G. C., Blanchard, E. B., & Becker, J. V. (1976). Psychological treatment of rapists. In M. Walker & S. Brodsky (Eds.), *Sexual assault: The victim and the rapist.* Lexington, MA: Lexington Books.

Abel, G. C., Blanchard, E. B., & Becker, J. V. (1978). An integrated treatment program for rapists. In R. Rada (Ed.), *Clinical aspects of the rapist.* New York: Grune and Stratton.

Abel, G. C., & Rouleau, J. L. (1990). The nature and extent of sexual assault. In W. L. Marshall, D. R. Laws, & H. E. Barbaree (Eds.), *Handbook of sexual assault: Issues, theories and treatments of the offender* (pp. 9–21). New York: Plenum Press.

Abelson, H., Cohen, R., Heaton, A., & Suder, C. (1971). National survey of public attitudes toward and experience with erotic materials. *Technical Report of the Commission on Obscenity and Pornography, Vol. 6.* Washington, DC: Government Printing Office.

Abramson, P. R., & Mechanic, M. B. (1983). Sex and the media: Three decades of best-selling books and major motion pictures. *Archives of Sexual Behavior, 12*(3), 198–204.

Abramson, P. R., & Hayashi, H. (1984). Pornography in Japan: Cross-cultural and theoretical considerations. In N. M. Malamuth & E. Donnerstein (Eds.), *Pornography and sexual aggression* (pp. 173–183). Orlando, FL: Academic.

Abramson, P. R., Perry, L., Seeley, T., Seeley, D., & Rothblatt, D. (1981). Thermographic measurement of sexual arousal: A discriminant validity analysis. *Archives of Sexual Behavior, 10*(2), 175–176.

Adamson, J. D., Romano, K. R., Burdeck, J. A., Corman, C. L., & Chebib, F. S. (1972). Physiological responses to sexual and unpleasant film stimuli. *Journal of Psychosomatic Research, 16*, 153–162.

Ageton, S. S. (1983). *Sexual assault among adolescents.* Lexington, MA: Lexington Books.

Alan Guttmacher Institute. (1991). *Preventing pregnancy, protecting health: A new look at birth control choices in the United States.* New York: Author.

Alcohol and Sports. (1992, Summer). *Bottom Line in Alcohol in Society, 13*(2), 4.

Alder, C. (1985). An exploration of self-reported sexually aggressive behavior. *Crime and Delinquency, 31,* 306–331.

Alexander, W. M., & Judd, B., Jr. (1978). Do nudes in ads enhance brand recall? *Journal of Advertising Research, 18*(1), 47–51.

Allen, M., D'Alessio, D., Emmers, T. M., & Gebhardt, L. (1996). The role of educational briefings in mitigating effects of experimental exposure to violent sexually explicit material: A meta-analysis. *Journal of Sex Research, 33*(2), 135–141.

Alvaro, E., Reichert, T., & Ahern, R. K. (1997, February). *The impact of sexually orienappealppeals in advertising are cognition, memory and persuasion.* Paper presented at the annual meeting of the Western States Communication Association, Monterey, CA.

Amoroso, D. M., Brown, M., Pruesse, M., Ware, E. E., & Pilkey, D. W. (1971). An investigation of behavioral, psychological, and physiological reactions to pornographic stimuli. In *Technical Report of the Commission on Obscenity and Pornography* (Vol. 8, pp. 1–40). Washington, DC: U. S. Government Printing Office.

Archer, D., Iritani, B., Kimes, D., & Barrios, M. (1983). Face-ism: Five studies of sex differences in facial prominence. *Journal of Personality and Social Psychology, 45,* 725–735.

Archer, D., Kimes, D., & Barrios, M. (1978, September). Face-ism. *Psychology Today, 12,* 65–66.

Athanasiou, R., & Shaver, P. (1971). Correlates of heterosexuals' reactions to pornography. *Journal of Sex Research, 7,* 298–311.

Atkin, D. (1991). The evolution of television series addressing women, 1966–1990. *Journal of Broadcasting and Electronic Media, 35*(4), 517–523.

Attorney General's Commission on Pornography. (1986). *Final report.* Washington, DC: U. S. Government Printing Office.

Atwood, E. A., Zahn, S. B., & Webber, G. (1986). Perceptions of the traits of women on television. *Journal of Broadcasting, 30,* 95–101.

Axelrod, J. N. (1963). Induced moods and attitudes towards products. *Journal of Advertising Research, 3*(2), 19–24.

Babrow, A. S. (1987). Student motives for watching soap operas. *Journal of Broadcasting and Electronic Media, 31,* 309–321.

Baker, M. J., & Churchill, G. A., Jr. (1977). The impact of physically attractive models on advertising evaluations. *Journal of Marketing Research, 14,* 538–555.

Baker, S. (1961). *The effects of pictures on the subconscious: Visual persuasions.* New York: McGraw Hill.

Baldwin, W. (1982). Trends in adolescent contraception, pregnancy and child-bearing. In E. A. McAnarney (Ed.), *Premature adolescent pregnancy and parenthood.* New York: Grove and Stratton.

Bancroft, J., & Mathews, A. (1971). Autonomic correlates of penile erection. *Journal of Psychosomatic Research, 15,* 159–167.

Bandura, A. (1973). *Aggression: A social learning analysis.* Englewood Cliffs, NJ: Prentice-Hall.

Bandura, A. (1977). *Social learning theory.* Englewood Cliffs, NJ: Prentice-Hall.

Bandura, A. (1986). *Social foundations of thought and action.* Englewood Cliffs, NJ: Prentice-Hall.

Bandura, A. (1994). Social cognitive theory of mass communication. In J. Bryant & D. Zillmann (Eds.), *Media effects: Advances in theory and research* (pp. 61–90). Hillsdale, NJ: Lawrence Erlbaum Associates.

Bandura, A., & Walters, R. H. (1963). *Social learning and personality development*. New York: Holt, Rinehart and Winston.

Barak, A., & Fisher, W. A. (1997). Effects of interactive computer erotica on men's attitudes and behavior toward women: An experimental study. *Computer in Human behavior, 13*(3), 353–369.

Baran, S. J. (1976a). How TV and film portrayals affect sexual satisfaction in college students. *Journalism Quarterly, 53*(3), 468–473.

Baran, S. J. (1976b). Sex on TV and adolescent sexual self-image. *Journal of Broadcasting, 20*, 61–68.

Barbaree, H. E., Marshall, W. L., & Lanthier, R. D. (1979). Deviant sexual arousal in rapists. *Behavior Research and Therapy, 17*, 215–222.

Baron, L. (1990). Pornography and gender equality: An empirical analysis. *Journal of Sex Research, 27*, 363–380.

Baron, L., & Straus, M. (1984). Sexual stratification, pornography and rape in the United States. In N. M. Malamuth & E. Donnerstein (Eds.), *Pornography and sexual aggression* (pp. 185–209). New York: Academic Press.

Baron, L., & Straus, M. (1989). *Four theories of rape in American society: A state-level analysis.* New haven, CT: York University Press.

Baron, R. A,. (1974a). The aggression-inhibiting influence of heightened sexual arousal. *Journal of Personality and Social Psychology, 30*, 318–322.

Baron, R. A. (1974b). Sexual arousal and physical aggression: The inhibiting influence of "cheese-cake" and nudes. *Bulletin of the Psychonomic Society, 3*, 337–339.

Baron, R. A. (1977). *Human aggression.* New York: Plenum Press.

Baron, R. A. (1979). Heightened sexual arousal and physical aggression: An extension to females. *Journal of Research in Personality, 13*, 91–102.

Baron, R. A., & Bell, P. A. (1977). Sexual arousal and aggression by males: Effects of erotic stimuli and prior provocation. *Journal of Personality and Social Psychology, 35*(2), 79–87.

Bart, P. B., Freeman, L., & Kimball, P. (1984, June). *The different worlds of women and men: Attitudes toward pornography and responses to "Not a Love Story"—A film about pornography.* Paper presented at the Second International Interdisciplinary Conference on Women, Groningen, The Netherlands.

Bartell, G. (1971). *Group sex.* New York: New American Library.

Bass, A. R., & Firestone, I. J. (1980). Implications of representativeness for generalisability of field and laboratory research findings. *American Psychologist, 35*, 463–464.

Baxter, D. J., Barbaree, H. E., & Marhsall, W. L. (1986). Sexual responses to consenting and forced sex in a large sample of rapists and nonrapists. *Behavior Research and Therapy, 24*(1), 513–520.

Baxter, R. L., De Riemer, C., Landini, A., Leslie, L., & Singletary, M. W. (1985). A content analysis of music videos. *Journal of Broadcasting & Electronic Media, 29*, 333–340.

Becker, M. A., & Byrne, D. (1985). Self-regulated exposure to erotica, recall errors and subjective reactions as a function of erotophobia and type A coronary-prone behavior. *Journal of Personality and Social Psychology, 48*, 760–767.

Becker, J., & Stein, R. M. (1991). Is sexual erotica associated with sexual deviance in adolescent males? *International Journal of Law and Pornography, 14*, 85–95.

Belch, G. E., Belch, M. A., & Villareal, A. (1987). Effects of advertising communications: Review of research. In J. Sheth (Ed.), *Research in marketing* (Vol. 9, pp. 59–117). New York: JAI Press.

Belch, M. A., Holgerson, B. E., Belch, G. E., & Koppman, J. (1981). Psychological and cognitive responses to sex in advertising. In A. Mitchell (Ed.), *Advances in consumer research* (Vol. 9, pp. 424–427). Ann Arbor, MI: Association for Consumer Research.

Bello, D. C., Pitts, R. E., & Etzel, M. J. (1983). The communication effects of controversial sexual content in television programs and commercials. *Journal of Advertising, 12,* 32–42.

Bem, S. L. (1981). Gender scheme theory: A cognitive account of sex typing. *Psychological Review, 88*(4), 354–364.

Bem, S. L. (1993). *The lenses of gender: Transforming the debate on sexual inequality.* New Haven, CT: Yale University Press.

Ben-Veniste, R. (1971). Pornography and sex crime: The Danish experience. In *Technical Report of the Commission on Obscenity and Pornography* (Vol. 7, pp. 245–261). Washington, DC: U.S. Government Printing Office.

Berkowitz, L. (1984). Some effects of thoughts on anti- and prosocial influences of media events: A cognitive neoassociation analysis. *Psychological Bulletin, 95,* 410–427.

Berkowitz, L., & Donnerstein, E. (1982). External validity is more than skin deep: Some answers to criticism of laboratory experiments. *American Psychologist, 37,* 245–257.

Berkowitz, L. (1993). Towards a general theory of anger and emotional aggression: Implications of the cognitive-neoassociationistic perspective for the analysis of anger and other emotions. In R. S. Wyer & T. R. Srull (Eds.), *Perspectives on anger and emotion: Advances in social cognition* (Vol. 6, pp. 1–46). Hillsdale, NJ: Lawrence Erlbaum Associates.

Berscheid, E., & Walster, E. (1974). Physical attractiveness. In L. Berkowitz (Ed.), *Advances in experimental social psychology* (pp. 157–215). New York: Academic Press.

Beschloss, S. (1990, May 7). Making the rules in prime-time. *Channels,* 23–77.

Beuf, F. A. (1974). Doctor, lawyer, household drudge. *Journal of Communication, 24,* 110–118.

Biblow, E. (1973). Imaginative play and the control of aggressive behavior. In J. L. Singer (Ed.), *The child's world of make-believe: Experimental studies of imaginative play* (pp. 104–128). New York: Academic Press.

Bigler, M. O. (1989, October/November). Adolescent sexual behavior in the eighties. *SIECUS Report,* pp. 6–9.

Billy, J., & Udry, J. R. (1983). *The effects of age and pubertal development on adolescent sexual behavior.* Chapel Hill, NC: Carolina Population Centre.

Blanchard, G. (1989). *Sex offender treatment: A psychoeducational model.* Golden Valley, MN: Golden Valley Institute for Behavioral Medicine.

Boddewyn, J., & Kunz, H. (1991). Sex and decency issues in advertising: General and internal dimensions. *Business Horizons, 34,* 13–20.

Bogaert, A. F. (1993). *The sexual media: The role of individual differences.* Unpublished doctoral dissertation, University of Western Ontario, London, Ontario, Canada.

Borchert, J. (1991, April). *The impact of sexual and violent films on women viewers.* Paper presented at the meeting of the Western Psychological Association, San Francisco.

Brannigan, A., & Goldenberg, S. (1986). Social science versus jurisprudence in Wagner: The study of pornography, harm and the law of obscenity in Canada. *The Canadian Journal of Sociology, 11,* 419–431.

Brannigan, A., & Goldenberg, S. (1987a). The study of aggressive pornography: The vicissitudes of relevance. *Critical Studies in Mass Communication, 4,* 262–283.

Brannigan, A., & Goldenberg, S. (1987b). Pornography studies: The second wave [A review essay]. *Law in Context, 5,* 56–72.

Braverman, P. K., & Strasburger, V. C. (1993). Adolescent sexual activity. *Clinical Pediatrics, 32,* 658–668.

Bretl, D., & Cantor, J. (1988). The portrayal of men and women in U.S. television commercials: A recent content analysis and trends over 15 years. *Sex Roles, 18,* 595–609.

Briere, J., Corne, S., Rintz, M., & Malamuth, N. M. (1984, August). *The rape arousal inventory: predicting actual and potential sexual aggression in a university population.* Paper presented at the annual meeting of the American Psychological Association, Toronto.

British Board of Film Classification. (1998). *Annual report 1997–98*. London: Author.

Broadcasting Standards Commission (1998, June). *Codes of guidance*. London: Author.

Brosius, H-B., Weaver, J. B., & Staab, J. F. (1993). Exploring the social and sexual "reality" of contemporary pornography. *Journal of Sex Research, 31*(2), 161–170.

Brown, D., & Bryant , J. (1989). The manifest content of pornography. In D. Zillmann & J. Bryant (Eds.), *Pornography: Research advances and policy considerations* (pp. 3–24). Hillsdale, NJ: Lawrence Erlbaum Associates.

Brown, J. D., & Campbell, K. (1986). Race and gender in music videos: The same beat but a different drummer. *Journal of Communication, 36*, 94–106.

Brown, J. D., Childers, K. W., & Waszak, C. S. (1990). Television and adolescent sexuality. *Journal of Adolescent Health Care*, 11, 62–70.

Brown, J. D., Greenberg, B. S., & Buerkel-Rothfuss, N. L. (1993). Mass media, sex and sexuality. *Journal of Adolescent Health Care, 14*, 62–70.

Brown, J. D., & Newcomer, S. F. (1991). Television viewing and adolescents' sexual behavior. *Journal of Homosexuality, 21*, 77–91.

Brown, J. D., & Steele, J. R. (1995). *Sex and the mass media*. Menlo Park, CA: Kaiser Family Foundation.

Brown, J. D., White, A. B., & Nikopoulou, L. (1993). Disinterest, intrigue, resistance: Early adolescent girls' use of sexual media content. In B. S. Greenberg, J. D. Brown, & N. L. Buerkel-Rothfuss (Eds.), *Media, sex and the adolescent* (pp. 177–195). Cresskill, NJ: Hampton Press.

Brown, L. K., DiClemente, R. J., & Peck, T. (1992). Predictors of condom use in sexually active adolescents. *Journal of Adolescent Health, 13*(8), 651–657.

Brownmiller, S. (1975). *Against our will: Men, women and rape*. New York: Simon and Schuster.

Brownmiller, S. (1984, November). The place of pornography: Packaging eros for a violent age [Comments to a forum held at the new School for Social Research in New York City, moderated by L. H. Lapham]. *Harper's*, pp. 31–39.

Bryant, J. (1985, September 11). *Effects of massive exposure to sexually-explicit television fare on adolescents moral judgement*. Testimony presented before the U.S. Attorney General's Commission of Pornography, Houston, TX.

Bryant, J., & Brown, D. (1989). Use of pornography. In D. Zillmann & J. Bryant (Eds.), *Pornography: Research advances and policy considerations* (pp. 35–55). Hillsdale, NJ: Lawrence Erlbaum Associates.

Bryant, J. ,& Comisky, P. W. (1978). The effect of positioning of a message within differentially cognitively involving portions of a television segment on recall of the message. *Human Communication Research, 5*(1), 63–75.

Bryant, J., & Rockwell, D. (1994). Effects of massive exposure to sexually oriented prime-time television programming on adolescents' moral judgements. In D. Zillmann, J. Bryant, & A. C. Huston (Eds.), *Media, children and the family: Social scientific psychodynamic and clinical perspectives* (pp. 183–195). Hillsdale, NJ: Lawrence Erlbaum Associates.

Buerkel-Rothfuss, N. L., & Mayes, S. (1981). Soap opera viewing: The cultivation effect. *Journal of Communication, 31*(3), 108–115.

Buerkel-Rothfuss, N. L., & Strouse, J. S. (1993). Media exposure and perceptions of sexual behaviors: The cultivation hypothesis moves to the bedroom. In B. S. Greenberg, J. D. Brown, & N. L. Buerkel-Rothfuss (Eds.), *Media, sex and the adolescent* (pp. 225–247). Cresskill, NJ: Hampton Press.

Buerkel-Rothfuss, N. L., Strouse, J. S., Pettey, G., & Shatzer, M. (1993). Adolescents' and young adults' exposure to sexually oriented and sexually explicit media. In B. S. Greenberg, J. D. Brown, & N. L. Buerkel-Rothfuss (Eds.), *Media, sex and the adolescent* (pp. 99–114). Cresskill, NJ: Hampton Press.

Burgess, A. (1984). Pornography victims and perpetrators. In D. Scott (Ed.), *Symposium on media violence and pornography: Proceedings resource book and research guide* (pp. 173–183). Toronto: Media Action Group.

Burt, M. R. (1980). Cultural myths and support for rape. *Journal of Personality and Social Psychology, 38,* 217–230.

Bushman, B. J. (1998). Effects of television violence on memory for commercial messages. *Journal of Experimental Psychology: Applied, 4*(4), 291–307.

Bushman, B. J., & Stack, A. D. (1996). Forbidden fruit versus tainted fruit: Effects of warning labels on attraction to television violence. *Journal of Experimental Psychology: Applied, 2,* 207–226.

Buss, D. M. (1995). Evolutionary psychology: A new paradigm for psychological science. *Psychological Inquiry, 6,* 1–30.

Buss, D. M., & Schmidt, D. P. (1993). Sexual strategies theory: An evolutionary perspective on human mating. *Psychological Review, 100,* 204–232.

Butler, M., & Paisley, W. (1980). *Women and the mass media.* New York: Human Sciences Press.

Buvat, J., Buvat-Berbaut, M., Lemare, A., Marcolin, G., & Quittelier, E. (1990). Recent developments in the clinical assessment and diagnoses of erectile dysfunction. *Annual Review of Sex Research, 1,* 265–308.

Byrne, D. (1977). Social psychology and the study of sexual behavior. *Personality and Social Psychology Bulletin, 3,* 3–30.

Byrne, D. (1982). Predicting human sexual behavior. In A. G. Kraut (Ed.), *The G. Stanley Hall Lecture Series* (Vol. 2, pp. 207–254). Washington, DC: American Psychological Association.

Byrne, D. (1983). The antecedents, correlates, and consequences of erotophobia-erotophilia. In C. Davies (Ed.), *Challenges in sexual science: Current theoretical issues and research advances* (pp. 53–75). Philadelphia: Society for the Scientific Study of Sex.

Byrne, D., Fisher, J. D., Lamberth, J. & Mitchell, H. E. (1974). Evaluations of erotica: Facts or feelings? *Journal of Personality, 41,* 385–394.

Byrne, D., & Kelley, K. (1981). *An introduction to personality* (3rd ed.). Englewood Cliffs, NJ: Prentice Hall.

Byrne, D., & Lamberth, J. (1971). The effect of erotic stimuli on sex arousal, evaluative responses, and subsequent behavior. In *Technical Report of the Commission on obscenity and Pornography* (Vol. 8). Washington, DC: U.S. Government Printing Office.

Caballero, M. J., Lumpkin, J., & Madden, J. (1989). Using physical attractiveness as an advertising tool: An empirical test of the attraction phenomenon. *Journal of Advertising Research, 29,* 16–21.

Canary, D. J., & Spitzberg, B. H. (1993). Loneliness and media gratifications. *Communication Research, 20,* 800–821.

Cantor, J., Harrison, K., & Krcmar, M. (1996). Ratings and advisories for television programming. *National Television Violence Study Scientific Papers 1994–95.* Studio City, CA: Mediascope.

Cantor, J., Harrison, K., & Nathanson, A. (1998). Ratings and advisories for television programming. *National Television Violence Study Year 2.* Newbury Park, CA: Sage.

Cantor, J., Stutman, S., & Duran, V. (1996, November 21). *What parents want in a television rating system: Results of a national survey.* Chicago, IL: National Parent-Teacher Association.

Cantor, J. R., Zillmann, D., & Einsiedel, E. F. (1978). Female responses to provocation after exposure to aggressive and erotic films. *Communication Research, 5*(4), 395–411.

Carnes, P. J. (1984). *Out of the shadows: Understanding sexual addiction*. Minneapolis: Comp Care.

Carnes, P. J. (1989). *Contrary to love: Helping the sexual addict*. Minneapolis: Comp Care.

Carnes, P. J. (1991). *Don't call it love*. New York: Bantam.

Carrol, J. L., Volk, K. D., & Shibley-Hyde, J. (1985). Differences between males and females in motives for engaging in sexual intercourse. *Archives of Sexual Behavior, 14*, 131–139.

Carveth, R., & Alexander, A. (1985). Soap opera viewing motivations and the cultivation process. *Journal of Broadcasting and Electronic Media, 29*, 259–273.

Ceniti, J., & Malamuth, N. (1984). effects of repeated exposure to sexually violent or nonviolent stimuli on sexual arousal to rape and non-rape depictions. *behavior Research & Therapy, 22*, 535–548.

Ceulemans, M., & Fauconnier, G. (1979). *Mass media: The image, role and social conditions of women* (Report No. 84). Paris, France: United Nations Educational, Scientific and Cultural Organisation.

Chaiken, S. (1979). Communicator physical attractiveness and persuasion. *Journal of Personality and Social Psychology, 37*, 1387–1394.

Champion, H., & Furnham, A. (1999). The effect of the media on body satisfaction in adolescent girls. *European Eating Disorders Review, 7*, 213–228.

Charting the Adult Video Market (1989). *Adult video news: 1989 buyer's guide*, 6–7.

Check, J. V. P. (1984). *The effects of violent and nonviolent pornography*. (Contract No. 955V, 19200-3-0899). Ottawa, Ontario: Canadian Department of Justice.

Check, J. V. P. & Guloien, T. H. (1989). Reported proclivity for coercive sex following repeated exposure to sexually violent pornography, nonviolent dehumanising pornography, and erotica. In D. Zillmann & J. Bryant (Eds.), *Pornography: Research advances and policy considerations* (pp. 159–184). Hillsdale, NJ: Lawrence Erlbaum Associates.

Check, J. V. P., & Malamuth, N. M. (1983). Sex role stereotyping and reactions to depictions of stranger versus acquaintance rape. *Journal of Personality and Social Psychology, 45*, 344–356.

Check, J. V. P., & Malamuth, N. M. (1984). Can participation in pornography experiments have positive effects? *Journal of Sex Research, 20*, 14–31.

Check, J. V. P., & Malamuth, N. M. (1986). Pornography and sexual aggression: A social learning theory analysis. *Communication Yearbook, 9* (pp. 181–213). Beverly Hills, CA: Sage.

Check, J. V. P., & Maxwell, D. (1992). *Pornography consumption and pro-rape attitudes in children*. Paper presented at the XXVth International Congress of Psychology, Brussels.

Chestnut, R., LaChance, C., & Lubitz, A. (1977). The 'decorative' female model: Sexual stimuli and the recognition of advertisements. *Journal of Advertising, 6*, 11–14.

Christensen, F. (1987). Effects of pornography: The debate continues. *Journal of Communication, 37*(1), 186–188.

Christensen, F. M. (1990). Cultural and ideological bias in pornography research. *Philosophy of the Social Sciences, 20*(3), 351–375.

Cline, V. B. (Ed.). (1974). *Where do you draw the line? An exploration into media violence, pornography, and censorship*. Provo, UT: Brigham Young University Press.

Cline, V. B. (1994). Pornography effects: Empirical and clinical evidence. In D. Zillmann, J. Bryant, & A. C. Huston (Eds.), *Media, children and the family: Social scientific, psychodynamic and clinical perspectives* (pp. 229–247). Hillsdale, NJ: Lawrence Erlbaum Associates.

Cohen, D. (1981). *Consumer behavior*. New York: Random House, Inc.

Colman, E. J. (1988). Sexual compulsivity: Definition, etiology, and treatment consider-ations. In E. Colman (Ed.), *Chemical dependency and intimacy dysfunction* (pp. 189–204). New York: Haworth Press.

Commission on Obscenity and Pornography (1970). *U.S. presidential commission on obscenity and oornography.* New York: Bantam Books.

Commission on Obscenity and Pornography (1971). *Technical reports of the U. S. Commission on obscenity and pornography* (Vols. 1–9). Washington, DC: U.S. Government Printing Office.

Committee on Sexual Offences Against Children and Youths (1984). *Sexual offences against children.* Ottawa: Canadian Government Publishing Center.

Compesi, R. J. (1980). Gratifications of daytime TV serial viewers. *Journalism Quarterly, 57,* 155–158.

Cook, R. F., & Fosen, R. H. (1971). Pornography and the sex offender: patterns of exposure and immediate arousal effects of pornographic stimuli. In *Technical report of the commission on obscenity and pornography* (Vol. 7). Washington, DC: U.S. Government Printing Office.

Cook, R. F., Fosen, R. H., & Pacht, A. (1971). Pornography and the sex offender: Patterns of previous exposure and arousal effects of pornographic stimuli. *Journal of Applied Psychology, 55,* 503–511.

Cope, K., & Kunkel, D. (1999, May). *Sexual messages in the television shows most frequently viewed by adolescents.* Paper presented at the annual conference of the International Communication Association, San Francisco.

Copeland, G. A., & Slater, D. (1985). Television, fantasy and vicarious catharsis. *Critical Studies in Mass Communication, 2,* 352–362.

Corder-Bolz, C. R. (1980). Mediation: The role of significant others. *Journal of Communication, 30*(3), 106–118.

Cosmides, L., & Tooby, J. (1987). From evolution to behavior: Evolutionary psychology as the missing link. In J. Dupre (Ed.), *The latest are the best: Essays on evolution and optimality* (pp. 277–306). Cambridge, MA: MIT Press.

Costlin, X., Kibler, K. J., & Crank, S. (1982, August). *Beliefs about rape and women's social roles.* Paper presented at the meeting of the American Psychological Association, Washington, DC.

Court, J. H. (1977). Pornography and sex crimes: A re-evaluation in the light of recent trends around the world. *International Journal of Criminality and Penology, 5,* 129–157.

Court, J. H. (1980). *Pornography and the harm condition.* Adelaide: Flinders University.

Court, J. H. (1984). Sex and violence: A ripple effect. In N. M. Malamuth & E. Donnerstein (Eds.), *Pornography and sexual aggression* (pp. 143–172). New York: Academic Press.

Courtney, A. E. & Whipple, T. W. (1983). *Sex stereotyping in advertising.* Lexington, MA: D.C. Heath and Company.

Courtright, J. A., & Baran, S. J. (1980). The acquisition of sexual information by young people. *Journalism Quarterly, 57,* 107–114.

Cowan, G. (1979). *See no evil: The backstage battle over sex and violence on television.* New York: Simon & Schuster.

Cowan, G. (1992). Feminist attitudes toward pornography control. *Psychology of Women Quarterly, 16,* 165–177.

Cowan, G., & Campbell, R. R. (1995). Rape causal attitudes among adolescents. *Journal of Sex Research, 32*(2), 145–153.

Cowan, G., Chase, C. J., & Stahly, G. B. (1989). Feminist and fundamentalist women's attitudes toward pornography control. *Psychology of Women Quarterly, 13,* 97–112.

Cowan, G., & Dunn, K. F. (1994). What themes in pornography lead to perceptions of the degradation of women? *Journal of Sex Research, 31*(1), 11–21.

Cowan, G., Lee, C., Levy, D., & Snyder, D. (1988). Dominance and inequality in X-rated videocassettes. *Psychology of Women Quarterly, 12,* 299–312.

Cowan, G., & O'Brien, M. (1990). *Gender survival versus death in slasher films: A content analysis.* Unpublished manuscript, California State University, San Benardino.

Cowan, G., & Stahly, G. B. (1992). Attitudes toward pornography control. In J. C. Chrisler & D. Howards (Eds.), *New directions in feminist psychology: Practice, theory and research* (pp. 200–214). New York: Springer.

Crabbe, A. (1988). Feature-length sex films. In G. Day & C. Bloom (Eds.), *Perspectives on pornography: Sexuality in film and literature* (pp. 44–66). London: Macmillan.

Davies, K. (1997). Voluntary exposure to pornography and men's attitudes toward feminism and rape. *Journal of Sex Research, 34*(2), 131–151.

Davis, D. M. (1990). Portrayals of women in prime-time network television: Some demographic characteristics. *Sex Roles, 23,* 325–332.

Davis, K. E., & Braucht, G. N. (1971a). Exposure to pornography, character, and sexual deviance: A retrospective survey. In *Technical report of the commission on obscenity and pornography* (Vol. 7). Washington, DC: U.S. Government Printing Office.

Davis, K. E., & Braucht, G. N. (1971b). Reactions to viewing films of erotically realistic heterosexual behavior. In *Technical report of the commission on obscenity and pornography* (Vol. 8). Washington, DC: U.S. Government Printing Office.

Day, G. (1988). Looking at women: Notes toward a theory of porn. In G. Day & C. Bloom (Eds.), *Perspectives on pornography: Sexuality in film and literature* (pp. 83–100). London: Macmillan.

Debevec, K., Madden, T. J., & Kernan, J. B. (1986). Physical attractiveness, message evaluation and compliance: A structural examination. *Psychological Reports, 58,* 503–508.

Demare, D. (1985). *The effects of erotic and sexually violent mass media on attitudes towards women and rape.* Unpublished manuscript, University of Winnipeg, Winnipeg, Manitoba.

Demare, D., Briere, J., & Lips, H. M. (1988). Violent pornography and self-reported likelihood of sexual aggression. *Journal of Research in Personality, 22,* 140–155.

Devaney, B. (1981). *An analysis of the determinants of adolescent pregnancy and childbearing.* (Final Report to NICHD). Bethesda, MD.

DHSS/Welsh Office (1987). *AIDS: Monitoring Response to the Public Advertising Campaign—February 1986–February 1987.* London: Her Majesty's Stationery Office.

Diamond, S. (1985). Pornography: Image and reality. In V. Burstyn (Ed.), *Women against censorship* (pp. 40–57). Vancouver, BC: Douglas & McIntyre.

Diamond, M., & Dannemiller, J. E. (1989). Pornography and community standards in Hawaii: Comparisons with other states. *Archives of Sexual Behavior, 18,* 475–495.

Dienstbier, R. A. (1977). Sex and violence: Can research have it both ways? *Journal of Communication, 27,* 176–188.

Dietz, S. R., Blackwell, K. T., Daley, P. C., & Bentley, B. J. (1982). Measurement of empathy for rape victims and rapists. *Journal of Personality and Social Psychology, 43,* 372–384.

Dietz, P. E., & Evans, B. (1982). Pornographic imagery and prevalence of paraphilia. *American Journal of Psychiatry, 139,* 1493–1495.

Dietz, P. E., Harry, B., & Hazelwood, R. R. (1986). Detective magazines: Pornography for the sexual sadist? *Journal of Forensic Sciences, 31*(1), 197–211.

Dipboye, R. L., & Flanagan, M. F. (1979). Research settings in industrial and organisational psychology: Are findings in the field more generalisable than in the laboratory? *American Psychologist, 34,* 141–150.

Dodd, D., Harcar, V., Foerch, B., & Anderson, H. (1989). Face-ism and facial expressions of women in magazine photos. *The Psychological Record, 39,* 325–331.

Donnerstein, E. (1980). Aggressive erotica and violence against women. *Journal of Personality and Social Psychology, 39,* 269–277.

Donnerstein, E. (1983). Erotica and human aggression. In R. Geen & E. Donnerstein (Eds.), *Aggression: Theoretical and empirical reviews* (Vol. 2, pp. 127–154). New York: Academic Press.

Donnerstein, E. (1984). Pornography: Its effect on violence against women. In N. M. Malamuth & E. Donnerstein (Eds.), *Pornography and sexual aggression* (pp. 53–81). Orlando, FL: Academic Press.

Donnerstein, E., & Barrett, G. (1978). Effect of erotic stimuli on male aggression toward females. *Journal of Personality and Social Psychology, 36,* 180–188.

Donnerstein, E., & Berkowitz, L. (1981). Victim reactions in aggressive erotic films as a factor in violence against women. *Journal of Personality and Social Psychology, 41,* 710–724.

Donnerstein, E., Donnerstein, M., & Evans, R. (1975). Erotic stimuli and aggression: Facilitation or inhibition? *Journal of Personality and Social Psychology, 32,* 237–244.

Donnerstein, E., & Hallam, J. (1978). Facilitatory effects of erotica on aggression toward women. *Journal of Personality and Social Psychology, 36,* 1270–1277.

Donnerstein, E., & Linz, D. (1988). A critical analysis of "A critical analysis of recent research on violent erotica." *Journal of Sex Research, 24,* 348–352.

Donnerstein, E., Linz, D., & Penrod, S. (1987). *The question of pornography: Research findings and policy implications.* New York: The Free Press.

Donovan, D. M. (1988). Assessment of addictive behaviors: implications of an emerging biopsychological model. In D. M. Donovan & G. A. Marlatt (Eds.), *Assessment of addictive behaviors.* New York: Guilford Press.

Dorr, A., & Kunkel, D. (1990). Children and the media environment: Change and constancy amid change. *Communication Research, 17,* 5–25.

Dow, B. J. (1990). Hegemony, feminist criticism and "The Mary Tyler Moore Show." *Critical Studies in Mass Communication, 7,* 261–274.

Downs, A. C., and Harrison, S. K. (1985). Embarrassing age spots or just plain ugly? Physical attractiveness as an instrument on sexism on American television commercials. *Sex Roles, 13,* 9–19.

Dunkley, C. (2000, February 17). Is nothing too sexually explicit for TV now? *Daily Mail,* p. 12.

Durkin, K. (1985a). Television and sex-role acquisition: 2—Effects. *British Journal of Social Psychology, 24,* 221–222.

Durkin, K. (1985b). *Television, sex roles and children.* Milton Keynes, UK: Open University Press.

Dworkin, A., & Mackinnon, C. A. (1988). *Pornography and civil rights.* Minneapolis, MN: Organising Against Pornography.

Earnest, K. D. (1988). *Jealousy threat: Affect and coping in men and women.* Unpublished doctoral dissertation, University of Connecticut, Storrs.

Eccles, A., Marhsall, W. L., & Barbaree, H. E. (1988). The vulnerability of erectile measures to repeated assessments. *Behavior Research & Therapy, 26*(2), 179–183.

Einsiedel, E. F. (1988). The British, Canadian, and U.S. pornography commissions and their use of social science research. *Journal of Communication, 38*(2), 108–121.

Elkind, D. (1993). *Parenting your teenager in the 90's.* Rosemont, NJ: Modern Learning Press.

Eysenck, H. J. (1972). Obscenity—Officially speaking. *Penthouse, 4,* 69–76.

Eysenck, H. J. (1976). *Sex and personality.* Austin: University of Texas Press.

Eysenck, H. J. (1978). *Sex and personality.* London: Sphere.

Eysenck, H. J., & Nias, D. K. B. (1978). *Sex, violence and the media.* London: Maurice Temple Smith.

Fabes, R. A., & Strouse, J. S. (1984). Youth's perceptions of models of sexuality: Implications for sexuality education. *Journal of Sex Education and Therapy, 10,* 33–37.

Fabes, R. A., & Strouse, J. S. (1987). Perceptions of responsible and irresponsible models of sexuality: A correlational study. *Journal of Sex Research, 23,* 70–84.

Family Planning Perspectives. (1990). HIV rates among U.S. teenagers. *Family Planning Perspectives, 22*(5), 196.

Farrell, D. (1994, August). Password: Pornography. *Women's Day,* pp. 28, 31, 36.

Feild, H. S. (1978). Attitudes towards rape: A comparative analysis of police, crisis counsellors and citizens. *Journal of Personality and Social Psychology, 36,* 156–179.

Fernandez-Collado, C. F., Greenberg, B. S., Korzenny, F., & Atkin, C. K. (1978). Sexual intimacy and drug use in TV series. *Journal of Communication, 28*(3), 30–37.

Ferrante, C. L., Haynes, A. M., & Kingsley, S. M. (1988). Image of women in television advertising. *Journal of Broadcasting and Electronic Media, 32,* 231–237.

Feshbach, S. (1955). The drive-reducing function of fantasy behavior. *Journal of Abnormal and Social Psychology, 5,* 3–11.

Feshbach. S. (1961). The stimulating versus catharsis effects of a vicarious aggressive activity. *Journal of Abnormal and Social Psychology, 63,* 381–385.

Feshbach, S., & Malamuth, N. M. (1978). Sex and aggression: Proving the link. *Psychology Today, 12*(6), 111–122.

Feshbach, S., & Singer, R. D. (1971). *Television and aggression.* San Francisco: Jossey-Bass.

Fisher, W. A. (1983). Gender, gender-role identification, and response to erotica. In E. R. Allgeier & N. D. McCormick (Eds.), *Changing boundaries: Gender roles and sexual behavior* (pp. 261–284). Palo Alto, CA: Mayfield Publishing.

Fisher, W. A. (1986). A psychological approach to human sexuality: The sexual behavior sequence. In D. Byrne & K. Kelley (Eds.), *Alternative approaches to the study of sexual behavior* (pp. 131–171). Hillsdale, NJ: Lawrence Erlbaum Associates.

Fisher, W. A., & Barak, A. (1989). Sex education as a corrective: Immunizing against possible effects of pornography. In D. Zillmann & J. Bryant (Eds.), *Pornography: Research advances and policy considerations* (pp. 289–320). Hillsdale, NJ: Lawrence Erlbaum Associates.

Fisher, W. A., & Barak, A. (1991). Pornography, erotica and behavior: More questions than answers. *International Journal of Law and Psychiatry, 14,* 65–83.

Fisher, W. A., & Byrne, D. (1978a). Individual differences in affective, evaluative, and behavioral responses to in erotica films. *Journal of Applied Social Psychology, 8,* 355–365.

Fisher, W. A., & Byrne, D. (1978b). Sex differences in response to erotica. *Journal of Personality and Social Psychology, 36,* 117–125.

Fisher, W. A., & Byrne, D. (1981). Social background, attitudes, and sexual attraction. In M. Cook (Ed.), *The bases of sexual attraction* (pp. 23–63). New York: Academic Press.

Fisher, W. A., Byrne, D., White, L. A., & Kelley, K. (1988). Erotophobia-erotohpilia as a dimension of personality. *Journal of Sex Research, 45,* 123–151.

Fisher, R. D., Cook, I. J., & Shirkey, E. C. (1994). Correlates of support for censorship of sexual, sexually violent, and violent media. *Journal of Sex Research, 31*(3), 229–240.

Fisher, W. A., & Grenier, G. (1994). Violent pornography, antiwomen thoughts, and antiwomen acts: In search of reliable effects. *Journal of Sex Research, 31*(1), 23–38.

Fisher, W. A., Miller, C. T., Byrne, D., & White, L. A. (1980). Talking dirty: Responses to communicating a sexual message as a function of situational and personality factors. *Basic and Applied Social Psychology, 1,* 115–126.

Fiske, S. T., & Taylor, S. E. (1984). *Social cognition.* New York: Random House.

Fox, J. A. (1976). *Forecasting crime data: An econometric analysis.* Lexington: Lexington Books.

Franzblau, S., Sprafkin, J. N., & Rubinstein, E. A. (1977). Sex on TV: A content analysis. *Journal of Communication, 27*(2), 164–170.

Frazier, S. H. (1994, January). Psychotrends: Taking stock of tomorrow's family and sexuality. *Psychology Today, 27,* 32–40.

Freedman, J. L. (1984). Effect of television violence on aggressiveness. *Psychological Bulletin, 96,* 227–246.

Freedman, J. L. (1986). Television violence and aggression: A rejoinder. *Psychological Bulletin, 100,* 372–378.

Freund, K. (1967). Erotic preference in paedophilia. *Behavior Research and Therapy, 5,* 339–348.

Friedrich-Cofer, L., & Huston, A. C. (1986). Television violence and aggression: The debate continues. *Psychological Bulletin, 100*(3), 364–371.

Frueh, T., & McGhee, P. E. (1975). Traditional sex-role development and amount of time spent watching television. *Developmental Psychology, 11,* 109.

Furnham, A., Gunter, B., & Walsh, D. (1998). Effects of program context on memory of humorous television commercials. *Applied Cognitive Psychology, 12,* 555–567.

Furniss, M. (1993). Sex with a hard (disk) on: Computer bulletin boards and pornography. *Wide Angle, 15,* 19–37.

Furstenberg, F. F., Jr. (1976, July/August). The social consequences of teenage parenthood. *Family Planning Perspectives, 8,* 148–164.

Furstenberg, F. F., Moore, K. A., & Peterson, J. L. (1985). Sex education and sexual experience among adolescents. *American Journal of Public Health, 75,* 1331–1332.

Gagnon, J. H. (1977). *Human sexualities.* Glenview, IL: Scott, Foresman.

Gagnon, J. H. (1990). Gender preferences in erotic relations: The Kinset scale and sexual scripts. In D. P. McWhirter, S. A. Sanders, & J. M. Reinsch (Eds.), *Homosexuality/heterosexuality: Concepts of sexual orientation* (pp. 177–207). New York: Oxford University Press.

Gagnon, J. H., & Simon, W. (1973). *Sexual conduct: The sources of human sexuality.* Chicago: Aldine.

Gallup, G. (1985, March 18). A *Newsweek* poll: Mixed feelings on pornography. *Newsweek,* p. 60.

Garcia, L. T. (1986). Exposure to pornography and attitudes about women and rape: A correlational study. *Journal of Sex Research, 22,* 378–385.

Gebhard, P. H., Gagnon, J. H., Pomeroy, W. B., & Christenson, C. V. (1965). *Sex offenders: An analysis of types.* London: Heinemann.

Geis, G., & Geis, R. (1979). Rape in Stockholm: Is permissiveness relevant? *Criminology, 17*(3), 311–322.

Gerbner, G. (1985). Children's television: A national disgrace. *Pediatric Annals, 14,* 822–827.

Gerbner, G., & Gross, L. (1976). Living with television: The violence profile. *Journal of Communication, 26*(2), 173–199.

Gerbner, G., Gross, L., Jackson-Beeck, M., Jeffries-Fox, S., & Signorielli, N. (1978). Cultural indicators: Violence profile No. 9. *Journal of Communication, 28,* 176–207.

Gerbner, G., Gross, L., Morgan, M., & Signorielli, N. (1980). The "mainstreaming" of America: Violence profile No. 11. *Journal of Communication, 30,* 10–29.

Gerbner, G., Gross, L., Morgan, M., & Signorielli, N. (1986). Living with television: The dynamics of the cultivation process. In J. Bryant & D. Zillmann (Eds.), *Perspectives on media effects* (pp. 13–40). Hillsdale, NJ: Lawrence Erlbaum Associates.

Gerrard, M., & Gibbons, F. X. (1982). Sexual experience, sex guilt, and sexual moral reasoning. *Journal of Personality, 50*, 435–439.

Gilligan, C. (1982). *In a different voice.* Cambridge, MA: Harvard University Press.

Gilmour, R., & Duck, S. (1980). *The development of social psychology.* London: Academic Press.

Gitlin, T. (1994). The prime time ideology. In H. Newcomb (Ed.), *Television: The critical view.* New York: Oxford University Press.

Glassman, M. B. (1977). *A uses and gratifications approach to the study of sexual materials.* Unpublished doctoral dissertation, Columbia University, New York.

Godenne, G. D. (1974). Sex and today's youth. *Adolescence, 9*, 67–72.

Goldstein, A. (1984, November). The place of pornography: Packaging eros for a violent age [Comments to a forum held at the new School for Social Research in New York City, moderated by L. H. Lapham]. *Harper's* (pp. 31–39, 42–45).

Goldstein, M. J. (1973). Exposure to erotic stimuli and sexual deviance. *Journal of Social Issues, 29*(3), 197–219.

Goldstein, M. J., Kant, H. S., & Harman, J. J. (1974). *Pornography and sexual deviance.* Berkeley: University of California Press.

Goldstein, M. J., Kant, H. J., Judd, L. L., Rice, C. J., & Green, R. (1971). Exposure to pornography and sexual behavior in deviant and normal groups. In *Technical Report of the Commission on Obscenity and Pornography* (Vol. 7). Washington, DC: U.S. Government Printing Office.

Government of Canada, Special Committee on Pornography and Prostitution. (1985). *Pornography and Prostitution in Canada, Vol. 1.* Ottawa: Ministry of Supply and Services.

Gow, J. (1993, July). *Gender roles in popular music videos: MTV's "top 100 of all time."* Paper presented at the 1993 Popular Culture Association/American Culture association convention, New Orleans, LA.

Granello, D. H. (1997). Using *Beverly Hills 90210* to explore developmental issues in female adolescents. *Youth & Society, 29*(1), 24–53.

Grazer, W. F., & Keesling, G. (1995). The effect of print advertising's use of sexual themes on brand recall and purchase intention: A product specific investigation of male responses. *Journal of Applied Business Research, 11*, 47–58.

Green, S. E., & Mosher, D. L. (1985). A causal model of sexual arousal to erotic fantasies. *Journal of Sex Research, 21*, 1–23.

Greenberg, B. S. (1982). Television and role socialisation: An overview. In D. Pearl, L. Bouthilet, & J. Lazar (Eds.), *Television and behavior: Ten years of scientific progress and implications for the eighties* (pp. 179–190). Rockville, MD: National Institute of Mental Health.

Greenberg, B. S. (1994). Content trends in media sex. In D. Zillmann, J. Bryant, & A. C. Huston (Eds.), *Media, children and the family* (pp.165–182). Hillsdale, NJ: Lawrence Erlbaum Associates.

Greenberg, B. S., Abelman, R., & Neuendorf, K. (1981). Sex on the soap operas: Afternoon intimacy. *Journal of Communication, 31*(3), 83–89.

Greenberg, B. S., Brown, J. D., & Buerkel-Rothfuss, N. L. (1993). *Media, sex and the adolescent.* Cresskill, NJ: Hampton Press.

Greenberg, B. S., & Busselle, R. W. (1996). Soap operas and sexual activity: A decade later. *Journal of Communication, 46*, 153–160.

Greenberg, B. S., & D'Alessio, D. (1985). Quantity and quality of sex in soaps. *Journal of Broadcasting and Electronic Media, 29*, 309–321.

Greenberg, B. S., Graef, D., Fernandez-Collado, C., Korzenny, F., & Atkin, C. K. (1980). Sexual intimacy in commercial television during prime time. *Journalism Quarterly, 52*(2), 211–215.

Greenberg, B. S., Linsangan, R., & Soderman, A. (1993). Adolescents' reactions to television sex. In B. S. Greenberg., J. D. Brown, & N. L. Buerkel-Rothfuss (Eds.), *Media, sex and the adolescent* (pp. 196–224). Cresskill, NJ: Hampton Press.

Greenberg, B. S., Neuendorf, K., Buerkel-Rothfuss, N., & Henderson, L. (1982). The soaps: What's on and who cares? *Journal of Broadcasting, 26,* 519–535.

Greenberg, B. S., Perry, K., & Covert, A. (1983). The body human: Sex education, politics and television. *Family Relations, 32,* 419–425.

Greenberg, B. S., Richards, M., & Henderson, L. (1980). Trends in sex-role portrayals on television. In B. Greenberg (Ed.), *Life on television* (pp. 65–88). Norwood, NJ: Ablex.

Greenberg, B. S., Siemicki, M., Dorfman, S., Heeter, C., Stanley, C., Soderman, A., & Linsangan, R. (1986). *Project CAST: Adolescents and their reactions to television sex* (Report No. 5). East Lansing: Michigan State University.

Greenberg, B. S., Siemicki, M., Dorfman, S., Heeter, C., Stanley, C., Soderman, A., & Linsangan, R. (1993). Sex content in R-rated films viewed by adolescents. In B. S. Greenberg., J. D. Brown, & N. L. Buerkel-Rothfuss (Eds.), *Media, sex and the adolescent* (pp. 45–58). Cresskill, NJ: Hampton Press.

Greenberg, B. S., Stanley, C., Siemicki, M., Heeter, C., Soderman, A., & Linsangan, R. (1993). Sex content on soaps and prime-time television series most viewed by adolescents. In B. S. Greenberg, J. D. Brown, & N. L. Buerkel-Rothfuss (Eds.), *Media, sex and the adolescent* (pp. 29–44). Cresskill, NJ: Hampton Press.

Greenberg, B. S., & Woods, M. G. (1999). The soaps: Their sex, gratifications and outcomes. *Journal of Sex Research, 36*(3), 250–257.

Greendlinger, V., & Byrne, D. (1985). Authoritarianism as a predictor of response to heterosexual and homosexual erotica. *The High School Journal, 68,* 183–186.

Greeson, L. E., & Williams, R. A. (1986). Social implications of music videos for youth: An analysis of the contents and effects of MTV. *Youth & Society, 18,* 177–189.

Gross, A. E. (1978). The male role and heterosexual behavior. *Journal of Social Issues, 34*(1), 87–107.

Gross, L. (1983). Pornography and social science research. *Journal of Communication, 33*(4), 107–111.

Gunter, B. (1980). The cathartic potential of television drama. *Bulletin of the British Psychological Society, 33,* 448–450.

Gunter, B. (1985). *Dimensions of television violence.* Aldershot, UK: Gower.

Gunter, B. (1995). *Television and gender representation.* Luton, UK: John Libbey.

Gunter, B., Sancho-Aldridge, J., & Winstone, P. (1994). *Television: The public's view—1993.* London: John Libbey.

Gunter, B., & Stipp, H. (1992). Attitudes to sex and violence on television in the United States and in Great Britain: A comparison of research findings. *Medien Psychologie, 4*(4), 267–286.

Gunter, B., & Wober, M. (1990). *Television and advertising: The public's view.* London: Independent Broadcasting Authority.

Guttman, A. (1991). *Women's sports: A history.* New York: Columbia University Press.

Hall, C. C. I., & Crum, M. J. (1994). Women and "body-isms" in television beer commercials. *Sex Roles, 31*(5/6), 329–337.

Hall, C. R. (1990). Note on the erotic economy: The condom in the age of AIDS. *Journal of American Culture, Winter,* 23–28.

Hamilton, K., & Waller, G. (1993). Media influences on body size estimation in anorexia and bulimia: An experimental study. *British Journal of Psychiatry, 162,* 837–840.

Hansen, C. H., & Hansen, R. D. (1990). The influence of sex and violence on the appeal of rock music videos. *Communication Research, 17,* 212–234.

Harmon, A. (1993, November 20). Computers are newest market for pornography. *Los Angeles Times*.

Harre, R., & Secord, P. F. (1972). *The explanation of social behavior*. Oxford, UK: Blackwell.

Harris and Associates. (1986). *American teens speak: Sex myths, TV and birth control*. New York: Planned Parenthood Federation of America.

Harris, R. J. (1994). The impact of sexually explicit media. In J. Bryant & D. Zillmann (Eds.), *Media effects: Advances in theory and research* (pp. 247–272). Hillsdale, NJ: Lawrence Erlbaum Associates.

Harvey, O. (1999, July 14). Keep sex off our screens viewers tell TV bosses. *Daily Mail*, p. 27.

Hawkins, R., & Pingree, S. (1982). Television's influence on social reality. In D. Pearl., L. Bouthilet, & J. Lazar (Eds.), *Television and behavior: Ten years of scientific progress and implications for the eighties*. Rockville, MD: Institute of Mental Health.

Hawkins, R. P., & Pingree, S. (1986). Activity in the effects of television on children. In J. Bryant & D. Zillmann (Eds.), *Perspectives on media effects* (pp. 233–250). Hillsdale, NJ: Lawrence Erlbaum Associates.

Hayes, C. D. (Ed.). (1987). *Risking the future: Adolescent sexuality, pregnancy and child-bearing* (Vol. 1). Washington, DC: National Academic Press.

Hazelwood, R. (1985, August). *The men who murdered* (FBI law enforcement bulletin).

Hazen, H. (1983). *Endless rapture: Rape, romance, and the female imagination*. New York: Charles Scribner & Sons.

Head, H. (1954). Content analysis of television drama programs. *Quarterly of Film, Radio and Television, 9*, 175–194.

Hebditch, D., & Anning, N. (1988). *Porngold: Inside the pornography business*. London: Faber & Faber.

Heilbrun, A. B., Jr., & Loftus, M. P. (1986). The role of sadism and peer pressure in the sexual aggression of male college students. *Journal of Sex Research, 22*, 320–332.

Heilbrun, A. B., Jr., & Seif, D. T. (1988). Erotic value of female distress in sexually explicit photographs. *Journal of Sex Research, 24*, 47–57.

Heinberg, L. J., & Thompson, J. K. (1992). Social comparison: Gender, target importance ratings and relation to body image disturbance. *Journal of Social Behavior and Personality, 7*, 335–344.

Heintz-Knowles, K. E. (1996). *Sexual activity on daytime soap operas: A content analysis of five weeks of television programming*. Menlo Park, CA: Kaiser Family Foundation.

Hendren, R. L., & Strasburger, V. C. (1993). Rock music and music videos. *Adolescent Medicine: State of the Art Reviews, 4*, 577–587.

Herman, J. L. (1990). Sex offenders: A feminist perspective. In W. L. Marshall, D. R. Laws, & H. E. Barbaree (Eds.), *Handbook of sexual assault: Issues, theories and treatment* (pp. 177–194). New York: Plenum.

Herman, M. S., & Bordner, D. C. (1983). Attitudes toward pornography in a southern community. *Criminology, 21*, 349–374.

Herold, E., & Thomas, R. E. (1980). Sexual experience and responses to a birth control film. *The Journal of School Health, 50*(2), 66–68.

Hill, J. M. (1987). Pornography and degradation. *Hypatia, 2*, 39–54.

Hodges, K. K., Brandt, D. A., & Kline, J. (1981). Competence, guilt and victimization: Sex differences in ambition of causality in television dramas. *Sex Roles, 7*, 537–546.

Hogan, D., & Kitagawa, E. (1983, May). *Family factors in the fertility of Black adolescents*. Paper presented at the annual meeting of the Population Association of America, Minneapolis, MN.

Hopkins, J. R. (1977). Sexual behavior in adolescence. *Journal of Social Issues, 33,* 67–85.

Horn, J. (1985, October). Fan violence: Fighting the injustices of it all. *Psychology Today, 19,* 30–31.

Howard, J. L., Reifler, C. B., & Liptzin, M. B. (1971). Effects of exposure to pornography. In *Technical report of the Commission on Obscenity and Pornography* (Vol. 8, pp. 97–132). Washington, DC: U.S. Government Printing Office.

Hsu, B., Kling, A., Kessler, C., Knape, K., Diefenbach, P., & Elias, J. (1994). Gender differences in sexual fantasy and behavior in a college population: A ten-year replication. *Journal of Sex and Marital Therapy, 20,* 103–118.

Huston, A. C., Donnerstein, E., Fairchild, H., Feshbach, N. D. Katz, P. A., Murray, J. P., Rubinstein, E. A., Wilcox, B. G., & Zuckerman, D. (1992). *Big world, small screen: The role of television in American society.* Lincoln: University of Nebraska Press.

Independent Broadcasting Authority. (1988). *Attitudes to broadcasting in 1987.* London: Author.

Independent Broadcasting Authority. (1990). *Attitudes to broadcasting in 1988/89.* London: Author.

Independent Television Commission. (1991). *The ITC programme code.* London: Author.

Independent Television Commission. (1995). *Nudity in television advertising* (an ITC Research publication). London: Author.

Independent Television Commission. (1998). *Television: The public's view—1997.* London: Author.

Independent Television Commission. (1999). *Television: The Public's view—1998.* London: Author.

Independent Television Commission. (2000). *Annual report and accounts 1999.* London: Author.

Impoco, J. (1996, April 15). TV's frisky family values: In prime-time, there is more sex and sex talk than ever and Americans fear the consequences. *US News and World Report,* 58–62.

Intons-Peterson, M. J., & Roskos-Ewoldsen, B. (1989). Mitigating the effects of violent pornography. In S. Gubar & J. Hoff-Wilson (Eds.), *For adult users, only.* Bloomington: Indiana University Press.

Intons-Peterson, M. J., Roskos-Ewoldsen, B., Thomas, L., Shirley, M., & Blut, D. (1989). Will educational materials reduce negative effects of exposure to sexual violence? *Journal of Social and Clinical Psychology, 8,* 256–275.

Jaeger, B. (1984, April 22). Rock'n' roll indulges in sex and violence. *Raleigh News and Observer,* 1E, 8E.

Jaffe, Y., Malamuth, N., Feingold, J., & Feshbach, S. (1974). Sexual arousal and behavioral aggression. *Journal of Personality and Social Psychology, 30,* 759–764.

Jaffee, D., & Straus, M. A. (1987). Sexual climate and reported rape: A state-level analysis. *Archives of Sexual Behavior, 16,* 107–123.

Jakobovits, L. A. (1965). Evaluational reactions to erotic literature. *Psychological Reports, 16,* 985–994.

Jessor, S., & Jessor, R. (1975). Transition from virginity to nonvirginity among youth. *Developmental Psychology, 11*(4), 473–484.

Jessor, R., Costa, F., Jessor, L., & Donovan, J. E. (1983). Timing of first intercourse: A prospective study. *Journal of Personality and Social Psychology, 44*(3), 608–626.

Johnson, D. K., & Satow, K. (1978). Consumers' reaction to sex in TV commercials. In H. K. Hunt (Ed.), *Advances in consumer research* (Vol. 5, pp. 411–414). Chicago: Association for Consumer Research.

Johnson, P., & Goodchilds, J. (1973). Pornography, sexuality and social psychology. *Journal of Social Issues, 29,* 231–238.

Johnson, W. T., Kupperstein, L. R., & Peters, J. J. (1971). Sex offenders' experience with erotica. In *Technical report of the commission on obscenity and pornography* (Vol. 7). Washington, DC: U.S. Government Printing Office.

Joint Select Committee on Video Material (1988). *Report of the Joint Select Committee on Video Material*. Canberra: Australian Government Publishing Service.

Jones, S. G. (Ed.). (1995). *Cybersociety: Computer-mediated communication and community*. Thousand Oaks, CA: Sage.

Jones, S. S., Forest, J., Goldman, N., Henshaw, S., Lincoln, R., Rosoff, J., Westoff, C., & Wulf, D. (1985). Teenage pregnancy in developed countries: Determinants and policy implications. *Family Planning Perspectives, 17*(2), 53–63.

Joseph, W. B. (1982). The credibility of physically attractive communicators: A review. *Journal of Advertising, 11*, 15–24.

Judd, B. B., & Alexander, M. W. (1983). On the reduced effectiveness of some sexually suggestive ads. *Journal of the Academy of Marketing Science, 11*, 156–168.

Juvenal. (1958). *Satires* (R. Humphries, Trans.). Bloomington: Indiana University Press.

Kahle, L. R., & Homer, P. M. (1983). Physical attractiveness of the celebrity endorser: A social adaptation perspective. *Journal of Consumer Research, 11*, 954–061.

Kaiser Family Foundation. (1996, December). *The Family Hour focus groups: Children's responses to sexual content on TV*. Menlo Park, CA: Author.

Kaiser Family Foundation. (1998). *Parents, children and the television ratings system: Two Kaiser Family Foundation surveys*. Menlo Park, CA: Author.

Kamins, M. A. (1990). An investigation into the "Match-Up" hypothesis in celebrity advertising: When beauty may be only skin deep. *Journal of Advertising, 19*, 4–13.

Kannin, E. J. (1985). Date rapists: Differential sexual socialisation and relative deprivation. *Archives of Sexual Behavior, 14*, 219–231.

Kaplan, H. S. (1984, July). Have more fun making love. *Redbook*, 88–89, 166.

Katz, E., Blumler, J. G., & Gurevitch, M. (1973). Uses and gratifications research. *Public Opinion Quarterly, 37*, 509–523.

Kelley, K. (1985a). Sexual attitudes as determinants of the motivational properties of exposure to erotica. *Personality and Individual Differences, 6*(3), 391–393.

Kelley, K. (1985b). The effects of sexual and/or aggressive film exposure on helping, hostility, and attitudes about the sexes. *Journal of Research in Personality, 19*, 472–483.

Kelley, K., & Byrne, D. (1983). Assessment of sexual responding: Arousal, affect and behavior. In J. Cacioppo & R. Petty (Eds.), *Social psychopathology: A sourcebook* (pp. 467–490). New York: Guilford.

Kennedy, J. R. (1971). How program environment affects TV commercials. *Journal of Advertising Research, 11*(1), 33–38.

Kenrick, D. T, & Gutierres, S. E. (1980). Contrast effects and judgements of physical attractiveness: When beauty becomes a social problem. *Journal of Personality and Social Psychology, 38*(1), 131–140.

Kenrick, D. T., Gutierres, S. E., & Goldberg, L. L. (1989). Influence of popular erotica on judgments of strangers and mates. *Journal of Experimental Social Psychology, 25*, 159–167.

Kenrick, D. T., Stringfield, D. O., Wagenhals, W., Dahl, R., & Ransdell, H. (1980). Six differences, androgyny and approach responses to erotica: A new variation on the old volunteer problem. *Journal of Personality and Social Psychology, 38*, 517–524.

Kilbourne, J. (1989). Beauty and the beast of advertising. *Media and Values, 4*, 121–125.

Kilbourne, J. (Lecturer), & Lazarus, M. (Producer and Director). (1987). *Still killing us softly* [Film].

Kilbourne, J. (Lecturer), & Wunderlich, R. (Producer and Director). (1979). *Killing us softly* [Film].

Killoran, M. M. (1983). Sticks and stones may break my bones and images can hurt me: Feminists and the pornography debate. *International Journal of Women's Studies, 6,* 443–456.

Kimmel, M. S., & Linders, A. (1996). Does censorship make a difference: An aggregate empirical analysis of pornography and rape. *Journal of Psychology and Human Sexuality, 8*(3), 1–20.

Kinsey, A. C., Pomeroy, W. B., & Martin, C. E. (1948). *Sexual behavior in the human male.* Philadelphia: Saunders.

Kinsey, A. C., Pomeroy, W. B., Martin, C. E., & Gebhard, P. H. (1953). *Sexual behavior in the human female.* Philadelphia: Saunders.

Klemmack, S. H., & Klemmack, D. L. (1976). The social definition of rape. In M. J. Walker & S. L. Brodsky (Eds.), *Sexual assault.* Lexington, MA: D. C. Heath & Company.

Knill, B., Persch, M., Pursey, G., Gilpin, P., & Perloff, R. (1981). Sex role portrayals in television advertising. *International Journal of Women's Studies, 4,* 497–506.

Koop, C. E. (1987). Report of the Surgeon General's workshop on pornography and public health. *American Psychologist, 42,* 944–945.

Koss, M. P., & Dinero, T. E. (1988). Predictors of sexual aggression among a national sample of male college students. In R. A. Pentky & V. L. Quinsey (Eds.), *Sexual aggression: Current perspectives. Annals of the New York Academy of Sciences* (pp. 133–147). New York: New York Academy of Sciences.

Koss, M. P., & Leonard, K. E. (1984). Sexually aggressive men: Empirical findings and theoretical implications. In N. M. Malamuth & E. Donnerstein (Eds.), *Pornography and sexual aggression* (pp. 213–232). Orlando, FL: Academic Press.

Koss, M. P., Leonard, K. E., Beezley, D. A., & Oros, C. J. (1985). Nonstranger sexual aggression: A discriminant analysis of psychological characteristics of nondetected offenders. *Sex Roles, 12,* 981–992.

Krafka, C. L. (1985). *Sexually explicit, sexually violent, and violent media: Effects of multiple naturalistic exposures and debriefing on female viewers.* Unpublished doctoral dissertation, University of Wisconsin, Madison.

Krattenmaker, T. G., & Powe, L. A., Jr. (1978). Televised violence: First Amendment principles and social science. *Virginia Law Review, 64,* 1123–1297.

Krcmar, M., & Cantor, J. (1997). The role of television advisories and ratings in parent–child discussion of television viewing choices. *Journal of Broadcasting and Electronic Media, 41,* 3, 393–411.

Kruglanski, A. W. (1975). The human subject in the psychology experiment: Fact and artifact. In L. Berkowitz (Ed.), *Advances in experimental social psychology* (Vol. 8, pp. 101–147). New York: Academic.

Kuchenhoff, E. (1977). Die Darstellung der Frau im Fernsehen. In M. Furlan (Ed.), *Kinder und Jugendliche im Spannungsfeld der Massunmedien.* Stuttgart: Bonz Verlag.

Kunkel, D. (1997). Why content, not age of viewers, should control what children watch on TV. *The Chronicle of Higher Education,* XLIII(21), B4–B5, January 31.

Kunkel, D., Cope, K. M., & Colvin, C. (1996). *Sexual messages on family hour television: Content and context.* Menlo Park, CA: Kaiser Family Foundation.

Kunkel, D., Cope, K. M., Farinola, W. J., Biely, E., Roth, E., & Donnerstein, E. (1999). *Sex on TV: Content and context.* Menlo Park, CA: Kaiser Family Foundation.

Kunkel, D., Farinola, W. J. M., Cope, K. M., Donnerstein, E., Biely, E., & Zwanin, L. (1998). *Rating the TV ratings: One year out* [A report to the Kaiser Family Foundation]. Menlo Park, CA: Kaiser Family Foundation.

Kupperstein, L. R., & Wilson, W. C. (1971). Erotica and antisocial behavior: An analysis of selected indicator statistics. In *Technical report of the Commission on Obscenity and Pornography* (Vol. 7). Washington, DC: U.S. Government Printing Office.

Kutchinsky, B. (1971a). Towards an explanation of the decrease in registered sex crimes in Copenhagen. In *Technical report of the Commission on Obscenity and Pornography* (Vol. 7). Washington, DC: U.S. Government Printing Office.

Kutchinsky, B. (1971b). The effect of pornography: A pilot experiment on perception, behavior and attitudes. In *Technical report of the Commission on Obscenity and Pornography* (Vol. 8). Washington, DC: U.S. Government Printing Office.

Kutchinsky, B. (1973). The effect of easy availability of pornography on the incidence of sex crimes: The Danish experience. *Journal of Social Issues, 29,* 163–181.

Kutchinsky, B. (1977). *Pornography and sex crimes in Denmark: Early research findings.* London: Martin Robertson.

Kutchinsky, B. (1985). Pornography and its effects in Denmark and the United States: A rejoinder and beyond. *Comparative Social Research, 8,* 301–330.

Kutchinsky, B. (1991). Pornography and rape: Theory and practice? Evidence from crime data in four countries where pornography is easily available. *International Journal of Law and Psychiatry, 14,* 147–164.

Laan, E., & Everard, W. (1995). Habituation of female sexual arousal to slides and film. *Archives of Sexual behavior, 25,* 517–541.

Lafky, S., Duffy, M., & Berkowitz, D. (1996). Looking though gendered lenses: Female stereotyping in advertisements and gender role expectations. *Journalism Quarterly, 73,* 379–388.

Lahey, K. A. (1991). Pornography and harm: Learning to listen to women. *International Journal of Law & Psychiatry, 14*(1/2), 117–132.

Lang, A., & Sibrel, P. (1989). Psychological perspectives of alcohol consumption and interpersonal aggression: The potential role of individual differences in alcohol-related criminal violence. *Criminal Justice and behavior, 16,* 299–324.

Langevin, R., Lang, R. A., Wright, P., Handy, L., Frenzel, R. R., & Black, E. L. (1988). Pornography and sexual offenses. *Annals of Sex Research, 1,* 335–362.

LaPlante, M. N., McCormick, N., & Brannigan, G. G. (1980). Living the sexual script: College students' views of influence of sexual encounters. *Journal of Sex Research, 16,* 338–355.

LaTour, M. S. and Henthorne, T. L. (1994). Ethical judgments of sexual appeals in print advertising. *Journal of Advertising, 23,* 81–90.

LaTour, M. S., Pitts, R. E., & Snook-Luther, D. C. (1991). Female nudity, arousal and ad response: An experimental investigation. *Journal of Advertising, 19,* 51–62.

Laumann, E. O., Gagnon, J. H., Michael, R. T., & Michaels, S. (1994). *The social organization of sexuality: Sexual practices in the United States.* Chicago: University of Chicago Press.

Lawrence, K., & Herold, E. S. (1988). Women's attitudes toward and experience with sexually explicit materials. *Journal of Sex Research, 24,* 161–169.

Laws, D. R., & Rubin, H. B. (1969). Instructional control of an autonomic sexual response. *Journal of Applied behavior Analysis, 2,* 93–99.

Laws, J. L., & Schwartz, P. (1981). *Sexual scripts: The social construction of female sexuality.* Washington, DC: University Press of America.

Lederer, L. (1980). *Take back the night: Women on pornography.* New York: William Morrow.

Lenderking, W. R. (1991). *Deception about sexually-transmitted disease as a function of personality, guilt, and attitudes towards condoms: Sex lies and guided imagery.* Unpublished doctoral dissertation, University of Connecticut, Storrs.

Leonard, K. E., & Taylor, S. P. (1983). Exposure to pornography, permissive and nonpermissive cues and male aggression toward females. *Motivation and Emotion, 7,* 291–299.

Levy, M. R., & Windahl, S. (1985). The concept of audience activity. In K. E. Rosengren, L. A. Wenner, & P. Palmgreen (Eds.), *Media gratifications research: Current perspectives* (pp. 109–122). Beverly Hills, CA: Sage.

Liebert, R., Sprafkin, J., & Davidson, E. (1982). *The early window: Effects of television on children and youth* (2nd. ed.). New York: Pergamon.

Lin, C. A. (1997). Beefcake versus cheesecake in the 1990s: Sexist portrayals of both genders in television commercials. *Howard Journal of Communication, 8,* 237–249.

Lin, C. A. (1998). Uses of sex appeals in prime-time television commercials. *Sex Roles, 38*(5/6), 461–475.

Linz, D. (1985). *Sexual violence in the media: Effects on male viewers and implications for society.* Unpublished doctoral dissertation, University of Wisconsin, Madison.

Linz, D. (1989). Exposure to sexually explicit materials and attitude to rape: A comparison of study results. *Journal of Sex Research, 26,* 50–84.

Linz, D., Arluk, I., & Donnerstein, E. (1990). Mitigating the negative effects of sexually violent mass media through pre-exposure briefings. *Communication Research, 17*(5), 641–674.

Linz, D., & Donnerstein, E. (1988). The methods and merits of pornography research. *Journal of Communication, 38*(2), 180–184.

Linz, D., Donnerstein, E., & Adams, S. M. (1989). Physiological desensitization and judgments about female victims of violence. *Human Communication Research, 15,* 509–522.

Linz, D., Donnerstein, E., Bross, M., & Chapin, M. (1986). Mitigating the influence of violence on television and sexual violence in the media. In R. Blanchard (Ed.), *Advances in the study of aggression* (Vol. 2, pp. 165–194). Orlando: Academic.

Linz, D., Donnerstein, E., Land, K., McCall, P., Scott, J., Klein, L. J., Shafer, B. J., & Lance, L. (1991, Spring). Estimating community tolerance for obscenity: The use of social science evidence. *Public Opinion Quarterly,* 80–112.

Linz, D., Donnerstein, E., & Penrod, S. (1984). The effects of multiple exposures to filmed violence against women. *Journal of Communication, 34*(3), 130–147.

Linz, D., Donnerstein, E., & Penrod, S. (1987). The findings and recommendations of the Attorney General's Commission on Pornography: Do the psychological "facts" fit the political fury? *American Psychologist, 42,* 946–951.

Linz, D., Donnerstein, E., & Penrod, S. (1988). Effects of long-term exposure to violent and sexually degrading depictions of women. *Journal of Personality and Social Psychology, 55,* 758–768.

Linz, D., Fuson, I. A., & Donnerstein, E. (1990). Mitigating the negative effects of sexually violent mass communications through preexposure briefings. *Communication Research, 17,* 641–674.

Linz, D., Penrod, S., & Donnerstein, E. (1986). Issues bearing on the legal regulation of violent and sexually violent media. *Journal of Social Issues, 42*(3), 171–193.

Linz, D., Malamuth, N. M., & Beckett, K. (1992). Civil liberties and research on the effects of pornography. In P. Tetlock & P. Suedfeld (Eds.), *Psychology and social advocacy* (pp. 149–164). New York: Hemisphere.

Linz, D. & Malamuth, N. M. (1993). *Pornography.* Newbury Park, CA: Sage.

Lipkin, M., & Carns, D. E. (1970, Winter). *University of Chicago Division of Biological Sciences and Pritzker School of Medicine Reports.*

Longford, L. (Ed.). (1972). *Pornography: The Longford Report.* London: Coronet.

Longino, H. E. (1980). Oppression and freedom: A closer look. In L. Lederer (Ed.), *Take back the night* (pp. 40–54). New York: William Morrow.

Louis Harris & Associates. (1986). *American teens speak: Sex, myths, TV and birth control.* New York: Planned Parenthood Federation of America.

Lovdal, L. T. (1989). Sex role messages in television commercials: An update. *Sex Roles, 21,* 715–724.

Lowry, D. T., Love, G., & Kirby, M. (1981). Sex on the soap operas: patterns of intimacy. *Journal of Communication, 31,* 90–96.

Lowry, D. T. & Towles, D. E. (1988). Prime time TV portrayals of sex, contraception and venereal diseases. *Journalism Quarterly, 66,* 347–352.

Lyons, J., & Larsen, D. (1990, November). *A systematic analysis of the social science research on the effects of violent and non-violent pornography.* Paper presented at the meeting of the NFF, Pittsburgh, PA.

Mackinnon, C. (1984). Not a moral issue. *Yale Law and Policy Review, 2*(2), 321–345.

Malamuth, N. M. (1981). Rape fantasies as a function of exposure to violent sexual stimuli. *Archives of Sexual Behavior, 10,* 33–47.

Malamuth, N. M. (1984). Aggression against women: Cultural and individual causes. In N. M. Malamuth & E. Donnerstein (Eds.), *Pornography and sexual aggression* (pp. 19–52). New York: Academic Press.

Malamuth, N. M. (1986). Predictors of naturalistic sexual aggression. *Journal of Personality and Social Psychology, 50,* 953–962.

Malamuth, N. M. (1988a). A multidimensional approach to sexual aggression: Combining measures of past behavior and present likelihood. In R. A. Prentky & V. L. Quinsey (Eds.), *Sexual aggression: Current perspectives. Annals of the New York Academy of Sciences* (pp. 123–132). New York: Academy of Sciences.

Malamuth, N. M. (1988b). Predicting laboratory aggression against female vs male targets: implications for research on sexual aggression. *Journal of Research in Personality, 22,* 474–495.

Malamuth, N. M. (1988c). Research on "violent erotica": A reply. *Journal of Sex Research, 24,* 340–348.

Malamuth, N. M. (1989). Sexually violent media, thought patterns and antisocial behavior. *Public Communication and Behavior, 2,* 159–204.

Malamuth, N. M. (1993). Pornography's impact on male adolescents. *Adolescent Medicine: State of the Art Reviews, 4*(3), 563–576.

Malamuth, N. M. (1996a). Evolutionary psychology and the confluence model of sexual aggression. In D. Buss & N. Malamuth (Eds.), *Sex, power and conflict: Evolutionary and feminist perspectives* (pp. 269–295). New York: Oxford University Press.

Malamuth, N. M. (1996b). Sexually explicit media, gender differences and evolutionary theory. *Journal of Communication, 46*(3), 8–31.

Malamuth, N. M., & Billings, V. (1986). The functions and effects of pornography: Sexual communication versus the feminist models in light of research findings. In J. Bryant & D. Zillmann (Eds.), *Perspectives on media effects* (pp. 83–108). Hillsdale, NJ: Lawrence Erlbaum Associates.

Malamuth, N. M., & Briere, J. (1986). Sexual violence in the media: Indirect effects on aggression against women. *Journal of Social Issues, 42,* 75–92.

Malamuth, N. M., & Ceniti, J. (1986). Repeated exposure to violent and nonviolent pornography: Likelihood of raping ratings and laboratory aggression against women. *Aggressive behavior, 12,* 129–137.

Malamuth, N. M., & Check, J. V. P. (1980a). Penile tumescence and perceptual responses to rape as a function of victim's perceived reactions. *Journal of Applied Social Psychology, 10,* 528–547.

Malamuth, N. M., & Check, J. V. P. (1980b). Sexual arousal to rape and consenting depictions: The importance of the woman's arousal. *Journal of Abnormal Psychology, 89,* 763–766.

Malamuth, N. M., & Check, J. V. P. (1981a). Rape fantasies as a function of exposure to violent sexual stimuli. *Archives of Sexual Behavior, 10,* 33–47.

Malamuth, N. M., & Check, J. V. P. (1981b). The effects of mass media exposure on acceptance of violence against women: A field experiment. *Journal of Research in Personality, 15,* 436–446.

Malamuth, N. M., & Check, J. V. P. (1983). Sexual arousal to rape depictions: Individual differences. *Journal of Abnormal Psychology, 92,* 35–67.

Malamuth, N. M., & Check, J. V. P. (1985). The effects of aggressive pornography on beliefs in rape myths: Individual differences. *Journal of Research in Personality, 19,* 299–320.

Malamuth, N. M., Check, J. V. P., & Briere, J. (1986). Sexual arousal in response to aggression: Ideological, aggressive, and sexual correlates. *Journal of Personality and Social Psychology, 50,* 330–340.

Malamuth, N. M., & Donnerstein, E. (1982). The effects of aggressive-pornographic mass media stimuli. In L. Berkowitz (Ed.), *Advances in experimental social psychology* (Vol. 15, pp. 103–136). New York: Academic.

Malamuth, N. M., Feshbach, S., & Jaffe, Y. (1977). Sexual arousal and aggression: Recent experiments and theoretical issues. *Journal of Social Issues, 33,* 110–133.

Malamuth, N. M., Feshbach, S., & Heim, M. (1980). Ethical issues and exposure to rape stimuli: A reply to Sherif. *Journal of Personality and Social Psychology, 38*(3), 413–415.

Malamuth, N. M., Haber, S., & Feshbach, S. (1980). Testing hypotheses regarding rape: Exposure to sexual violence, sex differences, and the "normality" of results. *Journal of Research in Personality, 14,* 121–137.

Malamuth, N. M., Heim, M., & Feshbach, S. (1980). Sexual responsiveness of college students to rape depictions: Inhibitory and disinhibitory effects. *Journal of Personality and Social Psychology, 38,* 399–408.

Malamuth, N. M., Sockloskie, R., & Koss, M. (1991, August). *Testing the effects of sexually explicit media within a structural equation model of aggression against women.* Paper presented at the meeting of the American Psychological Association, San Francisco.

Malamuth, N. M., & Spinner, B. (1980). A longitudinal content analysis of sexual violence in the best-selling erotica magazines. *Journal of Sex Research, 16,* 266–287.

Manes, A. I. & Melnyk, P. (1974). Televised models of female achievement. *Journal of Applied Social Psychology, 4,* 365–374.

Mann, J., Berkowitz, L., Sidman, J., Starr, S., & West, S. (1974). Satiation of the transient stimulating effect of erotic films. *Journal of Personality and Social Psychology, 30,* 729–735.

Mann, J., Sidman, J., & Starr, S. (1971). Effects of erotic films on sexual behavior of married couples. In *Technical Report of the Commission on Obscenity and Pornography* (Vol. 8, pp. 170–254). Washington, DC: U.S. Government Printing Office.

Mann, J., Sidman, J., & Starr, S. (1973). Evaluating social consequences of erotic films: An experimental approach. *Journal of Social Issues, 29,* 113–131.

Marshall, W. L. (1988). The use of sexually explicit stimuli by rapists, child molesters and nonoffenders. *Journal of Sex Research, 25,* 267–288.

Marshall, W. L. (1989). Pornography and sex offenders. In D. Zillmann & J. Bryant (Eds.), *Pornography: Research advances and policy considerations* (pp. 185–214). Hillsdale, NJ: Lawrence Erlbaum Associates.

Marshall, W. L., & Barbaree, H. E. (1984). A behavioral view of rape. *International Journal of Law and Psychiatry, 7,* 51–77.

Marshall, W. L., & Barbaree, H. E. (1990). An integrated theory. In W. L. Marshall, D. R. Laws, & H. E. Barbaree (Eds.), *Handbook of sexual assault: Issues, theories and treatment of the offender* (pp. 257–275). New York: Plenum.

Mayerson, S. E., & Taylor, D. A. (1987). The effects of rape myth pornography on women's attitudes and the mediating role of sex role stereotyping. *Sex Roles, 17*(5/6), 321–338.

McConaghy, N. (1974). Penile volume responses to moving and still pictures of male and female nudes. *Archives of Sexual Behavior, 3,* 565–570.

McGaugh, J. L. (1983). Preserving the presence of the past. *American Psychologist, 38,* 161.

McGhee, P., & Frueh, T. (1980). Television viewing and the learning of sex-role stereotypes. *Sex Roles, 2,* 179–188.

McKay, H. B., & Dolff, D. J. (1985). *The impact of pornography: An analysis of research and summary of findings.* Working papers on Pornography and Prostitution, No.13. Ottawa: Ministry of Supply and Services.

McKenzie-Mohr, D. & Zanna, M. P. (1990). Treating women as sexual objects: look to the (gender schematic). male who has viewed pornography. *Personality and Social Psychology Bulletin, 16,* 296–308.

McNeil, J. (1975). Feminism, femininity and the television shows: A content analysis. *Journal of Broadcasting, 19,* 259–269.

Meischke, H. (1995). Implicit sexual portrayals in the movies: Interpretations of young women. *Journal of Sex Research, 32*(1), 29–36.

Meyer, T. P. (1972). The effects of sexually arousing and violent films on aggressive behavior. *Journal of Sex Research, 8,* 324–331.

Mifflin, L. (1997, March 19). The parents speak. *New York Times,* p. A18.

Milkman, H. & Sunderwirth, S. (1987). *Craving for ecstasy: The consciousness and chemistry of escape.* Lexington, MA: Lexington Books.

Miller, B., Downs, W., & Gondoli, D. (1989). Spousal violence among alcoholic women as compared to a random household sample of women. *Journal of Studies of Alcohol, 50,* 533–540.

Miller, C. (1992, November 23). Publisher says sexy ads are OK, but sexist ads will sink sales. *Marketing News, 26,* 8–9.

Miller, J. D. (1986). *Toward a new psychology of women* (2nd ed.). Boston: Beacon.

Millwood-Hargrave, A. (1992). *Sex and sexuality in broadcasting.* London: Broadcasting Standards Council and John Libbey.

Millwood-Hargrave, A. (1999, January). *Sex and sensibility.* London: Broadcasting Standards Commission.

Moffit, M. A. (1987, May). *Understanding the appeal of the romance novel for the adolescent girl: A reader response approach.* Paper presented at the annual meeting of the International Communication Association, Montreal. (ERIC Document Reproduction Service No. ED 284190.)

Molitor, F., & Sapolsky, B. S. (1993). Sex, violence and victimisation in slasher films. *Journal of Broadcasting & Electronic Media, 37*(2), 233–242.

Morgan, M. (1987). Television, sex-role attitudes and sex-role behavior. *Journal of Early Adolescence, 7*(3), 269–282.

Morgan, M., & Rothschild, N. (1983). Impact of the new television technology: Cable TV, peers and sex-role cultivation in the electronic environment. *Youth and Society, 15*(1), 33–50.

Morrison, D. (1999). *Defining violence: The search for understanding.* Luton, UK: University of Luton Press.

Mosher, D. L. (1971). Psychological reactions to pornographic films. In *Technical Report of the Commission on Obscenity and Pornography* (Vol. 8). Washington, DC: U.S. Government Printing Office.

Mosher, D. L. (1973). Sex differences, sex experiences, sex guilt and explicitly sexual films. *Journal of Social Issues, 29*(3), 95–112.

Mosher, D. L. (1980). A three dimensional theory of depth of involvement in human sexual response. *Journal of Sex Research, 16*, 1–42.

Mosher, D. L. (1988a). Pornography defined: Involvement theory, narrative context, and goodness of fit. *Journal of Psychology and Human Sexuality, 1*, 67–85.

Mosher, D. L. (1988b). Sexual Path Preferences Inventory. In C. M. Davis, W. L. Yarber, & S. L. Davis (Eds.), *Sexuality-related measures: A compendium* (pp. 188–192). Lake Mills, IA: Graphic Press.

Mosher, D. L. (1991). Macho men, machismo, and sexuality. *Annual Review of Sex Research, 2*, 199–247.

Mosher, D. L. (1994a). A script theory of human sexual response: Postulates, corollaries, and definitions. In D. L. Nathanson & A. M. Stone (Eds.), *Knowing feeling.* New York: Norton.

Mosher, D. L. (1994b). Gender. In V. L. Bullough & B. Bullough (Eds.), *Human sexuality: An encyclopedia* (pp. 470–477). New York: Garland Publishing.

Mosher, D. L., & Abramson, P. R. (1977). Subjective sexual arousal to films of masturbation. *Journal of Counselling and Clinical Psychology, 45*, 796–807.

Mosher, D. L., & Anderson, L. D. (1986). Macho personality, sexual aggression, and reactions to guided imagery of realistic rape. *Journal of Research in Personality, 20*, 77–94.

Mosher, D. L., & Katz, H. (1971). Pornographic films, male verbal aggression against women, and guilt. In *Technical report of the Commission on Obscenity and Pornography* (Vol. 81). Washington, DC: U.S. Government Printing Office.

Mosher, D. L., & MacIan, E. (1994). College men and women respond to X-rated videos intended for male or female audiences: Gender and sexual scripts. *Journal of Sex Research, 31*(2), 99–113.

Mosher, D. L., & O'Grady, K. E. (1979a). Homosexual threat, negative attitudes toward masturbation, sex guilt, and males' sexual and affective reactions to explicit sex films. *Journal of Counselling and Clinical Psychology, 47*, 860–873.

Mosher, D. L., & O'Grady, K. E. (1979b). Sex guilt, trait anxiety, and females' subjective sexual arousal to erotica. *Motivation and Emotion, 3*, 235–249.

Mosher, D. L., & Tomkins, S. S. (1988). Scripting the macho man: Hypermasculine socialisation and enculturation. *Journal of Sex Research, 25*, 60–84.

Mould, D. E. (1988). A critical analysis of recent research on violent erotica. *Journal of Sex Research, 24*, 326–340.

Muehlenhard, C. L., & Hollabaugh, L. L. (1988). Do women sometimes say no when they mean yes? The prevalence and correlates of women's token resistance to sex. *Journal of Personality and Social Psychology, 54*, 872–879.

Murphy, W. D., Coleman, E. M., & Haynes, M. R. (1986). Factors related to coercive sexual behavior in a nonclinical sample of males. *Violence and Victims, 1*, 255–278.

Murrin, M. R., & Laws, D. R. (1990). The influence of pornography on sexual crimes. In W. L. Marshall, D. R. Laws, & H. E. Barbaree (Eds.), *Handbook of sexual assault: Issues, theories, and treatment of the offender* (pp. 73–91). New York: Plenum Press.

Myers, P. N., & Biocca, F. A. (1992). The elastic body image: The effect of television advertising and programming on body image distortion in young women. *Journal of Communication, 42*(3), 108–133.

Neuman, W. L. (1994). *Social research methods: Qualitative and quantitative approaches* (2nd ed.). Boston: Allyn and Bacon.

Newcomer, S. F., & Brown, J. D. (1984, August). *Influences of television and peers on adolescents' sexual behavior.* Paper presented at the 92nd annual convention of the American Psychological Association, Toronto.

Norris, C. E., & Colman, A. M. (1992). Context effects on recall and recognition of magazine advertisements. *Journal of Advertising, 21*(3), 37–46.

Norris, C. E., & Colman, A. M. (1993). Context effects on memory for television advertisements. *Social Behavior and Personality, 21*(4), 279–296.

Norris, J. (1989). Normative influence effects on sexual arousal to nonviolent sexually explicit material. *Journal of Applied Social Psychology, 19,* 341–352.

Norris, J. (1991). Social influence effects on responses to sexually explicit material containing violence. *Journal of Sex Research, 28,* 67–76.

O'Donogue, W. T., & Geer, J. H. (1985). Habituation of sexual arousal. *Archives of Sexual behavior, 14,* 233–246.

Ogden, J., & Mundray, K. (1996). The effect of the media on body satisfaction: The role of gender and size. *European Eating Disorders Review, 4,* 171–181.

Olivia N. v National Broadcasting Company, Inc. (1978). *California Reporter, 141,* 511–515.

Olson, B. (1994). Soaps, sex and cultivation. *Mass Communication Review, 21,* 106–113.

Orne, M. T. (1962). On the social psychology of the psychological experiment: With particular reference to demand characteristics and their implications. *American Psychologist, 17,* 776–783.

Padgett, V. R., Brislin-Slutz, J., & Neal, J. A. (1989). Pornography, erotica and attitudes toward women: the effects of repeated exposure. *Journal of Sex Research, 26,* 479–491.

Paletz, D. L. (1988). Pornography, politics, and the press: The U. S. Attorney General's Commission on Pornography. *Journal of Communication, 38*(2), 122–136.

Palys, T. S. (1984). A content analysis of sexually explicit videos in British Columbia. *Working papers on pornography and prostitution* (Research Rep. No. 15). Ottawa: Canadian Department of Justice.

Palys, T. S. (1986). Testing the common wisdom: The social content of video pornography. *Canadian Psychology, 27,* 22–35.

Patzer, G. L. (1985). *The physical attractiveness phenomena.* New York: Plenum Press.

Pearson, J. L. (1992). *Cultural norms in mass communications: Influencing self-perceptions and self-satisfaction.* Unpublished master's thesis, Colorado State University.

Penrod, S., & Linz, D. (1984). Using psychological research on violent pornography to inform legal change. In N. M. Malamuth & E. Donnerstein (Eds.), *Pornography and sexual aggression* (pp. 247–275). Orlando, FL: Academic.

Percy, L., & Rossiter, J. R. (1992). Advertising stimulus effects: A review. *Journal of Current Issues and Research in Advertising, 14,* 75–90.

Perse, E. M. (1986). Soap opera viewing patterns of college students and cultivation. *Journal of Broadcasting and Electronic Media, 30,* 175–193.

Perse, E. M. (1994). Uses of erotica and acceptance of rape myths. *Communication Research, 21*(4), 488–515.

Perse, E. M., & Rubin, A. M. (1988). Audience activity and satisfaction with favorite television soap operas. *Journalism Quarterly, 65,* 368–375.

Perse, E. M., & Rubin, A. M. (1990). Chronic loneliness and television use. *Journal of Broadcasting and Electronic Media, 34,* 37–53.

Peterson, J. L., Moore, K. A., & Furstenberg, F. F. (1984, August). *Television viewing and early initiation of sexual intercourse: Is there a link?* Paper presented at the annual meeting of the American Psychological Association, Toronto.

Peterson, J. L., Moore, K. A., & Furstenberg, F. F. (1991). Television viewing and early initiation of sexual intercourse: is there a link? *Journal of Homosexuality, 21,* 93–119.

Peterson, R., & Kahn, J. (1984, August). *Media preferences of sexually active teens: A preliminary analysis*. Paper presented at the meeting of the American Psychological Association, Toronto.

Peterson, R. A., & Kerin, R. A. (1977). The female role in advertisements: Some experimental evidence. *Journal of Marketing, 41*, 59–63.

Petley, J. (1999, August 27). Sexual healing. *Broadcast*, p. 30.

Planned Parenthood of New York City, Inc. (1986, September 2). *Memorandum Re: The need for balanced messages in the media*. New York: Author.

Planned Parenthood Federation of America. (1987). *American teenagers speak: Sex myths, TV and birth control*. New York: Author.

Polskin, H. (1991, August 3). MTV at 10. *TV Guide*, 4–8.

Pope, D. (1987, September). *Hearing on women, violence and the law*. Testimony before the Select Committee on Children, Youth and Family.

Postman, N., Nystrom, C., Strate, L., & Weingartner, C. (1988). *Myths, men and beer: An analysis of beer commercials on broadcast television, 1987*. Washington, DC: AAA Foundation for Traffic Safety.

Press, A. (1991). *Women watching television: Gender, class and generation in the American television experience*. Philadelphia: University of Pennsylvania Press.

Press, A., Namuth, T., Agrest, S., Gander, M., Lubenow, G., Reese, M., Friendly, D. T., & McDaniel, A. (1985, March 18). The war against pornography. *Newsweek*, 58–66.

Preston, E. H. (1990). Pornography and the construction of gender. In N. Signorielli & M. Morgan (Eds.), *Cultivation analysis*. Beverly Hills, CA: Sage.

Pribram, D. (1988). *Female spectators: Looking at film and television*. New York: Verso.

Prince, S. (1990). Power and pain: Content analysis and the ideology of pornography. *Journal of Film and Video, 42*(2), 31–41.

Propper, M. M. (1972). Exposure to sexually oriented materials among young male prisoners. In *Technical report of the Commission on Obscenity and Pornography* (Vol. 9). Washington, DC: U.S. Government Printing Office.

Pytkowicz, A. R., Wagner, N., & Sarason, I. G. (1967). An experimental study of the reduction of hostility through fantasy. *Journal of Personality and Social Psychology, 5*, 295–303.

Quinsey, V. L. (1977). The assessment and treatment of child molesters: A review. *Canadian Psychological Review, 18*, 204–220.

Quinsey, V. L., & Chaplin, T. C. (1984). Stimulus control of rapists' and non-sex offenders' sexual arousal. *Behavioral Assessment, 6*, 169–176.

Quinsey, V. L., Chaplin, T. C., & Upfold, D. (1984). Sexual arousal to nonsexual violence and sadomasochistic themes among rapists and non-sex-offenders. *Journal of Consulting and Clinical Psychology, 52*, 651–657.

Quinsey, V. L., Chaplin, T. C., & Varney, G. (1981). A comparison of rapists' and non-sex-offenders' sexual preference for mutually consenting sex, rape, and physical abuse of women. *Behavioral Assessment, 3*, 127–135.

Rachman, S. (1966). Sexual fetishism: An experimental analogue. *Psychological Record, 16*, 293–296.

Rachman, S., & Hodgson, R. J. (1968). Experimentally-induced "sexual fetishism": Replication and development. *Psychological Record, 18*, 25–27.

Rak, D., & McMullen, L. M. (1987). Sex-role stereotyping in television commercials: A verbal response mode and content analysis. *Canadian Journal of Behavioral Science, 19*, 25–39.

Rapaport, R. (1984). *Sexually aggressive males: Characterological features and sexual responsiveness to rape depictions*. Unpublished doctoral dissertation, Auburn University, Auburn, AL.

Rapaport, K., & Buckhart, B. R. (1984). personality and attitudinal characteristics of sexually coercive college males. *Journal of Abnormal Psychology, 93,* 216–221.

Reed, M. D. (1990). *Research on pornography: The evidence of harm.* Cincinnati, OH: National Coalition Against Pornography.

Reed, M. D. (1994). Pornography addiction and compulsive sexual behavior. In D. Zillmann, J. Bryant, & A. C. Huston (Eds.), *Media, children and the family: Social scientific, psychodynamic and clinical perspectives* (pp. 249–269). Hillsdale, NJ: Lawrence Erlbaum Associates.

Reep, D. C., & Dambrot, F. H. (1987). Television's professional women: Working with men in the 1990s. *Journalism Quarterly, 64,* 376–381.

Reichert, T., Lambiase, J., Morgan, S., Carstarphan, M., & Zavoina, S. (1999). Cheesecake and beefcake: No matter how you slice it, sexual explicitness in advertising continues to increase. *Journalism and Mass Communication Quarterly, 76*(1), 7–20.

Reid, L. N., Salmon, C. T., & Soley, L. C. (1984). The nature of sexual content in television advertising. In R. W. Belk (Ed.), *Proceedings of the 1984 AMA Educators' meeting* (pp. 214–216). Chicago: American Marketing Association.

Reid, L. N., & Soley, L. C. (1981). Another look at the 'decorative' female model: The recognition of visual and verbal ad components. *Current Issues and Research in Advertising, 9,* 122–133.

Reid, L. N., & Soley, L. C. (1983). Decorative models and the readership of magazine ads. *Journal of Advertising Research, 23,* 27–32.

Reifler, C. B., Howard, J., Lipton, M. A., Liptzin, M. B., & Widmann, D. E. (1971). Pornography: An experiment study of effects. *American Journal of Psychiatry, 128,* 575–582.

Richins, M. L. (1991). Social comparison and the idealized images of advertising. *Journal of Consumer Research, 18,* 71–83.

Richmond, D., & Hartman, T. P. (1982). Sex appeal in advertising. *Journal of Advertising Research, 22,* 53–61.

Riley, A. (1992). Home sex therapy. *Journal of Sexual Health, 2,* 7–9.

Rimm, M. (1995). Marketing pornography on the information superhighway: A survey of 917,410 images, descriptions, short stories and animations downloaded 8.5 million times by consumers in over 2000 cities in forty countries, provinces and territories. *Georgetown Law Journal, 83*(5), 1849–1934.

Rimmer, R. H. (1986). *The X-rated videotape guide.* New York: Harmony.

Robert, L. (1971). *Les Gladiateurs dans L'Orient Grec* [The gladiators in the Greek Orient]. Amsterdam: Hakkert.

Roberts, E. (1982). Television and sexual learning in childhood. In D. Pearl, L. Bouthilet, & J. Lazar (Eds.), *Television and behavior: Ten years of scientific progress and implications for the eighties* (pp. 209–223). Rockville, MD: National Institute of Mental Health.

Roberts, E., Kline, D., & Gagnon, J. (1978). *Family life and sexual learning.* Cambridge, MA: Cambridge University Press.

Robertson, J. C. (1990). Sex addiction as a disease: A neurobehavioral model. *American Journal of Preventive Psychiatry and Neurology, 2*(3), 15–18.

Robinson, B. E., Scheltema, K., Koznar, J., & Mantheir, R. (1996). Attitudes of U.S. and Czeck/Slovak mental health and health professionals towards five types of sexually explicit materials. *Archives of Sexual Behavior, 25*(6), 601–628.

Rotter, J. B., Chance, J. E., & Phares, E. J. (Eds.). (1977). *Applications of a social learning theory of personality.* New York: Holt, Rinehart & Winston.

Rouner, D., Domenech-Rodriguez, M. M., & Slater, M. D. (1998, July). *Gender-role and sexual imagery in television advertisements: A message and adolescent audience processing analysis.*

Paper presented at the annual conference of the International Communication Association, Jerusalem, Israel.

Rubin, A. M. (1985). Uses of daytime television soap operas by college students. *Journal of Broadcasting and Electronic Media, 29*, 241–258.

Rubin, A. M., & Perse, E. M. (1987). Audience activity and soap opera involvement: A uses and effects investigation. *Human Communication Research, 14*, 246–268.

Russell, D. E. H. (1988). Pornography and rape: A causal model. *Political Psychology, 9*, 41–73.

Russo, A. (1987). Conflicts and contradictions among feminists over issues of pornography and sexual freedom. *Women's Studies International Forum, 10*, 103–112.

Salvosa, M. F. (1997, May 16–18). Readers rate TV worse than ever. *USA Weekend*, pp. 20–21.

Sandford, D. A. (1974). *Patterns of sexual arousal in heterosexual males. Journal of Sex Research, 10*, 150–155.

Sapolsky, B. S. (1982). Sexual acts and references on prime-time TV: A two-year look. *Southern Speech Communication Journal, 47*, 212–226.

Sapolsky, B. S. (1984). Arousal, affect and the aggression-moderating effect of erotica. In N. M. Malamuth & E. Donnerstein (Eds.), *Pornography and sexual aggression* (pp. 84–114). Orlando, FL: Academic Press.

Sapolsky, B. S., & Tabarlet, J. G. (1991). Sex in prime time television: 1979 vs. 1989. *Journal of Broadcasting and Electronic Media, 34*, 505–516.

Sapolsky, B. S., & Zillmann, D. (1981). The effect of soft-core and hard-core erotica on provoked and unprovoked hostile behavior. *Journal of Sex Research, 17*, 319–343.

Schaefer, H. H., & Colgan, A. H. (1977). The effect of pornography on penile tumescence as a function of reinforcement and novelty. *Behavior Therapy, 8*, 938–946.

Schmidt, G. (1975). Male–female differences in sexual arousal and behavior during and after exposure to sexually explicit stimuli. *Archives of Sexual Behavior, 4*, 353–365.

Schmidt, G. & Sigusch, V. (1970). Sex differences in response to psychosexual stimuli. *Journal of Sex Research, 6*, 268–273.

Schmidt, G., Sigusch, V., & Meyberg, V. (1969). Psychosexual stimulation in men: Emotional reactions, changes of sex behavior, and measures of conservative attitudes. *Journal of Sex Research, 5*, 199–217.

Schmidt, G., Sigusch, V., & Schafer, S. (1973). Responses to reading erotic stories: Male–female differences. *Archives of Sexual Behavior, 2*, 181–199.

Schorin, G. A., & Vanden Bergh, B. G. (1985). Advertising's role in the diffusion of country-western trend in the U.S. *Journalism Quarterly, 62*, 515–522.

Schumann, D. W. (1986). Programme impact on attitude toward TV commercials. In J. Seagert (Ed.), *Proceedings of the Division of Consumer Psychology* (pp. 67–73). Washington, DC: American Psychological Association.

Schwartz, N., Wagner, D., Bannert, M., & Mathes, L. (1987). Cognitive accessibility of sex roles concepts and attitudes toward political portrayals: the impact of sexist ads. *Sex Roles, 17*(9–10), 593–601.

Scott, J. E. (1986). An updated longitudinal content analysis of sex references in mass circulation magazines. *Journal of Sex Research, 22*, 385–392.

Scott, J. E., & Cuvelier, S. J. (1987). Sexual violence in *Playboy* magazine: A longitudinal content analysis. *Journal of Sex Research, 23*, 534–539.

Scott, J. E., & Schwalm, L. A. (1988a). Pornography and rape: An examination of adult theater rates and rape rates by state. In J. E. Scott & T. Hirschi (Eds.), *Controversial issues in crime and justice* (pp. 40–53). Beverly Hills, CA: Sage.

Scott, J. E., & Schwalm, L. A. (1988b). Rape rates and the circulation rates of adult magazines. *Journal of Sex Research, 24*, 241–250.

Senn, C. Y., & Radtke, H. L. (1990). Women's evaluations of and affective reactions to mainstream violent pornography, non-violent pornography and erotica. *Violence and Victims, 5,* 143–155.

Severn, J., Belch, G. E., & Belch, M. A. (1990). The effects of sexual and non-sexual advertising appeals and information level of cognitive processing and communication effectiveness. *Journal of Advertising, 19*(1), 14–22.

Shaw, C. (1999). *Deciding what we watch: Taste, decency and media ethics in the UK and the USA.* Oxford, UK: Clarendon Press.

Shemberg, K. M., Leventhal, D. B., & Allman, L. (1968). Aggression machine performance and rated aggression. *Journal of Experimental Research in Personality, 3,* 117–119.

Sherif, C. (1980). Comments on ethical issues in Malamuth, Heim, and Feshbach's "Sexual responsiveness of college students to rape decisions: Inhibitory and disinhibitory effects." *Journal of Personality and Social Psychology, 38,* 409–412.

Sherman, B. L., & Dominick, J. R. (1986). Violence and sex in music videos: TV and rock 'n' roll. *Journal of Communication, 36,* 79–93.

Sherr, L. (1987). An evaluation of the UK government health education campaign on AIDS. *Psychology and Health, 1,* 61–72.

Showers, R. (1994). Research, public policy and law: Combination for change. In D. Zillmann, J. Bryant, & A. C. Huston (Eds.), *Media, children and the family: Social scientific, psychodynamic and clinical perspectives* (pp. 327–339). Hillsdale, NJ: Lawrence Erlbaum Associates.

Signorielli, N., & Lears, M. (1992). Children, television and conceptions about chores: Attitudes and behaviors. *Sex Roles, 27*(3/4), 157–170.

Sigusch, V., Schmidt, G., Reinfeld, A., & Weidemann-Sutor, I. (1970). Psychosexual stimulation: Sex differences. *Journal of Sex Research, 6,* 10–24.

Silbert, M. H. (1989). The effects on juveniles of being used for pornography and prostitution. In D. Zillmann & J. Bryant (Eds.), *Pornography: Research advances and policy considerations* (pp. 215–235). Hillsdale, NJ: Lawrence Erlbaum Associates.

Silbert, M. H., & Pines, A. M. (1984). Pornography and sexual abuse of women. *Sex Roles, 10*(11–12), 857–867.

Silverman, L. T., Sprafkin, J. N., & Rubinstein, E. A. (1979). Physical contact and sexual behavior on prime time TV. *Journal of Communication, 29*(1), 33–43.

Silverman-Watkins, L. T. (1983). Sex in the contemporary media. In J. Q. Maddock, G. Neubeck & M. B. Sussman (Eds.), *Human sexuality and the family,* (pp. 125–140). New York: Haworth.

Simpson, P. M., Horton, S., & Brown, G. (1996). Male nudity in advertisements: A modified replication and extension of gender and product effects. *Journal of the Academy of Marketing Science, 24,* 257–262.

Singer, J. L. (1961). Imagination and waiting ability in young children. *Journal of Personality, 29,* 396–413.

Singer, J. L. (1966). *Daydreaming: An introduction to the experimental study of inner experience.* New York: Random House.

Singer, J. L., Wilensky, H., & McGraven, V. (1956). Delaying capacity, fantasy, and planning ability: A factorial study of some basic ego functions. *Journal of Consulting Psychology, 20,* 375–383.

Sintchak, G., & Geer, J. (1975). A vaginal plethysmograph system. *Psychophysiology, 12,* 113–115.

Singh, D. (1995). Female judgment of male attractiveness and desirability for relationships: Role of waist-to-hip ratio and financial status. *Journal of Personality and Social Psychology, 69,* 1089–1101.

Singh, D., & Luis, S. (1995). Ethnic and gender consensus for the effect of waist-to-hip ratio on judgments of women's attractiveness. *Human Nature, 6*, 51–65.

Singh, D., & Young, R. (1995). Body weight, waist-to-hip ratio, breasts and hips: Role in judgments of female attractiveness and desirability for relationships. *Ethology and Sociobiology, 16*, 483–507.

Sirkin, M. I. (1985). *Sexual involvement theory, sexual trance, and hypnotizability: The experimental use of guided imagery.* Unpublished doctoral dissertation, University of Connecticut.

Skinner, B. F. (1953). *Science and human behavior.* New York: Macmillan.

Skinner, B. F. (1974). *About behaviorism.* New York: Knopf.

Slade, J. (1984). Violence in the hard-core pornographic film: An historical survey. *Journal of Communication, 26*, 16–33.

Smith, D. G. (1976). The social content of pornography. *Journal of Communication, 26*, 16–33.

Smith, G. & Engel, R. (1968). Influence of a female model on perceived characteristics of an automobile. In *Proceedings of the 76th annual convention of the American Psychological Association* (pp. 681–682). Washington, DC: American Psychological Association.

Smuts, B. (1995). The evolutionary origins of patriarchy. *Human Nature, 6*, 1–32.

Snyder, M., & Ickes, W. (1985). Personality and social behavior. In G. Lindzey & E. Aronson (Eds.), *Handbook of social psychology, 3rd. ed.* (Vol. 2, pp. 883–947). New York: Random House.

Soldow, G. F., & Principe, V. (1981). Response to commercials as a function of program context. *Journal of Advertising Research, 21*(2), 59–65.

Soley, L., & Kurzbard, G. (1986). Sex in advertising: A comparison of 1964 and 1984 magazine advertisements. *Journal of Advertising, 15*(3), 46–54, 64.

Soley, L. C., & Reid, L. N. (1988). Taking it off: Are models in magazine ads wearing less? *Journalism Quarterly, 65*, 960–966.

Special Committee on Pornography and Prostitution (1985). *Report of the Special Committee on Pornography and Prostitution.* Ottawa: Canadian Government Publishing Center.

Spence, J., & Helmreich, R. (1972). The attitudes toward women scale: An objective instrument to measure attitudes toward rights and roles of women in contemporary society. *JSAS Catalogue of Selected Documents in Psychology, 2*, 66.

Sprafkin, J. N., & Silverman, L. T. (1981). Update: Physically intimate and sexual behavior on prime time television: 1978–1979. *Journal of Communication, 31*(1), 34–40.

Stanley, C., & Greenberg, B. S. (1993). Family structure and adolescents' orientation to TV and movie sex. In B. S. Greenberg, J. D. Brown, & N. L. Buerkel-Rothfuss (Eds.), *Media, sex and the adolescent* (pp. 153–162). Cresskill, NJ: Hampton Press.

Stauffer, J., & Frost, R. (1976). Male and female interest in sexually-oriented magazines. *Journal of Communication, 26*(1), 25–30.

Steadman, M. (1969). How sexy illustrations affect brand recall. *Journal of Advertising Research, 9*(1), 15–19.

Steele, D. G., & Walker, C. E. (1976). Female responsiveness to erotic film and the 'ideal' erotic film from a feminine perspective. *Journal of Nervous and Mental Disease, 162*, 266–273.

Steenland, S. (1990). *What's wrong with the picture? The status of women on screen and behind the camera in entertainment TV.* Washington, DC: National Commission on Working Women of Wider Opportunities for Women.

Steinem, G. (1980). Erotica and pornography: A clear and present difference. In L. Lederer (Ed.), *Take back the night: Women on pornography*, (pp. 35–39. New York: William Morrow.

Stengel, R. (1986, July 21). Sex busters: Meese Commission and the Supreme Court echo a new moral militancy. *Time*, 12–22.

Stice, E., & Shaw, H. E. (1994). Adverse effects of the media portrayed thin-ideal on women and linkages to bulimic symptomatology. *Journal of Social and Clinical Psychology, 13,* 288–308.

Stock, W. (1991, August). *Differential responses of women and men to pornography: A feminist interpretation.* Paper presented at the annual meeting of the American Psychological Association, San Francisco.

Stoller, R. (1976). Sexual excitement. *Archives of General Psychiatry, 33,* 899–909.

Strasburger, V. C. (1985). When parents ask about ... the influence of TV on their kids. *Contemporary Pediatrics, 2,* 18–27.

Strasburger, V. C. (1995). *Adolescents and the media: Medical and psychological impact.* Thousand Oaks, CA: Sage.

Strickland, L. J., Aboud, F. E., & Gergen, K. J. (Eds.). (1976). *Social psychology in transition.* New York: Plenum.

Strouse, J. S., & Buerkel-Rothfuss, N. L. (1987). Media exposure and the sexual attitudes and behaviors of college students. *Journal of Sex Education and Therapy, 13,* 43–51.

Strouse, J., & Fabes, R. (1985). Formal versus informal sources of sex education: Competing forces in the sexual socialisation of adolescents. *Adolescence, 20*(78), 251–263.

Sullivan, G., & O'Connor, O. (1988). Women's role portrayals in magazine advertising: 1958–1983. *Sex Roles, 18,* 181–188.

Svennevig, M. (1998). *Television across the years: The British public's view.* Luton, UK: University of Luton Press and Independent Television Commission, London.

Swan, J. (1994). *Sex, lies and computer networks: Playing down power and violence in virtual worlds.* Panel discussion held on 20 January, 1994, at the Johannes Keppler University, Linz, Austria.

Tan, A. (1979). TV beauty ads and role expectations of adolescent female viewers. *Journalism Quarterly, 56,* 283–288.

Tannenbaum, P. H. (1971). Emotional arousal as a mediator of erotic communication effects. In *Technical Report of the Commission on Obscenity and Pornography* (Vol. 8, pp. 326–356). Washington, DC: U.S. Government Printing Office.

Tavris, C., & Sadd, S. (1978). *The Redbook report on female sexuality.* New York: Dell.

Tedesco, N. (1974). Patterns in prime-time. *Journal of Communication, 74,* 119–124.

Thompson, M. E., Pingree, S., Hawkins, R. P., & Draves, C. (1991). Long-term norms and cognitive structures as shapers of television viewer activity. *Journal of Broadcasting and Electronic Media, 35,* 319–334.

Thornburg, H. (1981). Adolescents source of information on sex. *Journal of School Health, 51,* 274–277.

Tinkham, S. F., & Reid, L. N. (1988). Sex appeal in advertising revisited: Validation of a typology. In J. D. Leckenby (Ed.), *Proceedings of the 1988 conference of the American Academy of Advertising.* Austin, TX.

Tjaden, P. G. (1988). Pornography and sex education. *Journal of Sex Research, 24,* 208–212.

Tomkins, S. S. (1979). Script theory: Differential magnification of affects. In H. E. Howe, Jr. (Ed.), *1978 Nebraska Symposium on Motivation* (pp. 201–236). Lincoln: University of Nebraska Press.

Tomkins, S. S. (1987). Script theory. In J. Arnoff, J. Rodin, & R. Zucker (Eds.), *The emergence of personality* (pp. 147–216). New York: Springer Publishing.

Tomkins, S. S. (1991). *Affect, imagery and consciousness. Vol. 3: The negative affects—Anger and fear.* New York: Springer.

Tong, R. (1987, September–October). Women, pornography, and the law. *Academe,* 14–22.

Tooby, J., & Cosmides, L. (1990). On the universality of human nature and the uniqueness of the individual: The role of genetics and adaptation. *Journal of Personality, 58,* 17–68.

Townsend, J. K. (1968). The relation between Rorschach signs of aggression and behavioral aggression in emotionally disturbed boys. *Journal of Projective Techniques and Personality Assessment, 31,* 13–21.

Trachtenberg, J. A. (1986, May 5). It's become a part of our culture. *Forbes,* 134–135.

Trussel, J. (1988). Teenage pregnancy in the United States. *Family Planning Perspectives, 20*(6), 262–272.

Tuchman, G., Daniels, A., & Benet, J. (Eds.). (1978). *Hearth and home: Images of women in the mass media.* New York: Oxford University Press.

Turow, J. (1974). Advising and ordering: Daytime, prime time. *Journal of Communication, 24,* 135–141.

Tversky, A., & Kahneman, D. (1973). Availability: A heuristic for judging frequency and probability. *Cognitive Psychology, 5,* 201–232.

Tversky, A., & Kahneman, D. (1974). Judgment under uncertainty: Heuristics and biases. *Science, 185,* 1124–1131.

U.S. Commission on Obscenity and Pornography. (1970). *Report of the Commission on Obscenity and Pornography* (Vol. 7). Washington, DC: U.S. Government Printing Office.

Vance, C. (Ed.). (1984). *Pleasure and danger: Exploring female sexuality.* Boston: Routledge and Kegan Paul.

Van der Voort, T. H. A. (1986). *Television violence: A child's eye view.* Amsterdam, Holland: Elsevier Science.

Venkatesan, M., & Losco, J. (1975). Women in magazine ads. *Journal of Advertising Research, 15*(5), 49–54.

Vincent, R. C. (1988). Clio's consciousness raised? Portrayal of women in rock videos, re-examined. *Journalism Quarterly, 65,* 155–160.

Vincent, R. C., Davis, D. K., & Bronszkowski, L. A. (1987). Sexism on MTV: A content analysis of rock videos. *Journalism Quarterly, 64,* 750–755.

Wagner, G. (1985). Penile erection provoked by vibration and intracorporeal injection. *Nordisk Sexology, 3,* 113–118.

Walker, C. E. (1971). Erotic stimuli and the aggressive sexual offender. In *Technical Report of the Commission on Obscenity and Pornography* (Vol. 7). Washington, D.C: U.S. Government Printing Office.

Wallace, D. H., & Wehmer, G. (1973). Evaluation of visual erotica by sexual liberals and conservatives. *Journal of Sex Research, 8,* 147–153.

Wallace, J., & Mangan, M. (1996). *Sex, lies and cyberspace: Freedom and censorship on the frontiers of the online revolution.* New York: Holt.

Waller, G., Hamilton, K., & Shaw, J. (1992). Media influences on body size estimation in eating disordered and comparison subjects. *British Review of Bulimia and Anorexia Nervosa, 6,* 81–87.

Walsch-Childers, K. (1991, May). *Adolescents' interpretations of the birth control behavior of a soap opera couple.* Paper presented at the meeting of the Health Communication Division of the International Communication Association, Chicago.

Ward, M. (1995). Talking about sex: Common themes about sexuality in the prime-time television programs children and adolescents view most. *Journal of Youth and Adolescence, 24,* 595–615.

Wartella, E., Heintz, K. E., Aidman, A. J., & Mazzarella, S. R. (1990). Television and beyond: Children's video media in one community. *Communication Research, 17*(1), 45–64.

Warwick, Walsh & Miller, Inc. (1981). *Study of consumer attitudes toward TV programming and advertising.* New York: Author.

Watson, C. A. (1993). *Sophie's sex: An analysis of the responses of ten focus groups to one programme from the series Sex presented by Sophie Lee.* Wellington, New Zealand: Broadcasting Standards Authority.

Watson, C., Bassett, G., Lambourne, R., & Shuker, R. (1991). *Television violence: An analysis of the portrayal of 'violent acts' on the three New Zealand broadcast television channels during the week of 11th–17th February, 1991.* Research project for the Broadcasting Standards Authority by the Educational Research and Development Centre, Massey University.

Wattleton, F. (1987). American teens: Sexually active, sexually illiterate. *Journal of School Health, 57,* 379–380.

Weaver, J. (1992). The perceptual and behavioral consequences of exposure to pornography: The social science and psychological research evidence. In I. C. Itzin (Ed.), *Pornography: Women, violence and civil liberties* (pp. 284–309). Oxford: Oxford University Press.

Weaver, J. B. (1987). Effects of exposure to horror film violence on perceptions of women (Doctoral dissertation, Indiana University). *Dissertation Abstracts International, 48*(10), 2482-A.

Weaver, J. B. (1988, November). *A content analysis of ten commercially successful 'teenage slasher' horror films.* Paper presented at the annual meeting of the Speech Communication Association, New Orleans, LA.

Weaver, J. B. (1991). Responding to erotica: perceptual processes and dispositional implications. In J. Bryant & D. Zillmann (Eds.), *Responding to the screen: Reception and reaction processes* (pp. 329–354). Hillsdale, NJ: Lawrence Erlbaum Associates.

Weaver, J. B., Masland, J. L., & Zillmann, D. (1984). Effects of erotica on young men's aesthetic perception of their female sexual partners. *Perceptual and Motor Skills, 58,* 929–930.

Weber, S. J., & Cook, T. D. (1972). Subject effects in laboratory research: An examination of subject roles, demand characteristics, and valid inferences. *Psychological Bulletin, 77,* 273–295.

Wells, W. D. (1973). *Television and aggression: Replication of an experimental field study.* Unpublished manuscript, Graduate School of Business, University of Chicago.

West, C. (1994). Market culture run amok: The '80s.' *Newsweek, 3,* 46–49.

White, L. A. (1979). Erotica and aggression: The influence of sexual arousal, positive affect and negative affect on aggressive behavior. *Journal of Personality and Social Psychology, 37,* 591–601.

Wilcox, B. L. (1987). Pornography, social science, and politics: When research and ideology collide. *American Psychologist, 42,* 941–943.

Wiley, R. (1977). Family viewing: A balancing of interests. *Journal of Communication, 27*(2), 188–192.

Williams Committee Report. (1979, November). *Report of the Departmental Committee on Obscenity and Film Censorship.* London: Her Majesty's Stationery Office.

Williams, J., Meyerson, L., & Eron, L. (1967). Peer-rated aggression and aggressive responses elicited in an experimental situation. *Child Development, 38,* 181–189.

Willis, E. (1983). Feminism, moralism and pornography. In A. Snitow, C. Stansell, & S. Thompson (Eds.), *Powers of desire: The politics of sexuality* (pp. 460–467). New York: Monthly Review Press.

Wilson, B., Donnerstein, E., Linz, D., Kunkel, D., Potter, J., Smith, S. L., Blumenthal, E., & Gray, T. (1996, June). *Content analysis of entertainment television: The importance of context.* Paper presented at the Duke University Conference on Media Violence and Public Policy in the Media, Durham, NC.

Wilson, B., Linz, D., Donnerstein, E., & Stipp, H. (1992). The impact of social issue television programming on attitudes toward rape. *Human Communication Research, 19*(2), 179–208.

Wilson, B. J., Linz, D., & Randall, B. (1990). Applying social science research to film ratings: A shift from offensiveness to harmful effects. *Journal of Broadcasting & Electronic Media, 34*(4), 443–468.

Wilson, J. (1972). Violence, pornography, and Social science. *The Public Interest, 27,* 45–61.

Wilson, M., & Daly, M. (1992). The man who mistook his wife for a chattel. In J. H. Barkow, L. Cosmides, & J. Topoby (Eds.), *The adapted mind: Evolutionary psychology and the generation of culture.* New York: Oxford University Press.

Wilson, W. C. (1978). Can pornography contribute to the prevention of sexual problems? In C. B. Quals, J. P. Wincze, & D. H. Barlow (Eds.), *The prevention of sexual disorders: Issues and approaches* (pp. 159–179). New York: Plenum Press.

Wilson, M., & Daly, M. (1992). The man who mistook his wife for a chattel. In J. H. Barkow, L. Comsmides, & J. Topoy (Eds.), *The adapted mind: Evolutionary psychology and the generation of culture.* New York: Oxford University Press.

Wimmer, R. D., & Dominick, J. R. (1994). *Mass media research: An introduction* (4th ed.). Belmont, CA: Wadsworth Publishing Company.

Winick, C. (1971). Some observations on characteristics of patrons of adult theatres and bookstores. In *Technical report of the Commission on Obscenity and Pornography* (Vol. 4). Washington, DC: U.S. Government Printing Office.

Winick, C. (1985). A content analysis of sexually explicit magazines sold in an adult bookstore. *Journal of Sex Research, 21,* 206–210.

Wober, J. M. (1980, September). *Attitudes towards advertisements on television: Survey and diary evaluation.* London: Independent Broadcasting Authority.

Wober, J. M. (1987). *Evaluating the broadcast campaign on AIDS.* London: Independent Broadcasting Authority.

Wober, J. M. (1988). Informing the British public about AIDS. *Health Education Research, 3,* 19–24.

Wober, J. M. (1990). *Sex in the corner: Viewing of and attitudes concerning television programmes on sex.* London: Independent Broadcasting Authority.

Wober, M., & Gunter, B. (1988). *Television and social control.* Aldershot, UK: Avebury.

Wolmuth, R. (1983, October 17). Rock 'n' roll 'n' video: MTV's music revolution. *People,* 96–99.

Wood, M., & Hughes, M. (1984). The moral basis of morale reform: Status discontent vs. culture and socialisation as explanations of anti-pornography social adherence. *American Sociological Review, 49,* 86–99.

Woods, M. G. (1998, July). *Teen viewing of soaps: A uses and gratifications/cultivation study.* Paper presented at the 48th annual conference of the International Communication Association, Jerusalem.

Wydra, A., Marshall, W. L., Earls, C. M., & Barbaree, H. E. (1983). Identification of cues and control of sexual arousal by rapists. *Behavior Research and Therapy, 21,* 469–476.

Wylie, K. R. (1996). Use of erotic videos for assessments of sexual functioning. *Sexual and Marital Therapy, 11*(4), 353–357.

Yaffe, M. (1982). Therapeutic uses of sexually explicit material. In M. Yaffe & E. C. Nelson (Eds.), *The influence of pornography on behavior* (pp. 50–65). London: Academic.

Yang, N., & Linz, D. (1990). Movie ratings and the content of adult videos: The sex–violence ratio. *Journal of Communication, 40*(2), 28–42.

Zabin, L. S., Hirsch, M. B., Smith, E. A., & Hardy, J. B. (1984). Adolescent sexual attitudes and behavior: Are they consistent? *Family Planning Perspectives, 16,* 181–185.

Zelnick, M., & Kantner, J. (1980). Sexual activity, contraceptive use and pregnancy among metropolitan-area teenagers: 1971–1979. *Family Planning Perspectives, 12*(5), 230–237.

Zillmann, D. (1978). Attribution and misattribution of excitatory reactions. In J. H. Harvey, W. J. Ickes, & R. F. Kidd (Eds.), *New directions in attribution research* (Vol. 2, pp. 335–368). Hillsdale, NJ: Lawrence Erlbaum Associates.

Zillmann, D. (1982). Transfer of excitation in emotional behavior. In J. T. Cacioppo & R. E. Petty (Eds.), *Social psychophysiology*. New York: Guilford.

Zillmann, D. (1979). *Hostility and aggression*. Hillsdale, NJ: Lawrence Erlbaum Associates.

Zillmann, D. (1984). *Connections between sex and aggression*. Hillsdale, NJ: Lawrence Erlbaum Associates.

Zillmann, D. (1989). Effects of prolonged consumption of pornography. In D. Zillmann & J. Bryant (Eds.), *Pornography: Research advances and policy considerations* (pp. 117–157). Hillsdale, NJ: Lawrence Erlbaum Associates.

Zillmann, D. (1994). Erotica and family values. In D. Zillmann, J. Bryant, & A. C. Huston (Eds.), *Media, children and the family: Social scientific, psychodynamic and clinical perspectives* (pp. 199–214). Hillsdale, NJ: Lawrence Erlbaum Associates.

Zillmann, D., & Bryant, J. (1982). Pornography, sexual callousness and the trivialisation of rape. *Journal of Communication, 32*(4), 10–21.

Zillmann, D., & Bryant, J. (1983). Colloquy: Pornography and social science research ... higher moralities. *Journal of Communication, 32*(4), 111–114.

Zillmann, D., & Bryant, J. (1984). Effects of massive exposure to pornography. In N. M. Malamuth & E. Donnerstein (Eds.), *Pornography and sexual aggression* (pp. 115–141). Orlando: Academic Press.

Zillmann, D., & Bryant, J. (1986). Shifting preferences in pornography consumption. *Communication Research, 13*(4), 560–578.

Zillmann, D., & Bryant, J. (1987). Pornography and behavior: Alternative explanations: A reply. *Journal of Communication, 37*(3), 189–192.

Zillmann, D., & Bryant, J. (1988a). Effects of prolonged consumption of pornography on family values. *Journal of Family Issues, 9*, 518–544.

Zillmann, D., & Bryant, J. (1988b). Pornography's impact on sexual satisfaction. *Journal of Applied Social Psychology, 18*, 438–453.

Zillmann, D., & Bryant, J. (1988c). The methods and merits of pornography research: A response. *Journal of Communication, 38*, 185–192.

Zillmann, D., & Bryant, J. (Eds.). (1989). *Pornography: Research advances and policy considerations*. Hillsdale, NJ: Lawrence Erlbaum Associates.

Zillmann, D., Bryant, J., & Carveth, R. A. (1981). The effect of erotica featuring sadomasochism and bestiality on motivated intermale aggression. *Personality and Social Psychology Bulletin, 7*, 153–159.

Zillmann, D., Bryant, J., Comisky, P. W., & Medoff, N. J. (1981). Excitation and hedonic valence in the effect of erotica on motivated intermale aggression. *European Journal of Social Psychology, 11*, 233–252.

Zillmann, D., Hoyt, J. L., & Day, K. (1974). Strength and duration of the effect of aggressive, violent and erotic communications on subsequent aggressive behavior. *Communication Research, 11*(3), 286–306.

Zillmann, D., & Mundorf, N. (1987). Image effects in the appreciation of video rock. *Communication Research, 14*, 316–334.

Zillmann, D., & Sapolsky, B. S. (1977). What mediates the effect of mild erotica on annoyance and hostile behavior in males? *Journal of Personality and Social Psychology, 35*, 587–596.

Zillman, D., & Weaver, D. (1989). Pornography and men's sexual callousness toward women. In D. Zillmann & J. Bryant (Eds.), *Pornography: Research advances and policy considerations* (pp. 95–125). Hillsdale, NJ: Lawrence Erlbaum Associates.

Zuckerman, D. M., Singer, D. G., & Singer, J. L. (1980). Television viewing, children's reading and related classroom behavior. *Journal of Communication, 30*, 166–174.

Zurcher, L. A., Kirkpatrick, R. G., Cushing, R. G., & Bowman, C. K. (1973). Ad hoc anti-pornography organisations and their active members: A research summary. *Journal of Social Issues, 29,* 69–94.

Author Index

Subject Index

A